The Many Faces of Slavery

The Many Faces of Slavery: New Perspectives on Slave Ownership and Experiences in the Americas

Edited by Lawrence Aje and Catherine Armstrong

BLOOMSBURY ACADEMIC
LONDON • NEW YORK • OXFORD • NEW DELHI • SYDNEY

BLOOMSBURY ACADEMIC
Bloomsbury Publishing Plc
50 Bedford Square, London, WC1B 3DP, UK
1385 Broadway, New York, NY 10018, USA
29 Earlsfort Terrace, Dublin 2, Ireland

BLOOMSBURY, BLOOMSBURY ACADEMIC and the Diana logo are
trademarks of Bloomsbury Publishing Plc

First published in Great Britain 2020
This paperback edition published in 2021

Copyright © Lawrence Aje and Catherine Armstrong, 2020

Lawrence Aje and Catherine Armstrong have asserted their right under the Copyright, Designs and Patents Act, 1988, to be identified as the Editors of this work.

Cover image: Bowles's New One-Sheet Chart of the Atlantic or Western Ocean, Laid down from the Latest Discoveries, and Regulated by Numerous Astronomical Observations. (Courtesy of the John Carter Brown Library)

All rights reserved. No part of this publication may be reproduced or transmitted in any form or by any means, electronic or mechanical, including photocopying, recording, or any information storage or retrieval system, without prior permission in writing from the publishers.

Bloomsbury Publishing Plc does not have any control over, or responsibility for, any third-party websites referred to or in this book. All internet addresses given in this book were correct at the time of going to press. The author and publisher regret any inconvenience caused if addresses have changed or sites have ceased to exist, but can accept no responsibility for any such changes.

A catalogue record for this book is available from the British Library.

A catalog record for this book is available from the Library of Congress.

ISBN: HB: 978-1-3500-7142-1
PB: 978-1-3502-9868-2
ePDF: 978-1-3500-7143-8
eBook: 978-1-3500-7144-5

Typeset by RefineCatch Limited, Bungay, Suffolk

To find out more about our authors and books visit www.bloomsbury.com and sign up for our newsletters.

Contents

List of Figures   vii
List of Tables   viii
List of Contributors   ix

    Introduction   *Lawrence Aje and Catherine Armstrong*   1

Part 1 Documenting Non-traditional Slavery and Slaveholding

1. Many Faces of Slaveholding Sephardim   *Seymour Drescher*   13
2. Something Close to Freedom: The Case of the Black Seminoles in Florida   *Brent R. Weisman*   25
3. 'Adventure in a Wigwam': Henry Bibb's Account of Slavery among the Cherokees in *Narrative of the Life and Adventures of Henry Bibb, An American Slave* (1849)   *Sandrine Ferré-Rode*   39
4. To 'make a good Mistress to my servants': Unmasking the Meaning of Maternalism in Colonial South Carolina   *Inge Dornan*   55
5. Resident Female Slaveholders in Jamaica at the End of Emancipation: Evidence from the Compensation Claims   *Ahmed Reid*   71

Part 2 The Politics and Economics of Atypical Forms of Slavery and Slaveholding

6. Corporate Slavery in Seventeenth-Century New York   *Anne-Claire Faucquez*   89
7. Militarized Slavery: The Creation of the West India Regiments   *Tim Lockley*   101
8. 'A question between hiring and selling': Slave Leasing at Thomas Jefferson's Monticello, 1780–1830   *Christa Dierksheide*   115
9. Turmoil in the Cocoa Groves: Slave Revolts in Ocumare de la Costa, Venezuela, 1837 and 1845   *Nikita Harwich*   133

Part 3 Social Mobility on the Margins of Slavery, Freedom and Slave Ownership

10. Keeper of the Keys: Creole Management of a Nineteenth-Century French Plantation in New Orleans   *Nathalie Dessens*   151

11 João de Oliveira's Atlantic World: Mobility and Dislocation in Eighteenth-Century Brazil and the Bight of Benin   *Mary E. Hicks*   165
12 Gilbert Hunt, the City Blacksmith: Slavery, Freedom and Fame in Antebellum Richmond, Virginia   *Elizabeth Kuebler-Wolf*   183
13 Nominal Slavery, Free People of Colour and Enslavement Requests: Slavery and Freedom at the 'Edges' of the Regime in the Antebellum South   *Emily West*   199
14 The Transition from Plantation Slave Labour to Free Labour in the Americas   *Herbert S. Klein*   211

Index   229

List of Figures

10.1 *Topographical Map of New Orleans and its Vicinity*, 1834. By Charles F. Zimpel. 154

12.1 Cook Studio, *Gilbert Hunt*. Glass-plate negative. The Valentine, Richmond, Virginia. 184

12.2 *Isaac Granger Jefferson*, c. 1845. Tracy W. McGregor Library of American History, Special Collections, University of Virginia Library. 185

12.3 *Gilbert Hunt*. Salt print, taken by Julian Vannerson, 5.25 × 7.375 in., 77 Main St, Richmond, Virginia, c. 1859–60. Image courtesy of Cowan's Auctions, Cincinnati, Ohio. 187

12.4 Joseph Lossing Benson, *The Burning of the Theatre in Richmond, Virginia, on the Night of the 26th. December 1811*. Philadelphia: Benjamin Tanner, 25 February 1812. 189

12.5 Smith and Vannerson, *Portrait of Gilbert Hunt*. Smith & Vannerson, 77 Main St, Richmond, Virginia, c. 1859. 191

List of Tables

5.1	Parish distribution of compensation claims for Jamaica	72
5.2	Descriptive statistics of resident slaveholders in Jamaica	73
5.3	Sugar produced in Jamaica relative to other British West Indian Islands	75
5.4	Breakdown of claims submitted by resident slaveholders in Jamaica	76
5.5	Females buying real estate in Kingston by select year	79
5.6	Parish distribution of resident female pen-keepers	81
5.7	Parish distribution of resident female estate owners	82
9.1	List of the runaway slaves from the *Obra Pía de Cata Hacienda*	138
11.1	Slaves arriving in the north-eastern ports of Brazil	168

List of Contributors

Lawrence Aje is Associate Professor of United States History at the University Paul-Valéry, Montpellier, specializing in African American history. His current research explores the interconnection between law, race and group identity formation, as well as the migration and circulation of free people of colour in the United States and in the Atlantic World during the nineteenth century. He also specializes in historiography and more specifically on the political, methodological, and epistemological stakes involved in the writing of the history of slavery. His publications include *La Mémoire de l'esclavage: traces mémorielles de l'esclavage et des traites dans l'espace atlantique* (2018), which he co-edited with Nicolas Gachon; 'Fugitive Slave Narratives and the (Re)presentation of the Self? The Cases of Frederick Douglass and William Brown' (2013); and '"Africa the land of our fathers": The Emigration of Charlestonians to Liberia in the Nineteenth Century', in *Pan-Africanism, Citizenship and Identity*, edited by Toyin Falola and Kwame Essien (2013).

Catherine Armstrong is Senior Lecturer in Modern History at Loughborough University, having previously spent six years at Manchester Metropolitan University. She has published two monographs on colonial North America, specifically about print culture and representations of the landscape and identity, and is also interested in the boundaries of enslavement in the southern United States. She published an article on the cultural geography of southern slave autonomy in the work of Frederick Law Olmsted in *Slavery and Abolition* (2017) and is currently researching the ways in which conceptions of global slavery changed in the United States after emancipation. Her work on viewing slavery and abolition with a long chronological lens has been published in *The Conversation*, and she has also published on the pedagogical methodologies of slavery in the classroom.

Nathalie Dessens is a Professor of American History and Civilization at the University of Toulouse-Jean Jaurès (France). After conducting research on ideology in the antebellum American South, on the myth of the Old South in literature and popular culture, and on the history of the slave societies of the Americas, she has refocused her research on nineteenth-century New Orleans and the consequences of the Haitian Revolution. She has co-edited, with Jean-Pierre le Glaunec, *Haïti, regards croisés* (2007) and *La Louisiane au carrefour des cultures* (2016). She has authored *Myths of the Plantation Society: Slavery in the American South and the West Indies* (2003), *From Saint-Domingue to New Orleans: Migration and Influences* (2007) and *Creole City: A Chronicle of Early American New Orleans* (2015). After editing *French Colonial History*, she became vice-president then president of the French Colonial Historical Society. She is currently vice-president of her university, in charge of Dissemination of Scientific Knowledge.

Christa Dierksheide is Assistant Professor of History and a Kinder Professor of Constitutional Democracy at the University of Missouri. She is also Senior Fellow at the Robert H. Smith International Center for Jefferson Studies at Monticello. Since 2006, she has conceptualized and written exhibitions for Monticello, including *The Boisterous Sea of Liberty* (2008), *Mulberry Row: The Landscape of Slavery* (2012) and *The Life of Sally Hemings* (2018). Christa's current research focus is on race, nationalism, and Thomas Jefferson's legacy in early nineteenth-century America. She has published several articles and essays on slavery and imperialism in the American South and British Caribbean and is the author of *Amelioration and Empire: Progress and Slavery in the Plantation Americas* (2014).

Inge Dornan is Lecturer in American History at Brunel University London, UK. Her research focuses on slavery and abolition in Britain, America and the Caribbean in the eighteenth and nineteenth centuries, and she has published widely on the experiences of enslaved women and women slaveholders. Inge is currently undertaking a research project on the education of enslaved and emancipated children in the British West Indies, which forms the subject of her most recent publication, '"Book don't feed our children": Nonconformist Missionaries and the British and Foreign School Society in the Development of Elementary Education in the British West Indies Before and After Emancipation', in *Slavery and Abolition* (March 2019). She is also working on a monograph on women, slavery and emancipation in the Atlantic world.

Seymour Drescher is Distinguished Professor of History emeritus at the University of Pittsburgh. He was also the inaugural Secretary of the European Program of the Woodrow Wilson International Center for Scholars in Washington, DC. His research focuses on the history of slavery and abolition in a global context, and his works include *From Slavery to Freedom: Comparative Studies in the Rise and Fall of Atlantic Slavery* (1999), *Abolition: A History of Slavery and Abolition* (2009) and *Pathways from Slavery: British and Colonial Mobilizations in Global Perspective* (2018). Drescher is also a co-editor of the *Cambridge World History of Slavery, Vol. IV: 1804–2016* (2017).

Anne-Claire Faucquez is Associate Professor in American Civilization and History at University Paris 8. She is currently preparing the manuscript of her thesis entitled 'From New-New Netherland to New York: The Birth of a Slavery Society 1624–1712'. Anne-Claire works on New York's colonial space and more specifically on the issues of class and race in colonial America by comparing dependent populations of forced labourers (slaves, indentured servants, apprentices, soldiers). She is also interested in the commemoration and representations of slavery in museums, monuments and contemporary art.

Sandrine Ferré-Rode is an Associate Professor in American and Canadian Studies at the University of Versailles–Saint-Quentin-en-Yvelines, France. Her research interests focus on the narratives of American slaves who fled to Canada during the age of emancipation. Sandrine has recently completed, with Anne-Laure Tissut as translator, a critical edition in French of Henry Bibb's 1849 *The Life and Adventures of Henry Bibb,*

An American Slave, published as *Récit de la vie et des aventures de Henry Bibb, esclave américain* (2018).

Nikita Harwich is Professor of Latin American History and Civilization in the Department of Applied Foreign Languages at the University of Paris Nanterre, France. His research interests focus on Latin American commodity trade, foreign investments in Latin America, as well as on the history of ideas and contemporary Latin American historiography. His recent publications include '1910 en Venezuela: Una renovada alborada?', in Paul-Henri Giraud, Eduardo Ramos-Izquierdo and Miguel Rodríguez (eds), *1910: México entre dos épocas* (2014); 'Barcelona beyond the Seas: A Catalan Enclave in Colonial Venezuela', *European Review* (2017); 'Las guerras de Independencia en Ocumare de la Costa. Continuidad y cambios estructurales : 1800–1830', *Boletín de la Academia Nacional de la Historia* (2017) and *Historia del chocolate* (2018).

Mary E. Hicks is an Assistant Professor at Amherst College in the Departments of Black Studies and History. Her research focuses on the transatlantic slave trade in colonial and imperial Brazil. Her current book project explores the maritime dimension of the African diaspora in the South Atlantic, and details how African-born seafarers spearheaded multiple commercial, cultural, and intellectual exchanges between Bahia and the Bight of Benin in the eighteenth and early nineteenth centuries. Mary has published in the *Journal of Global Slavery*.

Herbert S. Klein is Gouverneur Morris Professor Emeritus of History at Columbia University, and Hoover Research Fellow and Latin American Curator at the Hoover Archives and was Professor of History and Director of the Center for Latin American Studies at Stanford University. He has published some 180 articles and authored several books on Bolivia: *Parties and Political Change in Bolivia, 1880–1952* (1969, 2009); *Revolution and the Rebirth of Inequality* (co-author, 1981); *Haciendas and Ayllus* (1993); and *A Concise History of Bolivia* (2nd edition, 2011). His recent work on slavery includes *African Slavery in Latin American and the Caribbean* (2nd edition, co-authored, 2007); *The Middle Passage: Comparative Studies in the Atlantic Slave Trade* (1969); *The Atlantic Slave Trade* (2nd edition, 2009); *Escravismo em São Paulo e Minas Gerais* (co-authored, 2009); and *Slavery in Brazil* (co-authored, 2009). On Brazil, his most recent books include the co-authored *Economic and Social History of Brazil Since 1889* (2014), *Brazil 1964–1985: The Military Regimes of Latin America in the Cold War* (2017) and *Feeding the World: The Rise of Modern Brazilian Agriculture* (2019). He has also written on Latin American colonial fiscal history and *A Population History of the United States* (2nd edition, 2012).

Elizabeth Kuebler-Wolf is Associate Professor of Art History at the University of Saint Francis, Fort Wayne, Indiana, United States. Her research interests include the rhetoric and material lives of images and objects, particularly as applied to antebellum slavery. Kuebler-Wolf has published on images of slavery and the history of collections. Her most recent publication is '"Born in America, in Europe bred, in Africa travell'd and in Asia wed": Elihu Yale, Material Culture, and Actor Networks from the Seventeenth Century to the Twenty-first', *Journal of Global History* 11, no. 3 (2016): 320–43.

Tim Lockley is Professor of North American History at the University of Warwick and associate editor of *Slavery & Abolition*, the leading journal in slave and post-slave studies. He is the author of *Lines in the Sand: Race and Class in Lowcountry Georgia* (2001), *Welfare and Charity in the Antebellum South* (2007) and *Maroon Communities in South Carolina* (2009), as well as numerous articles on slavery, race, class and gender in the American South, including one article on American cricket. Tim has recently completed a four-year collaborative research project on the West India Regiments, black soldiers recruited to fight in the British Army from 1795, focusing on the physicians attached to the regiments and their writings about race. He is currently completing a monograph on the subject entitled *Military Medicine and the Making of Race*.

Ahmed Reid is Associate Professor of Caribbean History at Bronx Community College (City University of New York). He is currently a member of the United Nations Working Group of Experts on People of African Descent, where he sits as the representative for Latin American and Caribbean States. Reid's research interests include Caribbean economic and social history, comparative slavery in the Americas, the transatlantic trade in Africans, and reparation. He is the author and co-author of several articles, the most recent being 'Sugar, Slavery and Productivity in Jamaica, 1750–1807', *Slavery and Abolition* 37, no. 1 (2016). He has also published 'Sugar, Land Markets and the Williams Thesis: Evidence from Jamaica's Property Sale', *Slavery and Abolition* 34, no. 3 (2013): 401–24 (co-author David Ryden) and 'West Indian Economic Decline', in Trevor Burnard (ed.), *Oxford Bibliographies in Atlantic History* (2013). He is the recipient of several awards including, a prestigious research fellowship from Yale University's Gilder Lehrman Center for the Study of Slavery, Resistance and Abolition, and a research fellowship from the John Carter Brown Library, Brown University.

Brent R. Weisman is Emeritus Professor of Anthropology at the University of South Florida, Tampa. His research interests include North American Indians, particularly of the Southeast and Florida, Florida archaeology and museum studies. His most recent publication (co-edited) is *We Come For Good: Archaeology and Tribal Historic Preservation at the Seminole Tribe* (2016).

Emily West is Professor of American History at the University of Reading, UK. Her research interests focus on slavery and gender in the antebellum American South, especially the lives of enslaved spouses, motherhood under slavery, and free people of colour in the slave South. She is the author of *Enslaved Women in America: From Colonial Times Through Emancipation* (2014), *Family or Freedom: People of Color in the Antebellum South* (2012) and *Chains of Love: Enslaved Couples in Antebellum South Carolina* (2004), as well as several articles and book chapters.

Introduction

Lawrence Aje and Catherine Armstrong

This volume broadens our conception of both slaveholding and enslaved experience in the Americas. It acknowledges that by the eighteenth century, racial slavery had matured into a fully-fledged, firmly established, profitable form of labour. In slave societies, the development of the plantation unit led both to the geographical concentration of the slave population and to a growing homogenization of the activities bondsmen performed. However, throughout the Atlantic world, the existence of phenomena such as urban slavery, slave self-hiring, quasi-free or nominal slaves, domestic slave concubines, slave vendors, slave soldiers and sailors, slave preachers, slave overseers and many other types of 'societies with slaves', broadens our traditional conception of slavery by complicating the slave experience. Further, the book explores slaveholding by poor whites, women, free blacks, Native Americans, Jewish Americans, corporations and the state.

This edited collection stems from two conferences, co-organized by the editors of this book and Lydia Plath and held in London (2014) and Montpellier (2015), that sought to examine the plurality of slaveholding and slave experience in the Atlantic world.[1] This book does not challenge the significance of the plantation system, where 90 per cent of the slaves toiled, but, by using it as a paradigm, seeks to offer new perspectives on the nature of atypical forms of slavery and slaveholding in the context of the historical evolution of labour in the Americas, which we qualify as being *non-traditional*. By focusing on marginal forms of slavery and of slaveholding, the volume enriches existing historiography by bringing to the fore the complexities within the 'peculiar institution'.

The Many Faces of Slavery assesses how widespread the phenomenon of slaveholding was among the non-white and poor white populations of the Americas. In the process, it demonstrates the ways in which these slaveholders were distinct from more conventional slave holders in their attitudes and behaviour towards the institution and towards their slaves. Indeed, regional specificities, historical contexts and legal frameworks encouraged atypical forms of slaveholding and influenced the nature of bondage. The book's approach allows for an examination of the nature of the enslaved cultures and enslaved agency which emerged in this context.

The book confronts a series of questions about the plurality of experiences of the enslaved population. Were certain locations, historical periods and economic conditions more favourable to the diversification of the slave experience? How does the variety of slave experience inform the essence of slavery itself? What strategies did slaves employ to negotiate or manoeuvre themselves into different relationships with their masters or with their societies? Did the privileges that certain slaves enjoy, such as geographic or social mobility, undermine the slave system by subverting the established social and racial order? At what point did slave autonomy develop from an act of the assertion of agency to become an act of rebellion? Could it be argued that the development of atypical forms of slavery was the result of deliberate political choices? What are the epistemological consequences of acknowledging slave ownership by slaveholders who belonged to various subaltern groups? How does slave holding and slave trading by persons of colour alter our understanding of 'the colour line'?

The conferences from which this book emerges were conceived as places to bring together scholarship on a wide variety of slaveholding and slave experience. Challenging the idea that all slaveholders were wealthy white men, this book explores the historiographical origins of the study of slave ownership by corporations, by poor whites, by Native Americans, by free blacks and by women. It also discusses methods of control of the black population that operated at the boundaries of slave ownership, such as slave hiring and permanent supervision of slaves by managers and overseers. Finally, by exploring the different ways that slave purchase was used to buy one's freedom or that of relatives, the volume lays special focus on experiences that cross boundaries between enslavement and freedom. The concept of freedom itself is interrogated, as it is acknowledged that free blacks – 'slaves without masters' in Ira Berlin's famous phrase – were caught in a perpetual legal and cultural struggle to maintain their precarious status. However, other varieties of autonomy are explored, such as the way that the geographical, military and economic mobility of the enslaved person provided relief from the oppression of the regime.

Methodologically, this book builds on two approaches: placing slavery in the context of Atlantic history and examining slavery through the lens of multidisciplinarity. In recent years the Atlantic paradigm has made an important contribution to understanding the long chronological story of the region, and facilitates the notion that transnational rather than national histories are most enlightening when considering the evolution of economic networks and their accompanying power structures. The methodological approach adopted in the book borrows David Armitage's concept of the 'cis-Atlantic': the idea that fruitful comparative history can be undertaken by exploring several unique locations within the Atlantic alongside one another to produce a regional understanding of the topic.[2] It does not deny important regional specificities, some of which are created because of divergent experiences driven at national level, but rather seeks to broaden the scope of historical enquiry by explicitly and methodologically reclaiming hidden and hitherto silenced voices in the region in an attempt to stretch and diversify concepts of resistance to hegemonic power by bringing to the fore, in James Scott's famous phrase, the 'weapons of the weak', deployed either by slaves in non-traditional contexts, or slave owners not normally considered part of the elite.[3]

The present edited collection also contrasts different methodological approaches to three types of sources: visual, material and textual culture, and explores what scholars from the disciplines of history, art history, literature and archaeology contribute to this new, non-traditional approach to the study of slavery. Using diverse disciplinary approaches allows a single volume to gather together pieces of research foregrounding different types of evidence, as well as using different analytical tools, with the result that the picture presented of the many faces of slavery is thus richer and multivalent.

Few studies tackle the diverse experiences of the enslaved and slaveholders in the same volume and with such a wide lens as this book. Some recent works looking at slavery in an Atlantic context include Laird Bergad, *The Comparative Histories of Slavery in Brazil, Cuba and the United States*; Michael Gomez, *Reversing Sail: A History of the African Diaspora*; and Gwendolyn Hall, *Slavery and African Ethnicities in the Americas*.[4] Recent edited collections comparing thematic aspects of slavery over wide geographical areas include David Barry Gasper and Darlene Clark Hine (eds), *Beyond Bondage: Free Women of Color in the Americas*; Herbert S. Klein and Ben Vinson, *African Slavery in Latin America and the Caribbean*; Pamela Scully and Diana Paton (eds), *Gender and Slave Emancipation in the Atlantic World*; and Cora Kaplan and John Oldfield (eds), *Imagining Transatlantic Slavery*.[5] Recent influential books focusing on slave experience in the British colonial world include Philip D. Morgan and Sean Hawkins (eds), *Black Experience and the Empire*; James Walvin, *Britain's Slave Empire*; and Peter H. Wood, *Strange New Land: Africans in Colonial America, 1526–1776*.[6] Contrary to some of the aforementioned books which provide a general comparative introductory history to slavery in the Americas (Bergad) and target an undergraduate readership (Gomez), while others study the survival and persistence of African ethnic identities (Hall), or largely focus on abolitionist discourse by examining literary and visual material (Kaplan and Oldfield), *The Many Faces of Slavery* examines atypical forms of slaveholding and slavery in different locales in the Americas.

Much recent scholarship has focused on the plantation showing that it is still a paradigm worth working with, examining, for example, relations between white and black women there, as in Thavolia Glymph's *Out of the House of Bondage*, or exploring the variety of labour systems in the British Atlantic, as in Simon Newman's *A New World of Labour*.[7] In recent years there have been many new works on non-plantation slavery, and our book complements these by bringing together new stories from across the Americas. Exploring urban slavery are works by Mariana Dantas, *Black Townsmen: Urban Slavery in the Eighteenth Century Americas*; Herman Bennett, *Africans in Colonial Mexico: Absolutism, Christianity and Afro-Creole Consciousness*; and Christine Hunefeldt, *Paying the Price of Freedom: Family and Labor among Lima's Slaves, 1800– 1854*.[8] Examining Atlantic slavery on the boundaries between enslavement and freedom are Kathleen Higgins, *Licentious Liberty in a Brazilian Gold-Mining Region: Slavery, Gender and Social Control in 18th Century Sabara, Minas Gerais*; Seth Rockman, *Scraping By: Wage Labor, Slavery, and Survival in Early Baltimore*; James Brooks, *Captives and Cousins: Slavery, Kinship and Community in the Southwest Borderlands*; and Jorge Canizares-Esqguerra, Matt Childs and James Sidbury (eds), *The Black Urban Atlantic in the Age of the Slave Trade*.[9] Jeffrey Bolster, *Black Jacks: African American Seamen in the Age of Sail*, explores the way that autonomy might be asserted in certain labour contexts, with some spaces offering more freedom than others.[10] Some of these monographs take as an example one family or individual, mirroring the approach of some of the chapters in this volume, such as Rebecca Scott and Jean Hébrard, *Freedom Papers: An Atlantic Odyssey in the Age of Emancipation*, and Tiya Myles, *Ties that Bind: The Story of an Afro-Cherokee Family in Slavery and Freedom*.[11]

Some books have focused on slave owning by 'others', but again, these focus on one specific time and/or place, examples being Kimberly Hanger, *Bounded Lives, Bounded Places: Free Black Society in Colonial New Orleans, 1769–1803*; Stewart King, *Blue Coat or Powdered Wig: Free People of Color in Pre-Revolutionary Saint Domingue*; Gad Heuman, *Between Black and White: Race, Politics and the Free Coloureds in Jamaica, 1792–1865*; or Larry Koger, *Black Slaveowners: Free Black Slave Masters in South Carolina, 1790–1860*.[12] More recently, Stephanie E. Jones-Rogers's book has revealed the scope of female slaveholding in the United States South and highlighted how the role of women in the slave system had hitherto been largely underestimated.[13] Unlike these volumes, our book addresses local specificities to enrich the scholarship on slavery by bringing together examples from many different slaveholding societies in the Americas. At once this book reveals the plethora of stories still left to be told about slavery, while retaining chronological and regional coherence, examining the complexities within one specific form of enslavement, which used those from the African diaspora and their descendants as chattels.

The Many Faces of Slavery is arranged in three sections: 'Documenting Non-traditional Slavery and Slaveholding', 'The Politics and Economics of Atypical Forms of Slavery and Slaveholding' and 'Social Mobility on the Margins of Slavery, Freedom and Slave Ownership'.

By combining the use of multiple sources in an effort to reconstruct master–slave interactions, **Part One, Documenting Non-traditional Slavery and Slaveholding**, poses the fundamental question of how the phenomena of non-traditional forms of slaveholding or slave experiences can be documented and retraced in the archives. Perhaps more significantly, it seeks to explore the specificities of slave ownership by historical actors who, as a result of their comparative absence in the primary sources, have consequently been historiographically marginalized. The different chapters in Part 1 interrogate the evolutionary nature of the relationship between race and slavery, in addition to understanding how determining factors such as gender, religion and cultural and legal transfers shaped the forms of slavery that were practised.

Seymour Drescher's contribution opens the collection with the remarkable endeavour of analysing salient aspects of the diverse spectrum of Sephardim slaveholding in the Atlantic world, from the early modern period to the nineteenth century. Drescher illumines the nature of the relationship between African slaves and New Christian slaveholders (*judeoconversos*) through the prism of the theo-politics of descent and blood purity, which relegated both groups to a lower status – albeit to different degrees of social degradation. Drescher shows that, compared to their Christian counterparts in the Iberian empires, New Christian slaveholders were vulnerable as they were liable to accusations of Judaizing made against them by their slaves. Drescher takes us to the Dutch colony of Suriname to examine the situation of the Sephardim slaveholders of Portuguese origin. He concludes that the rabbinical *responsas*, which regulated slaveholding by Jewish slaveholders east of the Atlantic, were not implemented in the Americas. Drescher complicates the divisions along racial lines which characterized the social organization of slave societies in the Americas by showing how, in Suriname, added to racial origin, the variable of religion constituted a determining factor in terms of ascribing social and legal status. He concludes his chapter by retracing the atypical personal and family trajectory of Moses Levy, who, in the 1820s, developed a project for the gradual abolition of the slaves he had purchased in order to establish a settlement in Florida that would serve as a safe haven for oppressed Jews from Russia. Drescher's contribution highlights that except for a few minor differences, which primarily stemmed from the observance of Jewish religious practices, Sephardic slaveholding in the Americas did not particularly distinguish itself from its Christian counterpart in the treatment of African-descended slaves.

In the same fashion, although with a focus on a different group, **Brent Weisman** seeks to ascertain the specificities of Native American slaveholding by analysing the case of enslaved and slaveholding Black Seminoles in Florida. Weisman argues that a fuller understanding of the complexities of the history of slavery requires that we focus less on issues of dominance and control and more on behavioural systems of mutualistic interaction. He convincingly proposes that, in addition to relying on historical documentary evidence, which is oftentimes lacking, scholars of slavery and of historically marginalized groups should integrate archaeological, ethnographic, geographic and linguistic evidence to reconstruct cultural landscapes. According to Weisman, it is only by developing contextualized culturally-based constructions of ownership, defined through the processes of adaptation and acculturation and an evolutionary perspective in which historical circumstances act on traditional cultural forms, that a more accurate depiction can be obtained of the many 'hidden faces of slavery'. He offers a set of interpretations to define the relationships and interactions between Seminoles and Black Seminoles thanks to the implementation of archaeological and anthropological investigation, while warning against temptations of drawing definitive conclusions.

Sandrine Ferré-Rode's chapter also provides a reflection on the means to gain further insight into the scantily documented history of the specificities of Native American slaveholding of African Americans. In order to do so, she examines fugitive slave Henry Bibb's account of his enslavement among the Cherokees in Indian Territory, an episode he relates in his 1849 slave narrative, *The Life and Adventures of Henry Bibb, An American Slave*. While showing how Bibb endeavoured to appear as a trustworthy and articulate first-hand witness of Cherokee slaveholding and Indian customs, Ferré-Rode highlights the unreliability of his testimony, which is framed in a dichotomic comparison between white southern slavery and Native American slavery. Although Bibb's account is informative in many respects, Ferré-Rode emphasizes its subjective, politicized and mediatized nature, thus raising the question and limits of its historical value.

Inge Dornan sets out to shed light on another facet of slavery by exploring the historical and legal factors which contributed to the emergence of a white female slaveholding class and ideology in South Carolina during the colonial era. Dornan analyses the extent to which South Carolinian white female slave ownership differed in practice from its male counterpart. She argues that, in addition to economic power, slaveholding gave white South Carolinian women socio-political obligations and responsibilities in the development of the colony. Dornan contends that female slave ownership translated into an ideology – maternalism – which was inspired by a combination of pragmatism, gendered mores, religious sentiment and enlightenment sensibility, which manifested itself in the enterprising initiatives of the colony's widows and in their management of their slaves.

Quite similarly, by shifting the focus from large male absentee slave owners to resident Jamaican female slaveholders who received compensation after the abolition of slavery by Great Britain in 1833, **Ahmed Reid** fills a historiographical gap. Reid mined the British compensation records – which concern the allocation of £20 million to slave owners for the loss of their slave property – to undertake a gender analysis and delineate the profile of the female recipients who represented 45 per cent of the total claims filed by residents. In so doing, he provides a gendered insight into the nature of slave ownership in Jamaica by assessing the numerical importance of the phenomenon, the monetary value of the compensation, the spatial distribution of the claimants and the economic activities they engaged in.

Part Two reflects on **The Politics and Economics of Atypical Forms of Slavery and Slaveholding** by particularly focusing on the systemic contexts within which they operated. It shows how specific historical contexts, such as periods of territorial settlement or of gradual manumission of slavery, which respectively signalled the introduction or the end of coerced forms of labour, fostered specific forms of slavery, thus highlighting the evolving, malleable and adaptable nature of slavery.

Through the examination of the enslaved who were employed by the Dutch West India Company in seventeenth-century New York, **Anne-Claire Faucquez** explores how corporate slave ownership impacted the nature of slavery in New Netherland. By examining the case of the first corporate slaves who were partially manumitted after having served eighteen years, Faucquez sheds light on their intermediate legal status – half-slave and half-free – which differed from that of term slaves who later appeared in Northern states after the gradual abolition of slavery in the wake of the American Revolution. An analysis of the different rights these corporate slaves enjoyed, and the paths to social integration the Dutch authorities offered them, leads Faucquez to interrogate cultural specificities which may have led to a comparatively more lenient form of slavery.

Tim Lockley also focuses on collective and public slave ownership by historicizing the factors which led British authorities to create the black West India Regiments. He reveals that, in the context of the campaigns against Saint Domingue, between 1793 and 1798, the British increasingly resorted to what he refers to as 'militarized slavery' to address the issue of the high death toll among white soldiers, primarily due to disease, principally yellow fever. However, as concern was expressed regarding the recruitment of plantation slaves from British colonies, the army eventually engaged in the purchase of Africans directly from the slave trade before later employing recaptured slaves after the British slave trade was abolished in 1807. Lockley complexifies the reasons why these black soldiers received equal treatment with their white counterparts over time by retracing the historical heterogeneity of the West India Regiments.

Christa Dierksheide's contribution investigates the little known phenomenon of slave leasing at Thomas Jefferson's Monticello from 1780 to 1830. Dierksheide argues that instead of weakening slavery, the liberalization of property laws, coupled with the decline of Virginia's staple crop, tobacco, resulted in a dramatic rise in slave ownership, slave selling and slave leasing, thus entrenching the 'peculiar institution' in post-revolutionary Virginia. She contends that even a so-called 'traditional' slaveholder like Jefferson increasingly turned to a 'non-traditional' practice like renting slaves to incur profits. In the process of demonstrating how the ownership or hiring of slaves was democratized in post-revolutionary Virginia, Dierksheide conclusively shows that individuals who had hitherto not been able to purchase, inherit or employ slaves – such as women, orphans and poor white men – were offered unprecedented opportunities to attain social status and accumulate wealth.

Nikita Harwich presents a detailed account of two nineteenth-century slave revolts that took place in Ocumare de la Costa, in the cocoa cultivating region of Venezuela. Harwich contends that the implementation of the 1821 gradual Manumission Law, which provided that the future offspring of bond women would be liberated at age eighteen, involuntarily led to an increasing subordination among the enslaved population as the legislation signalled the ultimate extinction of slavery in the long run. Through a minute analysis of two slave revolts that occurred in 1837 and 1845, Harwich precisely reconstructs the actual working conditions of the enslaved and sheds new light on the peculiar type of master–slave relationship which characterized the cocoa-growing plantations in post-independence Venezuela. He argues that during the transitional period which preceded the general abolition of slavery in 1854, the limited nature of the repression of these slave uprisings resulted from the authorities' wish to maintain a certain form of political and economic stability.

By focusing on personal or group trajectories, with a particular emphasis on the dynamic and evolving nature of slavery and slaveholding, **Part Three** examines the question of **Social Mobility on the Margins of Slavery, Freedom and Slave Ownership**.

Nathalie Dessens's chapter complicates the practice of absentee slaveholding in Louisiana by examining the trajectory of Henri de Ste-Gême, a refugee from Saint-Domingue who became a slaveholder through marriage and, after 1818, left for France with his family and never returned. Ste-Gême left the supervision of his plantation and twenty slaves to Auvignac Dorville, a Louisianan Creole of modest social origin, who assumed full decision-making in the managerial choices of the estate. Through analysis of the epistolary correspondence between Ste-Gême and Dorville, Dessens manages to piece together in minute detail the interactions between the absentee slaveholder, the *de facto* slave owner and the enslaved who were left under his care.

By taking João de Oliveira's as a case in point, **Mary Hicks** examines how seamen of Africa descent who were employed onboard Bahian vessels travelling to West Africa's Slave Coast exercised a surprising degree of geographic mobility and economic agency. She analyses how these enslaved Preto (black or African) mariners who engaged in the West African slave trade in goods and the slave trade enjoyed a privileged access to the transatlantic trade and employed the profits generated from their time as enslaved seamen to purchase their manumission and establish themselves as independent transatlantic slave traders (*cabeceiras*), residing in the Brazilian port city of Salvador da Bahia. By exposing the convoluted life trajectory of Oliveira, Hicks's contribution complicates the notion of slave agency while also exemplifying the precariousness of free black status in Brazil.

Elizabeth Kuebler-Wolf retraces the exceptional life story of Gilbert Hunt, a Richmond, Virginia, enslaved blacksmith, who, after being manumitted by self-purchase in 1829, rose to fame. In 1811, while still a slave, Hunt saved family members of his owner from a deadly fire that engulfed the Richmond Theater. After this heroic rescue, Hunt became a local celebrity. Through the examination of a body of texts and images, Kuebler-Wolf shows how the white population of Richmond instrumentalized Gilbert Hunt's life in order to offer a positive representation of slavery that emphasized its benevolent nature. By comparing Hunt's fictionalized life to the historical record, Kuebler-Wolf exposes the modalities which enabled Hunt to navigate the waters between slavery and freedom. With this forceful case study in slave social mobility, and how Hunt's legacy has been passed been down to the present, Kuebler-Wolf underscores the tension between history and collective memory and, more specifically, how atypical and exceptional forms of slavery have been memorialized.

As we draw nearer to the general abolition of slavery, **Emily West** proposes an exploration of the nominal slaves or free people of colour who lived on the margins of the slave regime in a precarious situation. Through the examination of US census and legislative records across several slave states, West explains why a significant number of free black people lived within the households of white slaveholders and, in many instances, laboured for them under informal, unrecorded systems of bondage. However, she shows that as Southern state legislatures imposed increasingly restrictive legislation against free people of colour which limited their mobility and sometimes sought to expel them, some individuals made (re-)enslavement requests as a means to remain in their home state. West's contribution clearly reveals how despite the slaveholding states' repeated efforts to demarcate the boundaries between socio-racial statuses, there remained diverse middle grounds in between slavery and freedom where the enslaved, free blacks and poorer whites interacted in personal and economic relationships.

Herbert Klein concludes the book with a chapter of magisterial scope which describes the crucial period of transition from slavery to freedom in the Americas. He provides insightful comparisons to reveal patterns in the regional solutions that were adopted in post-emancipation societies to maintain the plantation system and its pre-emancipation level of productivity. By analysing multiple variables such as the level of competency of the coloured population, free and enslaved, as well as the demographic share of the racial and legal categories before emancipation, Klein examines the labour choices post-slave societies made, the degree of government involvement in planning this economic transition and the fate of former slaves and free coloured people in terms of their political and social integration.

Taken as a whole, the chapters in *The Many Faces of Slavery* seek to offer new perspectives on slave ownership and experiences in the Americas, as the subtitle of the book indicates. The overarching thesis of this edited volume is to examine the practice of slaveholding and the experience of slavery as it evolved over time and space. By placing emphasis on the dynamic nature of the history of slavery and of slaveholding, this book seeks to broaden the perspective of more conventional studies by uniquely bringing together a large collection of cutting-edge research from scholars in the US,

UK and continental Europe, drawing on both junior and experienced academics. One of its main assets lies in the broad geographical outlook, with chapters covering all regions of the Atlantic, with a particular emphasis on the Americas. *The Many Faces of Slavery* should be read as a modest but valuable addition to the growing body of works that interrogate the complex nature of slavery and help further our understanding while raising new questions.

Notes

1. The editors of this book wish to acknowledge the work of Lydia Plath in helping to organize the events that brought together the scholars working on this volume and in participating in framing early drafts of the book.
2. David Armitage and Michael J. Braddick, *The British Atlantic World 1600–1800* (Basingstoke: Palgrave Macmillan, 2002).
3. James C. Scott, *Weapons of the Weak: Everyday Forms of Peasant Resistance* (New Haven, CT: Yale University Press, 1985).
4. Laird Bergad, *The Comparative Histories of Slavery in Brazil, Cuba and the United States* (New York: Cambridge University Press, 2007); Michael Gomez, *Reversing Sail: A History of the African Diaspora* (Cambridge: Cambridge University Press, 2005); Gwendolyn Hall, *Slavery and African Ethnicities in the Americas* (Chapel Hill: University of North Carolina Press, 2005).
5. David Barry Gasper and Darlene Clark Hine (eds), *Beyond Bondage: Free Women of Color in the Americas* (Urbana-Champaign: University of Illinois Press, 2004); Herbert S. Klein and Ben Vinson, *African Slavery in Latin America and the Caribbean*, 2nd edn (New York: Oxford University Press, 2007); Pamela Scully and Diana Paton (eds), *Gender and Slave Emancipation in the Atlantic World* (Durham, NC: Duke University Press, 2005); Cora Kaplan and John Oldfield (eds), *Imagining Transatlantic Slavery* (Basingstoke: Palgrave Macmillan, 2010).
6. Philip D. Morgan and Sean Hawkins (eds), *Black Experience and the Empire* (Oxford: Oxford University Press, 2004); James Walvin, *Britain's Slave Empire* (Stroud: History Press Ltd., 2000); Peter H. Wood, *Strange New Land: Africans in Colonial America, 1526–1776* (Oxford: Oxford University Press, 1996).
7. Thavolia Glymph, *Out of the House of Bondage* (Cambridge: Cambridge University Press, 2008); Simon Newman, *A New World of Labour: The Development of Plantation Slavery in the British Atlantic* (Philadelphia: University of Pennsylvania Press, 2013).
8. Mariana Dantas, *Black Townsmen: Urban Slavery in the Eighteenth Century Americas* (Basingstoke: Palgrave Macmillan, 2008); Herman Bennett, *Africans in Colonial Mexico: Absolutism, Christianity and Afro-Creole Consciousness* (Bloomington: Indiana University Press, 2003); Christine Hunefeldt, *Paying the Price of Freedom: Family and Labor among Lima's Slaves, 1800–1854* (Berkeley: University of California Press, 1994).
9. Kathleen Higgins, *Licentious Liberty in a Brazilian Gold-Mining Region: Slavery, Gender and Social Control in 18th Century Sabara, Minas Gerais* (University Park: Penn State University Press, 1999); Seth Rockman, *Scraping By: Wage Labor, Slavery, and Survival in Early Baltimore* (Baltimore, MD: Johns Hopkins University Press, 2009); James Brooks, *Captives and Cousins: Slavery, Kinship and Community in the Southwest Borderlands* (Chapel Hill: University of North Carolina Press, 2002); Jorge

Canizares-Esqguerra, Matt Childs and James Sidbury (eds), *The Black Urban Atlantic in the Age of the Slave Trade* (Philadelphia: University of Pennsylvania Press, 2013).
10 Jeffrey Bolster, *Black Jacks: African American Seamen in the Age of Sail* (Cambridge, MA: Harvard University Press, 1998).
11 Rebecca Scott and Jean Hébrard, *Freedom Papers: An Atlantic Odyssey in the Age of Emancipation* (Cambridge, MA: Harvard University Press, 2014); Tiya Myles, *Ties that Bind: The Story of an Afro-Cherokee Family in Slavery and Freedom* (Berkeley: University of California Press, 2015).
12 Kimberly Hanger, *Bounded Lives, Bounded Places: Free Black Society in Colonial New Orleans, 1769–1803* (Durham, NC: Duke University Press, 1997); Stewart King, *Blue Coat or Powdered Wig: Free People of Color in Pre-Revolutionary Saint Domingue* (Athens: University of Georgia Press, 2001); Gad Heuman, *Between Black and White: Race, Politics and the Free Coloureds in Jamaica, 1792–1865* (Westport, CT: Praeger, 1981); Larry Koger, *Black Slaveowners: Free Black Slave Masters in South Carolina, 1790–1860* (Jefferson, NC: McFarland, 1985).
13 Stephanie E. Jones-Rogers, *They Were Her Property: White Women as Slave Owners in the American South* (New Haven, CT, and London: Yale University Press, 2019).

Part One

Documenting Non-traditional Slavery and Slaveholding

1

Many Faces of Slaveholding Sephardim

Seymour Drescher

East of the Atlantic

During the period that Europe underwent its expansion to the shores of Africa and the western Atlantic, a book on Jewish practices devoted a brief chapter to slavery. In his *Historia dei riti Ebraice*, Leone da Modena noted that Jews held and sold slaves 'according to the custom of the place in which they live'.[1] This was a traditional extension of the Halachic principle for Jews in the diaspora that, in all non-religious matters, 'the law of the land is the law'. North of the Alps, whether under Catholic or Protestant rulers, Jews were not permitted to maintain ownership where slave law no longer existed.

Where the laws permitted, Jews could either hire Jewish or non-Jewish servants or purchase slaves. The enslaved could not be members of the dominant Christian or Muslim community. In the absence of constraining laws, such slaves could also be converted to Judaism. Since most slaves of Jews were household domestics, they or their children by their master might then be converted and integrated into the family and the community.[2]

Black slaves comprised a small proportion of the total slave population in this Mediterranean world. On the basis of the limited available evidence, Jonathan Schorsch concludes that the treatment of black slaves, mostly women in Jewish homes, hardly differed at all from those in non-Jewish homes and cultures. They seem to have been frequently converted by ritual immersion (or circumcised if male) and absorbed into the community. Some married their masters. Again, there appears to be no evidence that this domestic slavery created additional distinctions of treatment between Blacks and Whites, whether enslaved or manumitted.[3]

Confessing Conversos and practising Jews: navigating the world of Atlantic slavery

If one had to choose a non-traditional cohort of slaveholders in the Atlantic world, none would be more appropriate than those in the Sephardic diaspora who were forcibly converted to Christianity in Spain and Portugal at the end of the fifteenth century. They and their descendants were legally identified as 'Conversos' or 'New Christians'. One must approach the study of this diaspora by noting its variability both in terms of internal relations with the state and with other groups, including slaves. There is a historiographical tendency in diaspora studies to consider these descendants as secret, or crypto-Jews (*judeoconversos* or *marranos*). Viewed by authorities as a perpetual threat, members of this group likewise felt perpetually threatened.[4]

These New Christians played an important role in the commercial networks of the early modern era, including the transportation of enslaved Africans across the Iberian Atlantic to the Spanish and Portuguese settlements in the Americas. At the same time they became the most vulnerable of slaveowners. They remained constantly under the scrutiny of the Inquisition, spending their entire lives as potential suspects and subverters of the Catholic communities in which they lived. They were vulnerable to anonymous denunciation from any member of the community, including slaves. Such denunciations could lead to repeated imprisonment and examination, including methods now referred to as enhanced interrogation.[5]

To demonstrate their situation, I offer a documented procedure that exemplifies their judicial and existential situation. In 1567, Elvira del Campo, a resident of Toledo, Spain, was accused of 'Judaizing', one of the most serious crimes coming under the jurisdiction of the Spanish Inquisition. Elvira was a descendant of Jews who had converted to Catholicism during the previous century. Born, baptized and married to a Catholic, she was also still legally a *judeoconverso*. She was therefore also a carrier of 'impure blood'. Her anonymous accuser (or accusers) testified that she clandestinely engaged in Jewish practices. Elvira did not eat pork and wore fresh clothing on Saturdays. As a potential 'crypto-Jew' she was carried to the torture chamber and admonished to confess. As the official record states:

> Elvira was ordered to be stripped ... When stripped she said, 'Señores, I have done all that is said of me, and I bear false-witness against myself, for I do not want to see myself in trouble, please God, I have done nothing' ... She was told ... to tell the truth ... When a cord was tied to her arms and twisted, she screamed and said of her accusers, ... 'I have done all they say.' Another twist ... she screamed and said, 'Tell me what to say.' Another turn of the cord was ordered. She cried, 'Loosen me Señores and tell me what to say: I do not know what I have done.' Another turn and she said, 'Loosen me a little that I may remember what I have to tell ... I did not eat pork for it made me sick; ... I have done everything ...' She was told to tell what she had done contrary to our holy Catholic faith ... More turns were ordered ... she cried 'Oh! Oh! Loosen me for I don't know what to say – Oh my arms! I don't know what I have to say – If I did I would tell it.' Then she was put on the *escalera*: 'Señores why will you not tell me what I have to say? ... I did all that the witnesses *say* ...' Then she said, 'Señores I did it to observe the *Law*.' She was asked what Law. She said, 'The Law that the witnesses say – I declare it all Señor and don't *remember* what Law it was – Oh wretched was the mother that bore me.' Then came 'the water in her throat ...'[6]

The last of Elvira's stream of screams was true beyond any doubt. The mother who had given birth to her had endowed her with the curse of vulnerability. The social conditions of the New Christians in the Iberian empires that first created the Atlantic slave system were defined by the legacy of forced mass conversions. The founding of the Inquisitions of Spain and Portugal coincided with the culmination of the *Reconquista* in Iberia and the creation of their transoceanic empires. By the mid-fifteenth century the idea of the 'secret Jew' took its place alongside its 'old Christian' counterpart.

When non-Europeans also began to be incorporated into the Iberian Atlantic, the blood of Blacks, like those of ex-Jews and Muslims, was deemed to be too impure to be completely assimilated. This expanded the ideological formation of a category of Christians whose descendants were legally ineligible for most political and religious positions and whose blood was eternally tainted. The extension of this religious-cultural identity coincided with the emergence of a lexicon of loaded words like race, caste lineage, reinforced by popular notions about social reproduction.[7]

What did this entail for relationships between Iberian New Christian *judeoconversos* and their African slaves? For New Christians and slaves who were connected only through the slave trade, it meant very little. One group passed through the hands of the other in a long chain of collective transactions. Even slavers who escorted their captives all the way from Africa to Peru would view most of them only as a mass of captive human commodities. Those dealing in such human beings might accumulate enormous fortunes without recalling a single face or a name of their commodities.

Where are we likely to find glimpses of interaction or communication between two groups stigmatized in their own way by the theo-politics of descent and blood purity? Precisely where we met Elvira del Campo – in the records of the Inquisition. There we encounter verbatim testimonies of both masters and slaves. But Elvira's very own words warn us to exercise caution in assuming that they offer clear evidence of how individuals within the two groups actually interacted with each other. The Inquisitors' procedures were, after all, invitations to a range of discursive strategies by both accusers and accused.

It was as captives themselves that Sephardic Iberians first became involved in the founding of Atlantic slave colonies. In 1492 the majority of Jews who fled Spain crossed the frontier to Portugal. Most entered as illegal aliens, unable to pay the high price demanded by Portugal's ruler from each refugee. King Manual declared all such defaulters to be his debt-slaves. Five years later he ordered the roundup of 2,000 Jewish children from families who refused his royal order to convert. They were dispatched to the island of São Tomé off the African coast in order to help found a new colony. The 600 who reportedly survived to adulthood were offered African partners.[8] In turn, their Luso-African progeny participated in turning the island into a sugar colony and a major entrepôt for the transatlantic slave trade. Subsequent generations of 'New Christians' in Portugal similarly found that participation in the transatlantic slave trade allowed them to relocate to imperial frontiers where the gaze of the Inquisition was easier to evade. Their status was not. A century and a half after the Iberian forced conversions, an Italian monk observed that the Portuguese were still making use of *Judeoconversos* as forced labour in Luanda.[9] Generations of Christianized free Afroiberians also remained targets of the Inquisition.

For slaves, however, the Inquisitions offered a potential weapon. Excessive punishment by masters might lead them to retaliate with accusations of Judaizing.

Slaves denounced owners for actions ranging from ordering them to wash floors on Good Friday or who whipped them severely. The accusations could be lurid. In Bahia, Brazil, a New Christian was denounced for fornicating with a black slave who was allegedly forced to lie on a crucifix. Masters could strike back against their own brutal agents. Manuel Bautista Perez in Peru, a wealthy Portuguese slave trader, warned his Lima inquisitors that one of his stewards always went around complaining that Perez was threatening to have the steward punished for beating one of his African slaves to death.[10]

In this way the Inquisition added a new dimension to traditional slave–master relations. Black and mulatto slaves used the Inquisition for protection from, or leverage against, masters. Clashes over servitude might have been more important catalysts than divisions between Old and New Christians, but 'Judaizing' was clearly a potent weapon of the weak. The accused always had to defend themselves against anonymous accusers. Affluence could actually increase vulnerability. Large numbers of servants meant increasing possibilities for anonymous denunciation. One Spanish family defended itself by identifying more than thirty former servants who were potentially hostile witnesses. Correctly identifying an anonymous accuser might nullify their credibility, so it was tempting for the accused to strike back in every direction.[11]

If one were both a foreigner *and* a New Christian, the hurdles could be insuperable. Manuel Batista Perez was tortured and executed in Lima in the course of an *autodafé* in 1639. He had the misfortune to be both Portuguese and *Judeoconverso* during a great Spanish purge of Portuguese. Perez's eating habits were provided by his domestics. They attested to his warnings against purchasing the hind quarters of animals, and his orders to soak meat overnight. These were warning signs periodically publicized by the Inquisition, and domestics could credibly testify to their veracity. The combination of slave accusations and refusal to confess even under torture could lead to the most painful of deaths. For his stubborn insistence on his enduring faith in the 'law of Jesus' and his desire to die as 'a soldier of Jesus Christ', Perez was burned at the stake.[12]

Slaves themselves remained vulnerable accusers. The Inquisition could not allow itself 'complete faith and credit' in someone who was 'a slave and vile person'. A juridical commentator affirmed that the gravity of heresy permitted the acceptance of slaves' testimony, but only with care, because 'in general they bear extreme malice against their masters'. However, the same 'gravity' allowed the court to torture a slave who showed himself reluctant to denounce his master. Since an accusing slave could be tortured if the court suspected his or her testimony, it is likely that many slaves stayed as far as they could from the tribunal unless their situation was desperate.[13]

Since slaves remained embedded in a status that made their testimony suspect, ambiguous testimony might lead the tribunal to decide that the slave must be put to the 'procedure'. Suspicious that a female slave had lied against her masters, a Mexico City tribunal decided that she needed to be faced with torture to see whether she would alter her testimony. Suspicious masters could pre-empt accusation by dispatching a hostile slave to a plantation where they might soon die as a result of severe punishment or hard labour. Denunciations from plantations were exceedingly rare. It was only slaves who could readily observe the daily behaviour of masters who could credibly describe the subtle signs of 'Judaizing' within the domestic circle. In this respect, field slaves remained as remote from the intimate lives of their masters as were the cargoes of Africans transported by slaving merchants.[14]

Domestic slaves were vulnerable in other respects. They could be charged by the Inquisition to act as agents of surveillance against masters at home or in prison, watching for signs of Judaizing practices. As one scholar noted, domestic slaves could observe their masters eating, sleeping, or dressing; drunk or sober; they could observe all visitors; they knew 'all the secrets'. Some agents of the Inquisition took pride in being able to discern the truth within the 'lies' of Blacks. As with masters, the temptation to please a powerful new inquisitorial master was always present.[15]

Other repertoires might be followed. A slave might feel deprived of the familial connections enjoyed by New Christian masters whether or not the family was free of the usual signs of Judaizing. Denunciation offered an escape from solitary isolation. The Inquisition offered slaves one more pathway to integration into the community. It opened a range of opportunities for slaves in the Iberian empires that was unavailable to those in the Protestant-dominated Atlantic. A small minority of newly Christianized slaves might have some leverage against a group of Europeans born and raised as 'New Christians'. Fervently religious masters correspondingly feared being thrust out of their religious community even as death loomed. One such mistress, about to die under accusation, requested that a crucifix be permanently placed upon her body in plain view of the black women at her funeral. Alternatively, some masters allegedly promised manumission to their slaves in exchange for silence.[16]

Jonathan Schorsch thus concludes that 'despite their subaltern status slaves often exercised disproportionate influence on their masters' behaviour'.[17] They certainly had leverage unavailable to the slaves of Old Christians. It is impossible to estimate the degree to which New Christian masters treated their domestic slaves with any less rigour or more caution than their Old Christian counterparts, but *Conversos* had reason to believe that the Inquisition would treat slaves' allegations of infidelity with greater seriousness than those directed toward Old Christian masters. In sum, given the legal consequences of both open enslavement and secret 'Judaizing', masters could become victims of slaves, slaves victims of masters, and both victims of the Inquisition. The range of possible behaviours under a regime of judicial torture is not unfamiliar to us.

The Dutch Caribbean

We turn from a society in which no Jewish slaveholders could live openly or securely even within the privacy of their own homes to one in which they lived with more public independence than anywhere else in the early modern world. During the seventeenth century a portion of the Sephardic diaspora began to escape to areas of the Atlantic dominated by Protestants interested in launching their own overseas empires. The Dutch were particularly prone to welcome refugees fleeing the Iberian Catholic empires. In the seventeenth century the Dutch had the highest standard of living, the lowest unemployment rate and the best welfare system in Europe. In short, the Netherlands was the most difficult area in Europe from which to entice volunteers for establishing colonies in the tropics of the Americas. Given their situation, descendants of 'New Christians' were offered the best terms anywhere on either side of the Atlantic to become pioneers in a new Dutch colony.[18] In the mid-seventeenth century, openly practising Jews were among the colony's earliest European settlers in Suriname. Under both Dutch and English rule they established the village of Jodensavanne, the largest Jewish agricultural community in the early modern world. As a virtually self-determining community, they created a society in which the highest form of social or political status was open to Jews as well as Christians. In Suriname, Sephardim thus found themselves at the opposite pole from descendants of Jews in the contemporary Iberian world, with a degree of autonomy unavailable even to their prosperous co-religionists in Amsterdam.[19]

How then did Jewish slaveholders, marginalized elsewhere in the world, relate to their slaves? On the eastern side of the Atlantic in the Mediterranean, where *domestic* slaveholding was the rule, there was an extensive body of rabbinical *responsas* with rules for the treatment of slaves, including issues related to religious integration and manumission. By contrast, barely any analogous record of rabbinical writings can be found for the treatment of slaves anywhere in the Americas. Large-scale plantations increased the social distance between European masters and the mass of their African slaves. Suriname's Jewish slaveowners closely resembled their Christian counterparts. Like their neighbours, they made no sustained effort to convert or to manumit the overwhelming majority of enslaved Africans.[20]

The only major impact of Jewish law on slave labour in Jodensavanne was that Jewish planters in Suriname rested their slaves on their Sabbath and festivals. This shift, of course, meant that Sundays were days full of working. Sparse anecdotal evidence indicates that Jewish masters could be as demanding of their slaves as were those of any other religious group. The most important opportunities for variation of treatment of slaves in Suriname arose in relation to their masters' vastly different social status from the New Christians of the Iberian world. As Aviva Ben-Ur notes, since Jodensavanne was virtually a self-governing village, it was a place in which 'the highest form of social climbing for a slave meant becoming a Jew rather than a Christian or a Muslim'.[21]

Demography, not religion, offered status mobility. As early as the last quarter of the seventeenth century, Africans represented three-quarters of the colony's population. A century later the proportion had reached 96 per cent. From the beginning, the Jewish population, like their European counterparts, had at least two males to every female. This, above all, 'opened doors to mixed race "Suriname marriage"'. Only in the case of 'children of affection' (mulatto offspring of slave women and Europeans) was there any effort to religiously incorporate such individuals through traditional circumcision or conversion. This created a pattern of not-fully-formalized but very durable relationships between black women and white men. The outcome was an Afro-European population with recognized claims to paternal white descent. The children usually grew up as privileged slaves, were frequently manumitted and continued to have good relationships with their fathers. These Afro-Europeans represented 60 per cent of the slaves manumitted between 1760 and 1836. Occasionally, they might inherit slaves of their own or, more rarely, an entire plantation. However, for the overwhelming majority of Suriname slaves in each generation, this pathway to liberation was a narrow one.[22]

From early on in the settlement, the *Mahamad* (the autonomous governing body of Suriname's Jews) made provision for recognizing Afro-European unions, while simultaneously creating a new hierarchy of status. It divided the community between *jehidim* and *congregantes*. The former referred to full members of the Jewish community by European ancestry. The mulatto '*congregant*' was consigned to a lower status. This was not exclusively a colour line. Congregants consisted of both Eurafricans and descendants of male Europeans. The latter were also Europeans demoted as a penalty for formally marrying females of Afro-European lineage. This novelty was in direct contradiction to traditional rabbinic law. It was borrowed from a Dutch Calvinist doctrine that distinguished church 'members' from 'followers'. This arrangement only took cognizance of cases where 'Suriname marriages' occurred. There was no restriction against extramarital relations. Moreover, the *Mahamad* provided for a 'fallen' *jahid* to be readmitted to his old status if his children and grandchildren married white women.[23]

One significant legal omission evidenced the dramatic difference between Old and New World traditions. Rabbinical law provided that Jewish identity was from the mother. Yet Suriname law said absolutely nothing about the status of the offspring of a Jewish mother and an African father. In the New World the very mention of such a transgression was suppressed. One rare text suggests that in Suriname (and Curaçao) slaves were allowed to convert to Judaism during their enslavement. While religiously ignoring their field labourers, Jewish masters seem to have taken the lead among white colonists in converting household slaves to their religion.[24]

The existence of marronage from Jewish masters' and snippets of responses from runaways' testimony offer evidence that cruelty played its usual prominent role in the treatment of plantation slaves. On the other hand, nowhere in the entire corpus of Maroon oral histories collected by anthropologist Richard Price (many of which relate to Jewish plantation owners) does there exist expressed hostility against Jews as Jews. They were not differentiated by slaves from Christian masters. Jonathan Schorsch concludes that the lack of anti-Jewish animus on the part of Suriname's slaves is further evidence of the unremarkable nature of Jewish slaveholders' behaviour within the plantation economy. Otherwise, the contrast of Suriname with the Iberian empires is clear. This underscores the role of Iberian ruling class ideology in sustaining the framework for religio-racial denunciations of New Christian masters. The difference in slave attitudes in territories under Inquisition surveillance from those in orbits, where it had no jurisdiction, offers a striking comparative perspective.[25]

While the demands of sugar cultivation and the enormous disparity between slaves and free people in Suriname caused the planters to replicate the plantation rigour and brutality of the plantation system, the Sephardic experience under Iberian rule impacted the slave–master relationship in one particular moment of ritual leisure. Whether in the major city of Paramaribo or the rural Jodensavanne, the holiday of Purim lasted for a week or more. Crowds of masked celebrants poured into the streets. They marched, danced, sang, drank, costumed as Maroons, Indians, soldiers and sailors. Christian observers identified the holiday as a *bacchanalia judaeorum* – a Jewish carnival.

Purim, however, was more than a carnival for the descendants of the Portuguese Jews. Purim was a story of escape – the Book of Esther. Esther, the heroine, masqueraded as a non-Jew while laying a trap to ensnare an enemy of the Jews who had planned their annihilation. When Suriname's slaves massively joined the boisterous celebration, they did not merely imitate their masters. They were fully aware of its implicit message of reversal and liberation. They performed and cultivated their own traditions. The popularity of naming children Purim and Esther may also have followed the African practice of naming a child after an important legend. The popularity of Purim or Esther was an opportunity to link their own meaning and wishes to the unbridled joy which they poured into the celebration. This was implicitly recognized by government authorities. Purim was the only Jewish holiday continually policed by Dutch colonial law in anticipation of its potential to get out of control.[26]

Transatlantic Jewish abolitionism

Finally, we turn to the period when the slave trade and slavery first began to come under major sustained political and moral challenge at the end of the eighteenth century. Slavers and planters were unlikely to be at the forefront of any movement against institutions that provided them with their livelihood and prestige. One must also take note of the fact that the emergence of abolitionism occurred at the very moment when slavery in the tropics still appeared to be a most attractive institution to Euro-Americans on both sides of the Atlantic. The transatlantic slave trade slavery reached peaks of volume and value to Europeans, even to whose polities lacked direct access to the Atlantic slave system. They envied 'the mountain of sugar being brought to Europe by other Europeans'. Johann David Michaelis, a German academic living in a kingdom without tropical colonies or slaving entrepôts on the coast of Africa, advocated a unique German solution to satisfy its growing craving for sugar. He proposed that Germany establish a tropical colony with its Jews as the plantation labour force. This would simultaneously solve both Germany's sweet tooth and its metropolitan 'Jewish problem'. Since Jews were, in his view, 'an unmixed race of more southern people', they would be well suited to grow cane alongside African slaves.[27]

With a very different end in mind, a Sephardic Jew in America came up with another colonization plan to solve another Jewish problem, Tsarist oppression in Russia. Moses Elias Levy of Florida was not cut in the mold of other abolitionists in the early nineteenth century. A true Atlantic navigator, he was descended from Jews who fled to Morocco in 1492. Born in 1782, he was the son of a favoured courtier and a royal merchant of the Sultan. In 1790 the family was imperiled after the sudden death of the Sultan, and they fled to British Gibraltar. At age eighteen, Moses Levy moved to the Danish West Indian island of St Thomas, successfully engaging in the trade between Gibraltar and the West Indies.[28]

In 1821, Levy moved to Florida, just acquired by the United States. His abolitionist commitment had already crystalized. While he was a devout Jew, Levy embraced a dissident vision of orthodoxy. Heavily influenced by the Anglo-American evangelical Protestantism of the 1820s, his anti-slavery project resembled many communitarian projects of early nineteenth-century socialism. He differed from most by proposing to found a demonstration settlement that would ultimately raise sugar by free white labour on the St Johns river. In one respect, Levy's Florida prospect was utterly different from all other planters of his time. He proposed to make a free labour plantation to serve as an asylum for European Jewry, suffering under the authority of Tsar Nicholas of Russia.[29]

In order to clear the land, however, Levy's initial workers were leased slaves from their Seminole masters; others were purchased. They were paid wages and allowed considerable 'personal liberty'. As his biographer observes:

> To the casual observer the practice of slavery at Levy's settlement probably did not appear all that unconventional. Yet brutal excesses were apparently not part of the plantation regimen. Levy abhorred the 'wantonness and caprice' of those slaveholders who inflicted 'horrible cruelty' ... and looked to the Hebrew Bible and its humane laws ... as his paradigm.[30]

In other respects, Levy was, like most British and North American abolitionists in the early nineteenth century, a gradualist. He believed that adult slaves would suffer more if suddenly liberated after a lifetime of bondage. He favoured the method already adopted in the Northern US states for slave children. Final liberation would be delayed until slaves reached age twenty-one and had completed their educational and agricultural training. In the early 1820s, this trajectory was clearly in accord with the position of most prior emancipations and gradualist anti-slavery associations throughout the Atlantic world. In a Florida slave territory, even such a gradualist project would have appeared threatening to most of his slaveholding neighbours. Levy kept his anti-slavery ideas out of public view.[31]

Desperately needing funds to subsidize the migration of refugees to his new community, Levy journeyed to London in 1825. He sought for philanthropic aid from his transatlantic co-religionists. Three years of appeals proved to be unsuccessful. However, during his stay he became the first Southern plantation owner and probably the only employer of slaves in America to offer both a series of abolitionist lectures in London and to publish a tract in favour of abolition. His fundraising venture in London coincided almost precisely with the emergence of a British gradualist movement campaigning for gradual emancipation. In *A Plan for the Abolition of Slavery, Consistently with the Interests of all Parties Concerned* (1828), Levy expanded his own solution to a degree that few abolitionists on either side were yet prepared to consider. He drew attention to the long-term problem of post-emancipation racialism that would certainly endure long after the legal abolition of the institution. He recommended interracial marriage as the solution. To his British audience he likewise suggested that the flow of convicts to Australia should be diverted to the West Indies in order to assure the long-term economic success of British emancipation.[32]

In the end, Levy's project foundered. His one Florida settlement was destroyed during the Second Seminole War in the 1830s. In order to preserve the remains of his wealth, Levy first mortgaged, then sold, the last of thirty-one slaves who had survived its destruction. His son David broke with Moses, converted to Christianity, married the daughter of a former Kentucky governor and changed his name from Levy to Yulee. As a (New) Christian, but without the crushing legal burden of Iberian disability, David

Yulee established a 5,000-acre sugar plantation, built and fully maintained by slaves. Yulee became a United States senator from Florida, the first American born a Jew to enter that body. After serving two terms, he renounced his allegiance to the United States and joined the Confederacy. His memory was enshrined in the Florida town and county of Yulee.[33]

Perhaps the principal conclusion that one might draw from these histories is that, with rare exceptions, most Sephardic slaveholders behaved much like their traditional counterparts. Minorities in every empire that they inhabited, they acted, as Leone da Modena had written, 'according to the custom of the place in which they live'. Differences in their relations with slaves varied within the range of opportunities and constraints imposed upon them. The same conclusion probably holds true for those whom they held in bondage.[34]

Notes

1 Rendered into English as *The History of the Rites, Customes, and Manner of Life of the Present Jews, Throughout the World*, trans. Edmund Chilmead (London: Printed by J.L. and are to be sold by Jo: Martin, and Jo: Ridley, at the Castle in Fleet-street, by Ram-Alley, 1650).
2 Jonathan Schorsch, *Jews and Blacks in the Early Modern World* (New York: Cambridge University Press, 2004), chapter 2.
3 Schorsch, *Jews and Blacks*, chapter 3.
4 For the most recent examinations of the Sephardic diaspora and slavery, see Jonathan Schorsch and Sina Rauschenbach (eds), *The Sephardic Atlantic: Colonial Histories and Postcolonial Perspectives* (Basingstone: Palgrave Macmillan, 2018). On the complexities of identifying and assessing the Sephardic Jewish and New Christian diasporas, see, inter alia, Paolo Bernardini and Norman Fiering (eds), *The Jews and the Expansion of Europe to the West, 1450–1800* (New York: Berghahn Books, 2001); Richard L. Kagan and Philip D. Morgan (eds), *Atlantic Diasporas: Jews, Conversos, and Crypto-Jews in the Age of Mercantilism* (Baltimore, MD: Johns Hopkins University Press, 2008); Daviken Studniki-Gisbert, *A Nation Upon the Ocean Sea: Portugal's Atlantic Diaspora and the Crisis of the Spanish Empire, 1492–1640* (Oxford: Oxford University Press, 2007); Peter Mark and José da Silva Horta (eds), *The Forgotten Diaspora: Jewish Communities in West Africa and the Making of the Atlantic World* (Cambridge: Cambridge University Press, 2011). For some critique on the uses of the term identity itself, see Rogers Brubaker and Frederick Cooper, 'Beyond Identity', *Theory and Society* 29 (2000): 1–47.
5 On the Inquisition, see Henry Kamen, *The Spanish Inquisition: A Historical Revision* (New Haven, CT: Yale University Press, 1998); and Irene Silverblatt, 'Colonial Conspiracies', *Ethnohistory* 53, no. 2 (Spring 2006): 260–1.
6 Marvin Perry and Frederick M. Schweitzer (eds), *Antisemitic Myths: A Historical Account and Contemporary Anthology* (Bloomington: Indiana University Press, 2008), 35–7; transl. from Henry Charles Lea, *A History of the Inquisition of Spain*, 4 vols (New York: Macmillan, 1907), III, 24–6. See also Jonathan Kirsch (ed.), *The Grand Inquisitor's Manual: A History of Terror in the Name of God* (New York: Harper One, 2008).
7 See María Elena Martínez, *Genealogical Fictions: Limpieza de Sangre, Religion, and Gender in Colonial Mexico* (Stanford, CA: Stanford University Press, 2008).

8 See Robert Garfield, 'Public Christians, Secret Jews: Religion and Political Conflict on São Tomé Island', *Sixteenth Century Journal* 21, no. 4 (1990): 645–54; and François Soyez, 'King João II of Portugal O Príncipe Perfeito' and the Jews', *Sefarad* 69, no. 1 (2009): 75–99.
9 David Eltis, 'Identity and Migration, The Atlantic in Comparative Perspective', in Wim Klooster and Alfred Pedula (eds), *The Atlantic World: Essays on Slavery: Migration and Immigration* (Upper Saddle River, NJ: Pearson Prentice Hall, 2005), 122, cited in Jonathan Schorsch, *Swimming the Christian Atlantic: Judeoconversos, Afroibereans, and Amerindians in the Seventeenth Century* (Leiden and Boston: Brill, 2009), 55.
10 Schorsch, *Swimming the Christian Atlantic*, chapter 4.
11 For the incidents described in the context of the Inquisition, I have relied primarily on Jonathan Schorsch, *Swimming the Christian Atlantic*, passim.
12 Nathan Wachtel, *La Foi du Souvenir: Labyrinthes Marranes* (Paris: Seuil, 2001), 79–101.
13 Schorsch, *Swimming the Christian Atlantic*, 184.
14 Schorsch, *Swimming the Christian Atlantic*, 188.
15 Schorsch, *Swimming the Christian Atlantic*, 185–7.
16 Schorsch, *Swimming the Christian Atlantic*, 184. See Diana Luz Ceballos Gomez, *Quyen tal haze que tal pague: Sociedad y practicas mágecas en la Nuevo Reino de Granada* (Bogota: Ministerio de Cultura, 2002), 298–9; cited in Schorsch, *Swimming the Christian Atlantic*, 189.
17 Schorsch, *Swimming the Christian Atlantic*, 207: 'Ultimately, mistresses and masters had no way of knowing whether slaves, even seemingly loyal ones, could be trusted under the stare of the inquisitorial gaze.'
18 On the Dutch situation in comparative terms, see David Eltis, *The Rise of African Slavery in the Americas* (New York: Cambridge University Press, 2000), 9, Table 1.1; Seymour Drescher, 'White Atlantic? The Choice for African Slave Labour in the Plantation Americas', in D. Eltis, F. D. Lewis and Kenneth L. Sokoloff (eds), *Slavery in the Development of the Americas* (New York: Cambridge University Press, 2004), 31–69.
19 Aviva Ben-Ur, 'A Matriarchal Matter: Slavery, Conversion, and Upward Mobility in Suriname's Jewish Community', in Richard L. Kagan and Philip D. Morgan (eds), *Atlantic Diasporas: Jews, Conversos, and Crypto-Jews in the Age of Mercantilism, 1500–1800* (Baltimore, MD: Johns Hopkins University Press, 2009), 152–69.
20 See Rosemary Brana-Shute, 'The Manumission of Slaves in Suriname, 1760–1828', PhD diss., University of Florida, 1985, 231.
21 Ben-Ur, 'A Matriarchal Matter', 156–62.
22 Ben-Ur, 'A Matriarchal Matter', 156–62.
23 Ben-Ur, 'A Matriarchal Matter', 156–62.
24 Schorsch, *Jews and Blacks*, chapter 4.
25 Schorsch, *Jews and Blacks*, 299, and Richard Price, *Alabi's World* (Baltimore, MD: Johns Hopkins University Press, 1983); Richard Price, *The Guiana Maroons* (Baltimore, MD: Johns Hopkins University Press, 1976); and Richard Price, *To Slay the Hydra: Dutch Colonial Perspective on the Saramaka Wars* (Ann Arbor, MI: Karoma Publishers, 1983).
26 On Slaves and Purim, see Aviva Ben-Ur, 'Purim in the Public Eye: Leisure, Violence and the Cultural Convergence in the Dutch Atlantic', *Jewish Social Studies: History, Culture, Society* 20, no. 1 (Fall 2013): 32–76.
27 For all quotations, see Jonathan M. Hess, *Germans, Jews, and the Chains of Modernity* (New Haven, CT: Yale University Press, 2002), 79–84.
28 C. S. Monaco, *Moses Levy of Florida: Jewish Utopian and Antebellum Reformer* (Baton Rouge: Louisiana State University Press, 2005), 12–38.

29 Monaco, *Moses Levy*, 39–51, 95–114, 123–9. On Russian Jewry, see Michael Stanislawski, *Tsar Nicholas I and the Jews: The Transformation of Jewish Society in Russia, 1825-1855* (Philadelphia: Jewish Publication Society of America, 1983); and Salo W. Baron, *The Russian Jew Under Tsars and Soviets* (New York: Schocken Books, 1987), 30–1.
30 Monaco, *Moses Levy*, 109.
31 Monaco, *Moses Levy*, chapter 7.
32 Moses Levy, *A Plan for the Abolition of Slavery, Consistently with the Interest of all Parties Concerned* (London: n.p., 1828).
33 David Yulee's own son distanced himself even further from his religious heritage, claiming that his grandfather was not a Jew after all, but 'a Mohammedan by the name of Yulee'. A subsequent historian repositioned the family into the genealogical racialism of the Inquisition, casually observing that 'David Levy can be regarded as a Jew by race only', and concluded that he deserved to be remembered because he was 'the first of his race' to be a member of the United States Senate. As for Moses, another passing observation by the same author mentioned that he 'created a stir by a plan he devised for the abolition of Negro slavery'. See Leon Hühner, 'David L. Yulee, Florida's First Senator', in Leonard Dinnerstein and Mary Dale Palsson (eds), *Jews in the South* (Baton Rouge: Louisiana State University Press, 1973), 52–74, 52, 56, 74.
34 Leone da Modena, *Historia dei riti Ebraice* (Vienna: n.p., 1867), 174–5.

2

Something Close to Freedom: The Case of the Black Seminoles in Florida

Brent R. Weisman

There is no easy way to think about African slavery among the Indians in what is now the Southeastern United States. Our sympathies lie with those peoples whose homelands were invaded, whose population suffered traumatic and culturally transformative loss from disease and warfare, who were dispossessed of their territories and forced to move to ground alien to them. We cast the adaptive response of the Southeastern Indians to the swelling tide of European occupation in a number of ways: resistance, accommodation, acculturation, assimilation, creolization, all of them strategies to ensure cultural or biological survival but none of them done with complete free will, that is, in the absence of opposition. Likewise we are sympathetic with those peoples ripped from their homes and families, boated as freight across the ocean, sold in the marketplace like bales of cotton or tobacco, and destined for a life of subhuman servitude. And bringing these Africans and Indians into the frame with Europeans, we would like to think that the former two groups would bond in alliance against a common enemy. Indeed, sometimes this did happen, in very historically specific circumstances. But this is not the larger story. This is the story that is hard for us to think about. How can we make sense of the fact that Southeastern Indians came to own African slaves, viewing them as property just as their European-American neighbours did?[1] The answer defies our sympathies and we must set them aside, even knowing that the same sympathies were held by many people of the time; indeed, Americans have always been divided on the morality of slavery and the legitimacy of Indian rights and were confounded even in the early 1800s by the nature of the relationship between Indians and Africans. When the notion of Indians owning human property could not be reconciled with notions of the rightful place of Indians in the social order, white Americans often made poor decisions that escalated into armed conflict.[2]

It is hard to think about slavery among the Indians because it is hard to talk about, to find the right words to hold a conversation. Our case, that of the Black Seminoles in Florida, is especially hard because it doesn't fit into any standard classification. No existing term adequately captures the relationship between Seminole and Black. The conventional 'Black Seminole' implies that these people were Seminoles who happened to be Black.[3] This was not the case; they were not integrated into the all-important clan system nor did they participate in the annual social and religious cycle culminating in the Green Corn Dance. They dressed like Seminoles and allied with them in fights against a common enemy, but they lived apart, had their own codes of behaviour, their own beliefs and rituals. The term 'maroon'[4] has been applied but it too misses the mark by ignoring the fact that the Blacks were, as recognized by everyone at the time, owned by the Seminoles. 'Seminole Negroes', the term most commonly used at the time, best describes the relationship because it implies ownership by the Seminoles, but the word 'negro' has fallen out of favour in recent years. 'Seminole Freedmen' applies only to their post-Removal status in Indian Territory (Oklahoma) after emancipation following the Civil War.[5] To my knowledge, these people had no collective term for themselves before they organized into political bands in Oklahoma. And so we are left with a host of unsatisfactory alternatives. Choosing one over another also suggests a particular perspective on the subject, a choosing of sides, polarizing rather than unifying the discussion. Having said this, I will use Black Seminoles here because it is the most widespread both popularly and in scholarship within the last fifty years.

But back to our core concern: how can we best understand the relationship between the Seminole Indians and the Black Seminoles? What conceptual tools do we need to place this relationship in the contexts of the time, from about the 1780s through 1842 in Florida, then through 1865 in Oklahoma? How do we need to think to make sense of the world as those who lived at the time saw it, what they saw as normal? In this chapter I will suggest several ways in which we can challenge our thinking, then go on to place the critical concept of ownership in its cultural and historical contexts. Because I was trained as an archaeological anthropologist, I will use evidence from the ground to argue that we can offer interpretations of those past realities but no conclusions, that enigma and ambiguity remain and that we need to be cautious about casting the past in our own image.

Rethinking conventional ideas about American slavery

We are concerned here with slaveholding by people we do not expect to be slaveholders. We begin our understanding by contrasting it to 'traditional' slaveholding, the iconic slaveholding of textbooks and popular media. What is the first image that comes to mind when thinking about slavery? For most of us, this will be plantation slavery of the antebellum American South; the first figure looming large the wealthy landowning white man. This is the slavery of the English-influenced South entangled in the web of a global economy.[6] We can acknowledge the undeniable horrors of the chattel system and its vile perpetrators, accepting it as a major blemish in American history before looking away. But to do so is to miss the smaller stories of different forms of slavery, hidden from view upon first glance, but visible there between the lines in context-specific documents or in the dirt sifting through an archaeologist's screen.

We must break apart our monolithic perception of the prevailing dominance of the traditional system and the strong-chested whip-wielding white man coercing a captive labour force into a grinding manual daily routine. Although such circumstances no doubt were real, perpetuating that stereotype will not gain us further insight into the historical and cultural contexts that created the opportunities for variant forms of slavery to exist.

In what would become the American South, English influence that stressed social hierarchy based on racial dichotomy and the complete control of captured labour in the service of commerce was strong and persistent and indeed has been melded into the mainstream of American history.[7] But England, its cultures and peoples, was not the only colonial influence in the South. The Spanish presence, although largely written out of the American historical narrative, dominated Florida for most of its colonial history and that Spain still held Florida during the early decades of the American republic was a festering sore for those Americans living just beyond her northern border.[8] It was in Spanish Florida that the Seminoles first settled and it was in Spanish Florida that their unique version of slavery was shaped. To understand how the relationship between the Seminoles and Black Seminoles came to be, we need to look first at forms of slavery that existed in Spanish Florida.[9] The Spanish model adopted by the Seminoles set it apart both from slavery practised in the former British colonies to the north and from the other slaveholding Southeastern Indians whose interactions had been primarily with the English.[10]

Florida became a territory of the US in 1821; before that it had been mostly in Spanish hands except for a brief 20-year hiatus of British rule between 1763 and 1783.[11] During the pre-American years, and especially after 1763, the plantation way of life became well established, particularly along the Atlantic coast. Cotton, citrus and rice were the major crops.

Owners of English or Spanish descent held slaves, many of whom were of African birth.[12] Under weak Spanish rule on a very unstable colonial frontier and with Spain's liberal policies toward slavery, owners and slaves developed a uniquely close bond, born of survival, mutual dependence and mutual self-interest. Although the rights of ownership were not contested (slaves as property could be and were bought and sold), an almost 'corporate' sense of group identity emerged, a co-dependence of 'us vs. them' more so than slave vs. master.

Owners (admittedly to the consternation of colonial authorities) encouraged their slaves to carry firearms to protect against marauders (human or otherwise). Again, Spain was a weak overlord; any astute property owner would realize that their security from British (or American) aggressors was in their own hands. Owners with business interests elsewhere often left their plantations, for months at a time, in the care of black overseers, themselves slaves. Manumission was possible and did occur as a reward for faithful and trusted service.

The case of Zephaniah Kingsley, although not exactly typical, shows what was permissible in the protocol of social relations in Spanish Florida of the early nineteenth century.[13] Kingsley, a British-born Quaker, sea captain and slave trader, owned one of the largest plantation holdings in Florida on which he created largely self-sufficient agricultural villages stocked with Africans specially selected from his larger slave trade. He organized labour in a task system but also believed in education and the benefits of material wellbeing for his slaves. Kingsley married a Wolof woman purchased in Africa, had children by her, set her free and set her up on her own plantation which she managed with the help of twelve slaves of her own.

Later in life, Kingsley sympathized with abolitionism, but as a businessman had no trouble justifying the need for enslaved Africans in semitropical Florida (praising their superior endurance) while at the same time stating 'color ought not to be the badge of degradation; the only distinction should be between slave and free, not between white and colored'.[14] Up until recent times, and virtually universally across human experience in both space and time, human beings saw no moral violation in relegating some people to the status of slaves. It is hard for many of us today, particularly those of us living in the American South and coming of age in the Civil Rights era and for whom the Civil War is living history, not to conflate race and slavery. The history of race relations in the US, born out of slavery, has been the central perennial challenge to the flowering of American democracy.

To the Indians, Europeans and Africans who inhabited eighteenth- and nineteenth-century Southeastern US, 'all understood enslavement as a legitimate fate for a particular group of individuals'.[15] Indians were made slaves before the establishment of the African slave trade, Indians were enslavers on behalf of the colonists in the Divide and Rule world of the colonial Southeast, and became slaveowners again as they adapted and prospered in the global mercantile economy.[16]

Kingsley's statement forces us to confront the relationship between race and slavery. To what extent does our association between the two dim our potential to understand slaveholding by non-white peoples? We can take colour (race) as a shorthand for justifying our understanding of history or contemporary society, but in so doing we mistake effect for cause. This is surely one of the lessons of anthropology. Colour has been and will continue to be used as a tool for legitimizing the naturalness of social inequality, but this is a legacy of the historical contingencies that resulted in black Africans being enslaved by white Americans and the contingent circumstances that gave white Americans global ascendancy by the mid-twentieth century. We need to critique our own position in the study of the process of racialization and our intellectually inherited perspectives through full immersion into the depths of time and place-specific context.

The three groups that we are concerned with – European-derived peoples, African-derived peoples and American Indians – all engaged in slavery as slaveowners and, whether slave or free, accepted the condition of slavery (at least until the mid-1840s) as the legitimate fate of at least some human beings.[17] Colour coding this reality might obscure rather than clarify our view of the underlying processes that gave shape and meaning to the reality in which these people lived.

The cultural construction of ownership

Common to all forms of slavery is the concept of ownership. Ownership at its most basic means the ability to possess property. Slavery then, in any form, means that for societies in which it exists, some people have the ability, conferred as socially legitimized rights, to consider other people as their property. The relationship between ownership and control that is negotiated through the medium of property can be time- and place-specific and is given form through the social institutions of status, kinship, inheritance and the division of labour. Differences in the range of control can at first be attributed to fundamental cultural differences. Again, compare the total coercion and oppression typically associated with chattel slavery in the plantation South with the contemporaneous open autonomous relationship between the Seminole Indians and the Black Seminoles. But we must be careful in what we choose to compare and how far we extend our generalizations. Many American Indian societies with a ranked form of social hierarchy had a slave class or caste at the bottom of the ranking, usually consisting of captives obtained in warfare or raiding.[18] To the Cherokee, for example, these people were 'atsi nahsa'I, one who is owned'. They were excluded from the matrilineal clan-based kinship system and were therefore not truly human. In 1774, perhaps ten years before they had Black Seminoles, the Seminoles of the Alachua area south of today's Gainesville held captured Indians as slaves.[19]

The actual treatment of slaves varied circumstantially and opportunistically but the aboriginal owners, either individually or corporately, held the power of life and death over the slaves. This power could be as absolute as that exercised by a Southern white plantation owner. Some North American archaeologists have tried to push this practice back into deep prehistory by looking for material evidence of a slave class and examples of violent death in populations of skeletal remains[20] such as we see in the retainer sacrifice in Pharaonic Egypt or the Mayan dynasties. Students in my classes get upset when they learn that American Indians held slaves but then rationalize it as a product of acculturation in the historic period and therefore not really 'Indian'. There is no doubt that Indians as slaveowners in the historic period were responding to, and were influenced by, the larger realm of commercial capitalism into which they had been drawn, but there is little doubt that prototypical forms of slaveholding already existed in their cultural repertoire.

Further, concepts of property, both corporate and private, existed aboriginally in culturally defined terms. People as property would not have been an alien concept, especially in the tribal worldview where true human beings were those people to whom you were linked through obligation and reciprocity and with whom you shared common ancestry (as in a clan or band, or what we call today ethnic groups). Bringing this native cultural template into contact with the Euroamerican world provided a point of convergence where the two worlds made sense to each other. Although the legitimacy of slaveowning was unquestioned by the European colonists and then by the Americans, the issue of slaveowning by Indians became increasingly problematic.

Certainly in the American period, regarding Indians as slaveowners, there was no unanimous or even commonly agreed upon point of view as to its rightness. Government authorities were not of one mind, politicians were not of one mind, the multi-interested general public was not of one mind. Policies and directives arising from any one of these sectors were often in conflict with and were contested by the others, which makes for a rich documentary record but thwarts easy generalization.

Again, the core issue was not moral, but one of ownership and property. An example from the Second Seminole War (1835–1842) will illustrate this. The Second Seminole War was a war of Indian Removal, ignited by Indian resistance to US government efforts to deport them from Florida to Indian Territory west of the Mississippi.[21] At the centre of the conflict was the disposition of the Indian slaves, known then as Indian or Seminole Negroes. The Seminoles did not want to leave Florida without them and insisted on monetary compensation for any loss of property. Ownership turned out to be a many-shaded thing. The government recognized that Seminoles could own Blacks legally, but that all Black Seminoles might not be legally owned. The question was: which ones? The government's compromise position was to document the claims made by the Seminoles, returning slaves to their rightful owners where Seminole ownership could not be substantiated. For example, in March 1838 a thirty-year-old man named Bob, his presumed wife Patience (also thirty years old) along with four slaves who were believed to be her children (ages two to twenty-four) were returned to a Mr Depeyster of Florida after being captured near Fort Jupiter.[22]

General Thomas Jesup describes these efforts in some detail in a report submitted to President John Tyler on December 28, 1841.[23] In accounting for all of the negroes (to use Jesup's term) captured by his troops in the Florida campaign, Jesup explains that the majority were Indian negroes (again, following Jesup's usage), either the property of the Seminoles or claimed by them. He writes of four distinct classes of Indian negroes. First, there were those descended from slaves taken by the Creek Indians in Georgia years before and to whom the Seminoles now had legitimate ownership through treaty. Next, those purchased legitimately from Spaniards in Florida during Spanish rule, some of whom were property confiscated from the British but legal under Spanish law. Third, there were those taken from citizens of Florida prior to the Treaty of Paynes Landing (1832), whose individual cases were subject to investigation. This circumstance was stated directly in Article 6 of that treaty, as follows:

> The Seminoles being anxious to be relieved from repeated vexatious demands for slaves and other property, alleged to have been stolen and destroyed by them, so that they may remove unembarrassed to their new homes; the United States stipulate to have the same property investigated, and to liquidate such as may be satisfactorily established, provided the amount does not exceed seven thousand (7,000) dollars.[24]

Finally, there were those purchased by the Seminoles from persons who in fact were not the owners, or sold by the Seminoles to citizens of the US who now wanted to make a claim. Jesup considered these alleged purchases to be fraudulent, and perhaps unwittingly upholding Indian sovereignty, stated that the Constitution gave Congress alone the ability to engage in and regulate commerce with Indian nations.

To Jesup's categories we must add one more layer of complexity. By 1821 when the Americans took possession of Florida, you could be Black and not in any of the four classes of Indian negroes described by Jesup. You could be free. There were several paths to freedom, none of which involved passage through the system as a Black Seminole. Under Spanish governance, you could be a legally purchased slave who was subsequently freed by your owner. Those freed by Kingsley, for example, started their own enterprises, farming their own plantations or opening shops or stores.

You could also have escaped from slavery by moving south from American states to the north, fleeing to Spanish Florida and achieving Spanish citizenship by serving in the militia and accepting the Catholic faith. The process from slave to free is best described as maroon or marronage; when these people came together they formed maroon communities, most famously at Fort Mose just north of St Augustine.[25] Marronage is best thought of as a process, a condition that someone passed through, not a static or final condition. Conceivably, a person could enter Florida as an escaped slave, become a maroon in association with others in establishing a community, achieve Spanish citizenship, be captured by the Seminoles to become a Black Seminole, get deported to Indian Territory, there to eventually be granted freedman status at the end of the Civil War.

Modern scholarship has not responded well to these complexities. The contemporary novels *The Good Lord Bird* and *Song of the Shank* do a much better job of revealing nuance and enigma, but this is history in the hands of gifted storytellers.[26] Novelists can unstrap themselves from the bonds of scholarship as needed. We cannot. For us, uncertainty can be an earned conclusion. I was talking with a man at a local Florida heritage event in 2014 who claims Black Seminole ancestry. He was complaining about what he perceived as racism among the contemporary Seminole Indians but then went on to say that even Africans enslaved other Africans, so 'maybe it's just human nature'. Human nature is where we often end up when the complexities of human behaviour defy easy thought (or 'common sense'). But this is the very place that we as scholars should start. We need to avoid our own easy generalizations and intellectual conveniences. This is a history that might be hard to explain in a sound bite or in an elevator or as we sip cocktails.

Specific context of the Black Seminoles

The relationship between the Seminole Indians and the Black Seminoles was conditioned by the mutual needs and expectations that both groups brought to the encounter. Mutualism is clearly one of its hallmarks. The Seminoles as Southeastern Indians had a long ancestral slave tradition and had adopted the ownership of Blacks as essential to their economic wellbeing and to the agreed upon ranking of social status in the colonial Southeast.

Those Blacks that sought refuge among the Seminoles through the process of marronage accepted ownership only if it meant autonomy and non-coercion, something close to freedom in daily lived experience. Those taken by capture or purchase in Spanish Florida certainly expected the same. Indeed there is no evidence that the Seminoles used coercion or force of any kind to control their human property. Both parties got what they needed from the relationship. For the Black Seminoles this was protection and security. Travellers moving into Indian Country from points east, from the St Johns river or from St Augustine, first had to pass through a ring of Seminole towns, checking in, stating their intent, receiving permission or at least making their presence known before proceeding further to the locations of the Black Seminole towns.

For the Seminoles the relationship provided a measure of status and wealth, the accumulation of real property that could be transferred or passed down through inheritance. Black Seminole labour also created a potential surplus of agricultural yield for the Seminoles, a surplus that could be used for their own subsistence or as an overage that could be converted to cash or trade goods in the colonial economy.[27] It is in this labour-based interaction between Seminoles and Black Seminoles that we can look for the efforts of the Black Seminoles to achieve 'freedom' not in the sense of life and liberty but in the use and control of their labour. How did the Black Seminoles arrange their lives to achieve something close to freedom?

The Black Seminoles define and control their own labour

The Black Seminoles performed two kinds of work. They performed the physical labour of working the fields. They also did knowledge work, knowledge gained from their up-close and inside experiences in the white plantation world usefully applied for the benefit of their Seminole masters. The Black Seminoles knew how this world worked beyond the experience of most Seminoles. Knowledge became a commodity. It took on value as a thing that could be offered or withheld and it could be exchanged for things or conditions that the Black Seminoles desired.

This knowledge existed in two domains. The first was technological knowledge: how to do work, how to plant and harvest rice, how to husband livestock, how to smith metal, how to build things. The plantation experience served the Black Seminoles well in giving them something they could own and convert or transfer for their own purposes. The lushness and bounty of Black Seminole fields, the fullness of their corn cribs and their overall industriousness compared to the neighbouring Seminoles, were often praised by travellers and traders in the years leading up to the Second Seminole War. Even their houses were said to be better framed. Not exactly Southern plantations in their layout but close, Black Seminole settlements did seem to comprise residential areas surrounded by large single-crop tracts.[28]

Did the Black Seminoles have a sex-based division of labour? And if so, to what extent did it reflect plantation, Creek-Seminole, or African influences and to what extent were these distinct traditions creolized into the Black Seminole way of life? We can begin to answer these questions by combining historical references and the archaeological record. When we do this we can see that there was a strong division of labour among the Black Seminoles based on sex. Women worked the fields: planting, cultivating, harvesting. In the words of one observer, writing of Pilaklikaha in 1823, '[m]ost of the labor is performed by the women, the men are indulged in following the habits of their women and pass most of their time in idleness, occasionally hunting'.[29] This daily pattern of life did not differ significantly from that of their Seminole masters.

The women prepared and served the food, and generally minded hearth and home. Black Seminole men interacted with the outside world, trading for the goods that eventually would enter the archaeological record. These goods moved into a domestic economy controlled by women through their labour. If you were a Black Seminole, how you spent your days depended on whether you were a man or a woman. Black

Seminole society depended on both. But men had far greater access to the larger world (as traders, hunters and warriors) and could wield their knowledge of it as a form of capital to leverage control over their own lives.

Adding to their cosmopolitanism was fluency in English (and Spanish) and in the Seminole languages. To their credit, they found opportunity to use that skill to their advantage. Knowing English put them in the white man's head; knowing the Indian languages did the same. They were culturally fluent in three worlds: the Indian world, their own and that of the Whites. Black Seminoles gained status and respect by serving as interpreters and translators in relations between the Seminoles and governmental, military and commercial interests. They became diplomats by shuttling the finer points of negotiation back and forth between the two sides. Abraham was particularly noted for this ability, accompanying Micanopy on a visit to Washington, DC, in 1825 and ten years later seeing service as a battlefield diplomat on the Seminole side in General Gaines's failed offensive against the Seminoles in the Cove of the Withlacoochee.[30]

Abraham and his extended family were granted freedom by the Seminole chief Micanopy at the time of deportation on 6 March, 1839 as reward for his service. He was also rewarded with a wife, a black woman who had been the wife of Micanopy's deceased brother Bowlegs. The muster rolls of Black Seminoles deported to Indian Territory show several instances where Black Seminoles are indicated as being owned by others listed as 'coloured', suggesting that this reward might have been accepted practice.[31]

When Black Seminoles were captured by troops in the Second Seminole War they often served as guides to the locations of Seminole villages.[32] Although not without coercion, and in some cases duping the unsuspecting troops on a path to nowhere, Black Seminole men took this role as an opportunity not just to survive but to win their freedom. Here they traded in not only their language abilities but their detailed knowledge of the lay of the land, much of it tactically unknown to the soldiers. Just as they had in the pre-war years in their dealings with government officials and traders, the Black Seminoles were again acting as agents of information on the margins of contact.

How did the Black Seminoles and Seminoles co-evolve in response to increasing contact with capitalist economy?

By the late 1700s many of the Seminoles had adopted their own version of the plantation system common across the agricultural South.[33] Archaeological and historical evidence suggest these settlements resembled Southern plantations and were distinctly different from the first Seminole towns established in Spanish Florida in the middle decades of the 1700s. A visitor's description of Opauney's Town east of present-day Tampa provides a nice visual: 'Two miles east of Opauney's residence you come to his field on which the Negro houses are built. This field is planted with corn and rice and attended in the same manner one would expect in Plantations under the direction of white people.' Opauney 'held about 20 slaves who perform the same labour that is generally expected on plantations in Florida'.[34] Corn and rice from Seminole fields and cattle from Seminole herds made their way to colonial governments in St Augustine.

While the sugar, rice and indigo plantations of the St Johns river were competing in international markets, the Seminole plantations were helping to feed the colony.

At the archaeologically excavated Black Seminole site of Pilaklikaha, unearthed artefacts attest to the possessions once held by its residents. Shards of English-made pottery in transfer print or shell edged patterns, slivers of heavy, dark green glass wine bottles, broken pipe stems from white kaolin pipes, and fragments of brushed-surface earthenwares made by the Seminoles are all typical artefacts found at Seminole sites of the early nineteenth century.[35] If archaeology is to be trusted and the historical documentation of the Black Seminole occupation of Pilaklikaha is solid, Black Seminoles there had access to the same sorts of goods available to the Seminoles and acquired them with much the same frequency. And clearly they were not going to St Augustine or to the trading houses to get them, nor is it likely that traders were frequently coming to them, particularly with the increasingly hostile environment leading up to and including the early years of American control. Strictly as measured by artefacts, the Black Seminoles were Seminoles. We have not always been happy with that conclusion. Surely they must be different, distinct in some material way if we look hard enough or deep enough or wide enough? We look for Africanisms in the archaeological record as indications of their persistent identity as Africans, we look for signs that the Black Seminoles were using material culture to generate their own ethnicity. But this is not what I read from the archaeological record.

At Southern plantations, archaeology shows us that the slaves had many of the same consumer goods as their owners and overseers, given to them as hand-me-downs or perhaps salvaged.[36] Historical sources are not sufficiently precise for us to know if this same kind of process was operating between Seminoles and Black Seminoles. But archaeological evidence shows that Seminoles and Black Seminoles interacted in some regular way, and that some type of exchange was taking place through which the Black Seminoles received their transfer print plates and bottled wine. Does this mean the Black Seminoles thought of themselves as Seminole?

The presence of Seminole pottery in its traditional style and forms begins to give us a picture of the people behind the process. This is Seminole pottery, not the so-called colonoware made by slaves on the coastal plantations of South Carolina and Georgia.[37] Seminole pottery typically was made in jar, bowl and open 'casuela' forms and was used for cooking, serving and storing food.[38] Several distinct decorative styles were used on the rims of jars such as fingernail pinching and punctated appliqué clay strips. Although historical accounts of Seminole pottery-making are extremely rare and do not specifically mention women as the potters, references to women potters in other Southeastern groups in the historic period suggests that it is a safe bet that they were.[39] The question then becomes: how did these pots get into Black Seminole villages?

Anthropology can offer several different explanations for the presence of this pottery. First, and most direct, Seminole women themselves were living in the Black Seminole villages, perhaps as marriage partners and in a family setting with Black Seminole men. This is a standard anthropological model, but in the matrilineal kinship system of the Seminoles would mean that children born from the union of Seminole women and Black Seminole men would become members of a Seminole clan and therefore fully integrated into Seminole society, which with possible rare exceptions seems not to have been the case.

It is also possible that the pots moved in as exchange items, changing hands from Seminole women to Black Seminole women as goods and services moved the other way in much the same process through which English tablewares ended up at Black Seminole sites. This is economically feasible, but might not adequately address the social reality that existed between Black and Seminole. To get to the nature of this relationship we need to explore the question: in what social context does it make sense to have traditional Seminole pottery in a Black Seminole setting?

A government report from 1930 gives us a glimpse of historic marriage patterns that place Black Seminole women in the households of Seminole men:

> In MacCauley's day [1880s] there were still 3 negro women living as Seminole wives, relics of slavery days, and 7 mixed bloods, all Indian–Negro crosses. At one time the Seminoles possessed a considerable number of slaves, all the Negro blood in the tribe traces back to that fact. The males of the superior economic order never have difficulty in finding mates among the females of an inferior economic group; the Indian–Negro crosses were invariably Indian men who mated with Negro women, never vice versa. No Indian woman, so far as I can learn, ever accepted a Negro male as the father of her children.[40]

If Seminole men historically had Black Seminole wives, would the wives' identity be discernible in the archaeological record? Certainly, as Black Seminoles, these women would be living in two worlds. In one, they are wives to Seminole men, belonging to them. But they also lived in the Seminole world, hence the Seminole pottery. Using Seminole pottery made them Seminole. Still, they had no place in the Seminole clan system and must have identified strongly with other Black Seminoles. They worked between the worlds of the Seminole and the Black Seminole and helped to join the interests of these distinct societies.

Most of the estimated 500 or so Black Seminoles were deported to Indian Territory by the end of the Seminole Wars.[41] In the West, the peculiar institution got even stranger. Some believed, mistakenly, that they would be freed if they agreed to emigrate. To effect removal the government acknowledged legal claims to the Blacks by the Seminoles, essentially transferring this unresolved issue 'out of sight, out of mind'. So for the first decades after Removal and until Emancipation at the close of the Civil War, the uncertain relationship between Blacks and Seminoles persisted in Indian Territory, always poised to be reinvented as both parties settled into the new land. Still awaiting archaeological investigation, the Black Seminole towns in Indian Territory (present-day Oklahoma) seem, based on historical maps, to have reproduced the pre-Removal settlement pattern of separation and distance from the Seminole towns.[42]

What new perspectives on slavery do we gain from research into the Black Seminoles?

To see the hidden faces of slavery we need to challenge our own assumptions and not let theory or comfort shape what we see. The words we choose can limit or doom our endeavour. Resistance, diaspora, freedom-seeking and other terms have all put in hard work in making our case, but they also serve as shields and in continuing to use them we suggest that we already know the conclusion and primary causes before we have actually done the research. Yes, an analytical framework is necessary, what anthropologists call an 'etic approach' because after all we are outsiders to the process. But as scholars we need to put people at the centre of the story, in an 'emic' approach, trying to get at the world they saw and how they positioned themselves in it. This comes not from a single voice or from only one side, but from looking at the process of interactions through which people shape who they are and how they become in response to all the people around them. Slavery has many faces; sometimes these faces belonged to people talking to each other.

Of course reconstructed interactions do not animate themselves. This requires our very careful attention to model-building based on context, again, through deep and specific immersion into every conceivable line of evidence: historical, ethnographic, cartographic, archaeological, linguistic, geographic, oral historical. That these lines of evidence resist easy synthesis provides both a frustration and a challenge.

Notes

1 Barbara Krauthamer, *Black Slaves, Indian Masters: Slavery, Emancipation, and Citizenship in the Native American South* (Chapel Hill: University of North Carolina Press, 2013).
2 John K. Mahon, *History of the Second Seminole War* (Gainesville: University Press of Florida, 1967).
3 Kenneth W. Porter, *The Black Seminoles: History of a Freedom-Seeking People*, rev. and ed. Alcione M. Amos and Thomas P. Senter (Gainesville: University Press of Florida, 1996).
4 Herbert Aptheker, 'Maroons Within the Present Limits of the United States', in Richard Price (ed.), *Maroon Societies* (Baltimore, MD: Johns Hopkins University Press, 1996), 155; Terrance M. Weik, *The Archaeology of Antislavery Resistance* (Gainesville: University Press of Florida, 2012); Kevin Mulroy, 'Seminole Maroons', in *Handbook of North American Indians*, vol. 14: *Southeast* (Washington, DC: Smithsonian Institution Press, 2005), 465–77.
5 Kevin Mulroy, *The Seminole Freedmen: A History* (Norman: University of Oklahoma Press, 2007).
6 David Eltis, *The Rise of African Slavery in the Americas* (Cambridge: Cambridge University Press, 2000); James Walvin, *Black Ivory: Slavery in the British Empire* (London: HarperCollins, 1992); Philip D. Curtin, *The Rise and Fall of the Plantation Complex: Essays in Atlantic History* (Cambridge: Cambridge University Press, 1990).
7 James Oliver Horton and Lois E. Horton, *Slavery and the Making of America* (Oxford: Oxford University Press, 2004); Michael Gannon (ed.), *The History of Florida* (Gainesville: University Press of Florida, 2013).
8 James G. Cusick, *The Other War of 1812: The Patriot War and the American Invasion of Spanish East Florida* (Athens: University of Georgia Press, 2003).
9 Jane Landers, 'Free and Enslaved', in Michael Gannon (ed.), *The History of Florida* (Gainesville: University Press of Florida, 2013), 179–94.

10 Annie Heloise Abel, *The American Indian as Slaveholder and Secessionist* (Lincoln: University of Nebraska Press, 1992); Theda Perdue, *Slavery and the Evolution of Cherokee Society, 1540-1866* (Knoxville: University of Tennessee Press, 1979); Daniel F. Littlefield, Jr, *Africans and Seminoles: From Removal to Emancipation* (Jackson: University of Mississippi Press, 1977).
11 Robin F. A. Fabel and Daniel L. Schafer, 'British Rule in Florida', in Michael Gannon (ed.), *The History of Florida* (Gainesville: University Press of Florida, 2013), 144–61.
12 William S. Willis, Jr, 'Divide and Rule: Red, White, and Black in the Southeast', in Charles M. Hudson (ed.), *Red, White, and Black: Symposium on Indians in the Old South*, Southern Anthropological Proceedings No. 5 (Athens: University of Georgia Press, 1971), 99–115.
13 Abel, *The American Indian as Slaveholder*.
14 Quoted in Daniel L. Schafer, 'Zephaniah Kingsley's Laurel Grove Plantation, 1803–1813', in Jane Landers (ed.), *Colonial Plantations and Economy in Florida* (Gainesville: University Press of Florida, 2000), 112; H. F. Hunt, 'Slavery Among the Indians of the Northwest Coast', *Washington Historical Quarterly* 9, no. 4 (1918): 276–83; James F. Brooks, *Captives and Cousins: Slavery, Kinship, and Community in the Southwest Borderlands* (Chapel Hill: University of North Carolina Press, 2002).
15 Perdue, *Slavery and the Evolution of Cherokee Society*, 17–18; William Bartram, *Travels of William Bartram*, Library of America series (New York: Penguin Books, 1996), 166.
16 William H. Sears, 'The Sociopolitical Organization of Pre-Columbian Cultures on the Gulf Coastal Plain', *American Anthropologist* 56 (1954): 339–46.
17 Jane Landers, 'Free and Enslaved'.
18 Schafer, 'Zephaniah Kingsley's Laurel Grove Plantation, 1803–1813', 98–120.
19 Allan Gallay, *The Indian Slave Trade: The Rise of the English Empire in the American South, 1670-1717* (New Haven, CT: Yale University Press, 2002), 8.
20 Willis, 'Divide and Rule'.
21 Mahon, *History of the Second Seminole War*.
22 It seems however unlikely that Nancy the 24 year-old female slave was Patience's daughter who was thirty. 'List of Negroes who Have been Captured by the Troops at Fort Jupiter, East Florida from the 22nd Feb. 1838 to the Present Day', http://www.seminolenation-indianterritory.org/negroes_captured_2.htm: M. M. Cohen, *Notices of Florida and the Campaigns* (Gainesville: University Press of Florida, 1964, facsimile reproduction of 1836 edition), 88.
23 'Seminole War–Slaves Captured', Report of Major General Thomas S. Jesup, 27th Congress, 2nd Session, Doc. No. 55, 28 December 1841.
24 Charles Kappler, *Indian Affairs: Laws and Treaties*, vol. 2: *Treaties*, Treaty With the Seminole 1832 (Washington, DC: Government Printing Office, 1904), 344–5.
25 Kathleen Deagan and Darcie MacMahon, *Fort Mose: Colonial America's Black Fortress of Freedom* (Gainesville: University Press of Florida, 1995).
26 Jeffrey Renald Allen, *Song of the Shank* (Minneapolis: Graywolf Press, 2014); James McBride, *Good Lord Bird* (New York: Riverhead Books, 2013).
27 Brent R. Weisman, 'The Plantation System of the Florida Seminole Indians and Black Seminoles During the Colonial Era', in Jane Landers (ed.), *Colonial Plantations and Economy in Florida* (Gainesville: University Press of Florida, 2000), 136–49; George A. McCall, *Letters From the Frontiers* (Philadelphia: J.B. Lippincott, 1868), 166; William Simmons, *Notices of East Florida with an Account of Seminole Nation of Indians by a Recent Traveler in the Province* (Charleston, SC: privately printed, n.d.); Cohen, *Notices*, 87, 90, 96, 108, 141 n.

28 Simmons, *Notices*, 43–5, 67.
29 Mark F. Boyd, 'Horatio S. Dexter and Events Leading to the Treaty of Moultrie Creek With the Seminole Indians', *Florida Anthropologist* 11, no. 3 (1958): 65–95; Horatio Dexter, 'Observations on the Seminole Indians, 1823', US National Archives Microfilm, M271, Record Group 75, Records of the Office of Secretary of War, Letter Received, 1800–1823, roll 4, frames 505–19; Brent R. Weisman, 'Labour and Survival among the Black Seminoles of Florida', in Robert Cassanello and Melanie Shell-Weiss (eds), *Florida's Working Class Past* (Gainesville: University Press of Florida, 2009), 78.
30 Kenneth W. Porter, 'The Negro Abraham', *Florida Historical Quarterly* 25 (1946): 1–44.
31 Littlefield, *Africans and Seminoles*, Lists A–K.
32 Frank Laumer (ed.), *Amidst a Storm of Bullets* (Tampa, FL: University of Tampa Press, 1998), 90–4; Kenneth W. Porter, 'Florida Slaves and Free Negroes in the Seminole War, 1835–1842', *Journal of Negro History* 28, no. 4 (1943): 390–421; Cohen, *Notices*, 72, 73, 78, 192–5, 216, 218.
33 Weisman, 'The Plantation System'.
34 Albert Devane, *Early Florida History*, vol. 2 (Sebring, FL: Sebring Historical Society, 1929).
35 Weik, *The Archaeology of Antislavery Resistance*; Weisman, 'Labour and Survival', 64–5, 71, 78. Cohen, *Notices*, 174–5.
36 John Solomon Otto, *Cannon's Point Plantation, 1794–1860: Living Conditions and Status Patterns in the Old South* (Orlando, FL: Academic Press, 1984).
37 Leland Ferguson, *Uncommon Ground: Archaeology and Early African America, 1650–1800* (Washington, DC, Smithsonian Institution Press, 1992).
38 John M. Goggin, 'Seminole Pottery', in William C. Sturtevant (ed.), *A Seminole Source Book* (New York: Garland Press, 1987).
39 Goggin, 'Seminole Pottery'.
40 Roy Nash, 'Survey of Seminole Indians in Florida', in W. C. Sturtevant (ed.), *A Seminole Source Book* (New York: Garland, 1987).
41 Dexter, 'Observations'; Simmons, *Notices*, 75.
42 Abel, *The American Indian as Slaveholder*, 25.

3

'Adventure in a Wigwam': Henry Bibb's Account of Slavery among the Cherokees in *Narrative of the Life and Adventures of Henry Bibb, An American Slave* (1849)

Sandrine Ferré-Rode

Introduction

This chapter is an exploration of the representation of African American slavery among the Cherokees in Indian Territory in the 1840s. It is based upon an analysis of Henry Bibb's *Narrative of the Life and Adventures of Henry Bibb, An American Slave*, published in 1849, which is one of the few extant first-hand accounts of African American enslavement among Native Americans. It seeks to highlight that Henry Bibb's retelling of his experience must be read not only through the lens of the author's defiance of the racial hierarchies that prevailed in antebellum America, but also through the prism of the author's specifically and pre-eminently abolitionist discourse. It thus makes the atypical or non-traditional nature of Indian slaveholding a highly unstable, if not an utterly invalid, truism.

In its issue of 22 January 1847, William Lloyd Garrison's *The Liberator* carried a note advertising the recent presence in Boston's Faneuil Hall of a 'runaway slave' whose identity was encapsulated in one paragraph:

> The last person who has occupied it [Faneuil Hall] is a runaway slave: Henry Bibb, formerly of Kentucky, and last from the Cherokee nation. On Friday and Saturday evenings, in the presence of a large and sympathetic audience, he gave a thrilling narrative of his sufferings and adventures as a slave. He was sold no less than six times, and has now a wife and child in slavery. He is so light in his complexion, and his hair is so straight, that he would pass easily for a white man. He is probably allied to the best blood in Kentucky. He is a young man, of very interesting appearance, and remarkably gifted in language and elocution.[1]

The description clearly aims at portraying an exceptional person, whose relationship with the 'Cherokee nation' serves as a hallmark, as well as a promise for an eventful life and, incidentally, a sensational story. The 'runaway slave' was Henry Walton Bibb, born into slavery in northern Kentucky probably in 1814,[2] the son of a slave woman and a white man. Bibb spent his teenage years as a hired-out slave, whose masters' cruel oppression made him an early practitioner of what he called 'the art of running away'.[3] He remained a relentless fugitive even after marrying a slave woman and becoming a father, though he repeatedly failed to rescue his wife and child and was sold to various masters across the South.[4] After he gave up hope for a reunion with his family in the early 1840s, he settled in Detroit, Michigan, remarried, lectured for the Michigan State Anti-Slavery Society,[5] and was involved in the fledgling Liberty Party.[6] In 1850, Bibb chose to settle in Canada West,[7] where he became a vocal anti-slavery activist, the promoter of a land settlement project known as the Refugee Home Society,[8] and the publisher of the first African Canadian newspaper, *Voice of the Fugitive*,[9] until his premature death on 1 August 1854 at his home in Windsor.[10]

As the news brief in *The Liberator* suggests, Henry Bibb toured the Northeastern United States in the second half of the 1840s to promote abolition, telling his 'thrilling' story to rally supporters. In 1849, Bibb published his *Narrative of the Life and Adventures of Henry Bibb, An American Slave* in New York City, with the sponsorship of patrons belonging to the American and Foreign Anti-Slavery Society,[11] a branch of abolitionism opposed to Garrison's American Anti-Slavery Society, and by members of the Wesleyan Connection, a group of Methodists (including Lucius Matlack, Bibb's editor) whose anti-slavery activism had led to their exclusion by the church authorities.[12]

The volume comprises twenty chapters, fifteen of which chronicle Bibb's painful experience of twenty-seven years in bondage. At the end of Chapter XIII, in Chapter XIV and at the beginning of Chapter XV, Henry Bibb describes why and how, from December 1840 to the spring of 1841, he was the property of a Cherokee master in Indian Territory. That almost two chapters should be devoted to his six-month Indian slavery is a sign that the narrator wished to showcase this part of his enslaved life. And indeed, in the only lengthy study of Bibb's Cherokee slavery, Keith Michael Green argues that because of its 'structural location in his narrative, [Bibb's] representation of Native slavery is as important as Frederick Douglass's much more well-known duel with the slave breaker, Covey'.[13] In his analysis, Green focuses on the complex processes used by Bibb to assert his black masculinity and attempt to repossess his frustrated roles of husband and father, especially in those periods of his life when he was incarcerated in Southern prisons and when he was the slave of a Cherokee. As Green so aptly demonstrates, Bibb's 'reclamation project' unfolded 'within a heteropatriarchal, racist and imperialist social order', with a view 'to prove his harmlessness to and affiliation with white men'.[14] As a result, 'to fashion his own idealized masculinity', Bibb's discourse on imprisonment and Indian slavery 'relegated incarcerated white men, dislocated Native Americans, and enslaved black women and children to precarious positions'.[15]

This chapter will seek to expand on Green's reading of Bibb's controversial construction of his manhood by focusing on the issue of Bibb's authority in the account of his Cherokee slavery. Authority will first be understood as synonymous with power.

Indeed, the episode of his Indian slavery appears at a crucial moment in Bibb's life, not just because he finally manages to escape once and for all from bondage and from the South: never before had he, as a slave, been in such a situation of empowerment as when he became the property of an Indian man. The episode thus underscores how slave agency could emerge in that context, though we will argue that Bibb's empowerment relies on a rather ambiguous strategy, not uncommon in classic slave narratives: that of treachery and disguise, or 'trickster tactics'. Second, Bibb's positioning as an author will be explored – that is, his authorial control over his narrative of Indian captivity. In *To Tell a Free Story*, William L. Andrews commends Bibb's idiosyncratic skills as a black autobiographer who, along with other narrators such as Frederick Douglass or William Wells Brown, 'infused into their writing a quality that the dictated Afro-American narratives of earlier decades rarely communicated: a sense of an individual authorial personality, the sound of a distinctive authorizing voice'.[16] However, if Bibb's account of his personal experience of Cherokee slavery evinces an effort at describing, for the benefit of his readers, some of the major characteristics of Indian slaveholding, we would like to argue that by portraying Indian slavery as 'non-traditional' and distinct from its white counterpart, Bibb jeopardizes his authority over his own text. Infused with the tropes of abolitionist discourse, Bibb's account of his Indian slavery is indeed conceived *primarily* as an indirect but vigorous attack on the 'peculiar institution' of the white South, and this objective takes precedence over all other possible considerations, including truthfulness and trustworthiness. The African American narrator's voice, as a result, ends up becoming virtually inaudible, while it weakens his pledge, made in the preface to his book, not to 'attempt by any sophistry to misrepresent slavery in order to prove its dreadful wickedness'.[17]

Slave agency: empowerment through 'trickster tactics'

In the opening chapter to his story, Bibb claims that 'the only weapon of self defense that I could use successfully, was that of deception'.[18] The circumstances in which Bibb was bought by an Indian master illustrate Bibb's powerful practice of deceit in order to pursue his sole objective: freedom. Only a year before, Bibb, his wife and child had been bought on the New Orleans slave market by Deacon Francis Whitfield. The latter proved to be one of the most violent and cruel slaveowners that Bibb had ever belonged to. Severely harsh treatment as well as lack of food and adequate shelter prompted Bibb to attempt escape with his family twice, but their second recapture led to their ultimate separation. Bibb alone was bought by two professional gamblers who took him from Louisiana to Texas and Arkansas, and from there to Indian Territory.

Indian Territory (approximately present-day Oklahoma) was then made up of tracts of land west of the Mississippi river, reserved to those Indian tribes that had been removed there by the United States' government after passage of the Indian Removal Act of 1830. Especially concerned by the policy of removal were the so-called 'Five Civilized Tribes', which included the Choctaws, Chickasaws, Cherokees, Creeks and

Seminoles who lived in the Southeast. Most prominent among those were the Cherokees, who lived in northeastern Georgia, northeastern Alabama and southeastern Tennessee. They had shifted at the end of the eighteenth century from a hunting to a subsistence farming economy, choosing as the model for their agricultural system that of the Southern slaveholding plantation.[19] It meant that some Cherokees, many of them actually of mixed race descent, owned increasing numbers of African American slaves, who worked in the fields to produce staple crops for commercial markets.[20] Before long, these planters accumulated substantial wealth and became the economic and political elite within Cherokee society.

Part of the slaveholding elite was instrumental in attempting to defend Cherokee rights to their traditional lands as well as Cherokee sovereignty, including by filing suit in the Supreme Court against the State of Georgia. In *Cherokee Nation v. Georgia* (1831), the federal Court, headed by Chief Justice John Marshall, ruled that it lacked jurisdiction to hear the claims of the Cherokees, as they were neither a state nor a foreign nation, while, in effect, it also limited tribal sovereignty by declaring Native populations to be 'domestic dependent nations' of the federal government instead of possible diplomatic equals. A year later, the Cherokees, with the cooperation of white missionaries, again challenged Georgia's attempt to destroy their sovereignty and seize their lands: in *Worcester v. Georgia* (1832), the Court struck down Georgia's laws trespassing on Cherokee sovereignty and land by decreeing that Natives were subject to federal, not state, laws, and by recognizing the Indian nation's legitimate title to its territory. Though the ruling seemed auspicious, the federal protection against Georgia's appetite for Cherokee land was undermined by President Andrew Jackson's determination to implement removal, officially for the sake of protecting Indians against white encroachment and violence. Besides, divisions intensified among the Cherokees themselves, as some argued in favour of selling their lands while they could get compensation, making resistance to removal increasingly disreputable. After a small faction of Cherokees eventually signed the Treaty of New Echota in 1835, ceding their lands, emigration could not be avoided.[21] In the spring of 1838, the US Army forcibly sent approximately 15,000 Cherokees onto the infamous 'Trail of Tears': the long and excruciating trek to Indian Territory claimed 4,000 lives, including, though historical records are few, those of African American slaves brought along by their Indian masters.[22]

It is difficult to assert whether Henry Bibb fails to provide this important context intentionally or not. Green argues that Bibb's 'ability to elicit white sympathy is dependent on the colonial trick of "remembering to forget" Native American dispossession'.[23] In other words, Bibb focuses on reminding his readership that he was first and foremost a victim of Indian oppression, while he withholds important knowledge not only about the white oppression of Indians themselves, but also about the unstable nature of Indian (and especially Cherokee) identity in what was then a period of difficult transition geographically, politically, economically and socially. Such neglect for contextualization and historicity confronts Bibb's readers with a narrative void that, inevitably, makes them more amenable to sharing stereotypical representations of Native people and more responsive to buying into generalizations, for want of more refined historical evidence.

The persuasiveness of Bibb's portrayal of himself as a victim of Indian oppression is, however, limited. When he recalls the circumstances in which he was brought to Indian Territory, he says that he and his masters went to an important social gathering, horse races, which were attended by 'a very wealthy half Indian of that tribe, who became much attached to me, and had some notion of buying me, after hearing that I was for sale, being a slaveholder'.[24] And Bibb suggests that it was his own decision and his own willpower that allowed him to be purchased by the Indian slaveholder. Indeed, he asserts that, prior to reaching Indian Territory, he had made a bargain with the gamblers who had bought him to make a profit:

> [The sportsmen] said they had bought me to speculate on, and were not able to lose what they had paid for me. But they would make *a bargain with me, if I was willing*, and would lay a plan, by which I might yet get free. If I would use *my influence* so as to get some person to buy me while traveling about with them, they would give me a portion of the money for which they sold me, and they would also give me directions by which I might yet run away and go to Canada.[25]

Bibb thus becomes an accomplice in white fraud, and, after being brought to the races in Indian Territory, the scene he describes offers a sharp contrast with his earlier experience as a powerless slave sold on the auction block only a few months before in New Orleans. There he had been deceived by the friendly appearance of Deacon Whitfield, who bought him and his family and 'looked like a saint, talked like the best of slaveholding Christians, and acted at home like the devil'.[26] As Bibb envisages his transfer to the Indian slaveholder, he is no longer the victimized slave, but in a position of taking precedence as a decision-maker. He thus presents himself not only as the one who makes the deal effective but also places special emphasis on the fact that it was substantiated by a sizeable amount of money:

> The idea struck me rather favorable, for several reasons. First, I thought I should stand a better chance to get away from an Indian than from a white man. Second he wanted me only for a kind of a body servant to wait on him – and in this case I knew that I should fare better than I should in the field. And my owners also told me that it would be an easy place to get away from. I took their advice for fear I might not get another chance as good as that, *and prevailed on the man to buy me*. He paid them nine hundred dollars, in gold and silver, for me. I saw the money counted out.[27]

Bibb's insistence on the amount of money paid for his acquisition must be qualified though: the value of a slave of his age would have been roughly equivalent throughout the South, and the investment was thus considerable but not exceptional.[28] Meanwhile, it underscores Bibb's ability to resist for his own subversive purposes by using the 'knowledge of slaveholders' incentives and ideology'.[29] Indeed, as Bibb manoeuvres to become the Cherokee's property, the stratagem of deceit moves to centre stage. In a powerful reversal of the image of the young slave boy who, at the very beginning of his narrative, is barred from knowing the rudiments of his own origins, Bibb becomes the master of his own fate by forbidding access to knowledge of who he really is – that is, an inveterate runaway, a literate slave and a tenacious achiever:

> I was to embrace the earliest opportunity of getting away, before they should become acquainted with me. I was never to let it be known where I was from, nor where I was born. I was to act quite stupid and ignorant.[30]

Thus the powerless slave has reached a position in which he can outwit his master. The slave's resistance is underscored as relying on either the retention or the disguise of personal intelligence. Such display of Bibb's ingenuity has allowed Charles H. Nichols to compare him to the typical Spanish rogue, the picaro, whose main characteristic is to perform immoral acts while presenting them as acceptable behaviour.[31] However, in the special relationship that develops between Henry Bibb and his Indian master, it is the figure of the trickster, borrowed from African lore (but also a familiar subject in the Native American folk tradition) and a relatively common motif in slave narratives, which more accurately befits Bibb's role in this part of the narrative.[32] Indeed, Bibb becomes more than a deceptive character, as his protean nature allows him to take various shapes: he is a changeling who is alternately hero or villain, but also navigates the black–white colour line and even, albeit briefly and symbolically, crosses gender boundaries.

As a result, Bibb's narrative in this passage becomes highly unstable, as the reader's trust is being tested by ambiguous assertions. Indeed, Bibb displays paradoxical feelings towards his Indian slaveowner, whom he first describes as 'the most reasonable, and humane slaveholder that I ever belonged to'.[33] He also willingly withholds information about his Indian master's identity:

> He was the last man that pretended to claim property in my person; and although I have freely given the names and residences of all others who have held me as a slave, for prudential reasons I shall omit giving the name of this individual.[34]

Bibb does not elaborate on his decision to favour discretion, invoking 'prudence' as his main motivation. Still legally a fugitive slave when he was writing his narrative, he might have feared for his own safety and thus made sure no one could claim him as their property: this hypothesis is validated by the publication in the *Western Citizen* of 20 November 1849 of a brief and rather elliptical note in which Bibb asked his fellow abolitionists to 'sound the alarm' in his favour as, according to him, the slaveholders were after him, having bought him from the Indian's heirs.[35] His decision not to reveal his Indian master's name, in this case, would reflect a wish for self-preservation, rather than kindness, if not gratitude, for his former and last owner. Good feelings were also possible though, because, by voluntarily disallowing the identification of his former Indian master, Bibb shielded him from subsequently being brought to symbolic trial by public opprobrium, a favour he did not grant to his other masters, including William Gatewood, John and Albert G. Sibley and Francis Whitfield. All of them are personally and virulently attacked throughout the narrative and Bibb even made his private letters to Gatewood and Albert G. Sibley accessible to a larger audience by publishing them later in the abolitionist press and his own *Voice of the Fugitive*.[36]

However, Bibb's benevolence towards his Indian master becomes clearly equivocal when the latter becomes terminally ill. Bibb asserts that he attended to his master in his home and on their long trek to visit an Indian doctor, day and night, taking care of the ailing man to his last breath. Bibb, incidentally, obliterates the Indian master's wife from his story (though her presence is acknowledged) and acts as a substitute for her, challenging traditional gender roles:

> While he lived, I waited on him to the best of my ability. I watched over him night and day until he died, and even prepared his body for the tomb, before I left him. He died about midnight and I understood from his friends that he was not to be buried until the second day after his death. I pretended to be taking on at a great rate about his death, but I was more excited about running away, than I was about that, and before daylight the next morning I proved it, for I was on my way to Canada.[37]

The description of Bibb's patient care for his agonizing Indian master also significantly clashes with another episode in the narrative where Bibb insists that Southern slaveholders do not allow for sick slaves to receive appropriate healthcare. If a slave dies, Bibb says that a decent funeral cannot be provided, as the slave has 'no Bible, no family altar, no minister to address to him the consolations of the gospel, before he launches into the spirit world'.[38] The circumstances of Bibb's final escape are thus decidedly awkward, not just because he has to acknowledge that his devotion to his sick master was entirely fake and hollow: the sham also served his purpose to escape from a dead man. But Bibb turns this predicament into a mercy, as it gives him an opportunity to portray himself as one endowed with the greatest moral virtues and as one who truly defends Christian values and charity. As classic heroic standards require, he is torn between his own personal desire for emancipation and his responsibility to his fellow man, even though the latter may be his enslaver. Meanwhile, though he remains the trickster who eventually cheats on the deceased, he insists that he never allowed himself to rob his master even when opportunities for such mischief arose. The slave's empowerment, in other words, is closely intertwined with his unflinching morality but also his physical energy and his self-willed decision to remain on the side of the living, all of which allow for a halfway step to self-emancipation: 'But all this I had passed through, and my long enslaved limbs and spirit were then in full stretch for emancipation. I felt as if one more short struggle would set me free.'[39]

The episode thus serves to reveal a crucial facet of Bibb's persona, as he is in a position of authority and control never experienced before, exerting his clever though deceitful influence to determine important choices he had so far been unable to make, all geared towards freedom. His *tour de force* consists of becoming a nineteenth-century avatar of the trickster figure of African traditional tales, as described by Lawrence Levine:

> In large part African trickster tales revolved around the strong patterns of authority so central to African cultures. As interested as they might be in material gains, African trickster figures were more obsessed with manipulating the strong and reversing the normal structure of power and prestige.[40]

In the specific context of his Indian slavery, however, Bibb's match with Levine's model of the African trickster must be qualified, first by the need to assess how strong 'the strong' might be, for in many ways Bibb suggests that 'the strong', in other words, the slaveholder, is actually weak, *because* he is an Indian. Meanwhile, it is impossible to read his representation of Indian slavery *only* as the dichotomy between 'the strong' and 'the weak': Bibb's obviously racialist commentary is informed by white abolitionist discourse, which undermines the strictly binary nature of the power struggle hinted at in the narrative. Instead, it reveals the intricate web of cultural and racial prejudice, settler colonialism and white middle-class influence as the backdrop against which Bibb's metamorphosis occurs.

Indian slavery: non-traditional?

> All things considered, if I must be a slave, I had by far, rather be a slave to an Indian, than to a white man, from the experience that I have had with both.[41]

Bibb's account of his Cherokee slavery begins with several remarks which, taken together, suggest that Indian slavery was mild compared to Southern white slavery. His arguments are based on economic, human, institutional and religious criteria. They are, nevertheless, consistently general, lacking details, sometimes even potentially contradictory. They are also to be read as explicitly or implicitly contrasting with Bibb's experience of Southern white slavery as it is abundantly recounted in the preceding pages of his narrative. Bibb first suggests that the economic wellbeing of Indian slaveholders was a rationale for their relatively good treatment of their slaves. He describes his master as a wealthy man who owned a large plantation and numerous slaves, but he also affirms, quite surprisingly if not paradoxically, that his master was not using his agricultural production for market-oriented, capitalistic purposes, as he 'raised corn and wheat for his own consumption only'.[42] From this observation, he is quick to assert about the Cherokees that, as a general rule, 'there was no cotton, tobacco or anything of the kind produced among them for market'.[43] Since Bibb arrived in Indian Territory a couple of years after removal, it is possible that Cherokee slaveholders had not yet developed their economy, and especially their agricultural production, to reach commercial markets. According to Theda Perdue, western relocation on land that was less fertile and less suitable to traditional crops indeed forced the Cherokees to adapt their agriculture or to find other sources of income in new activities.[44] Either way, slave labour made the transition easier and an integral part of Cherokee resettlement, while, according to William G. McLoughlin, it also sharpened social divisions among the Cherokees:

> After removal to the West, Cherokees who owned slaves found it far easier to resettle than those who had no slaves. Slave labour built their new homes, cleared their land, fenced their gardens and pastures, cultivated their fields, planted and gathered their crops, and tended their herds of cattle, horses and sheep. Slave

owners made a quantum leap forward in wealth and influence in the years after 1839. Poor, full-blood, non slave-owning families (most of them the last to arrive and choose land in the new country) fared badly after removal.⁴⁵

Meanwhile, whereas earlier in his narrative Bibb insisted on the recurrent lack of food that he and his family suffered from in the white South, he observes that Indian slaveholders did provide for the basic necessities of their slaves with sufficient food and proper clothing: 'And I found this difference between negro slavery among the Indians, and the same thing among the white slaveholders of the South. The Indians allow their slaves enough to eat and wear.'⁴⁶ His comment relies on his presentation of the economic wellbeing of Indian slaveholders, thus leading the reader to understand it as the source of the Cherokees' fair treatment of their slaves, because Bibb fails to observe that their wealth *originated* from the slaves themselves. The contrast with the other portions of his narrative is astounding, as his text teems with references to the exploitation of slaves and to Bibb's deep personal frustration that he was 'a wretched slave, compelled to work under the lash without wages'.⁴⁷

Besides, according to Bibb, Indian slaveholders were also less prone to violent treatment and corporal punishment of their slaves. Perdue's analysis cautiously corroborates Bibb's assessment of Indian leniency, arguing that although 'Cherokee planters required hard work from their bondsmen, they probably treated their slaves much better on the average than did their white counterparts'.⁴⁸ Meanwhile, Perdue also provides examples of Indian slaveholders lynching their slaves and, more importantly, she makes a clear distinction between Cherokee slaveholding in the Southeast and in the chaos that followed removal, insisting on 'a hardening of attitudes towards African Americans and a strengthening of the slave code'.⁴⁹ Indeed, starting in the year 1841, the year when Bibb escaped from his Indian master, and until the Civil War, a series of slave codes adopted by the Cherokee Nation led to the deterioration of the status of slaves as well as black freedmen.⁵⁰ Recent work has also highlighted that slave rebellions did occur in Indian Territory, indicating increased pressure on slaves and the corollary disposition of the slaves themselves to resist by absconding from their masters.⁵¹ Bibb's comments must thus be read with caution when confronted with historical evidence. His intention to focus on contrasting Indians and Whites in their practice of slavery creates the need for clear-cut distinctions, even if that means undue emphasis, exaggeration, or ellipsis. His narrative, like other antebellum slave narratives, abounds with examples of cruel treatment of himself but also of his wife and child in the white South, and the daily violence of slavery is recurrently brought vividly to life by the many emotionally-loaded illustrations in the book, whose 'graphic' language echo the horror transcribed in written words.⁵² Incidentally, the chapters devoted to Bibb's Indian slavery are not illustrated. Though the cause could be that Bibb, who relied on stock images already produced mostly for other anti-slavery publications, could not find any that might suit his needs, his decision not to have one made to order raises questions: outside of financial considerations, did that mean that visual representations of Indian slavery did not differ enough from slavery among white Southerners? Besides, the contrast that Bibb offers as he describes the master–slave relationship is arresting, for the black slave is shown as potentially shifting into a physically dominant position:

They have no overseers to whip nor drive them. If a slave offends his master, he sometimes, in a heat of passion, undertakes to chastise him; but it is as often the case as otherwise, that the slave gets the better of the fight, and even flogs his master, for which there is no law to punish him; but when the fight is over that is the last of it.[53]

The significance of this passage is crucial, as it shows the master–slave relationship among Cherokees challenged by the slaves themselves, who can be in a position to overpower their masters. It is so hard to believe, in fact, that Bibb's editor, Lucius Matlack, contributes a footnote (being one out of four throughout the book) to comment and assert Bibb's truthfulness: 'This singular fact is corroborated in a letter read by the publisher, from an acquaintance while passing through this country in 1849.'[54] But Matlack's direct intervention also serves as a reminder that Bibb's text must be envisaged as, at least, the site of negotiation between the former slave and his white abolitionist sponsor.[55] Meanwhile, the way in which the slave is described as dominating his master is through a hand-to-hand combat, without the interference of any other person, including the often powerful and cruel overseer of the slaveholding white South. Bibb also insists on the lack of punishment enforced by law, making Cherokee slavery reliant on *de facto* tradition rather than statutory rules.

Finally, paramount among Bibb's concerns, as his whole narrative emphasizes so clearly, is the Indian slaveholder's attitude towards kinship ties: Bibb asserts that Indian slaveholders did not 'separate husbands and wives, nor parents and children'.[56] Such a brief comment sharply contrasts with Bibb's focus, throughout his narrative, on presenting white slavery as an institution that destroys his own marriage and his family. As Green suggests, Bibb makes Indians 'treat their slaves as benevolent fathers would treat their children', while 'white abolitionist critiques of slavery in the antebellum era centered on its failures to live up to its paternalistic standards'.[57] Bibb combines his sketch of the preservation of the domestic ideal with the Indian slaveowners' practice of allowing slaves to worship in church without distinction of colour:

> So far as religious instruction is concerned, they have it on terms of equality, the bond and the free; they have no respect of persons, they have neither slave laws nor negro pews.[58]

McLoughlin provides the time frame necessary to validate Bibb's comment by arguing that 'most Christian slaveholders allowed their slaves to attend church and Sabbath schools until the Cherokee Council passed the law in 1841 prohibiting the teaching of slaves to read and write'.[59] If Bibb's comment on the Indian masters' consent to integrated religious practice thus hardly passes the test of historical accuracy, it must instead be seen as another powerful opportunity for Bibb to denounce white Southern norms as a corruption of Christian values and to portray Southern slaveholders as base hypocrites who deserved neither pity nor compassion. It must also be read as a subtext informing Bibb's struggle, fought alongside abolitionist and Wesleyan allies like James G. Birney and Lucius Matlack, to indict American churches for their complacent support of slaveholders.[60]

In the end, Bibb's overall intention becomes clearly apparent, as his narrative aims at depicting the various devices allowing the South to function as a slave society, whereas Cherokee slavery is shown as anything but an institution, as it lacked the legal foundations, economic justification and social ramifications defining the slaveholding white South. The apparent leniency and weakness of the hold of slavery in post-removal Cherokee society serves instead as a foil to amplify the deep-rooted and thoroughly institutionalized cruelty and inhumanity of white slaveholders. Such arguments bolstered those of a faction of Northern abolitionists who supported the Cherokees in their resistance to removal and criticized Andrew Jackson's policy as compliant with the South's tyrannical slaveocracy. These abolitionists portrayed African American slavery among Indians as a practice imposed by Whites. They also argued that it was temporary and should disappear once Native people came to embrace higher standards of civilization.[61] Meanwhile, in their struggle against white encroachment and in their attempt to save their political sovereignty, Cherokee planters were obviously serving vested interests as they became accomplices in portraying their practice of slavery as less rigid and less violent than its white counterpart. For example, William Potter Ross, a nephew of Cherokee Nation Chief John Ross and a slaveowner like his uncle, would insist that Cherokees treated their slaves 'in a just and liberal manner' and 'more generously ... than anywhere else'.[62] Henry Bibb's narrative of Indian slavery thus serves as a mouthpiece disseminating specifically radical abolitionist propaganda, succumbing in many ways to the 'sophistry' its author had pledged he would avoid.

Conclusion: black over red or, challenging the South's racial hierarchy

Although it was brief, Henry Bibb's Indian slavery was of paramount importance in allowing for his long-winded transition from a slave to a free man who pledged, in the concluding lines of his narrative, 'ever to contend for the natural equality of the human family, without regard to color, which is but fading *matter*, while *mind* makes the man'.[63] Bibb's eloquent promise of engagement in favour of racial equality strikes the reader as a powerful though precarious commitment, because one of the most important sources of Bibb's empowerment as a slave is his perception of his Indian master's race as decadent and inferior. Indeed, Bibb readily acknowledges that, when he became the slave of an Indian, he saw the best opportunity for escape. Moreover, Bibb takes utmost care in describing the Indians generally as primitive people, omitting to make clear distinctions between slaveholding and non-slaveholding Indians. For example, after his escape from his master, Bibb crosses the Indian Territory and meets Indians who cannot speak English, live in overcrowded houses and sleep on a dirt floor, and who, while obviously suffering from hunger themselves, prove their hospitality by sharing their scant food.[64] Bibb endeavours to showcase the Indians' primitiveness, referring disparagingly to 'a majority of Indians' being 'uneducated' who 'still followed up their old heathen traditional *notions*'.[65] In his performance at Faneuil Hall, Bibb revealed that his master's death had been caused by dropsy, commenting that the Indian doctor they had travelled many miles to see had 'soon finished his Indian master':[66] the suggestion that his master's death had been precipitated by shamanic medicine was clearly meant to be derogatory and to highlight the inferiority of such practices. The reader, however, might recall that Bibb, as a younger slave, describes early in his narrative his own interest and belief in black conjure, either to help him escape successfully, get a slave girl to fall in love with him, or evade his masters' punishment. Similarly, as he describes a typical Indian dance, Bibb denounces the Indians' lack of propriety and temperance as a sign of moral degradation.[67] Again, a striking contrast emerges between this elliptical, disparaging description of Native American customs and that of the dance or games performed by black slaves early in his book: while he recognizes the ignorance and degradation of the slaves, Bibb also insists that those traits originate from the masters' oppression, not from some possible intrinsic failing in African American identity. With the Indians, he does not allow for such attenuation. Besides, building on the white stereotype of the drunken Indian, Bibb fails to remark that it was white men who smuggled liquor into Indian Territory.[68] Bibb reinforces the perception of the Indian as a degraded human when he points out that, fearing for his safety after his escape, he passed as a drunken white man to evade detection as a fugitive, for he 'knew the Indians were generally drunkards, and that occasionally a drunken white man was found straggling among them, and that such an [sic] one would be more likely to find friends from sympathy than an upright man'.[69]

As a light-skinned, mixed-race man, Bibb used what Green calls 'his racial ambiguity' as 'an asset in Indian Territory':[70] he passes for white knowingly and intentionally, and it is his alertness and his shrewdness that allow him to outwit the Indians and secure his freedom. Bibb thus shows himself as a superior character, powerfully challenging preconceived notions of the inferiority of African American people, not only as developed by Southern whites who thus relied on them to promote and develop slavery, but also adopted by the Indians themselves, according to William G. McLoughlin:

> Having been conquered by superior European numbers, firepower, technology and cunning, the Indian was ready to admit that the white man had certain advantages which stemmed from his knowledge of how to read and write. But in order to save himself from total degradation, the Indian gave himself a position in the human hierarchy above that of the black slave. The Great Spirit, while changing his people from white to red and denying them the knowledge of reading and writing, nevertheless wrote the divine law in their hearts. Only the black man was reduced to the spiritual blankness of animals.[71]

Finally, as he closes the chapter on his 'adventure in a wigwam' (the expression is one of the subtitles in Chapter XV), Bibb presents a heroic portrait of himself as a man equipped with true grit and enough resourcefulness to face many terrible dangers amidst Indians:

> I had doubtless gone through great peril in crossing the Indian territory, in passing through the various half civilized tribes, who seemed to look upon me with astonishment as I passed along. Their hands were almost invariably filled with

bows and arrows, tomahawks, guns, butcher knives, and all the various implements of death which are used by them. And what made them look still more frightful, their faces were often painted red, and their heads muffled with birds feathers, bushes, coons tails and owls heads.[72]

As Green has shown, Bibb relies on 'stock images of Native American depravity found in colonial and contemporary accounts of Indian captivity' to construct 'an image of his own masculinity in contrast to, but created through, the prism of misconceptions surrounding Native Americans'.[73] Insisting on Indian savagery was also possibly Bibb's answer to the expectations of a white, middle-class northern readership who, in the mid-nineteenth century, showed renewed interest in the Indian captivity narrative.[74] Simultaneously, Bibb's perplexing use of the indigenous word 'wigwam' to refer to his Indian 'adventure', his insistence on the 'red' faces of Indians, and his portrayal of bloodthirsty warriors emphasize the racial features of Native Americans. Such characterization makes them clearly distinct and incompatible with Bibb's own race, justifying his brief association with them as merely 'passing', while confirming his obvious status as an alienated, though superior, 'other'. Incidentally and paradoxically, Bibb's adherence to a racial hierarchy that clearly disassociated white and black people from 'red' can be seen as the ultimate justification for the Southeastern tribes' removal to Indian Territory, which some white Americans had so long defended and which Bibb's fellow radical abolitionists had so vigorously opposed.[75]

Notes

1   'A Runaway Slave in Faneuil Hall', *The Liberator*, 22 January 1847.
2   In his narrative, Bibb says he was born in 1815, but recent archival research has revealed that he was born either in the spring of 1814 or in late 1813. See Diane Perrine Coon, 'Project Report 2.0 Second Stakeholders' Meeting National Henry Bibb Heritage Trail, Bedford, Kentucky, October 26, 2005', http://www.academia.edu/14439495/Project_Report_2_National_Henry Bibb_Heritage_Trail.
3   Henry Bibb, *The Life and Adventures of Henry Bibb, an American Slave* (Madison: University of Wisconsin Press, 2001/1849), 14. All subsequent references are to this edition.
4   Because of its structure based on escapes, returns and recaptures, Bibb's story has been described as 'the narrative of recursion'. See Charles J. Heglar, *Rethinking the Slave Narrative: Slave Marriage and the Narratives of Henry Bibb and William and Ellen Craft* (Westport, CT: Greenwood Press, 2001), 33–6.
5   During the 1830s and 1840s in Michigan, the Michigan State Anti-Slavery Society was the first and predominant anti-slavery organization, whose members urged active participation in politics and contributed to the creation of the Liberty Party. See Carol E. Mull, *The Underground Railroad in Michigan* (Jefferson, NC: McFarland & Co., 2010), 41–5.
6   On the Liberty Party, see Manisha Sinha, *The Slave's Cause: A History of Abolition* (New Haven, CT: Yale University Press, 2016), 463–8.
7   Canada West was one of the provinces of British North America until Canada was formed as a dominion in 1867.

8   On the RHS, see Robin Winks, *The Blacks in Canada: A History*, 2nd edn (Montreal and Kingston: McGill-Queen's University Press, 1987), 204–8.
9   See Afua Cooper, 'The *Voice of the Fugitive*: A Transnational Abolitionist Organ', in Karolyn Smardz Frost and Veta Smith Tucker (eds), *A Fluid Frontier: Slavery, Resistance, and the Underground Railroad in the Detroit River Borderland* (Detroit: Wayne State University Press, 2016), 135–53.
10 'Henry Bibb Is Dead', *Frederick Douglass' Paper*, 11 August 1854.
11 See Sihna, *The Slave's Cause*, 256–65.
12 On the publishing history of the narrative, see Michaël Roy, *Textes fugitifs: le récit d'esclave au prisme de l'histoire du livre* (Lyon: ENS Editions, 2018), 191–7.
13 Keith Michael Green, 'Am I Not a Husband and a Father?: Remembering Black Masculinity, Slave Incarceration, and Cherokee Slavery in *The Life and Adventures of Henry Bibb, an American Slave*', *MELUS* 39, no. 4 (Winter 2014): 35.
14 Green, 'Am I Not a Husband and a Father?', 24.
15 Green, 'Am I Not a Husband and a Father?', 41.
16 William L. Andrews, *To Tell a Free Story: The First Century of Afro-American Autobiography, 1760–1865* (Urbana: University of Illinois Press, 1986), 158.
17 Bibb, *Narrative*, 11.
18 Bibb, *Narrative*, 17.
19 Theda Perdue, *Slavery and the Evolution of Cherokee Society, 1540–1866* (Knoxville: University of Tennessee Press, 1993/1979), 97.
20 On the eve of removal, there were 15,000 Cherokees and 1,592 slaves. See William G. McLoughlin, 'Red Indians, Black Slavery and White Racism: America's Slaveholding Indians', *American Quarterly* 26, no. 4 (Summer 2001): 380.
21 Mary Young, 'The Cherokee Nation: Mirror of the Republic', *American Quarterly* 33, no. 5 (Winter 1981): 502–24.
22 For the slave testimonies on the 'Trail of Tears', see Patrick Minges, 'Beneath the Underdog: Race, Religion and the Trail of Tears', *American Indian Quarterly* 25, no. 3 (Summer 2001): 468.
23 Green, 'Am I Not a Husband and a Father?', 40.
24 Bibb, *Narrative*, 150.
25 Bibb, *Narrative*, 149 (my emphasis).
26 Bibb, *Narrative*, 110.
27 Bibb, *Narrative*, 110 (my emphasis).
28 See Walter Johnson, *Soul by Soul: Life Inside the Antebellum Slave Market* (Cambridge, MA: Harvard University Press, 1999), 45–77.
29 Johnson, *Soul by Soul*, 30.
30 Bibb, *Narrative*, 150.
31 Charles H. Nicols, 'The Slave Narrators and the Picaresque Mode: Archetypes for Modern Black Personae', in Charles T. Davis and Henry Louis Gates, Jr (eds), *The Slave's Narrative* (Oxford: Oxford University Press, 1985), 739–55.
32 Andrews, *To Tell a Free Story*, 144–5.
33 Bibb, *Narrative*, 152.
34 Bibb, *Narrative*, 152.
35 'Henry Bibb and the Slaveholders', *Western Citizen*, 20 November 1849.
36 In one of his letters to Albert G. Sibley, Bibb writes, 'I confess that I have been a little disappointed at your very singular defense, which has been only an unbroken silence. Perhaps you have had the vanity to think that in this way you could shield your official character from the execrations of the Christian public: but vain is

your hope.' See Henry Bibb, 'A Letter to my Old Master', *Voice of the Fugitive*, 2 December 1852.
37 Bibb, *Narrative*, 154–5.
38 Bibb, *Narrative*, 118.
39 Bibb, *Narrative*, 158.
40 Lawrence W. Levine, *Black Culture and Black Consciousness: Afro-American Folk Thought from Slavery to Freedom, 30th Anniversary Edition* (New York: Oxford University Press, 2007), 105.
41 Bibb, *Narrative*, 153.
42 Bibb, *Narrative*, 152.
43 Bibb, *Narrative*, 152.
44 See Perdue, *Slavery and the Evolution of Cherokee Society*, 99–105.
45 William G. McLoughlin, *After the Trail of Tears: The Cherokees' Struggle for Sovereignty, 1839–1880* (Chapel Hill: University of North Carolina Press, 1993), 125.
46 McLoughlin, *After the Trail of Tears*, 125.
47 Bibb, *Narrative*, 14.
48 Perdue, *Slavery and the Evolution of Cherokee Society*, 98.
49 Perdue, *Slavery and the Evolution of Cherokee Society*, 96.
50 Perdue (*Slavery and the Evolution of Cherokee Society*, 79) highlights the significant lack of runaway ads in the *Cherokee Phoenix*, the newspaper published in Georgia, when compared with the Indian Territory's *Cherokee Advocate*.
51 See Tiya Miles and Celia E. Naylor-Ojurongbe, 'African-Americans in Indian Societies', in *Handbook of North American Indians*, vol. 14: *Southeast* (Washington, DC: US Government Printing Office, 2004), 753–9.
52 On the complex nature of the narrative's illustrations, see Marcus Wood, *Blind Memory: Visual Representations of Slavery in England and America, 1780–1865* (Manchester and New York: Manchester University Press, 2000), 117–34.
53 Bibb, *Narrative*, 152–3.
54 Bibb, *Narrative*, 153.
55 Matlack's other interventions have been underlined by James Olney, '"I was Born": Slave Narratives, Their Status as Autobiography and as Literature', in Charles T. Davis and Henry Louis Gates, Jr (eds), *The Slave's Narrative* (Oxford: Oxford University Press, 1990/1985), 163–5, and by Sandrine Ferré-Rode, introduction, *Récit de la vie et des aventures de Henry Bibb, esclave américain, écrit par lui-même* (Rouen: Presses Universitaires de Rouen et du Havre, 2018).
56 Bibb, *Narrative*, 153.
57 Green, 'Am I Not a Husband and a Father?', 39.
58 Bibb, *Narrative*, 153.
59 McLoughlin, *After the Trail of Tears*, 133.
60 See James Gillepsie Birney, *The American Churches: The Bulwarks of American Slavery* (Newburyport, MA: Charles Whipple, 1842), and Lucius C. Matlack, *Narrative of the Anti-Slavery Experience of a Minister in the Methodist E. Church* (Philadelphia, PA: Merrihew and Thompson, 1845).
61 See Sinha, *The Slave's Cause*, 378–9, and Natalie Joy, 'Cherokee Slaveholders and Radical Abolitionists: An Unlikely Alliance in Antebellum America', *Common-Place* 10, no. 4 (July 2010), http://www.common-place-archives.org/vol-10/no-04/joy/.
62 Quoted in Celia E. Naylor, *African Cherokees in Indian Territory: From Chattel to Citizens* (Chapel Hill: University of North Carolina Press, 2008), 36.
63 Bibb, *Narrative*, 204.

64 Bibb, *Narrative*, 156.
65 Bibb, *Narrative*, 153 (my emphasis).
66 'Henry Bibb, the Fugitive Slave', *Western Citizen*, 28 December 1847.
67 Bibb, *Narrative*, 154.
68 See McLoughlin, *After the Trail of Tears*, 388.
69 Bibb, *Narrative*, 155.
70 Green, 'Am I Not a Husband and a Father?', 37.
71 McLoughlin, 'Red Indians', 379.
72 Bibb, *Narrative*, 158.
73 Green, 'Am I Not a Husband and a Father?', 34.
74 Andrews, *To Tell a Free Story*, 152.
75 On the Cherokees' 'invention' of Indian Territory as their country and their adherence to the notion of a separate 'red race', see James P. Ronda, '"We Have a Country": Race, Geography, and the Invention of Indian Territory', *Journal of the Early Republic* 19, no. 4 (Winter 1999): 739–55.

4

To 'make a good Mistress to my servants': Unmasking the Meaning of Maternalism in Colonial South Carolina

Inge Dornan

In 1745, Eliza Lucas Pinckney drew up a series of resolutions among which she promised to 'make a good wife to my dear Husband', to 'be a good Mother to my children' and to 'make a good Mistress to my servants'. She further vowed to treat her slaves 'with humanity and good nature; to give them sufficient and comfortable clothing and Provisions, and all things necessary for them. To be careful and tender of them in their sickness, to reprove them for their faults, to Encourage them when they do well, and pass over small faults; not to be tyrannical or peavish or impatient towards them, but to make their lives as comfortable as I can.' She concluded by resolving to 'be a universal lover of all mankind'. Her resolutions were intended to be kept private, to which end she marked them 'papers belonging to myself onely [sic]'.[1]

Pinckney's 'resolutions' point to the emergence of an ideology of maternalism in the colonial South that has heretofore received only limited recognition from scholars. With notable exceptions, including studies by William Foster, Kirsten Wood and Betty Wood, historians have largely concentrated on how patriarchy and paternalism shaped Southern colonial slave society and women's role and status within it.[2] This chapter places maternalism at the heart of Southern colonial women's relationship to slavery and in so doing seeks to unmask the meaning of 'maternalism' – to which Eliza Pinckney subscribed – in the context of female slaveholding in colonial South Carolina. Few colonial women slaveholders left personal records disclosing their relations with their slaves. Even Pinckney, whose record of correspondence is relatively voluminous, was despite the candidness of her resolutions, conspicuously tight-lipped about her interactions with her slaves. Careful combing through her correspondence nonetheless provides a glimpse into the nature of maternalism to which she aspired. Runaway slave notices in the colony's newspapers also shed light on women slaveholders' treatment of their slaves. Notwithstanding, it is not my intention here to debate the degree to which women slaveholders were or were not 'kind' or 'good mistresses'. Rather, my goal is to critique the meaning of maternalism as it shaped slaveholding women's identity and informed how they managed their slaves in colonial South Carolina.

English common law largely prevented married women from owning and managing property in their own right and therefore the majority of the colony's women slaveholders acquired their slaves in widowhood. There were, however, some notable exceptions to this. Pinckney's first experience of plantation management, for instance, occurred prior to marriage when, as a single woman legally able to transact business in her own name, her father placed her in charge of managing the family's South Carolina plantations while he was stationed in Antigua. In other instances, as a result of South Carolina's adoption of the rule of equity through the English Court of Chancery, married women could retain ownership and management of slaves through a marriage settlement or separate estate and could as well, with their husband's permission, operate in business as if they were a *feme sole* and not a *feme covert*.[3] That a small but conspicuous handful of the colony's married women took advantage of equity procedures is evident by their advertisements promoting their businesses in the colony's newspapers and buying and selling land and slaves in their own name. Such exceptions aside, however, most women who assumed the status of slaveowner did so in widowhood, just as Pinckney did after the death of her husband, Charles, in 1758.

It was the southern colonies' high mortality rates and the concomitant ubiquity of widowhood which led Edmund Morgan to coin the phrase 'widowarchy' to underscore the prevalence and relative socio-economic power of southern colonial widows.[4] The nature and form of widowarchy in South Carolina was shaped by the mores and customs that determined patterns of widows' inheritance. Where a husband died intestate in South Carolina (roughly one half of inventoried colonial estates were not accompanied by a will),[5] his widow's inheritance was decided by English common law: a widow's dower entitled her to use of her husband's land during her lifetime (primogeniture dictated that land ownership fell to her surviving eldest son) and she received one third (or one half if the couple had no children) of her husband's personalty (moveable goods) outright.[6] In colonial South Carolina, where slavery forced adaptations to English common law, it is important to note that personalty included slaves – in contrast to Virginia where widows possessed only a lifetime interest in the slaves they inherited as part of their dower rights.[7] In South Carolina's burgeoning economy where slaves were mortgaged, bought, sold and hired out for income, the award of outright ownership of slaves to widows under South Carolina's intestacy laws not only paved the way for women to own slaves, but also legally enshrined their role in the expansion and maintenance of slavery in the colony.

South Carolina's testate husbands further facilitated women's ownership of slaves and in so doing underwrote women's contribution to the development of slavery in the colony. John Crowley's analysis of the mathematics of life and death among parents and children in colonial South Carolina reveals that nearly one-third of testate husbands died childless and two-thirds of parents were survived by less than four children.[8] Furthermore, over three-quarters of testate parents died leaving behind young children and just less than 40 per cent had no surviving adult children at all.[9] These heartbreaking statistics had a staggering impact on widows' inheritance: most childless widows became appointed their husband's sole heir; most also inherited more than they would have been entitled to had their husband died intestate; almost 70 per cent of husbands appointed their wives their executrix (including Eliza's husband, Charles Pinckney, who nominated her his executrix).[10] Additionally, fully 80 per cent of widows were given their inheritance in fee simple – that is, to do with as they wished, as opposed to a lifetime use which prevented them from bequeathing or selling the property; over two-thirds of widows also received part of the residue of their testate husband's estate, which according to Crowley was often the most valuable share of his wealth.[11] Altogether, Crowley's findings persuaded him to press forth a bold conclusion: that patterns of female inheritance in colonial South Carolina signified a 'precocious liberalism'[12] which in turn reflected 'attitudes [that were] more pro-feminine than patriarchal'.[13] It is important to qualify Crowley's striking assertion. South Carolina's husbands were not driven to empower their widows with a view to undermine long-standing patriarchal ideals regarding women's role and place in society but, on the contrary, to provide them with the economic wherewithal to ensure that their family, which lay at the heart of patriarchal notions of government, authority and order, and the property which sustained it, remained intact. Empowering widows economically was not intended to beat a path towards women's independence in colonial South Carolina, but was aimed at strengthening their ability to support themselves and their children. By extending their widows' inheritance, more so than under the rules of intestacy, South Carolina's testate husbands revealed how much they trusted in their widows – more so than in anyone else – to manage the family's property and to care and provide for their children. And where they had no children, because they viewed their wives as rightfully deserving of the greatest share of their estate. Their actions thus represented an acknowledgement of their wives' role in the creation and maintenance of family wealth during marriage, more so than a conscious challenge to the patriarchal order. It was through converting their inheritance of slaves (and in some cases also land, plantations and businesses) into a source of income that South Carolina's widows became a visible and vital part of the economic and business life of the colony.

Pinckney's identity as a genteel slaveholder was key to the development of her vision of maternalism and her correspondence with family and friends illustrates how she harnessed the rhetoric of genteel maternalism in her management of the family's plantations. Writing to her friend Mary Boddicott, in 1740, she confided, 'I have the business of 3 plantations to transact wch. requires much writing and more business and fatigue of other sorts than you can imagine.'[14] The 'business' to which the young Eliza Lucas referred typically entailed correspondence with plantation overseers on a whole range of plantation matters, from crop planting and harvesting to the transporting of provisions and slaves between the family's plantations. A letter to her father in June 1741 underscores her confidence, knowledge and degree of involvement in the business of plantation management:

> I wrote this day to Starrat [overseer] for a barl butter. We expect the boat dayly from Garden Hill when I shall be able to give you an acct. of affairs there. The Cotton Guiney corn, and most of the Ginger planted here was cutt off by a frost. I wrote you in former letter we had a fine Crop of Indigo Seed upon the ground and since informd you ye. frost took it before it was dry I pickd out the best of it and had it planted but there is not more than a hundred bushes of it come up wch.

proves the more unluckey as you have sent a man to make it I make no doubt Indigo will prove a very valuable Commodity in time if we could have the seed from the west Indias time enough to plant the latter end of march that the seed might be dry enough to gather before our frost... The Lucern is yet but dwindleing, but Mr. Hunt tells me 'tis always so here the first year.[15]

Pinckney was accountable to her father on all aspects of plantation management, but as the above extract reveals, she did not run the family's plantations single-handedly; instead she relied upon overseers and also looked to neighbours to provide her with advice and guidance, like Mr Hunt, and also Mr Deveaux, who she noted, in another letter to her father, was 'very kind in Instructing me in planting affairs'.[16] Notwithstanding, she found the management of the family's plantations demanding as well as daunting, as she confided to her friend Mary Bartlett, in 1742: 'I have so much business on my hands at present I hardly know wch. to turn my self to first and most of it such as cant be deferred.'[17] Pinckney's correspondence illustrates how the business of plantation management compelled her to step into the 'affairs of the world', a phrase Cara Anzilotti employed to denote the public sphere of activity within which the colony's women planters operated.[18] This did not mean that, in so doing, Pinckney relinquished her claim to the ideals and mores of gentility that governed elite women's role and place in the colony. For as Pinckney's correspondence to her father, to her overseers and, in later years, to her husband and children shows, the 'business' of plantation management was commonly conducted – through letters – from within the household to the world of affairs outside the household. Kirsten Wood has argued of slaveholding widows in the revolutionary and antebellum era that correspondence formed the primary medium by which plantation business was transacted, particularly by those who ranked among the planter elite, and in this respect, as Wood keenly observes, women planters differed little from their male counterparts.[19] Indeed Pinckney once remarked to a friend that she set aside the whole of Thursdays for writing 'either on the business of the plantations, or letters to my friends'.[20] Stepping into the role of planter and slaveholder did not have the effect of transgressing southern (patriarchal) notions of a genteel woman's role and place in society where, in so far as the mode of plantation business was concerned, private and public spheres overlapped.

Pinckney strengthened her claim to rank among the colony's slaveholding elite in the self-image of maternalism she created in her correspondence with family and friends. Her response to Mary Bartlett's inquiry as to how she spent her days is a case in point:

In genl. then I rise at five o'Clock in the morning, read till Seven then take a walk in the Garden or field see that the Servants are at their respective business then to breakfast.

The first hour after breakfast is spend at my musick the next is constantly employd in recolecting something I have learnd ... such as french and short hand after that I devote the rest of the time till I dress for dinner to our little polly and two black girls who I teach to read, and if I have my papa's approbation (my Mamas I have got) I intend for school mistress's for the rest of the Negroe children

... the first hour after dinner as the first after breakfast at musick, the rest of the afternoon in Needle work till candle light, and from that time to bed time read or write.[21]

In representing her daily duties and responsibilities thus, Pinckney endeavoured to merge the customs and fashions of Lowcountry female gentility – music, reading, a walk in the garden – with plantation duties (a walk in the field) and slave management (seeing that the 'servants' were at their respective business). Even the management of her slaves was transformed into a genteel activity. Thus Pinckney confessed to Mary Bartlett to teaching two of her young female slaves to read and her desire to hire a school mistress to likewise instruct the rest of her family's enslaved children. The tone and content of this letter consciously avoids any direct reference to the fact that the children whom Pinckney instructed were in fact the family's chattel property. Instead, the image she invoked was that of a mother-figure tending to the instruction and raising of her children: just as she instructed her sister to read, so she instructed her slaves ('black girls'). The portrait of slaveholding and plantation business she cultivated in her correspondence with Mary Bartlett and other friends stands in marked contrast to the picture of plantation management she painted in her correspondence with her father and overseers quoted earlier, in which she keenly articulated her knowledge and engagement with plantation affairs.

Pinckney's love of the natural world and botany formed a further source of rhetoric to underline her status as a genteel female planter. To Mary Bartlett, she wrote, 'I have planted a large figg orchard with design to dry and export them, I have reckond my expence and the prophets to arise from these figgs ... I own I love the vegitable world extreamly I think it an innocent and useful amusement.'[22] Pinckney, whom we can fairly presume did not actually plant the fig orchard herself, justified her commercial venture not through any hard-nosed ambition to generate an income, but by framing it as a genteel 'amusement' born of a 'love of the vegitable world'. She wrote similarly of her intention to plant an oak plantation:

> I am making a large plantation of oaks wch. I look upon as my own property; whether my father gives me the land or not, and therefore I design many year hence when oaks are more valueable than they are now ... I intend I say 2 thirds of the produce of my oaks for a charity ... and the other 3d for those that shall have the trouble of puting my design in Execution.[23]

Although Pinckney vigorously staked her claim to the land she had set aside for the oaks and clearly intended to turn a profit from them, her end-goal was apparently not profit for profit's sake, but profit for the sake of charity and benevolence. In framing the economics of plantation management and the politics of managing her slaves in ways that bespoke her status as a genteel lady, Pinckney disclosed how maternalism was both rooted in, as well as reinforced by, her rank.

Pinckney's correspondence suggests that like many of her antebellum counterparts, her closest interactions and relationships were formed with slaves who laboured in and around her household, and it was in the sphere of domestic slave management that her vision of maternalism was most vividly manifest. This was nowhere more clearly expressed than in a letter she wrote to her daughter, Harriott, detailing the chores she delegated to her domestic slaves:

> Mary-Ann understands roasting poultry in the greatest perfection you ever saw, and old Ebba the fattening them to as great a nicety. Daphne makes me a loaf of very nice bread. You know I am no epicure, but I am pleased they can do things so well, when they are put to it ... I shall keep young Ebba to do the drudgery part, fetch wood, and water, and scour, and learn as much as she is capable of Cooking and Washing. Mary-Ann Cooks, makes my bed, and makes my punch, Daphne works and makes the bread, old Ebba boils the cow's victuals, raises and fattens the poultry, Moses is imployed from breakfast until 12 o'clock without doors, after that in the house. Pegg washes and milks. Thus I have formed my household, nobody eats the bread of idleness when I am here, nor are any overworked.[24]

Pinckney was keen to be seen to praise Mary-Anne, Old Ebba and Daphne's particular culinary talents and skills to her daughter, but she was even more keen to point out to her that she was 'pleased they can do things so well, *when they are put to it*'. In so many words, Pinckney encapsulated how the rhetoric of maternalism underscored genteel female mastery, and, furthermore, in this instance, how it was passed from mother to daughter. Pinckney's genteel maternalism was further inscribed by listing the domestic chores she delegated to each of her slaves, all of which by virtue of not being performed by her reinforced her status among the planter elite. Her closing sentence self-consciously epitomized as well as enforced her maternalism: '*nobody eats the bread of idleness when I am here, nor are any overworked*'. Pinckney's Christian faith was central to her self-image as a daughter, sister, wife and mother, as numerous letters to her family members throughout the course of her life testify. It was also, moreover, as she reveals here – in a reference to Proverbs 31.27, 'She looketh well to the ways of her household and not eateth the bread of idleness' – part of the rhetorical apparatus which underwrote her maternalism. It was by wedding her faith to the ideological fulfillment of her role and duties as a slaveholder that maternalism came to underpin Pinckney's identity as a genteel Christian planter.

Pinckney's maternalism found its most pronounced expression in the favouritism she displayed toward an enslaved woman named Sibb, who moved between her and her daughter Harriott's household. No other slave earned as much attention in Pinckney's correspondence with friends and family as Sibb: 'I hope Sibb's got better';[25] 'I am very sorry to hear poor Sibb is ill again';[26] 'Sibb was taken with a fever two days ago but it is luckily off this morning ... it would have distressd me a good deal to have left her so ill';[27] 'Sibby has been extremely ill with a Rheumatic fever ... I had her in the house and she has been well nursed tho' is still very weak.'[28] Favouritism, or 'personalism' as Suzanne Lebsock argues, formed a key characteristic of women slaveholders' treatment of their slaves and it figured prominently, I would argue, in the operation of maternalism. Pinckney owned and managed dozens of slaves over the course of her life, but only a tiny handful, like Sibb, received a special mention in her correspondence. It was, moreover, by no means incidental that on each occasion

Pinckney mentioned Sibb(y), it was in the context of Sibb's health, for this bespoke the maternalism that underpinned her resolutions: 'To be careful and tender of them [her slaves] in their sickness' and 'to make their lives as comfortable as I can.'

Pinckney's expressions of concern for her slaves' health and welfare embodied the maternalism to which she aspired and in so doing exposed how genteel notions of female domesticity blended with the economic realities of slave ownership. On the one hand, by making a conscious note of her slaves' illnesses to friends and family, she demonstrated her knowledge, control and authority (in some cases, intimately so) over her slaves and in the process signalled her maternalism. Thus she variously wrote, 'Juno's breast is a good deal better, her Child well';[29] 'We lost George and Phebe in a few day's [sic], and before I heard they were sick';[30] 'Abram and little Toby lay at the point of Death on Saturday'[31] – a fact which, she carefully noted, prompted her to send for a doctor to attend them. Elsewhere she wrote, 'Dye I hear complains of a pain in her knees . . . [and] her child has the thrush and I am told is but puny';[32] 'little Dick has been extremely ill I was afraid we should have lost him also. I believe taking him in ye house and good nursing was a means of saving him also.'[33] In each of these cases, Pinckney expressed her familiarity with her slaves by referring to them by name and also, most notably in the case of Juno, Dye and her child, by referring to the physically intimate illnesses from which they suffered. In this respect, Pinckney's maternalism was harnessed to signify her authority and control over her slaves. She made a point of knowing their particular illnesses and of saying so when she had not been informed they were unwell, as in the case of George and Phebe who died before *she* could administer care. She also made a point of deciding on their treatment: to call a doctor or not, or to care for them in her own house, as she did with Sibb and little Dick. Notwithstanding, it was in writing of the death of one of her carpenters during the 1760 smallpox epidemic that she betrayed the limits of maternalism: 'I lost one only a valuable Carpenter who took it ye natural way'[34] – referring to him not by his name but by his occupation and the impact his death had on her livelihood.

Only by reading against the grain as well as between the lines of Pinckney's correspondence do we catch a glimpse of the tensions and conflicts inherent in maternalism. Indeed, her resolution to be a 'good mistress' and treat her slaves with 'humanity' and 'good nature' rather implies, like all resolutions, that the ideal was not the norm. That maternalism was an ideology which she aspired to and not a reflection of the lived reality of slaveholding can be gauged by the one or two cases where Pinckney betrayed her frustration at her slaves' refusal to bend to her authority. Like many of her male and female slaveholding counterparts, she depended on her slaves to carry letters, messages and information back and forth between family, friends and neighbours; one such messenger was her slave Harry. In 1768, Pinckney received word via Harry that her son-in-law, Daniel Horry, had been injured; in the course of interrogating Harry for further information about Daniel's condition, she unwittingly disclosed the unsteadiness of her claim to maternalism when faced with slaves who undermined her authority. She wrote to her son-in-law:

> I don't believe Harry would utter a sentence more than he is commissiond to do for the world, I asked him many questions, particularly about your wound and whether

it was still bad, but I could not get anything out of him more than that it is a scratch, though Harriott calls it a deep Gash; had the Major such a servant I believe his secret never would have been discoverd.[35]

Although she does her best to mask the incident with a degree of humor, Pinckney was clearly irritated by Harry's tight-lipped refusal to be drawn on the details of her son-in-law's injury, despite a rigorous quizzing by his mistress. In another instance, Pinckney wrote to her daughter of her frustration at not being able to communicate with her slave, Ralph. 'Onia says he understands English very well, but I think he speaks it very badly, I cant understand him,' she wrote.[36] Not only was Onia bold enough to dispute Pinckney's judgment, but she also, in so doing, colluded with Ralph to frustrate Pinckney's claim to wield complete control over them.

The American Revolution fully exposed the myth of maternalism to which Pinckney cleaved in her identity as a genteel slaveholder and planter. Whether she was truly surprised when her slaves seized the chances afforded by the dislocations of war to challenge and contest her ownership and authority over them is hard to say, but there is little doubt about the impact of their actions on her livelihood and status. In a letter to her son, Thomas Pinckney, in 1779, she highlighted her complete loss of control and authority over her slaves: 'I sent Prince the Taylor from Goose Creek to order the Belmont people to Cross Scots ferry and come to me at Santee and I hear Mr. Horry did the same *but they are not come*'[37] (my italics). She further noted:

> I know not what to do in regard to the Beach hill and Belmont Negroes... for *they all do now what they please every where and several plantations of Negroes attatch'd to their homes and the little they have there have refused to remove* ... I think they are out of the way of being taken away [by the British] at present *unless they choose to go to them and in that case I fear we should not be able to prevent it*.[38] (my italics)

The Revolutionary War wrought severe disruption to the routines of plantation and slave management and discipline and exposed the fragile lines of authority that underpinned Pinckney's maternalism. After receiving word from her son that his house had been burned down to the ground and his slaves carried away, she observed, 'nor do I know whether they went volontarily [sic] with the Enemy or were taken by force.'[39] By conceding it was possible her slaves 'went' (absconded) voluntarily to the British, Pinckney acknowledged the reality of enslavement which maternalism did its best to mask. In a letter devoid of genteel niceties, she railed to her friend Rebecca Evance, in 1780, 'I tell you I have been Robbd and deserted by my slaves my property pulld to peieces [sic], burnt, and destroy'd, my money of no value, my Children sick and prisoners.'[40] Pinckney's maternalism collapsed in the face of her slaves' rejection of her authority and ownership, and she was finally forced to acknowledge the gulf that had in reality always separated 'my slaves' (her 'black girls') from 'my children'. Thereafter, her maternalism gave way to the true value and meaning of slave ownership, as she explained in a letter to a friend:

> I would sell some of my Negroes that remain in my possession; and make Instant paymt of the £200 I borrow'd of you with the Interest, but the slaves in this country

in genl. have behaved so infamously and even those that remaind at home so Insolent and *quite their own masters* that for this reason ye precariousness of the province & want of money – there are very few purchasers & their value is so trifling that it must be absolute ruin to sell at this time.[41] (my italics)

For all Pinckney's resolutions to be a 'good mistress' and to make her slaves' lives 'as comfortable as I can', her vision of maternalism was contingent, at heart, on her slaves acting as slaves. At the core of maternalism was the economic reality that slaves – acting as slaves – formed the basis of women slaveholders' livelihoods and their families' socio-economic status. Maternalism ceased to have any real meaning once slaves became 'quite their own masters'.

Pinckney was not alone in having to face up to the realities of maternalism when confronted by slaves who were intent on being their own masters or mistresses, as testified by the numerous runaway slave notices placed by women slaveholders in South Carolina's newspapers. Elizabeth Smith was one such slaveowner whose slave, Lancaster, was determined to be his own master. Like many of her slaveholding counterparts in Charleston who hired out their slaves, Smith sought to increase her income by hiring out Lancaster as a 'whitewasher' and fisherman. Lancaster clearly had other ideas about the value of his labour, for rather than hand his wages over to his mistress, he kept them to himself and Smith was prompted to place a notice in the *South Carolina Gazette* declaring that he had 'imposed upon his employers, and defrauded me of his wages'. In no uncertain terms, she forewarned anyone from employing him without her say-so on pain of being fined and threatened 'all negroes who carry Lancaster a Fishing, shall be rigorously prosecuted'.[42] Her remonstrance nonetheless fell on deaf ears because nine months later she placed another notice in the *Gazette*; not only had the public ignored her threats – 'Whereas I have formerly advised all person not to employ my negro man Lancaster … but to little purpose, since he constantly earns money'[43] – so too had Lancaster, who was spotted spending his/her wages on gambling and drinking, before settling on the ultimate act of self-mastery and running away.[44] Hiring out slaves was common among urban slaveholders and especially among women slaveowners to whom it offered a source of income (albeit not in Smith's case). Yet as a method of slave management it undercut the ideals of maternalism by devolving the daily care and supervision of slaves to another slaveholder. Nonetheless, as the case of Lancaster lucidly demonstrates, this did not relieve slaveowners of the need to assert their authority and ownership as well as issue punishment when their slaves refused to comply.

Elizabeth Bullock's treatment of her hired out slave, Hannah Bullock, is a case in point and provides a poignant example of the limits of maternalism. Unlike the majority of notices for runaway slaves in the *Gazette* which described slaves by their first name only, Elizabeth Bullock chose to refer to her slave as Hannah Bullock: assigning her own surname to her slave was not only a symbol of ownership, it was also filial. Hannah Bullock earned money for Elizabeth by selling 'cakes and other Things in the market' in Charleston, until, in 1751, she ran away. At some point between 1751 and 1766, Elizabeth Bullock succeeded in recapturing Hannah Bullock – and promptly sold her, in a not so filial or maternal act of punishment – for in 1766 Hannah

Bullock once again ran away and this time it fell to her new owner, Eliza Johnson, to place a notice in the *Gazette* demanding that she be caught and returned to her.[45] The hiring out of slaves and the numerous examples of hired out enslaved women and men who, determined to be their own masters and mistresses, kept their own wages and/or ran away illustrate the extent to which slaveholding practices and slave resistance operated to subvert maternalism.

In their treatment and punishment of the enslaved, moreover, South Carolina's slaveowners showed very little inclination to exercise much compassion and mercy. In grim detail, the descriptions of runaway slaves, which bear witness to the range of punishments meted out to them by their owners, overseers and the workhouse, point to the range of physical disfigurements induced by whipping, beating, branding, burning, shooting, as well as castration, which were highlighted to help identify runaways. Evidence of the brutal violence inflicted on the enslaved sits alongside evidence of injuries they sustained due to poor and hazardous working conditions and to general neglect, as in the case of Will, who lost all his toes due to frostbite,[46] and Richmond, who broke his arm (or had it broken) and 'wrong set'.[47] In some cases, signs of mental suffering and distress were so pronounced among some runaways that they too served as a means of identification: Elizabeth Harvey described her slave, Sack, as having a 'remarkable down look';[48] July had a 'sullen countenance';[49] and Isaac stuttered especially when 'scared'.[50] There is no evidence to suggest that slaves belonging to women suffered any more or less than those who belonged to men. Although some historians have pointed out that they may have suffered differently;[51] if we accept the view that enslaved women belonging to a woman may not have been as vulnerable to sexual violence as those belonging to men. This presumes that sexual assault was typically inflicted by a white male head of the household and that enslaved women were not similarly susceptible to sexual abuse from other men, free and enslaved, who lived and worked on plantations and in slaveholding households owned by women. Nor does it take into account that the practice of hiring out slaves, which was common among women slaveowners, left enslaved women vulnerable to sexual violence and ill-treatment from their employers. There is, then, little compelling evidence to indicate that slaves belonging to women fared significantly better or worse than those belonging to men.

In fact, there is plenty of evidence to suggest that in keeping with their male counterparts, South Carolina's women slaveowners did not flinch from punishing and disciplining their slaves, most especially when their slaves ceased to act as their slaves, as amply testified by their runaway notices. Recall Hannah Bullock who ran away from both Elizabeth Bullock and Eliza Johnson: in each case, her owners demanded she be taken to the workhouse in Charleston upon recapture.[52] Recall also Diana, who ran away with her two children: her owner, Anne Matthewes, also instructed that she was to be sent to the workhouse once caught.[53] By sending their recaptured slaves to the workhouse to be punished (whipped), women slaveowners, like their male counterparts who did likewise, avoided applying the whip to their slaves themselves. Delegating the punishment of their slaves to others – overseers, constables and the warden of the workhouse – may have been a preferable method of punishment to many slaveowners, and perhaps especially to women, not least because it reduced the threat of immediate physical retaliation. But it did not of course wash their hands clean of the violence that punishment by the workhouse warden or by overseers entailed. Rebecca Massey's notice for the recapture of her slave, Ruth, is a reminder that women slaveowners could be just as merciless as their male counterparts when it came to punishing their slaves: 'Whoever takes her up, gives her 50 *good* Lashes, and deliver her to me'[54] (my italics). Equally chilling was Mary Ellis's notice for the recapture of her slave, Catharina: 'dead or alive' – for which she offered a £10 reward.[55] Just as Pinckney's experience of slaveholding during the Revolution exposed the fault lines in her vision of maternalism, so the runaway notices placed by the likes of Massey and Ellis laid bare the limits of maternalism when slaves quit acting as slaves and challenged their owners' claim to their personhood and labour and in so doing 'robbed' them (Pinckney's word) of their livelihood.

In contrast to the majority of slaveowners who placed runaway notices in the colony's newspapers, a small handful explicitly resorted to the rhetoric of maternalism, not to recapture their slaves, but to persuade them to willingly return. In 1771, when Mary Simmons placed a notice in the newspaper to retrieve her runaway slave, she declared, '*If she returns of her own accord*, she shall be forgiven'[56] (my italics). In all, only twenty-one such notices offering runaway slaves forgiveness or the chance to avoid punishment appeared in the *South Carolina Gazette* between 1750 and 1775, although it is notable that no such offers of mercy appeared in runaway notices in the paper before that date.[57] Crucially, however, as Simmons' notice illustrates, clemency was not freely conferred; it came with strings attached and was contingent on the enslaved returning willingly and 'immediately', 'within 8 days', 'within the next ten days'. If not, woe betide them. John Forbes, for instance, was prepared to offer his slave Abram 'forgiveness if he will immediately come to Charles-Town', but 'if he does not speedily come in', Forbes wrote, 'he shall be when taken most rigorously punished'.[58] Maternalism/paternalism operated on a knife edge between forgiveness on the one hand and fear and threat of retribution on the other.

Maternalism was largely a myth that cloaked the harsh realities of slavery in colonial South Carolina. The maternalism to which Pinckney subscribed was not a reflection of her relationship with her slaves or of her attitude toward slavery. It was an ideology and rhetoric that by way of being rooted in and reinforced by Southern notions of gentility and a Christian ethos shored up her identity as a genteel slaveholder among the colony's planter elite. A dearth of testimony and detailed plantation records by the colony's women slaveowners makes it hard to say how much Pinckney's claim to maternalism was representative of other women slaveholders' approach to slaveownership and management in colonial South Carolina. However, there is no reason to suppose that the proportion of women slaveowners who began to embrace maternalism from the mid-eighteenth century significantly differed from the number of male slaveholders who in this same period similarly embraced paternalism. Philip Morgan has argued that paternalism ('enlightened patriarchalism') emerged in the Lowcountry and the Chesapeake 'in the second half of the eighteenth century'[59] – which dovetails with the examples cited here from mid-century onwards in the *South Carolina Gazette* of some slaveowners offering their slaves forgiveness if they voluntarily returned to them. Notably, Morgan, too, refrains from putting a figure on the numbers of slaveholders who began to adopt a paternalist approach to slave management in the colonial Lowcountry and Chesapeake.

Numbers aside, it is undeniable that there was a sea change in the attitude and approach toward slavery and slave management among a notable group of slaveholders in South Carolina from the mid-eighteenth century, and, as this chapter has argued, that this ideological shift was not exclusive to male slaveowners. Maternalism, like paternalism, underwrote the conceit of all slaveholders: that the terms of their relations with their slaves rested in their hands – to dispense food, clothes, healthcare, gifts, praise, instruction, favouritism, forgiveness, discipline, punishment and even freedom (notably, relatively few of the colony's women slaveowners manumitted their slaves).[60] But whereas paternalism rested on masculine notions of Southern honour and familial dependence and authority, maternalism paired itself with a vision of white Southern womanhood founded on female gentility, domesticity and the household, which in the nineteenth century found ultimate expression in idealized notions of the pedestalled Southern lady. This chapter has shown that it was frequently the enslaved themselves – Harry, Onia, Ralph and runaways like Diana, Lancaster and Hannah Bullock, as well as the many slaves who, as Pinckney noted, 'deserted' and 'robbed' their owners during the Revolution – who in countless ways exposed the myth of maternalism (and paternalism) by showing through their words and actions they could be 'quite their own masters'. Indeed, maternalism came apart at the seams when women slaveowners (like their male counterparts) came face to face with slaves who refused to act as slaves. The violent punishment customarily meted out to enslaved men and women by their owners – *50 good lashes* and *the workhouse* – along with other forms of cruelty, ill-treatment, general neglect and the sale and separation of slaves, betrayed the Janus-faced nature of maternalism, which the rhetoric of the 'good mistress' and offers of 'forgiveness' toward slaves who willingly returned to their owners (or else) wilfully masked. Ultimately, the real meaning of maternalism lay in an image of slaveholding that, by its very nature and creation, belied the reality of the conflict and cruelty that lay at the heart of slavery in colonial South Carolina.

Notes

1 Harriott Horry Ravenel, *Eliza Pinckney: Women of Colonial and Revolutionary Times* (New York: C. Scribner's Sons, 1896), 115–18.
2 William Henry Foster, *Gender, Mastery and Slavery: From European to Atlantic World Frontiers* (London: Palgrave Macmillan, 2010); William Henry Foster, 'Women Slave Owners Face their Historians: Versions of Maternalism in Atlantic World Slavery', *Patterns of Prejudice* 41, no. 3 (2007): 303–20; Kirsten Wood, *Masterful Women: Slaveholding Widows from the American Revolution through the Civil War* (Chapel Hill and London: University of North Carolina Press, 2004); Betty Wood, *Gender, Race, and Rank in a Revolutionary Age: The Georgia Lowcountry, 1750–1820* (Athens: University of Georgia Press, 2000).
3 For an extended discussion on the role of common law and equity on married women's property rights in South Carolina, see Marylynn Salmon, *Women and the Law of Property in Early America* (Chapel Hill: University of North Carolina Press,

1986); Marylynn Salmon, 'Women and Property in South Carolina: The Evidence from Marriage Settlements, 1730–1830', in Peter Charles Hoffer (ed.), *Colonial Women and Domesticity: Selected Articles on Gender in Early America* (New York and London: Garland Publishing, 1988), 238–68.
4   Edmund S. Morgan, *American Slavery, American Freedom: The Ordeal of Colonial Virginia* (New York: W.W. Norton & Company, 1975), 166–7. For a more recent discussion on widowarchy in Massachusetts, Maryland and South Carolina, see Vivian Bruce Conger, *The Widows Might: Widowhood and Gender in Early British America* (New York and London: New York University Press, 2009).
5   John E. Crowley, 'Family Relations and Inheritance in Early South Carolina', *Histoire Sociale – Social History* 17, no. 3 (1984): 40.
6   Crowley, 'Family Relations', 37; Thomas Cooper (ed.), *The Statutes at Large of South Carolina*, 5 vols (Columbia, SC: A. S. Johnston, 1837), vol. 2, 523–5.
7   Crowley, 'Family Relations', 38.
8   Crowley, 'Family Relations', 43.
9   John E. Crowley, 'The Importance of Kinship: Testamentary Evidence from South Carolina', *Journal of Interdisciplinary History* 16, no. 4 (1986): 567–8.
10 Charles Pinckney (1699–1758), Will, 13 February 1756, in *The Papers of Eliza Lucas Pinckney and Harriott Pinckney Horry Digital Edition*, ed. Constance Schulz (Charlottesville: University of Virginia Press, Rotunda, 2012) (Hereafter *Papers of Eliza Lucas Pinckney*), http://rotunda.upress.virginia.edu/PinckneyHorry/ELP0199.
11 Crowley, 'Family Relations', 45.
12 Crowley, 'Family Relations', 36.
13 Crowley, 'Family Relations', 57.
14 Eliza Lucas Pinckney to Mary Steer (Mrs Richard) Boddicott, 2 May [1740], in *Papers of Eliza Lucas Pinckney*, http://rotunda.upress.virginia.edu/PinckneyHorry/ELP0152.
15 Eliza Lucas Pinckney to George Lucas, 4 June 1741, in *Papers of Eliza Lucas Pinckney*, http://rotunda.upress.virginia.edu/PinckneyHorry/ELP0878.
16 Eliza Lucas Pinckney to George Lucas, 25 July [1740], in *Papers of Eliza Lucas Pinckney*, http://rotunda.upress.virginia.edu/PinckneyHorry/ELP0739.
17 Eliza Lucas Pinckney to Mary Bartlett, [1742], in *Papers of Eliza Lucas Pinckney*, http://rotunda.upress.virginia.edu/PinckneyHorry/ELP0118.
18 Cara Anzilotti, *In the Affairs of the World: Women, Patriarchy, and Power in Colonial South Carolina* (Westport, CT, and London: Greenwood Press, 2002).
19 Wood, *Masterful Women*, 84.
20 Eliza Lucas Pinckney to Mary Bartlett, [1742], in *Papers of Eliza Lucas Pinckney*, http://rotunda.upress.virginia.edu/PinckneyHorry/ELP0115.
21 Eliza Lucas Pinckney to Mary Bartlett, [1742], in *Papers of Eliza Lucas Pinckney*, http://rotunda.upress.virginia.edu/PinckneyHorry/ELP0115.
22 Eliza Lucas Pinckney to Mary Bartlett, [1742], in *Papers of Eliza Lucas Pinckney*, http://rotunda.upress.virginia.edu/PinckneyHorry/ELP0115.
23 Eliza Lucas Pinckney to Mary Bartlett, [1742], in *Papers of Eliza Lucas Pinckney*, http://rotunda.upress.virginia.edu/PinckneyHorry/ELP0115.
24 Eliza Lucas Pinckney to Harriott Pinckney Horry, n.d, in *Papers of Eliza Lucas Pinckney*, http://rotunda.upress.virginia.edu/PinckneyHorry/ELP0754.
25 Eliza Lucas Pinckney to Harriott Pinckney Horry, 1 March 1775, in *Papers of Eliza Lucas Pinckney*, http://rotunda.upress.virginia.edu/PinckneyHorry/ELP0442.
26 Eliza Lucas Pinckney to Harriott Pinckney Horry, 9 March 1775, in *Papers of Eliza Lucas Pinckney*, http://rotunda.upress.virginia.edu/PinckneyHorry/ELP0443.

27 Eliza Lucas Pinckney to Harriott Pinckney Horry, 28 May 1778, in *Papers of Eliza Lucas Pinckney*, http://rotunda.upress.virginia.edu/PinckneyHorry/ELP0446.
28 Eliza Lucas Pinckney to Harriott Pinckney Horry, 8 June 1778, in *Papers of Eliza Lucas Pinckney*, http://rotunda.upress.virginia.edu/PinckneyHorry/ELP0444.
29 Eliza Lucas Pinckney to Harriott Pinckney Horry, 12 May 1778, in *Papers of Eliza Lucas Pinckney*, http://rotunda.upress.virginia.edu/PinckneyHorry/ELP0445.
30 Eliza Lucas Pinckney to Harriott Pinckney Horry, 8 June 1778, in *Papers of Eliza Lucas Pinckney*, http://rotunda.upress.virginia.edu/PinckneyHorry/ELP0444.
31 Eliza Lucas Pinckney to Harriott Pinckney Horry, 8 June 1778, in *Papers of Eliza Lucas Pinckney*, http://rotunda.upress.virginia.edu/PinckneyHorry/ELP0444.
32 Eliza Lucas Pinckney to Harriott Pinckney Horry, [May 1774], in *Papers of Eliza Lucas Pinckney*, http://rotunda.upress.virginia.edu/PinckneyHorry/ELP0455.
33 Eliza Lucas Pinckney to Harriott Pinckney Horry, 8 June 1778, in *Papers of Eliza Lucas Pinckney*, http://rotunda.upress.virginia.edu/PinckneyHorry/ELP0444.
34 Eliza Lucas Pinckney to Rebecca Raven Evance (Mrs Branfill), 19 June 1760, in *Papers of Eliza Lucas Pinckney*, http://rotunda.upress.virginia.edu/PinckneyHorry/ELP0363.
35 Eliza Lucas Pinckney to Daniel Huger Horry, Jr, 9 March 1768, in *Papers of Eliza Lucas Pinckney*, http://rotunda.upress.virginia.edu/PinckneyHorry/ELP0401.
36 Eliza Lucas Pinckney to Harriott Pinckney Horry, [February 1775], in *Papers of Eliza Lucas Pinckney*, http://rotunda.upress.virginia.edu/PinckneyHorry/ELP0454.
37 Eliza Lucas Pinckney to Thomas Pinckney (1750–1828), 17 May 1779, in *Papers of Eliza Lucas Pinckney*, http://rotunda.upress.virginia.edu/PinckneyHorry/ELP0967.
38 Eliza Lucas Pinckney to Thomas Pinckney (1750–1828), 17 May 1779, in *Papers of Eliza Lucas Pinckney*, http://rotunda.upress.virginia.edu/PinckneyHorry/ELP0967.
39 Eliza Lucas Pinckney to Thomas Pinckney (1750–1828), 17 May 1779, in *Papers of Eliza Lucas Pinckney*, http://rotunda.upress.virginia.edu/PinckneyHorry/ELP0967.
40 Eliza Lucas Pinckney to Rebecca Raven Evance (Mrs Branfill), 25 September 1780, in *Papers of Eliza Lucas Pinckney*, http://rotunda.upress.virginia.edu/PinckneyHorry/ELP1013.
41 Eliza Lucas Pinckney to Rebecca Raven Evance (Mrs Branfill), 25 September 1780, in *Papers of Eliza Lucas Pinckney*, http://rotunda.upress.virginia.edu/PinckneyHorry/ELP1013.
42 *South Carolina Gazette*, 1–8 January 1741.
43 *South Carolina Gazette*, 10–17 October 1741.
44 *South Carolina Gazette*, 6 December 1751.
45 *South Carolina Gazette and Country Journal*, 30 September 1766.
46 *South Carolina Gazette*, 13 October 1757.
47 *South Carolina Gazette*, 29 May–5 June 1742.
48 *South Carolina Gazette*, 24 September 1772.
49 *South Carolina Gazette*, 12 February 1756.
50 *Georgia Gazette*, 20 December 1764.
51 See Wood, *Masterful Women*, 36–7, 48, 53.
52 *South Carolina Gazette*, 6 December 1751, and *South Carolina Gazette and Country Journal*, 30 September 1766.
53 *South Carolina Gazette*, 25 July–1 August 1761.
54 *South Carolina Gazette*, 1 February 1739.
55 *South Carolina Gazette*, 3 February 1757.
56 *South Carolina Gazette and Country Journal*, 17 December 1771.

57 This assessment is based on an analysis of runaway notices in the *South Carolina Gazette* in Lathan A. Windley, *Runaway Slave Advertisements – A Documentary History from the 1730s to 1790*, 4 vols (Westport, CT: Greenwood Press, 1983).
58 *South Carolina Gazette*, 25 September–2 October 1762.
59 Philip D. Morgan, *Slave Counterpoint: Black Culture in the Eighteenth-Century Chesapeake and Lowcountry* (Chapel Hill and London: University of North Carolina Press, 1998), 284.
60 Of all women who possessed slaves and recorded a will between 1750 and 1775, fifteen women (of 144) manumitted a slave(s). Four also gave their slaves money, three requested their slaves pay for their freedom, a further three fixed the age or period of time of their slave's freedom, and five attached no conditions at all but also offered no financial or material support to their manumitted slave(s). These figures derive from an analysis of all wills recorded by women slaveowners between 1750 and 1775 in *Records of the Secretary of State, Recorded Instruments, South Carolina Wills*, vol. NN, col. TT, vol. SS, vol. QQ, vol. PP, vol. RR, South Carolina Department of Archives and History, Columbia, South Carolina.

5

Resident Female Slaveholders in Jamaica at the End of Emancipation: Evidence from the Compensation Claims

Ahmed Reid*

The publication of Nicholas Draper's path-breaking study, *The Price of Emancipation*, and the research undertaken by the Legacies of British Slave-Ownership Project (hereafter LBS) are timely studies that have broadened our understanding of slaveholding at the crucial phase between slavery and freedom.[1] Based on a systematic analysis of the claims for compensation that were filed by slaveowners when slavery was abolished in 1834, they have shown that the ownership of enslaved people by British citizens was far more widespread than many believed and that a substantial amount of the compensation payments, over £10 million sterling, were paid to slaveowners living in Britain. Such legacies, they argue, are traceable to families and institutions in Britain today.[2]

A close reading of Draper's work and the LBS raises some important historiographical concerns that this chapter will address. One such concern is the continued historiographical focus on slaveholders living in Britain. As Draper admitted, his study sought to 'map more systematically the recipients of this compensation money in metropolitan Britain by geography, class and gender, and to explore their identities and places in British society'.[3] This historiographical tilt towards British slaveholders is evident in the structure of the LBS. The LBS has developed copious and sometimes detailed biographical notes on British absentee owners, but such level of detail is unavailable for enslavers living in the colonies. Though path-breaking in the use and manipulation of the compensation claims, the analysis of absentee owners by Draper and the LBS is part of a well-trodden historiographical focus. It is also an oversimplification of the true nature and patterns of slaveholding. Historians have been debating absentee contributions to the development of the plantation system. One school, spearheaded by Lowell Ragatz, is that absentee ownership was a drag on the development of the sugar plantation system. Absentee owners were accused of failing to institute new technology, or changes that were needed to improve the cultivation and manufacture of agricultural produce. According to Ragatz, such owners had 'an ingrained hostility to innovation, [and their] antiquated methods of production were stubbornly clung to'.[4] Douglas Hall rejected this stereotype and suggested instead that historians employ a more nuanced interpretation that considers the roles of absentees at various phases of Caribbean development. Recent work by Trevor Burnard and others have sought to diversify the experiences of absenteeism and have shown how they contributed to the spatial expansion of the plantation economy during the late eighteenth and early nineteenth century.

Slaveholding, however, was a far more complex and dynamic process that involved men and women crisscrossing the British Atlantic world in search of a fortune. It was a fluid concept that at any given time, an absentee owner (living in Britain) could become a resident owner (living in the colonies) and vice versa.[5]

Of the 16,114 claims that were filed for 568,047 enslaved people in Jamaica (Table 5.1), roughly 2,973, or 18.58 per cent, were filed by British absentee owners. The majority, 13,171, or 80.96 per cent, of claims were filed by resident slaveowners. In total, resident slaveowners filed claims for 209,471 enslaved people, or 37 per cent of the total. So even though absentee slaveholders owned larger productive units and by extension owned large numbers of enslaved people, the majority of slaveowners resided in the colonies.[6] Jamaica had a sizable white resident population comprised of those who, like their counterparts in Britain, filed claims and received substantial compensation. Therefore, to give prominence or pride of place to absentee owners, albeit the wealthiest and more influential, is to ignore patterns of slaveholding in the

Table 5.1 Parish distribution of compensation claims for Jamaica

Parish	No. of Claims	Total Enslaved Claimed	Compensation (£)
Clarendon	641	35,616	680,348
Hanover	748	35,271	671,076
Kingston	2,960	15,063	294,017
Manchester	668	32,079	625,039
Port Royal	275	9,959	199,706
Portland	362	12,529	224,064
St Andrew	710	22,356	459,557
St Ann	1,186	43,351	878,163
St Catherine	852	13,296	246,539
St David	203	13,900	275,345
St Dorothy	172	8,158	165,431
St Elizabeth	1,282	36,322	715,546
St George	520	18,949	348,848
St James	1,043	42,772	837,688
St John	360	9,787	181,134
St Mary	745	51,247	939,845
St Thomas-in-the-East	786	48,993	943,755
St Thomas-in-the-Vale	429	19,181	364,056
Trelawny	936	44,805	910,171
Vere	212	15,285	314,688
Westmoreland	1,024	39,128	723,495
Total	16,114	568,047	10,998,511

Sources: Legacies of British Slave-Ownership Project, University College London, www.ucl.ac.uk/lbs; National Archives, Kew, London, Claims for Compensation filed with the Assistant Commissioners for Jamaica T/71 92.

Table 5.2 Descriptive statistics of resident slaveholders in Jamaica

Parish	No. of Claims (M)	No. of Claims (F)	Enslaved Claimed (M)	Enslaved Claimed (F)	Total Compn (£) (M)	Total Compn (£) (F)	Avg. Enslaved Claims (M)	Avg Enslaved Claimed (F)	% Claims (M)	% Claims (F)
Clarendon	289	166	8,992	2,993	176,387	58,425	31	18	4	3
Hanover	322	265	6,988	1,903	139,084	41,167	22	7	4	5
Kingston	1,309	1,450	7,327	6,402	145,724	120,817	6	4	18	25
Manchester	303	178	13,218	3,087	251,110	61,892	44	17	4	3
Port Royal	111	78	2,590	446	54,176	9,826	23	6	2	1
Portland	181	113	3,955	1,017	73,770	19,069	22	9	2	2
St Andrew	358	241	9,449	3,366	200,102	73,281	26	14	5	4
St Ann	623	362	16,681	5,500	345,538	115,939	27	15	8	6
St Catherine	396	340	6,309	1,993	118,532	35,789	16	6	5	6
St David	95	53	4,882	415	97,376	8,512	51	8	1	1
St Dorothy	71	72	2,428	620	49,805	12,463	34	9	1	1
St Elizabeth	669	456	12,591	3,569	255,274	74,110	19	8	9	8
St George	288	146	7,161	1,362	133,967	25,912	25	9	4	3
St James	396	379	7,335	2,881	153,583	62,207	19	8	5	7
St John	213	110	4,544	900	95,781	19,124	21	8	3	2
St Mary	309	197	11,243	2,144	210,290	42,317	36	11	4	3
St Thomas-in-the-East	338	234	10,589	2,285	210,728	47,541	31	10	5	4
St Thomas-in-the-Vale	206	123	5,243	1,539	99,709	30,424	25	13	3	2
Trelawny	343	347	8,121	2,655	169,637	57,684	24	8	5	6
Vere	82	70	3,100	429	64,531	9,215	38	6	1	1
Westmoreland	437	327	8,887	2,332	173,191	45,614	20	7	6	6
Total	7,339	5,707	161,633	47,838	3,218,295	971,328	22	8	100	100

Sources: Legacies of British Slave-Ownership Project, University College London, www.ucl.ac.uk/lbs; National Archives, Kew, London, Claims for Compensation filed with the Assistant Commissioners for Jamaica T/71 92.

colonies. To put it bluntly, *The Price of Emancipation* and the LBS reinforces the historiographical bias towards absentee slaveowners living in Britain.[7]

In its focus on the gender, class and spatial distribution of British slaveowners, *The Price of Emancipation* fits within the emerging historiographical trend of studies that have sought to identify the extent to which the imperial metropole was formed and impacted by the experiences of the colonies.[8] The weakness of this 'new imperial' interpretation is that it is a retelling of British history. It is an approach that delimits an analysis of other actors in the British West Indian plantation system. It excludes, for example, the thousands of enslaved men, women and children who were oppressed, brutalized and exploited to provide the economic foundation on which modern British society was built. And while it is true that enslaved people were excluded from the compensation records, such exclusion should not prohibit an analysis of this important group. It excludes also an analysis of the pattern of slaveholding among the thousands of residents living in the colonies.

This chapter addresses this shortcoming. Very little is known of the claims filed and compensation received by resident Jamaican slaveowners. This chapter breaks new ground as it is the first quantitative analysis undertaken of slaveholding outside the metropole. Important works by Verene Shepherd, Christer Petley and Barry Higman have addressed some aspects of resident slaveowning in Jamaica. In her work on livestock farming, Shepherd examined the demographic composition and economic status of livestock farmers and showed how they navigated eighteenth-century plantation Jamaica. However, livestock farmers were not the major slaveholders in Jamaica. Jamaica's diversified economy included coffee planters and shopkeepers, for example, who are not accounted for in Shepherd's work. Petley's investigation of slaveholders in Jamaica focused more on the challenges and strategies employed by slaveholders to defend the institution of slavery during the 'turbulent' period of British abolitionism and enslaved resistance, while Higman examined the role of two attorneys during the growth of Jamaica's plantation economy. It is worth highlighting at this stage that Shepherd, Petley and Higman's analyses do not provide a complete account of the class, gender, economic and spatial distribution of resident slaveholders.[9] This chapter will also show that the majority of those who owned enslaved people lived in the colonies and that an analysis of the patterns of slaveholding by such a group is fundamental to our understanding of plantation slavery at this crucial period of transition from slavery to freedom. It will provide important answers on the gender and spatial distribution of slaveholding among resident slaveowners living in Jamaica.

Jamaica's plantation economy

Jamaica, Britain's largest and most productive plantation economy, was an important cog in Britain's burgeoning Atlantic trading system. The island's ability to outproduce its neighbours generated considerable wealth for slaveholders (see Table 5.3). Such was Jamaica's productive capacity that Richard Sheridan estimated its total wealth in 1775 at £18 million sterling.[10] Sheridan's estimates have since been revised by Trevor Burnard

Table 5.3 Sugar produced in Jamaica relative to other British West Indian Islands

Year	Jamaica	Other BWI Islands	% Jamaica
1793	80,300	163,500	49
1794	89,800	163,300	55
1795	83,200	128,300	65
1796	83,400	131,200	64
1797	80,030	121,074	66
1798	83,350	150,700	55
1799	95,000	193,000	49
1800	110,300	177,830	62
1801	143,200	228,150	63
1802	144,100	261,450	55
1803	125,000	212,300	59
1804	120,000	239,000	50
1805	132,000	224,700	59

Note: Return to the House of Commons, 6 May 1806, reproduced in Sir William Young, *West India Commonplace Book* (1807), p. 16 HHDs, where 1 HHD = 13 Long CWT.

who argues that the island's wealth was, at £25 million sterling, some £7 million (or 39 per cent) higher.[11] Such wealth was a testimonial to the island's productive capacity and, more importantly, its economic viability during the eighteenth century. When compared to mainland North America, Caribbean planters' per capita earnings were significantly greater than their mainland counterparts. Burnard argues that the aggregate wealth per White for the British West Indies was much higher than previous estimates. He suggested that per capita wealth among Whites in the Caribbean was £1,042.5 compared to only £60.2 per White in Britain's mainland territories.[12] The island's plantation economy was so strong by the early nineteenth century that Barry Higman suggested that its productive capacity could be compared to emerging industrial economies at the time.[13]

The benefits of this system of trade and exploitation to wider British society were significant: a vast amount of wealth generated from slavery was invested and reinvested in railroads, shipbuilding, insurance, the financial sector, arts, shopkeeping, building palatial country houses and just about every facet of British life. This level of wealth, and the way it pervaded British society, was the scaffold on which Britain achieved a second and more lasting Industrial Revolution.[14] The decision to abolish slavery in 1833 came as a huge financial blow to those who invested vast amounts of capital in slavery and the plantation system. Emancipation had far-reaching financial implications for the powerfully connected slaveowners. Many feared that they were about to lose their investments in the colonies. The passage of the Slavery Abolition Act mitigated this and awarded slaveholders (over 100 of whom were members of the House of Commons) £20 million plus interest from 1 August 1834. This bailout to enslavers represented a staggering 40 per cent of British public expenditure. A further stipulation of the act was the granting of apprenticeship, where the period of enforced labour was extended for a fixed term of six years.

Compensation claims

To facilitate these payments, the Slavery Abolition Act established the Commissioners of Arbitration or Compensation Commission. The commission consisted of five members (three of whom were salaried) and its main office was located at 25 Great George Street, London. The commission held its first meeting in October 1833 with representatives of the Colonial Office Slave Registration Office. Slaveholders were required to submit individual claims to the commission before any monies could be disbursed. These claims were then investigated to ascertain their veracity. To authenticate these claims, the commissioners relied heavily on data collected by assistant colonial boards of compensation located in the various colonies. Once all due diligence was done and the commissioners were satisfied that the claims submitted for enslaved people corresponded with the slave registry on July 1, 1835, the monies were then disbursed by the National Debt Office.[15]

Not every claim submitted to the commission was submitted by a slaveowner and this distinction must be highlighted. The types of claimants who were residents in Jamaica (see Table 5.4) is an indication of the varied nature of the claims that were submitted to the commissioners. Enslaved people were owned through direct purchases, mortgages, annuities, or as legatees, just to name a few examples. For the purposes of this chapter, two broad classifications of claimants are used: owners and agents.[16] So, for example, Eliza Rose Bucknor submitted a claim as owner-in-fee for thirty-four enslaved people on Friendship Grove Pen in the parish of Hanover, and received a compensation payment of £772.[17] The circumstances surrounding Isabella

Table 5.4 Breakdown of claims submitted by resident slaveholders in Jamaica

Types of Claimants	No of Claims	Male Claimants	Female Claimants	Enslaved Claim (Male)	Enslaved Claim (Female)
Administrator	6	6		330	
Annuitant	3	3		540	
Assignee	6	6		169	
Executor/Executrix	73	71	2	6,569	95
Guardian	3	3		111	
Judgement creditor	17	16	1	853	69
Legatee	1	1		320	
Mortgagee	4	4		452	
Owner-in-fee	423	324	99	25,363	4,079
Receiver	8	8		1,317	
Residuary Legatee	1	1		172	
Tenant-for-life	4		4	142	
Tenant-in-tail	1	1		31	
Trustee	26	26		2,909	
Type of Claimant not identified	12,471	6,869	5,602	122,355	43,590
Blank	124	51	73		
Total	13,171	7,390	5,781	161,633	47,833

Sources: Legacies of British Slave-Ownership Project, University College London, www.ucl.ac.uk/lbs; National Archives, Kew, London, Claims for Compensation filed with the Assistant Commissioners for Jamaica T/71 92.

Cockburn brings into sharp focus the importance of this classification. Cockburn's husband, Charles Seymour Cockburn, submitted a claim as owner-in-fee for thirty-nine enslaved people on Charlemount Pen, a mid-size livestock pen with forty-five livestock in St Andrew. Charlemount's economic function and importance to Jamaica's plantation economy was that it provided meat, manure and draught animals to neighbouring sugar plantations. Charles Cockburn died soon after the claim was submitted, leaving his wife, Isabella, as the executor of his will. Therefore, it was Isabella, as executor (and agent), who received the compensation payment of £906.[18] So, while Isabella Cockburn received compensation for thirty-nine enslaved people, she was not a resident female slaveowner.

A total of 46,000 claims were submitted for 850,000 enslaved people in twenty-one colonies, stretching from the Caribbean to Mauritius and the Cape Colony (part of modern-day South Africa). The compensation claims are a rich source of data and it is therefore surprising that so few studies have been undertaken of this consolidated source.[19] The claims were organized by name, from which the gender of the claimant can be inferred, the title of the claimant and the classification of the claimants (see Table 5.4). Next, is the colony for which each claim was made. The claims for Jamaica were unique in that it was the only colony which had the sub-category of parish (see Table 5.1). Data is also available on the type of property specific to each claim (livestock pens, coffee or sugar plantations, etc.), the number of enslaved people attached to each claim and, most importantly, the value or compensation that is awarded to each claim.

Resident female slaveholders in Jamaica's plantation economy

Contemporary writings on the British West Indies suggest that slavery was decidedly 'a male enterprise'.[20] British West Indian historiography, according to Hilary Beckles, 'focuses primarily on the entrepreneurship and politics of ruling class white males who are represented as having succeeded in fashioning with slave systems, a modern economic order'.[21] As such, women are usually represented in a supportive role. Such representation is evident in planter-historian Edward Long's *History of Jamaica*. In his assessment of the role of white females in Jamaica, he describes women as repeat brides, who benefited from the 'intemperance' of their husbands who typically met 'an untimely grave' due to their excesses.[22] Long highlighted the ease and frequency with which women accumulated wealth through matrimony. Sir Nicholas Lawes, a contemporary of Long, suggested 'that the female art of growing rich in a short time was comprised in two significant words, "*marry* and *bury*"'.[23] Such conceptual boundaries persist in the representation of women as dependent spinsters. The ensuing narrative of women being disconnected from the rigours of plantation production, and that their only connection with the plantation complex was as beneficiaries, is evident in Lucille Mair's *A Historical Study of Women in Jamaica*. In a chapter entitled 'The White Women in Jamaican Slave Society', Mair stated that 'women [were] carefully sheltered from the life of industry and commerce, [and were] recipients merely of the plantation proceeds'.[24] Mair's classification of white women fits with the oft-cited typology that in Caribbean plantation societies 'the black woman produced, the brown woman served, and the white woman consumed'.[25] The white woman as slaveowner or plantation owner is missing from James Walvin's *The Trade, The Owner, The Slave*. As such, some historians continue to treat women as marginal figures, despite evidence to the contrary. The emergence of 'women's history' coupled with the emergence of demographic and social historians focusing on women in Caribbean history have broadened our understanding of women, particularly women slaveowners.[26]

Slaveholding was widespread among women living in Jamaica, and resident female slaveholders were active participants in the island's robust plantation economy. Roughly 45 per cent of the 16,114 claims that were filed for enslaved people in Jamaica were filed by women. Approximately 2,973 of the total claims for Jamaica were submitted by absentees, of which 484, or 16 per cent, were claims filed by female slaveholders living in Britain. Clearly, women were less likely to be absentee slaveholders and the proportion of women filing claims as absentees was much lower than the proportion filing claims generally for Jamaica. Resident female slaveholders filed 5,707, or 35 per cent, of the total claims submitted by slaveowners (both absentees and residents), and 45 per cent of the total claims filed by residents. Overall, women owned and operated roughly 5 per cent of Jamaican sugar estates during the eighteenth century.[27] Many more were involved in the local market economy, such as livestock farming, lodging, huckstering, market-selling and shopkeeping. As such, their slaveholding was far more diverse.

Jamaica's heterogenous topography (mountainous in areas, savannah-like in others, and flat in some parts) facilitated specialized zonal distribution of crops. This also accounts for the diversified slaveholding pattern evident during the plantation period. The issue of crop and product diversification has been the focus of attention of revisionist historians.[28] The works of these revisionists are a counter-discourse to the early writings of Richard Sheridan, Richard Dunn and members of the 'plantation economy' school who have championed the concept of sugar monoculture.[29] The 'plantation economy' school has gone a long way to legitimize the concept of sugar monoculture on Caribbean plantations, an interpretation which gained momentum in the 1960s when development-economists in the Caribbean argued that contemporary Caribbean economies were monoculture export-oriented economies dominated by sugar. In their view, the structural dependence of these economies on the export of sugar was a profound legacy of colonization. The over-reliance on sugar exports and the continued dependence on the British market when colonization ended meant that alternatives to sugar were never sought. This, in their estimation, was the main cause of underdevelopment in the Caribbean.[30]

Revisionist scholars like Verene Shepherd have shown that diversification pre-dated the development of the plantation system in Jamaica and was a common feature of Jamaica's eighteenth-century economy. Sugar production never monopolized the spatial location within the island.[31] Coffee, livestock farming and the production of other minor staples like pimento, ginger, coca and trading and market-selling were important to Jamaica's economic development.[32] Diversification between sugar and non-sugar sectors provided an important entry point for many resident female slaveholders into Jamaica's economy. Livestock farming, for example, performed an important function in providing meat, draught animals and manure to the sugar estates. In this respect, the contribution of livestock farming to the development of Jamaica's plantation economy was invaluable.

The eighteenth-century practice of listing men by occupation and women by marital status poses some fundamental challenges when trying to reconstruct the contribution of women to Jamaica's plantation system. Difficult though this task might be, the compensation claims give us a window through which we can analyse the participation of resident female slaveowners in Jamaica's plantation economy, and one that deviates from the stereotype of the dependent spinster. As seen in Table 5.2, resident female slaveholders filed 5,707 claims for 161,633 enslaved Africans, which amounted to 35 per cent of the total claims filed for Jamaica and 45 per cent of the total claims filed by residents. Resident female slaveholders owned, on average, eight enslaved people compared to twenty-two per resident male, at a rate of 2.75 more than females. Relative to the other parishes, 25 per cent of claims filed by resident females were for enslaved people in Kingston.

By the mid-eighteenth century, Kingston was the most densely populated parish in Jamaica and, unlike most parishes, it had no rural area. The parish's rapid urban development was due in part to its unrivalled dominance as the leading port in the British West Indies and the eighteenth-century Atlantic economy. Colonial trade statistics show that it was the leading port in the frequency and tonnage of goods imported and exported from the British West Indies. It is estimated that over 80 per cent of sugar exports and 75 per cent of enslaved arrivals to Jamaica was through the port of Kingston. This level of trading activity accounted for Kingston's rapid rise during the eighteenth century. Between 1730 and 1788, the percentage of Whites living in Kingston rose from 16 to 36.[33]

Kingston's trading vibrancy and urban appeal was attractive to many women. The parish had the highest concentration of women in Jamaica, and Table 5.2 confirms this as 25 per cent of the claims filed by women were for Kingston.[34] Resident slaveowners like Charlotte Phillips Wynter submitted two claims for eleven enslaved people and received £214 in compensation. There were other women like Ann Moxham and Catherine Claypoole who respectively owned three and two enslaved each who actively

Table 5.5 Females buying real estate in Kingston by select year

Year	Number	% of Female Buyers
1750	96	6.25
1760	15	0
1770	30	6.67
1780	54	9.26
1790	90	13.33
1795	65	16.92
1800	219	18.72
1805	84	27.47
1810	91	15.48
All Years	774	15.46

Source: Land Deed, Island Record Office, Twickenham Park, Jamaica, Old Series Liber, Volumes 138–559.

participated in the commercial life of the parish as shopkeepers and lodgers.[35] This entrepreneurial spirit was evident in the fact that enslaved people were used as tradesmen and domestics in supporting female-headed business. Women contributed to the dynamism of Jamaica's non-plantation sector.

Recent work by David Ryden and myself on Jamaica's land market have shown that 7.7 per cent of Jamaica's property sales were made by women and 4.4 per cent of purchasers were women. Some 18 per cent of Kingston sellers and 15.5 per cent of Kingston buyers were female. Many resident female slaveowners were acquiring land to expand existing holding. This proves that women's involvement in Jamaica's land market is indicative of their economic independence in Kingston relative to the rest of the island. An analysis of the time-series distribution confirms this (see Table 5.5). Once we analyse the time-series distribution of women's active involvement in Jamaica's land market, we see a robust expansion of female buyers across the eighteenth century.[36]

Resident female slaveholders' involvement in Jamaica's plantation economy extended beyond Kingston's non-plantation sector. Some were involved in the daily rigours and uncertainties that accompanies the sugar plantation system. Table 5.6 provides a breakdown of resident females who owned and operated livestock pens. Overall, twenty-one women submitted claims for 1,057 enslaved people and received compensation of £21,663. As already noted, livestock farming performed an important function in providing meat, draught animals and manure to the sugar estates. The use of livestock farms as an adjunct to sugar estates is also evidence of diversification and cost-cutting strategies employed by planters.[37]

Many of these livestock pens were relegated to the agricultural fringes in preference for the larger and more capital-intensive sugar estates. The more fertile and cultivable land in Jamaica was given over to the production of sugar and its by-products. The common practice among planters was to purchase land to be used as adjuncts. In most cases, these lands were small acreages that were used as livestock pens. Here, the estate raised livestock to offset operating cost by providing meat to feed the enslaved population or manure to be used in the planting of sugar cane. This trend is confirmed by other evidence. In 1832, Andrew Colville, a London merchant, told a Parliamentary Select Committee investigating the state of trade and commerce in the British West Indies that it was customary for smaller holdings to fetch a higher price than larger holdings throughout the island. When questioned as to the price offered for small holdings, Colville cited an example where one acre of land was sold for £100, and it was sold to a planter who wanted the land for pasturage, or as an adjunct. In Colville's estimation, the price was justified since the land facilitated the expansion of the planter's estate, and that the benefits to be accrued from its use were significant.[38] The higher yield per acre of land gained by sugar estates meant that land devoted to cane cultivation offered a high economic return and was a more attractive alternative to other forms of agricultural activity. The economic rent that sugar cultivation enjoyed led to the exclusion of livestock pens and other crop types from the fertile plains of Jamaica. Because of this, a high percentage of pens were located along the savannah-like regions in St Elizabeth, or at elevations above 2,000 feet, and specialized livestock zones emerged in the parishes of St Ann and St Elizabeth, with high concentrations in Hanover, Vere and St Catherine.[39]

Table 5.6 Parish distribution of resident female pen-keepers

Parish	Name of Claimant	Name of Property	Number of Enslaved	Compensation (£)
Clarendon	Sarah Chevan	Bushy Park Pen	25	521
Hanover	Eliza Roe Bucknor	Friendship Grove Pen	34	772
Manchester	Sophia Scarlett Ashman	Pen's Lodge	44	916
Portland	Sarah Ross Hinchelwood	Providence Pen	28	736
St Andrew	Emily Ann Graham /Jane Green	Hermitage Pen	8	191
	Elizabeth Turner	White Hall Pen	28	675
	Caroline Hawker	Liberty Hall Pen	26	699
	Jane Campbell	Villa Pen	5	145
St Ann	Sarah Jane Keith Senior	Penshurst	53	1,073
	Barbara Hewson	Retreat Pen	250	4,718
St Catherine	Eleanor Dawson	Cottage Pen	28	514
	Elizabeth Williams Hanson	Hanson's Pen	98	1,704
	Marie Louise Darling	Turnsbull Pen	36	638
St Dorothy	Julia Ann Skelton	Folly Pen	43	996
St Elizabeth	Anna Williams	Luana Pen	38	856
	Jane Foster Greaves	Islington Pen	43	843
St George	Elizabeth Matthews	Redington Pen	34	533
St James	Barbara Hewan	Belmont Pen	64	1,437
St Thomas-in-the-East	Janes Noyes	Hopewell Pen	43	993
Vere	Hannah Tabbernorr	Mike Pen	21	518
Grand Total			949	19,478

Sources: Legacies of British Slave-Ownership Project, University College London, www.ucl.ac.uk/lbs; National Archives, Kew, London, Claims for Compensation filed with the Assistant Commissioners for Jamaica T/71 92.

When compared to male slaveholders, the percentage of female slaveholders who owned livestock farms was small. Resident males owned 145 of the 168, or 86 per cent of the livestock farms owned by residents. The same was true for resident plantation owners. Of the 82 sugar estates that were owned by resident slaveowners, only 5 or 6 per cent were owned by female slaveholders. In the competitive and risky world of the plantation system, female-headed livestock farms operated simultaneously, and competed with those owned by men. They jostled to supply large sugar estates with meat, manure and draught animals. Unlike livestock farms owned by absentees and operated and managed by a local agent, resident females owned, operated and managed their livestock farms. Many were small livestock farms with an average of fifty enslaved people. The outlier in Table 5.6, Retreat Pen, was not the typical livestock farm owned and operated by resident female slaveholders. Retreat Pen, which was owned by Barbara Hewson, was twice the size of livestock pens owned by resident female slaveholders.

As owner-in-fee, Oswan claimed compensation for 537 enslaved people and received payments totalling £10,006. Oswan clearly does not fit the stereotype of the dependent spinster and neither do the women in Tables 5.6 and 5.7. At various stages,

Table 5.7 Parish distribution of resident female estate owners

Parish	Name of Claimant	Name of Estate	Claim	Compensation (£)	Enslaved Claim
Hanover	Mary Capon	Saxham Estate	1	461	22
St Ann	Frances Cox	Carlton Estate	1	104	461
St Mary	Ann Horlock	Russell Hall Estate	1	4,246	215
Vere	Rebecca Ross	Pusey Hall Estate	1	618	32
Total			4	5,429	730

Sources: Legacies of British Slave-Ownership Project, University College London, www.ucl.ac.uk/lbs; National Archives, Kew, London, Claims for Compensation filed with the Assistant Commissioners for Jamaica T/71 92.

the number of livestock on Mammee Gully fluctuated between 350 and 450. When the claim was filed in 1836, the total livestock was 399. Oswan, like Andrew Colville testifying before the Parliamentary Select Committee earlier, used Mammee Gully Pen to offset operations costs by supplying the meat needed to feed the 429 enslaved people on Killets and the manure to facilitate a higher sugar yield.

Conclusion

The compensation records provide a clear portrait of the pattern of slaveholding in Britain's largest and most productive colony, Jamaica. What this highlights is the fact that the majority of slaveowners lived in the colony, yet they owned relatively fewer enslaved people. By contrast, a minority of slaveowners, or absentees living in Britain, owned most enslaved people. The records show that 25 per cent of Jamaican slaveholders were women living in Kingston's non-plantation sector. Resident female slaveowners, through their ownership of livestock pens and sugar plantations, were active participants in the island's economy. Though they did not hold superordinate positions in Jamaica's plantation economy, they constituted the majority of slaveholders. How their 'resident status' impacted their economic and social functions is critical to understanding the machinations of Jamaica's burgeoning plantation system. In focusing on resident slaveholders, one can now begin to investigate their contribution to Jamaica's plantation economy, the many internal linkages they created, their economic interests and whether they were ideologically different from sugar planters. The ongoing historiographical focus on absentees continues to marginalize this relatively important category of slaveholders.

Notes

* I would like to thank Scott McClelland, Nicholas Draper and Verene Shepherd for data on Jamaica. I wish to thank my colleague Prithi Kanakamadela for taking the time to read and comment on an earlier draft of this chapter.

1   Nicholas Draper, *The Price of Emancipation: Slave-Ownership, Compensation and British Society at the End of Slavery* (Cambridge: Cambridge University Press, 2010). See also, 'Legacies of British Slave-Ownership Project,' University College London. www.ucl.ac.uk/lbs.
2   Slaveowners argued that the freeing of enslaved people by the Slavery Abolition Act (1833) was a violation of their property rights and demanded compensation for the loss of their 'property'.
3   Draper, *The Price of Emancipation*, 2.
4   Lowell J. Ragatz, *The Fall of the Planter Class in the British Caribbean, 1763-1833: A Study in Social and Economic History* (New York: Octagon Books, 1963), 12.
5   For the purposes of this chapter, a resident slaveowner is a claimant living in the colonies at the time they submitted their compensation claim.
6   According to Barry W. Higman, the average size of a sugar plantation in the eighteenth century was 900 acres, with an average of 250 enslaved Africans. See B. W. Higman, *Jamaica Surveyed: Plantation Maps and Plans of the Eighteenth and Nineteenth Centuries* (Kingston: Institute of Jamaica Publications, 1988).
7   Lowell J. Ragatz, 'Absentee Landlordism in the British Caribbean, 1750-1833', *Agricultural History* 5, no. 1 (1931): 7-24; Ragatz, *The Fall of the Planter Class*; Douglass G. Hall, 'Absentee-Proprietorship in the British West Indies, to about 1850', *Jamaica Historical Review* 4 (1964): 15-35; Andrew Jackson O'Shaughnessy, *An Empire Divided: The American Revolution and the British Caribbean* (Philadelphia: University of Pennsylvania Press, 2000); Trevor Burnard, 'Passengers Only: The Extent and Significance of Absenteeism in Eighteenth Century Jamaica', *Atlantic Studies* 1, no. 2 (2004): 178-95; B. W. Higman, *Plantation Jamaica, 1750-1850: Capital and Control in a Colonial Economy* (Kingston: University of the West Indies Press, 2005); Christer Petley (ed.), 'Rethinking the Fall of the Planter Class', special issue, *Atlantic Studies* 9, no. 1 (2012); Keith Mason, 'The Absentee Planter and the Key Slave: Privilege, Patriarchalism, and Exploitation in the Early Eighteenth-Century Caribbean', *William and Mary Quarterly* 70, no.1 (2013): 79-102.
8   See, for example, Catherine Hall, *Civilising Subjects: Metropole and Colony in the English Imagination, 1830-1867* (Chicago: University of Chicago Press, 2002); Susan Dwyer Amussen, *Caribbean Exchanges: Slavery and the Transformation of English Society* (Chapel Hill: University of North Carolina Press, 2007); Simon Smith, *Slavery, Family and Gentry Capitalism in the British Atlantic: The World of the Lascelles, 1648-1834* (Cambridge: Cambridge University Press, 2010). For an overview of the Caribbean's impact on American society, see Edward Rugemer, *The Problem of Emancipation: The Caribbean Roots of the American Civil War* (Baton Rouge: Louisiana State University Press, 2009).
9   Verene Shepherd, *Livestock, Sugar and Slavery: Contested Terrain in Colonial Jamaica* (Kingston: Ian Randle Publishers, 2009); Christer Petley, *Slaveholders in Jamaica: Colonial Society and Culture During the Era of Abolition* (London: Pickering and Chatto, 2009); Higman, *Plantation Jamaica*.
10 Richard Sheridan, 'The Wealth of Jamaica in the Eighteenth Century', *Economic History Review*, 2nd Ser., 18, no. 2 (1965): 161-86, and 'The Wealth of Jamaica in the Eighteenth Century: A Rejoinder', *Economic History Review*, 2nd Ser., 21, no. 1 (1968): 292-311.
11 Trevor Burnard, '"Prodigious Riches": The Wealth of Jamaica before the American Revolution', *Economic History Review* 54, no. 3 (2001): 506-24.

12. Burnard, 'Prodigious Riches'. See also Barbara Solow, 'Caribbean Slavery and British Growth: The Eric Williams Hypothesis', *Journal of Developmental Economics* 17, nos. 1–2 (1985): 99–115, and Peter Coclanis, 'The Wealth of British America on the Eve of Revolution', *Journal of Interdisciplinary History* 21, no. 2 (1990): 245–60.
13. Higman, *Plantation Jamaica*, 1–6.
14. Eric Williams, *Capitalism and Slavery* (Chapel Hill: University of North Carolina Press, 1944). See also Joseph Inikori, *Africans and the Industrial Revolution in England: A Study in International Trade and Economic Development* (Cambridge: Cambridge University Press, 2002).
15. National Archives, Kew, London T/71 series, Office of Registry of Colonial Slaves and Compensation Commission.
16. The categories for claimants can be divided into two broad areas. The first category, owner, typically refers to the unqualified beneficial owners of enslaved people – in this case an owner-in-fee, tenant for life and a tenant-in-tail. The second category, agents, are claims that were filed by an executor/executrix, administrators/trustees, or guardians or receivers.
17. T71/915, p. 10. Claim submitted by Eliza Rose Bucknor.
18. T71/865, claim submitted by Charles Seymour Cockburn. See also Parliamentary Papers, p. 297.
19. R. E. P. Wastell, 'The History of Slave Compensation 1833 to 1845', MA thesis, London University, 1933; Williams, *Capitalism and Slavery*; Kathleen Mary Butler, *The Economics of Emancipation: Jamaica and Barbados, 1823–1843* (Chapel Hill: University of North Carolina Press, 1995).
20. Kamau Braithwaite, 'Caribbean Women During the Period of Slavery', Elsa Goveia Memorial Lecture, Cave Hill Campus, Barbados, 1984.
21. Hilary Beckles, *Centering Woman: Gender Discourses in Caribbean Slave Society* (Kingston: Ian Randle Publishers, 1999), xvi.
22. Edward Long, *History of Jamaica*, vol. 2 (London: T. Lowndes, 1774), 285.
23. Long, *History of Jamaica*, vol. 2, 286; Trevor Burnard, 'Inheritance and Independence: Women's Status in Early Colonial Jamaica', *William and Mary Quarterly*, 3rd Ser., 48, no. 1 (1991): 113.
24. See Braithwaite, 'Caribbean Women During the Period of Slavery'; Lucille Mathurin Mair, *A Historical Study of Women in Jamaica, 1755–1844* (Kingston: University of the West Indies Press, 2006), 171.
25. Beckles, *Centering Woman*, xv.
26. See, for example, Verene Shepherd (ed.), *Engendering History: Caribbean Women in Historical Perspective* (Kingston: Ian Randle Publishers, 1995) and *Women in Caribbean History* (Kingston: Ian Randle Publishers, 1999); Barbara Bush, '"White Ladies, Coloured Favourites and Black Wenches": Some Considerations on Sex, Race and Class Factors in the Caribbean', *Slavery and Abolition* 2 (1981): 245–62; Butler, *The Economics of Emancipation*; Hilary Beckles, 'White Women and Slavery in the Caribbean', *History Workshop Journal* 36 (1993): 65–82.
27. Butler, *The Economics of Emancipation*, 95.
28. B. W. Higman, *Slave Population and Economy in Jamaica 1807–1834* (Kingston: University of the West Indies Press, 1995), 16; B. W. Higman, 'Jamaica Coffee Plantations, 1780–1860: A Cartographic Analysis', *Caribbean Geography* 2 (1986): 73–91; Higman, *Jamaica Surveyed*; B. W. Higman, 'The Internal Economy of Jamaican Pens, 1760–1890', *Social and Economic Studies* 38 (1989): 61–86; Verene Shepherd, 'Pens and Pen-keepers in a Plantation Society: Aspects of Jamaican Social and

Economic History, 1740-1845', PhD diss., University of Cambridge, 1988; Verene A. Shepherd 'Livestock and Sugar: Aspects of Jamaica's Agricultural Development from the Late Seventeenth Century to the Early Nineteenth Century', *Historical Journal* 34 (1991): 627-43; Verene A. Shepherd 'Alternative Husbandry: Slaves and Free Labourers on Livestock Farms in Jamaica in the Eighteenth and Nineteenth Centuries', *Slavery and Abolition* 14 (1993): 41-66; Verene A. Shepherd (ed.), *Slavery Without Sugar: Diversity in Caribbean Economy and Society Since the 17th Century* (Gainesville: University of Florida Press, 2002); Kathleen Montieth 'The Coffee Industry in Jamaica 1750-1850', MPhil thesis, University of the West Indies, Mona, 1991.

29 Richard Sheridan, *Sugar and Slavery: An Economic History of the British West Indies, 1623-1775* (Kingston: University of the West Indies Press, 2012), 415-46.
30 See, for example, Lloyd Best 'Outlines of a Model of Pure Plantation Economy', *Social and Economic Studies* 17 (1968): 283-326; George Beckford, *Persistent Poverty: Underdevelopment in Plantation Economies of the Third World* (London: Oxford University Press, 1972); C. Y. Thomas, 'A Model of a Pure Plantation Economy', *Social and Economic Studies* 17 (1968): 339-48; Michael Craton 'The Historical Roots of the Plantation Model', *Slavery and Abolition* 5 (1984): 189-221; Richard Pryor 'The Plantation Economy as an Economic System', *Journal of Comparative Economics* 6 (1982): 288-317.
31 Shepherd, *Livestock, Sugar and Slavery*.
32 Barry Higman presented a widely accepted estimate of the labour participation ratio for the island, which is a clear indication of the level of diversification in Jamaica. He showed that in 1832, 49.5 per cent of the enslaved population worked on sugar estates; 14.4 per cent on coffee plantations; 12.8 per cent on livestock pens; 6.4 per cent on minor staples plantations; 6.4 per cent made up the jobbing gangs; and 8 per cent were located in the urban areas. Higman, *Slave Population and Economy in Jamaica*, 16.
33 See National Archives, Kew, London, CO 137/19 (Census 1730), CO/137/87 (Census 1788).
34 National Archives, Kew, London, CO 137/19 (Census 1730), CO/137/87 (Census 1788).
35 Parliamentary Papers: 26 and 29.
36 Ahmed Reid and David B. Ryden, 'Sugar, Land Markets and the Williams Thesis: Evidence from Jamaica's Property Sales, 1750-1810', *Slavery and Abolition* 34, no. 3 (2013): 401-24.
37 Shepherd, *Livestock, Sugar and Slavery*; Higman, *Slave Population and Economy in Jamaica*.
38 British Parliamentary Papers, Select Committee Reports and Correspondence on the Trade and Commerce of the West Indies with Minutes of Evidence and Appendices, 1806-1849, pp. 185-7.
39 Edward Long, *History of Jamaica*, vol. 1, 380; Higman, *Slave Population and Economy in Jamaica*, 25-6; Shepherd, *Livestock, Sugar and Slavery*.

Part Two

The Politics and Economics of Atypical Forms of Slavery and Slaveholding

6

Corporate Slavery in Seventeenth-Century New York

Anne-Claire Faucquez

New York and its Dutch predecessor New Netherland have been shaped since their foundation by the presence of African and Native American slaves. Yet, at first sight, New York, which was part of the Middle Colonies, did not seem to be favourable to the development of a harsh system of slavery.[1] Situated between New England and the South, endowed with an infertile soil that was not easily conducive to commercial agriculture and at the margin of the main transatlantic exchanges, the colony was known for its lenient slave system. For many historians, New York especially distinguished itself by the way the Dutch handled slavery. For example, in the 1960s, Edgar MacManus stated:

> In many ways, its operation was unique, for the system was as mild as the realities of chattel slavery probably allowed. There was none of the mutual hatred in New Netherland of the sort that brutalized slave relations in other colonies. The pragmatic Dutch regarded slavery as an economic expedient; they never equated it with social organization or race control.[2]

If Dutch slavery was characterized by an absence of legal codification, and the particular status of half-free slaves owned by the Dutch West Indian Company,[3] it was nevertheless far from being benign and insignificant. Indeed, in the course of the seventeenth century, New York concentrated the greatest proportion of black people north of the Mason–Dixon line, representing 20 per cent of the population of New Amsterdam in 1664 and around 15 per cent of New York City throughout the eighteenth century. Slavery quickly spread from the southern tip of the island of Manhattan to the surrounding counties and was practised at all levels of this young colonial society, from low-rank workers, to merchants, ministers, and governors. Far from being a 'peculiar institution' to the antebellum South, it became an ordinary practice among all the social strata of the population.[4] Until 1991, and the discovery of the African Burial Ground in lower Manhattan, the importance and impact of the institution on the colony had not been acknowledged.[5] In 2005, the New York Historical Society launched an exhibition on slavery in the city and declared that if New York had 'preeminently been the capital of American liberty, the freest city of the nation … it was also, paradoxically, for more than two centuries, the capital of American slavery'.[6]

If the influence of Dutch slavery has now been recognized by many scholars like Ira Berlin, Thelma W. Foote, Leslie Harris or Graham Hodges,[7] one needs to reconsider the institution within a more global context, from an Atlantic perspective, emphasizing the way European states used slavery to conquer and settle the New World. The introduction of this African labour force was partly due to the general policies of the Dutch and English empires to which the colony of New York belonged. Indeed, both the United Provinces and England conquered the New World principally in search of agricultural and commercial wealth. Contrary to the Spanish Empire in Central and South America, there was no gold or silver to extract in this northern region, so the lands needed to be productive. Hence their necessity to exploit an unfree labour force to develop their new territories, which in turn contributed to the growth and expansion of their empires. The exploitation of African slaves by European states and colonial governments thus served various political, economic, and religious goals. Slaves represented valuable goods that could be pillaged from enemy countries and sold to increase European countries' profits. Enslaved labour was employed to build the colonies and reinforce and assert the countries' political power, to better their positions and confront their empires in the Atlantic space. They also represented masses of potential converts who the countries could use in their religious battles following the Protestant Reformation.[8]

This chapter will question the peculiarity of Dutch slavery in seventeenth-century New York, from 1626, the date of arrival of the first slaves, to the English conquest of 1664. First, I will show the distinctiveness in the importation of slaves, who were for the most part brought into the colony by privateers who plundered Spanish ships. As these slaves became the property of the Dutch West India Company, they benefited from the particular status of corporate slaves, which granted them many singular rights.[9] Finally, I will qualify the apparent greater tolerance of Dutch slaveholders and assess the degree of integration of black people (slave and free) in colonial New York.

The Dutch West Indian Company, privateers and captives

The birth of the Dutch colony of New Netherland has to be understood in the context of European wars, especially the Thirty Years' War (1618–48), in which the Austrian Habsburgs, who were allied with Spain, opposed the United Provinces, Denmark, Sweden and France. The Dutch West India Company (hereafter WIC) was founded in 1621, after a twelve-year truce in the Dutch War of Independence, as a chartered company of Dutch merchants, whose explicit aim was to defeat Spain through commerce and Calvinist zeal.[10] New Netherland was thus founded in 1624 as a charter or corporate colony, administered and ruled by the WIC, which 'operated both as a commercial company and as a military institution with quasi-statelike powers'.[11]

The slave trade was, at the beginning of the seventeenth century, monopolized by the Portuguese who were granted the *asiento*[12] to supply Spanish colonies with slaves. The Dutch presence in West and Central Africa was still limited in the early decades of the century, so the United Provinces could only obtain slaves through war-making and plundering. Often, they would raid a Spanish or a Portuguese ship and, not knowing what to do with the slaves, would send them to their new colony in North America.[13] This practice was justified by the jurist Hugo Grotius who wrote in his *De jure belli ac pacis* ('On the Law on War and Peace'), published in 1625, that the practice of slavery was legal in times of war as 'the victors had a natural right to the possessions and labour of the defeated'. As the United Provinces was not at war with any African nation but rather with Spain, pillaging Spanish goods was thus perfectly justified.[14] This is how the first African slaves arrived in the colony in 1626, seven years after a Dutch ship had introduced the '20. and odd Negroes' to Point Comfort, Virginia.[15] The parallel is indeed relevant as the Dutch 'man of Warr' which came in 1619 had 'teamed up with the English corsair Treasurer to commandeer the Portuguese slave ship Sao Joao Bautista ... which was on its way to Vera Cruz, Mexico, directly from the Angolan port of Luanda'.[16] Indeed, that most New Netherland slaves came from Portuguese colonies in Central Africa can be traced through their names, which were reminiscent of their place of origin, such as Paulo d'Angola, Simon Congo, Pieter Santomee and Anthony Portuguese.[17]

It was only after the first slaves had been introduced to the colony that the WIC realized the advantage of using such a labour force, which could serve as a bait to attract new settlers while providing cheap workers to help build the colony. In 1639, the WIC indicated that it would 'allot to each Patroon [landowner] twelve Black men and women out of the prizes in which Negroes shall be found'.[18] It is interesting to notice here that the WIC, acting as the colonial government, officially encouraged the importation of war prizes from privateers as the only source of a labour force. Indeed, New Netherland was suffering from a chronic lack of labour and found it hard to attract new immigrants from the United Provinces as the new republic flourished economically and was famous for its peaceful and tolerant atmosphere. Slaves were considered to be more efficient and preferable to servants, all the more so as the Dutch had gained, after 1637, new access to the Portuguese forts in Elmina on the Gold Coast, as well to the regions of Angola and Congo.[19]

If privateers flourished until the end of the Thirty Years' War in 1648, the company had to fight against piracy[20] when the war was over. This was especially true after 1654, when the Dutch lost New Holland in Brazil to the Portuguese and were, at the same time, pressured by New Netherlanders to relinquish their trade monopoly.[21] On 9 March 1660, the directors finally agreed to open the slave trade to all inhabitants of the colony, but only if the slaves were confined to agriculture and were not sold out of the colony:

> As these Slaves are sent solely to be employed in agriculture, which is the only means whereby this State can be rendered flourishing, we expect and require most expressly that the aforesaid Slaves must be sold there to our inhabitants on express condition that they shall not be taken beyond our district, but kept specially there and be employed in husbandry, so that the great expense we are incurring herein may not be in vain; but the fruits we promise ourselves therefrom be abundantly reaped.[22]

If the directors of the WIC were at first reluctant to enter the slave trade, and relegated this immoral practice to the 'evil' Spaniards, the Dutch privateers, in their fight against the Spanish Crown, nevertheless introduced slaves to the Dutch colonies, which eventually prospered thanks to slavery.

The peculiarity of corporate slavery

The particular status of slaves in New Netherland was determined by the fact that most of them belonged to the Dutch West India Company and were thus considered 'corporate slaves'.[23] They were at the same time the property of a private merchant company and of the colonial government whilst also treated as real employees, who enjoyed specific rights and privileges. The Company housed, fed and clothed them and even allotted them a 50-to-100-feet garden that they were allowed to cultivate during their free time.[24] In 1658, a hospital was built for the slaves and the soldiers of the company.[25] Black people in New Amsterdam were accepted within the Dutch Reformed Church, and could get married and baptize their children despite its rigidity in requiring a good religious education and a confession of faith. Moreover, the company strove not to separate families. Looking at the Church registers, I have identified twenty-seven black marriages out of the 441 marriages that were celebrated between 1639 and 1664 (i.e. 6 per cent of all marriages)[26] and sixty-one black baptisms between 1639 and 1656 out a total of 880 baptisms (7 per cent).[27]

Company slaves also benefited from a whole range of legal rights: they could have grievances redressed in the courts and through petitions, give testimony in a trial, sign legal documents, and sue white people. In 1638, Anthony Portuguese obtained compensation after he sued Anthony Jansen de Salee, a Dutch merchant, because his pig had been attacked by the latter's dog. The following year, Pedro Negretto sued Jan Celes who had hired him to take care of his pigs and had never paid him for the service. That same Jan Celes was sued on another occasion, in 1643, based on the written declaration of two slaves, Groot Manuel and Manuel de Gerrit, who accused him of having injured Cleijn Manuel's cow with a knife. As a result, Celes had to pay damages to Cleijn Manuel.[28] In 1635, five slaves claimed they had been promised to be paid by Director Wouter van Twiller (who governed from 1633 to 1638) for having built the fort in New Amsterdam. Their petition was sent to the United Provinces, which finally agreed to pay them a wage of eight florins, corresponding to what a white worker earned in a month.[29] Some slaves even worked extra hours in the city to earn some money and went as far as to complain to the directors that the work they did for the company interfered with their other jobs. Company officials did not condemn this practice and even encouraged it, as the money the slaves could make reduced the financial burden on the WIC.[30] Yet, this situation might not be particular to New Netherland as it is similar to that of the 'service slaves', also called 'coast slaves' or 'castle slaves', who laboured on the coast of West Africa. Contrary to the 'trade slaves' who were sold and sent to America, these company slaves were charged with loading and unloading the ships, or could be employed as craftsmen. They were protected from being sold and were provided with housing and food. They could be emancipated if exchanged with another slave, or against a sum of money or as a reward granted by the company.[31]

On 17 January 1641, nine black men – Cleijn Antonio, Paulo d'Angola, Gracia d'Angola, Jan de Fort Orange, Manuel de Gerrit de Reus, Anthony Portuguese, Manuel Minuit, Simon Congo and Big (Groot) Manuel – who all worked on Fort Amsterdam, were charged with the murder of another African, Jan Primero. Out of solidarity, they all pleaded guilty to the murder. However, as the court didn't want the company to lose nine slaves, the accused were asked to cast lots to decide who would be executed. Fate chose Manuel de Gerrit, named 'the giant'. On 24 January 1644, he climbed onto the scaffold to be hanged, but the rope broke. The court took this as a sign that God was on his side, and Governor Kieft, under public pressure, finally agreed to pardon him.[32]

On 25 February 1644, the same group of slaves with two others petitioned the company to be granted their freedom, to which the directors consented 'on account of their long services'.[33] The company understood the need for slaves to be freed in order to take care of their families: 'they are burthened with many children so that it is impossible for them to support their wives and children, as they have been accustomed to do, if they must continue in the Company's service ... [We] do release, for the term of their natural lives, the above named and their Wives from Slavery'.[34] In exchange for their freedom, each man had to pay an annual tribute to the company (30 *skepels* of corn, wheat, peas, beans or a wild hog) and had to remain available to the company whenever they might be needed. They would then receive a salary and were promised not to be employed outside of the colony.[35] If they failed to respect this agreement, they would lose their liberty. Many historians have described this situation as 'half-freedom' because they were 'obligated to serve the Honorable WIC here, by water or on land where their services are required'.[36] Yet, the company never had to recall any slave, except on 20 April 1653, during the first Anglo-Dutch war, when the whole population, including soldiers and the company's servants, were impressed to defend Fort Amsterdam.[37]

These free blacks were given plots of farmland in southern Manhattan, west of the Bowery.[38] Some even hired white servants, as in the case of Manuel de Gerrit de Reus, who employed a Dutch farmer, Barent Hendricks, or Augustijn De Caper, who had Jan Owen's wife work for him as a domestic help.[39] Their land titles were confirmed in 1664 at the time of the English conquest through a patent letter, and they were given the title of freeholder, endowing them with the right to vote and to bequeath their lands to their children.[40] More than an act of benevolence, this was of course a way for the new English government to prevent free black people from falling into a state of indigence.[41]

A greater benevolence towards black people?

If Dutch slavery was considered to be benevolent because of the particular status of company slaves and in the absence of slave codes, one has to bear in mind that before the 1660s, slavery was not yet codified in any North American colony and slaves were usually referred to as 'servants'.[42] This doesn't mean, as Oscar and Mary Handlin put it, that they were treated as servants but rather that there was no clear-cut legal distinction between the two statuses in the first half of the seventeenth century.[43] Moreover, the Dutch authorities were more anxious about Native Americans who surrounded the Dutch settlement and who undoubtedly posed a greater threat to them. Indeed, in its early stages the colony was more a commercial outpost than a settlement colony. There were few slaveholders, since the majority of slaves were owned by the company. As historian Benjamin Quarles puts it, 'as a rule, a slave code was an accurate reflection of the fears and apprehensions of the colony. Hence the more numerous the blacks were, the stricter the slave codes were.'[44] Studying the laws (or the lack thereof) can thus be a good means to understand the reality of colonial experience. Acts were voted by colonial assemblies to prevent certain crimes from being committed and because these crimes represented society's strongest fears.

However, though slavery was not codified in New Netherland, it did not prevent black people from facing discrimination. As early as 1638, an ordinance seeking to control the behaviour of New Amsterdam's free residents ordered that 'each and every one must refrain from Fighting, Adulterous intercourse with Heathens, Blacks or other Persons, Mutiny, Theft, False Swearing, Calumny and other Immoralities'.[45] Here, the association of black people with Heathens and the criminalization of mixed intercourse is an indubitable proof of the will of the Dutch authorities to set black people apart.

Similarly, the 'half-freedom' status granted to eleven slaves in 1644 only applied to the oldest slaves, who had arrived in the colony eighteen years earlier and who had now become a financial burden to the company. The fact that their children remained enslaved also shows that the company was not ready to forfeit all its labour force.[46] Moreover, 1644 was a convenient time to get rid of the oldest slaves because the Dutch were now established in Elmina, Angola and Brazil, and could bring in fresh supplies of labourers.

From the very beginning of settlement, African slaves who had been imported mostly for agricultural work started to be segregated from other types of occupations. As early as 1628, the company directors announced in the Charter of Liberties and Exemptions that slaves would be excluded from the most skilled jobs, such as carpentry or bricklaying.[47] Indeed, slaves represented an unwanted form of competition for free workers as their average price amounted to a one-year salary for a free worker or six months' pay for an apprentice, so they were far more profitable for the company or the city of New York who employed them. In 1667, some trades like the cartmen formed guilds to exert a monopoly in the city and exclude slaves and free blacks from those types of employment.[48]

As slavery grew in the colony, black people started to become more and more despised. For example, the first Dutch minister, Johannes Michaelius, described his three Angolese servants as 'thievish, lazy and useless trash'.[49] In 1642, an ordinance stipulated that anyone convicted of drawing a knife would be fined 50 florins and, upon defaulting on this, be condemned 'to work three months with the Negroes in chains'.[50] This instance has made some historians speculate about the slaves' working conditions, suggesting that they were in shackles, but as no other source confirms this, it seems that we should rather interpret this ordinance as a special treatment reserved for criminals. Working alongside black criminals was a moral and physical condemnation. Progressively, the most degrading types of work became associated with slaves. The *fiscael*,[51] Hendrick van Dijck, complained for instance about the debasing work assigned to him by the company: 'The direction and management of all business, both Civil and Criminal, have been undertaken by the Director himself, who employed me very rarely and mostly as his boy; ordering me to look to the hogs and to keep these from the fort which a negro could have easily done.'[52] Jeremias Van Rensselaer expressed himself in similar terms when, in 1664, he wrote to his brother to inform him that his proposal regarding the boundary of the colony had not been accepted by the assembly, which, he said, 'cared as much about it as if [my] Negro had said it'.[53]

Far from living in a benevolent society, black slaves were not protected from violence at the hands of their masters. In his slave's act of manumission dated 17 February 1649, Philip Jansz Ringo declared that he was emancipating his slave of his own will and that this way he would never molest him again.[54] In April 1656, Nicholaes Boot bought a woman slave from Alexander d'Inoyoseph. Before being sent to her new master, the slave was severely beaten by Alexander's wife to the point that she could no longer work. Boot sued them to obtain financial compensation for the injured slave. But the judges declared that 'Boot was bound to receive back the said negress, on condition that d'Inoyossef shall prove, that the negress has received no injury by being beaten by his wife'. As no other trial followed, we might assume that the slave recovered and went to work with Boot.[55]

Colonial authorities also exerted power over the slaves. On 10 January 1659, Pieter Cornelis Van der Veen asked the *burgomeesters* for the right to 'chastise his Negress', which was duly granted to him.[56] This illustrates that masters did not have full control over their slaves' life and death but that moral policing was in the hands of the city authorities. Some slaves were even sentenced to capital punishment, like Lysbet Anthony from New Utrecht on Long Island, who was condemned for having set fire to her master's tavern on 5 February 1664. She received a last-minute pardon, saving her from the flames of the bonfire, but she was sold at public auction because her master wanted to get rid of her.[57] The severity of the Dutch masters towards their slaves combined with the authority of the directors of the West India Company were the necessary conditions to lay the foundations of slave society in the colony of New York.

Conclusion

Slaves in New Netherland benefited from a unique situation. As the property of a private merchant company that governed a Dutch colony in the name of the States General of the United Provinces, they embodied the will of the state to reinforce its power against enemy countries in the context of European wars. The Dutch were at first reluctant to get involved in the slave trade, despising that practice. Yet, they eventually became the largest slave traders in the first half of the seventeenth century, establishing slavery in all their American colonies (New Netherland, New Holland in Brazil, Curacao, Suriname and the Dutch Leeward islands of Saba, St Eustatius, and St Martin). As a matter of fact, the apparent benevolence of Dutch settlers in New Amsterdam is more circumstantial than anything else. As war prizes, slaves were the property of the company, so the way they were treated only depended on two factors:

its labour needs and economic welfare. When England took over New Netherland in 1664, the interests became different, and slaves were managed as in the rest of the English Empire. The Dutch had nevertheless succeeded in planting a burgeoning slave society[58] which paved the way for the English to set up a legal framework by progressively racializing society and definitely sealing the status of black people at the turn of the eighteenth century.

Notes

1   There are numerous studies of slavery in the Middle Colonies. See, for instance, Douglas Greenberg, 'The Middle Colonies in Recent American Historiography', *William and Mary Quarterly*, 3rd Ser., 36, no. 3 (1979): 396–427; Patricia U. Bonomi, 'The Middle Colonies: Embryo of the New Political Order', in Alden T. Vaughan and George Athan Billias (eds), *Perspectives on Early American History* (New York: Harper and Row, 1973), 63–92; Wayne Bodle, 'Themes and Directions in Middle Colonies Historiography, 1980–1994', *William and Mary Quarterly*, 3rd Ser., 51, no. 3 (1994): 355–88.
2   Edgar J. McManus, *A History of Negro Slavery in New York* (New York: Syracuse University Press, 1966), 11.
3   On 25 February 1644, Governor Kieft emancipated eleven slaves that belonged to the Dutch West India Company on condition that they 'shall be obligated to serve the Hon WIC here, by water or on land where their services are required, on receiving fair wages from the Company', in the 'Act of the Director and Council of New Netherland emancipating certain Negro slaves therein mentioned', in I. N. Phelps Stokes, *The Iconography of Manhattan Island, 1498–1909, Compiled from Original Sources and Illustrated by Photo-Intaglio Reproductions of Important Maps, Plans, Views, and Documents in Public and Private Collections* (New York: Robert H. Dodd, 1915–28), vol. 4, 101.
4   Kenneth Stampp, *The Peculiar Institution: Slavery in the Ante-Bellum South* (New York: Vintage, 1956). In this major work, the author defined slavery as an institution particular to the South, implying that slavery was non-existent in the Northern states.
5   Edna Green E. Medford (ed.), *The New York African Burial Ground History Final Report* (Washington, DC: Howard University, 2004), 17.
6   http://www.slaveryinnewyork.org/about_exhibit.htm.
7   Duncan Faherty, '"It Happened Here": Slavery on the Hudson', *American Quarterly* 58, no. 2 (2006): 455–66; Ira Berlin and Leslie Harris, *In the Shadow of Slavery in New York* (New York: New Press, W.W. Norton, 2005); Leslie Harris, *African Americans in New York City, 1626–1863* (Chicago: University of Chicago Press, 2003); Thelma Wills Foote, *Black and White Manhattan: The History of Racial Formation in Colonial New York City* (New York: Oxford University Press, 2004).
8   Protestant missionaries in frontier zones or areas that were colonized by multiple European nations fought hard to eradicate the spread of Catholicism and convert slaves to the 'True Religion'. See Katharine Gerbner, *Christian Slavery: Conversion and Race in the Protestant Atlantic World* (Philadelphia: University of Pennsylvania Press, 2018), 25–7; Robin Blackburn, *The Making of New World Slavery: From the Baroque to the Modern, 1492–1800* (London and New York: Verso, 1998), 64.

9   I owe the expression 'corporate slaves' to Morton Wagman, 'Corporate Slavery in New Netherland', *Journal of Negro History* 65, no. 1 (1980): 34–42.
10 Jonathan I. Israel, *Dutch Primacy in World Trade, 1585–1740* (Oxford: Clarendon Press, 1989), 84.
11 Herbert S. Klein, *The Atlantic Slave Trade* (Cambridge: Cambridge University Press, 2010), 79.
12 A license or contract granted by the Spanish Crown to foreign merchants providing a monopoly of supplying slaves for its colonies. The *asiento* was granted to the Portuguese from 1595 to 1640, to the Dutch from 1662 to 1713, and to the British from 1713 to 1750.
13 Elizabeth Donnan mentions three cases in which Dutch people freed the slave cargo after they had assailed foreign ships between 1624 and 1631, in Elizabeth Donnan, *Documents Illustrative of the History of the Slave Trade to America,* 4 vols (Washington, DC: Carnegie Institution of Washington, 1930–5), vol 3, 410.
14 Pieter Emmer, *The Dutch Slave Trade, 1500–1800* (New York: Berghahn Books, 2006).
15 We have not yet found any source relating this event, but as the company never expressed its will to import slaves, we can suppose they came from privateers. Historians have agreed on this arrival date for the first slaves since the slaves who petitioned for freedom in 1644 claimed they had been in the colony for eighteen years. E. Medford, *The New York African Burial Ground History Final Report*, 12; Robert J. Swan, 'First Africans into New Netherland, 1625 or 1626?', *De Halve Maen* 66, no. 4 (1993): 75–82.
16 Peter C. Mancall, *The Atlantic World and Virginia, 1550–1624* (Chapel Hill: University of North Carolina Press, 2012), 225.
17 Robert J. Swan, 'The Other Fort Amsterdam: New Light on Aspects of Slavery in New Netherland', *Afro-Americans in New York Life and History* 22 (1998): 27–8.
18 E. B. O'Callaghan and Berthold Fernow (eds and trans), *Documents Relative to the Colonial History of the State of New York*, 15 vols (Albany, NY: Weed, Parsons, 1865–87), vol. 1, 99. Items stolen by pirates could include food, water, alcohol, weapons, clothing or soap, rope and anchors, or even sometimes the whole ship, which they would sell off or keep (hereafter DRCHNY).
19 Linda M. Heywood (ed.), *Central Africans and Cultural Transformations* (Cambridge and New York: Cambridge University Press, 2002).
20 On 11 August 1656, the following ordinance against smuggling was passed: 'No skippers or anyone sailing with ships, yachts, barks, ketches, sloops or vessels, shall take with them or remove any of the Company's servants, any freemen or inhabitants of New Netherland, regardless of nationality or capacity, without the consent or permission of the Director General.' E. B. O'Callaghan, *Laws and Ordinances of New Netherland, 1638–1674* (Albany, NY: Weed, Parsons and Company, 1868), 64.
21 On 19 November 1654, two Dutch traders – Jan de Sweerts and Dirck Pietersen – were granted premission by the assembly to go to Africa on the *Witte Paert* in order to buy slaves and bring them back to New Netherland.
22 DRCHNY, vol. 14, 458–9; DRCHNY, vol. 2, 222.
23 It was only after 1640 that private settlers could start owning slaves, in 'Articles and Conditions of 1638' and then in the 'Charter of Liberties and Exemptions', dated 19 July 1640, in DRCHNY, vol. 1, 110–14, 119–23.
24 Robert J. Swan, *New Amsterdam Gehenna: Segregated Death in New York City, 1630–1801* (New York: Noir Verite Press, 2006), 230.
25 Stokes, *Iconography*, vol. 2, 263.

26 Thomas Grier Evans and Tobias Alexander Wright (eds), 'Records of the Reformed Dutch Church in New Amsterdam and New York, Marriages from 11 December 1639 to 26 August 1801' (New York: New York Genealogical and Biographical Society, 1890), vol. 1, 33–130; Thomas Grier Evans, 'Baptisms from 25 December, 1639, to 27 December, 1730' (New York: New York Genealogical and Biographical Society, 1890), vol. 2.

27 Jaap Jacobs, *The Colony of New Netherland, The Colony of New Netherland: A Dutch Settlement in Seventeenth-Century America* (Ithaca, NY: Cornell University Press, 2009), footnote 81, 282.

28 Petrus R. Christoph, 'The Freedmen of New Amsterdam', *Journal of the Afro-American Historical and Genealogical Society* 4 (1983): 109.

29 Graham Russell Hodges, *Root & Branch: African Americans in New York and East Jersey, 1613–1863* (Chapel Hill: University of North Carolina Press, 1999), 9; 'There was read a petition from five negroes arrived here from New Netherland, claiming to have earned eight guilders a month, requesting a settlement. Referred to the Commissioners for New Netherland', in Stokes, *Iconography*, vol. 4, 82.

30 Wagman, 'Corporate Slavery', 38.

31 Johannes Postma, *The Dutch in the Atlantic Trade, 1600–1815* (Cambridge: Cambridge University Press, 1992), 72–3.

32 Stokes, *Iconography*, vol. 4, 93.

33 DRCHNY, vol. 1, 343, 425; O'Callaghan, *Laws and Ordinances*, 36; Stokes, *Iconography*, vol. 4, 93.

34 O'Callaghan, *Laws and Ordinances*, 36–7.

35 O'Callaghan, *Laws and Ordinances*, 112; Edmund Bailey O'Callaghan, *Calendar of Historical Manuscripts in the Office of the Secretary of State, Albany, N.Y., Part I Dutch Manuscripts, 1630–1664* (Albany, NY: Weed, Parsons, 1865–6), 87 (hereafter CHMD).

36 Christoph, 'The Freedmen of New Amsterdam', 159 ; Ira Berlin, *Many Thousands Gone: The First Two Centuries of Slavery in North America* (Cambridge, MA: Belknap Press of Harvard University Press, 1998), 52; Berlin and Harris, *In the Shadow of Slavery*, 23; T. Foote, *Black and White Manhattan*, 39.

37 'That the soldiers and other servants of the Company, together with the free Negroes, no one excepted, shall complete the work on the fort by constructing a breastwork', in DRCHNY, vol. 14, 201.

38 Stokes, *Iconography*, vol. 1, 76; vol. 4, 97; CHMD, *Land Papers*, 368, 369, 370, 372, 374.

39 Christoph, 'The Freedmen of New Amsterdam', 114.

40 DRCHNY, vol. 2, 250–3; Stokes, *Iconography*, vol. 4, 266; vol. 2, 123.

41 Through all the English period, the colonial authorities seemed to worry about the free blacks' social condition, to such an extent that in 1712 they made it obligatory for slaveowners to post a £200 security bond and an additional yearly £20 bond to provide for their emancipated slaves' financial needs, *Colonial Laws of New York*, vol. 1, 464; Foote, *Black and White Manhattan*, 150.

42 The Barbados Slave Code of 1661 was the first code to be passed within the English colonies. It was later implemented in the American British colonies of Virginia, Maryland, and South Carolina.

43 'The status of Negroes was that of servants; and so they were identified and treated down to the 1660's', in Oscar and Mary Handlin, 'The Origins of the Southern Labour System', *William and Mary Quarterly*, 3rd Ser., 7 (1950): 203.

44 Quoted in Leon Higginbotham, *In the Matter of Color: Race and the American Legal Process: The Colonial Period* (New York: Oxford University Press, 1978), 116.

45 O'Callaghan, *Laws and Ordinances*, 12.
46 'With the express condition that all their children already born or yet to be born shall be obliged to serve the Company as slaves', E. B. O'Callaghan, *Calendar of Historical Manuscripts in the Office of the Secretary of State* (Albany, NY: Weed, Parsons, 1865–6), 87.
47 'Freedoms and Exemptions for the Patroons and Masters or Private Persons who would plant a colony and cattle in New Netherland'. The aim of this charter was to open colonization to private capital. See Oliver A. Rink, *Holland on the Hudson: An Economic and Social History of Dutch New York* (Ithaca, NY: Cornell University Press, 1986), 100–1.
48 Edwin G. Burrows and Mike Wallace, *Gotham: A History of New York City to 1898* (New York: Oxford University Press, 1999), 85.
49 James Franklin Jameson, *Narratives of New Netherland, 1609–1664* (New York: Charles Scribner's Sons, 1909), 129.
50 O'Callaghan, *Laws and Ordinances*, 12.
51 'A high official charged with upholding the rights of the WIC', in Jaap Jacobs, *New Netherland: A Dutch Colony in Seventeenth-Century America* (Leiden: Brill, 2005), xv.
52 E. B. O'Callaghan, *Journal of the Legislative Council of the Colony of New York* (Albany, NY: Weed, Parsons & Co., 1861), 333; Stokes, *Iconography*, vol. 4, 474–5.
53 A. G. F. Van Laer (ed. and trans.), *Correspondence of Jeremias van Rensselaer, 1651–1674* (Albany, NY: University of the State of New York, 1932), 353.
54 Willie F. Page, *The Dutch Triangle: The Netherlands and the Atlantic Slave Trade, 1621–1664* (New York: Garland Publishing, 1997), 204.
55 Berthold Fernow, *The Records of New Amsterdam from 1653–1674*, 7 vols (New York: Knickerbocker Press, 1897; Baltimore, MD: Genealogical Publishing Co., Inc., 1976), vol. 2, 87–8 (hereafter RNA).
56 RNA, vol. 7, 207.
57 CHMD, 258–9; Stokes, *Iconography*, vol. 2, 217.
58 Joyce D. Goodfriend spoke of an 'embryonic slave society' in New Amsterdam in 'Burghers and Blacks: The Evolution of a Slave Society at New Amsterdam', *New York History* 59, no. 2 (April 1978): 133.

7

Militarized Slavery: The Creation of the West India Regiments

Tim Lockley

On 17 April 1795, Henry Dundas, Secretary at War, wrote to General Sir John Vaughan, commander-in-chief in the Leeward Islands, authorizing him 'to raise two corps of mulattoes or Negroes to consist of 1,000 rank and file each'.[1] These were the first of what would, within five years, become twelve West India Regiments stationed throughout the British Caribbean. Many of these soldiers were recruited directly from slave ships and, as a result, the British Army became the largest slaveholder in the West Indies by 1802, owning several thousand men. This chapter explores the rationale for the British Army deciding to purchase (and arm) slaves, despite significant and persistent resistance from white planters, and concludes that rapidly spreading ideas about race, climate and disease resistance combined to create an environment whereby the recruitment of enslaved men became a logical, maybe even an inevitable, choice.

Roger Buckley, whose *Slaves in Redcoats* remains the best monograph on the West India Regiments despite being published in 1979, highlights the demographic equation that made military reliance on Whites in the Caribbean impossible. The West Indian islands had very small white populations, barely sufficient to form a small militia if required for defence, and certainly not large enough to repel a determined assault from an invader. The British Army stationed several regiments in the West Indies, but tended to concentrate forces in Jamaica and Barbados, leaving other territories vulnerable with only small garrisons. For Buckley, the use of enslaved men was a natural choice, and should be seen as an extension of the system of slavery that dominated the West Indies.[2] The elite white men who presided over island assemblies were accustomed to controlling the bodies of black people, using them however they saw fit, and therefore could easily justify using them to make up for a deficiency in military manpower. This argument holds true with regard to militia units, which were under the local control of each island. Indeed, white planters themselves served as officers in militia units, and would therefore most likely be supervising their own slaves. Surrendering enslaved men to the authority and control of an outside body, such as the British Army, was an entirely different matter. As this chapter will demonstrate, other factors were at play in the 1790s. Specifically, ideas about tropical diseases and their impact on British troops began to dominate the discourse about how best to defend imperial possessions in the West Indies.

Military expeditions in the West Indies throughout the eighteenth century faced an enemy far more deadly than rival European powers. According to John Bell, surgeon with the 94th Regiment, '[i]n every war, during the course of this century, in which the forces of Great Britain have been employed in the West Indies, it has unfortunately happened, that the number of those who have perished by disease has, in every instance, greatly exceeded the loss occasioned by the sword of the enemy.'[3] John Hunter, who managed the military hospitals in Jamaica between 1781 and 1783, agreed, calculating that 'in less than four years [1777–81], there died in the island of Jamaica 3,500 men; those that were discharged amounted to one half of that number, which make in all 5,250 men, lost to the service in that short period of time, from the climate and other causes of mortality, without a man dying by the hands of the enemy.'[4] The obvious conclusion was that 'the climate is certainly unfavourable to a British constitution, as it contains the causes of so many diseases, so far peculiar to itself, that those diseases are either not known, or very rarely met with in Britain'.[5]

The actual military impact of high rates of sickness and mortality among regiments in the West Indies prior to 1793 is debatable: it was never sufficient to seriously threaten British control of its possessions for example, but it was clear at the time that the blame could be attached to various tropical fevers that did not exist in Britain. Military surgeons quickly noticed that fevers impacted the various populations in the West Indies differently and that those of African descent were often highly resistant. John Hunter in Jamaica was not alone in thinking that 'the negroes afford a striking example, of the power acquired by habit of resisting the causes of fevers; for, though they are not entirely exempted from them, they suffer infinitely less than Europeans'.[6]

This perceived resistance possessed by those of African descent to tropical diseases had led the army to recruit enslaved men in small numbers since at least the 1740s, using them as 'pioneers' to undertake arduous physical labour. More than 400 participated in the Cartagena expedition of 1740, and during the siege of Havana in 1762 the army eventually obtained via purchase or hire about 2,000 enslaved men for military use. Regimental surgeons recommended '[a]ll drudgery and labour should be performed by negroes, and others, inured to the climate,' and thus the weaponry and ammunition for the siege was hauled into place by '500 blacks purchased ... at Martineco and Antigua for that purpose'.[7] In each instance, black soldiers were not formally embodied into regiments but instead simply attached to white regiments, and were confined to the sort of labouring work that enslaved people undertook throughout the West Indies. Most significantly, they were dispensed with once the campaign was over: hired slaves were returned to owners, purchased slaves were sold.

The first conclusion that many drew from these expeditions was that 'sickness will prevent European troops succeeding ... where the service exceeds six weeks'.[8] The second was that the British should look more seriously at using black troops more systematically. John Hunter recommended that throughout the Caribbean 'there should be a certain number of negroes attached to each regiment; or what perhaps would be better, a company of negroes and mulattoes should be formed in every regiment, to do whatever duty or hard work was to be done in the heat of the day, from which they do not suffer, though it would be fatal to Europeans'.[9] Significantly, it was through the published writings of military surgeons in the West Indies that ideas about the climatological suitability of those of African descent to West Indian service began to circulate in London, several years before the West India Regiments were founded in 1795. Thus British ministers would have had an awareness of the inhospitable Caribbean climate, and particularly its impact on the strength of white regiments stationed there. The idea of using black troops periodically resurfaced throughout the 1780s. Alex Dirom, Adjutant General to the Governor of Jamaica, believed an easy way to augment the militia with 'the strongest and most active people' would be for slaveowners to bring a few 'trusty' slaves with them to the regular musters 'to be trained and disciplined in the militia'.[10] In 1787, Lt. John Gosling, then serving with the 1st Regiment of Foot in the Caribbean, even outlined a scheme to the Foreign Secretary for recruiting a corps of 'free mulattoes and blacks' precisely because they were 'inured to the climate, [and] are not subject to those diseases so fatal to Europeans'. These men would be 'ever ready for any service' and in particular for 'all duty of fatigue which must ever be, as was the case in the last war in the West Indies, fatally destructive to our soldiery until they become reconciled to the climate'.[11]

One fully-fledged unit of black soldiers was actually stationed in the British Caribbean before 1795. The Carolina Corps had been created in the later stages of the American Revolutionary war in South Carolina. Fugitives from slave plantations 'attached themselves' to the army and were eventually given weapons and even mounted in order to strike terror among patriots. As the war drew to a close in 1782 and aware that 'many of them, which had taken an active part, had made themselves so obnoxious to their former owners' and now faced 'the severest punishment', army commanders instead decided to relocate 300 of them to St Lucia and, importantly, to retain them as a military unit. In 1783 they were posted to garrison Grenada, where they were deployed against fugitive slaves, and 'found more useful, than the other troops, from being better able to bear fatigue in that climate'.[12]

What forced British commanders in the Caribbean, and their political masters in London, to take the idea of wholesale black enlistment more seriously was the outbreak of a particularly virulent strain of yellow fever in 1793. The virus was transported from Bolama Island off the coast of West Africa by the ship *Hankey*.[13] The *Hankey* had led an idealistic British colonization effort that sought to demonstrate that slavery did not have to be the defining paradigm of European encounters with Africans. Instead, these colonists wished to establish a colony based on free labour, with native Africans being paid for any work they did. Their idealism proved to be misplaced, partly because of the mistrust of locals who had experienced several centuries of European incursions. What rapidly destroyed the colony, however, was disease. Within weeks of arriving on Bolama island, off the coast of Guinea-Bissau, in July 1792, the first colonists began to fall ill, and by the end of January 1793 only thirteen were left alive.[14] Not all colonists died of disease, some fled the island to take their chances on the mainland, but the majority succumbed to yellow fever, an endemic disease in tropical climates and found throughout West Africa. What made 'Bulam fever' particularly dangerous was that it had evolved on an island uninhabited by mankind with only monkeys as hosts. It proved to be even more deadly than the regular strains of yellow fever.

The Bolama strain of yellow fever would probably have remained in Africa but for the *Hankey*. The ship was anchored off the island between July and November 1792, giving plenty of time for a colony of *Aedes Aegypti* mosquitoes, responsible for spreading yellow fever, to establish themselves on the ship. In November and December 1792 the ship meandered around the West African coast before heading first for the Cape Verde islands and then the West Indies. The *Hankey* arrived in Barbados on 14 February 1793, before swiftly moving on first to St Vincent on 16 February and Grenada on 19 February where it would remain until July.[15] Colin Chisholm, surgeon to His Majesty's Ordnance in Grenada, documented the inevitable spread of a 'very fatal fever', firstly to the ships moored closest to the *Hankey* in the harbour of St George's, then to those a little further away. By mid-April the first cases appeared on shore and thereafter the disease became truly epidemic. Chisholm estimated that about two-thirds of the population of St George's became infected and that of those about a fifth perished.[16] Regiments stationed in Grenada also became infected. Worst affected were twenty-seven new recruits for the Royal Artillery who arrived in mid-July. By the middle of August, twenty-one of them were dead.[17]

The virus spread quickly throughout the Caribbean islands. The harbour of St George's was full, and some ships probably departed for other ports before the extent of the epidemic became fully known. Others fled in a vain attempt to escape the pestilence. A significant factor in the spread of yellow fever was the slave revolt in St Domingue, which created a large volume of refugees. It was those fleeing St Domingue that brought yellow fever to Philadelphia in the autumn of 1793. Another critical aid to the spread of the disease was the outbreak of hostilities between Britain and France in early 1793. The movement of troops between the various British islands in preparation for assaults on Guadaloupe and Martinique ensured that no island was spared this deadly virus.

Yellow fever had, of course, been a regular visitor to the Caribbean for more than a century but had been just one of a variety of tropical fevers, including malaria, that affected newly arrived Europeans. From 1793, however, this highly virulent strain of yellow fever took centre stage. In the first three months of the outbreak on Dominica, for instance, Dr James Clark recalled 'that eight hundred emigrants, including their servants and slaves, were cut off by this fever; and about two hundred English, including newcomers, sailors, soldiers, and negroes, also fell victims to it, in the same space of time. Few newcomers escaped an attack, and very few of those recovered.' No wonder that local physicians believed it to be 'as quick and fatal as the plague'.[18] The high mortality also began to be noticed in Britain. Whitehall officials naturally received communiqués from both island governors and military commanders, but such was the havoc caused by this outbreak that occasional reports also surfaced in the British press. In August 1793, the London *Times* reported 'the plague, brought from Bulam, which first made its appearance at Grenada, has spread most alarmingly. Eighty persons died in one day at Grenada of this disease.'[19] In early 1794, reports circulated that '[d]uring the last six months Grenada, Tobago, St Vincent's and Dominica, have lost, on the most moderate calculation, one third of their white inhabitants, principally by the yellow fever.'[20]

Almost immediately, military physicians noted that this strain of yellow fever followed other tropical fevers in affecting white people far more than black people. Observing the disaster unfolding in Grenada, Colin Chisholm commented, '[i]t is curious, and may be useful, to observe the gradation of this fatal malady, with respect to the various descriptions of people exposed to its infection. Neither age nor sex were exempted from its attack; but some were more obnoxious to it than others, and the colour had evidently much influence in determining its violence.'[21] The medical explanation for the selective impact of yellow fever is largely straightforward. Yellow fever was endemic in West Africa, generally manifesting itself as a comparatively mild childhood disease. Native West Africans therefore gained lifelong immunity to future infections because of a childhood illness, and obviously retained that immunity if enslaved and transported to the Caribbean. Children born to enslaved parents in the Americas might also have been infected with yellow fever during infancy, since the virus was certainly present if not continuously then fairly frequently throughout the eighteenth century, and therefore gained the same immunity as their parents.[22] This acquired immunity was widely interpreted as being innate by medical practitioners because they did not recognize the relatively mild childhood illness as yellow fever.[23] The error is entirely understandable since it bore little resemblance to the violent and often fatal version that affected adults.

The virulent strain of yellow fever that arrived in the West Indies in 1793 did not completely exempt black people but the mortality rate was comparatively low. Chisholm in Grenada recorded that while 'the disease began to appear among the negroes of the estates in the neighbourhood of town … [it] did not spread much among them, nor was it marked with the fatality which attended it when it appeared among the whites'. He estimated 'that only about one in four was seized with it; and the proportion of its mortality was still more trifling, viz, one to 83'.[24] Europeans, who were far less likely to have acquired immunity, suffered acutely from this more dangerous strain, with mortality rates upwards of 30 per cent.[25]

The impact on the British regiments stationed on the various islands was immediate and severe. These soldiers were nearly all born in Europe and few would have had a previous encounter with yellow fever. It is very likely that none had acquired immunity. Surgeon Thomas Reide recalled that the 'army in St Lucia suffered a great deal from sickness; and hardly an officer or private soldier escaped. The mortality was very great.'[26] William Pym, serving with the 70th Regiment in Martinique, reported that 'after the appearance of fever in Grenada in 1793, every station for troops, however healthy before, suffered severely from the contagion'. Using the muster rolls for each regiment, Pym documented the destruction wrought on the army by yellow fever. In 1794 the 9th Regiment in St Kitts lost 118 men, the 15th Regiment in Dominica lost 93 men, the 13th Regiment in Jamaica lost 136 men, and the 66th Regiment in St Domingue lost 249 men. The 69th Regiment lost 313 men within six months of arriving in St Domingue in 1795. These were exceptional losses, far above the usual mortality in the West Indies. The 9th Regiment, for instance, had lost only seventeen men in six years between 1787 and 1793.[27]

With hindsight, the decision by the British to invade St Domingue in September 1793 in the midst of a yellow fever epidemic was disastrous. Despite initial gains made in partnership with French royalist planters, outbreaks of yellow fever in 1794 and 1795 in particular, devastated newly-arrived regiments. David Geggus has estimated that more than 12,000 British soldiers perished in the five years of the St Domingue campaign. At one point, between August and December 1794, regiments were losing 10 per cent of their men each month. One French planter glumly informed the Duke of Portland that '[t]he small detachments of troops which you send out from time to time, are not even sufficient to supply the ravages of disease'.[28] The debilitated state of those who had survived yellow fever left regiments incapable of offensive operations.[29]

The rapid spread of the new strain of yellow fever among British troops quartered in St Domingue's ports proved especially devastating. *Aedes Aegyptii* is an urban mosquito and therefore it is unsurprising that in Port-au-Prince, according to one report, soldiers 'dropt like the leaves in autumn', and all this 'without a contest with any other enemy than sickness'.[30] One military surgeon stationed in St Domingue observed that 'our hospitals contain our garrisons, and the few who carry on duty are languid and convalescent; they are not fit for enterprize or hazard; and nominal armies will never achieve conquests'.[31] Spurred by the example of the French who had enlisted the support of many thousands of former slaves, and with operations 'unfortunately crippled by the unprecedented sickness prevailing among His Majesty's naval and military forces', British commanders in St Domingue began recruiting small numbers of local 'negroes to be embodied & to act against the Brigands'.[32] By late 1794, 400 slaves were 'performing all the most active and laborious services', which, it was hoped, 'would contribute in no small degree, to preserve the health of the regular troops'.[33] Less than a year later, the British forces in St Domingue were so weak they 'could hardly mount a sergeant's guard', and they completely relied on the 'black corps, [to] occupy all the advanced posts'.[34]

The consensus of medical professionals in St Domingue was that the only possible path to victory against those native to the island was 'by an army of negroes, possessed of the same habits as themselves, but more expert in arms, and led on by such a proportion of European troops as might animate and encourage them'. Hector M'Lean, assistant inspector of hospitals in St Domingue, believed that had this strategy been adopted early in the campaign it 'would have produced the most beneficial effects; the lives of thousands, who have fallen, not by the sword of the enemy, but by the climate, would have been spared; and the conquest of the island would become more certain and more rapid'. M'Lean was convinced that the embodiment of black soldiers as regular troops would 'more effectually ... diminish the mortality of British soldiers in St. Domingo ... than all the medical exertions of the most experienced and skilful physicians'.[35] Robert Jackson, resident in Port-au-Prince in November 1797 and who observed first-hand the 'blast of pestilence', estimated that about two-thirds of any European garrison would perish from disease each year in St Domingue.[36] The British withdrew ignominiously from St Domingue in 1798, having been unable to secure sufficient black troops to retain what little territory they still held.

The situation had been bad in St Domingue, and has attracted scholarly interest because the excessive mortality was concentrated in one place, but in reality was no worse than elsewhere in the Caribbean. Indeed more British soldiers perished collectively in Dominica, Grenada, St Lucia and other Leeward Islands than in

St Domingue. General Charles Grey was forced to postpone one planned attack on a French island, garrisoned by 'four thousand blacks and mulattoes in arms', due to the 'sickness and mortality' that prevailed amongst his troops. There was, he concluded, 'not even a prospect of success'.[37] Grey repatriated some units to Britain in late 1794 that were 'very weak, and almost reduced to skeletons' and Grey's replacement in the West Indies, General John Vaughan, reported that the 'great sickness and mortality which has prevailed since May last, has broken the strength of all the regiments'.[38] After more than a year of yellow fever whittling away at the army '[t]he whole force in all the islands does not exceed fifteen hundred men', with new regiments tending to 'fall victim to the climate or are in the hospital before another arrives; this renders me incapable of acting decisively and with vigour'.[39] Vaughan fretted that he did not know 'where this army may look for further reinforcements' since 'the climate will reduce it in some months, to a similar situation in which it now is'.[40]

The desperate situation of the army revitalized the idea of using black troops, and not just in support or auxiliary roles. With his army disintegrating around him, Vaughan came rapidly to 'the opinion that a corps of one thousand men, composed of blacks and mulattoes, and commanded by British Officers would render more essential service in the country, than treble the number of Europeans who are unaccustomed to the climate'.[41] Those of African descent were already known in military circles to be resistant to tropical diseases, particularly yellow fever. Dr Robert Jackson, who had extensive experience in the West Indies and later became surgeon-general of the army, claimed in 1791 with reference to yellow fever that 'it has never been observed that a negro, immediately from the coast of Africa, has been attacked with this disease'.[42] Established medical opinion therefore conveniently dovetailed with genuine military need.

In December 1794, having lost Guadaloupe to a French force consisting of 'four to five hundred whites, and four or five thousand blacks, who are all armed with muskets and bayonets', General Vaughan formally proposed to authorities in London that the army should 'avail ourselves of the service of the negroes' and, significantly, as regular troops 'to be in all respects upon the same footing as the marching regiments'. In purely military terms this made perfect sense: 'as the enemy have adopted this measure to recruit their armies, I think we should pursue a similar plan to meet them on equal terms'. It was simply foolish that 'we have been overlooking the support, which by exertion may be derived from opposing blacks to blacks'.[43] But the medical rationale was actually even more compelling. Vaughan urged that 'it may be taken into consideration, what great mortality ensues among our troops from the fatigues of service in this climate'. Each British soldier represented an investment of time, training and resources, thus each life saved was 'saving an extraordinary expence to the nation'. Vaughan was 'convinced that unless we can establish and procure the full effect of such a body of men, to strengthen our own troops, and to save them in a thousand situations, from service, which in this country will always destroy them; that the army of Great Britain is inadequate to supply a sufficient force to defend these colonies'.[44] Moreover military and medical necessity required the units to be properly organized and capable of functioning independently, since it was quite likely that they would be the single healthy regiment at each post.

While awaiting official approval for his plan, Vaughan tried to ensure that white troops 'should be spared on every possible occasion' and therefore dispatched the remnants of the Carolina Corps to tackle 'the revolted Negroes at St. Lucia ... to endeavor to drive them from their retreat on a mountain', which was deemed 'a proper enterprize on which to employ the blacks, and to save our own soldiers'.[45] He also authorized Capt. Robert Malcolm of the 34th Regiment to 'raise a considerable number ... [of] mulattoes and blacks, to be on the same footing as the troops of the line ... paying them as troops are paid'.[46] The case for black troops was strengthened by a letter, written by eight army physicians, that Vaughan received and duly forwarded to London. These men, 'having had too great occasion to observe the destructive effects of this climate on the health of the soldiers', deplored that 'too many of the soldiers in spite of our best endeavours fall sacrifices to acute disease'. Even those who did not die immediately were left to 'pine away under lingering chronic' illnesses because the unhealthy climate was an 'insuperable bar' to recovery.[47] These physicians held out no prospect that white troops would ever thrive in the West Indies.

The weight of opinion from both physicians and military commanders in the West Indies was thus that medical necessity required a formal shift in British strategy. It was not that Britain lacked sufficient troops. Time and again in the 1790s Britain managed to find, equip and train enough men to fight in pursuit of its imperial agenda. There were always jails that could be emptied, or men desperate enough to accept the King's shilling and join up. Men were not the problem, but finding the right kind of men, particularly for tropical service, proved far harder. In April 1795, Dundas wrote that after 'a full and deliberate consideration' the government had decided to accept 'the concurrent opinions of almost every officer of rank who has lately been employed in the West Indies' and proceed with the plan as quickly as possible.[48] In the intervening period, Dundas had received several letters from Vaughan indicating the effectiveness of black militia units that were operating in St Lucia and Guadaloupe.[49] Moreover, the issue was raised in a debate on the slave trade in the House Commons on 26 February. William Wilberforce pointed out the weakness of British power in the West Indies since the French 'had formed and disciplined them [their former slaves] to the use of arms' and that as a result they would 'acquire dominion in a climate, where labour, fatigue, and death to our men, were amusement to them'.[50] Approval from London finally arrived in Martinique on 16 June, providing Vaughan 'much satisfaction'. A letter to Vaughan from General Nicholls in Grenada, reporting that '[t]he dreadful fever raging here has weakened the militia of the town of St. George's so much that I have been obliged to call in two of the militia black compy', completely vindicated his persistence over the recruitment of black troops.[51] Sadly Vaughan's satisfaction was short-lived; he died at the end of July from the same disease, yellow fever, that had rendered his forces so ineffective.

Opposition from colonial legislatures unwilling to provide slaves for the army, as well as the logistical complexity of creating new regiments from scratch, meant that approval from London did not immediately transform the situation. Major-General Irving reported to Henry Dundas in August 1795 that the army was 'greatly diminished by death, exhausted by fatigue & the disorders incident to this inclement climate' and Vaughan's successor as commander-in-chief, Major-General Leigh, echoed this in

October: 'I cannot help lamenting the very distressing state of this army from present sickness and the great loss it has sustained by death.'[52] Even in Martinique, the headquarters of the army in the Leeward Islands and perhaps the most vulnerable to a French counter-attack, one corps had 'nearly three hundred sick out of five hundred and twenty rank and file'.[53] With the plan to raise black regiments 'having in no way succeeded' and 'not a man having been given by any one of the Islands towards completing them', Leigh co-opted the informal black militias that had been raised in Dominica and St Vincent by local commanders.[54] These men were to be used for 'local and temporary services' since they offered 'considerable advantages ... in the present state of the colonies'.[55] A month later, 1,109 black troops, drawn from the Royal Rangers, Guadaloupe Rangers and Dominica Rangers assembled in Barbados. Only eighty-four reported sick.[56]

Sir Ralph Abercromby, who assumed command of offensive operations in the Caribbean in 1796, was well aware of 'the many obvious advantages' offered by black troops, particularly when facing 'four thousand black troops at St Lucia' and 'eight thousand well disciplined troops of colour' in Guadaluope. As every regimental return seemed to record an ever-diminishing force, Abercromby's hopes of a rapid and successful military campaign against the French islands dwindled. Reporting that 'six British battalions have been nearly annihilated' by 'the great sickness', his only recourse was the 'completion of the Black Corps' as quickly as possible.[57] Continued opposition by local legislatures who refused to provide the men, fearing the 'most dangerous consequences' of arming enslaved men, ultimately forced Abercromby to conclude that '[t]he Black West India Regt have not gain'd an inch of ground, and there is no prospect of their being completed, unless the negroes are either purchased here, or upon the coast of Africa'.[58] Such a policy would involve expense, 'considerably beyond any calculation hitherto made', but nevertheless Henry Dundas agreed, authorizing Abercromby 'to procure in this manner the number that may be necessary for this purpose'.[59] Evidently the arguments in favour of black troops – that they had greater resistance to Caribbean diseases and were crucial to Britain's hopes of retaining its colonies – had not diminished in the slightest between 1795 and 1797.

Agents purchasing slaves were instructed to pay higher prices for a 'seasoned recruit' who had been in the West Indies for a period of time and was thus deemed to be accustomed to the disease environment, but the only viable way to assess this was by testing each recruit's knowledge of a European language.[60] Despite the premium offered for seasoned men, the army found it almost impossible to purchase prime male slaves in the Caribbean. Slavery remained hugely profitable and planters prized young men above all other enslaved people for the work that could be extracted from them. Men sold to the army would need to be replaced, a potentially troublesome business, and considering that many planters fundamentally disagreed with the principle of arming black men, it is not surprising that the army found few willing to sell. Unseasoned men, straight from Africa, were the only remaining recourse and by March 1798 General Cuyler was 'decidedly of opinion that it is preferable to purchase new negroes, rather than to enlist any who have been for a lengthy time in this country'.[61] The perils of this shift became obvious within weeks. The Governor of Dominica observed that at £56 each, 'the contract was too low, and bad negroes were in consequence given' and as a result 'they are now dying in dozens at Fort George and I am assured of consumption'.[62] Nevertheless this policy became the norm and, up to the closing of the transatlantic slave trade in 1807, Roger Buckley estimates that the army spent nearly £1 million on 13,400 enslaved men for the West India Regiments.[63]

The policy of purchasing men from slave ships to augment those already under arms in informal militia units increased the number of black troops in the British Army to more than 4,000 by 1800. The sickness and mortality statistics reported to the war office confirmed the massive immunity advantage enjoyed by those of African descent. In 1796 the mortality rate for white troops in the West Indies was 34 per cent, but for black troops it was just 3 per cent. Over the next six years mortality rates improved for Whites, and worsened for Blacks, but still the average mortality rate for Blacks of 6 per cent was less than a third of that of Whites at 19 per cent.[64] A survey of all the West India Regiments in 1798 listed 83.8 per cent of troops as fit and ready for duty, prompting Henry Dundas to urge commanders in the Caribbean 'to make every possible exertion for the completion of the black regiments'.[65] Completion of the West India Regiments up to their establishment of 500 men each would aid 'the preservation of the health of the European troops, by relieving them in those stations which, from the peculiar causes, are found most noxious to their constitutions, and by performing those duties of fatigue to which they are much better adapted than our own troops'.[66]

Although the army owned these men as slaves, it did not treat them like enslaved people were usually treated in the West Indies. All the men were paid, for instance, and those injured or otherwise incapable of performing their military duties were pensioned off and not sold. The British Army was a curious slaveholder: it fed, housed and equipped its black soldiers in a very similar manner to its white soldiers, and both were subject to (admittedly harsh) military discipline. The problem for the army was that many of the initial recruits to the West India Regiments were not enslaved. A number were free blacks from conquered French islands such as Martinique and Guadaloupe; a few were free blacks from British islands or from British North America who had been evacuated to the West Indies following the American Revolution; some even listed their place of birth as India, England, Scotland and especially Ireland.[67] The West India Regiments were not as uniformly African in their earliest years as they would later become. With a heterogeneous mix of free and slave, creole and African, and Black and White, it would have been impossible for commanders to try to treat the men they had purchased differently to the other men. Far easier to treat all equally and in line with established military practice.

When John Poyer wrote his *History of Barbados* in 1808 the rationale for the creation of the West India Regiments was absolutely clear in his mind: 'the extraordinary mortality among the British troops in the West Indies, induced the ministry to adopt the scheme of raising black regiments, who, being inured to the climate, were thought to be better adapted to the service than Europeans'.[68] Increased awareness of black resistance, and white vulnerability, to tropical diseases (particularly yellow fever) was therefore the imperative behind the creation of the West India Regiments. The opposition of local colonial legislatures to armed and trained black men, who might act as an encouragement to the enslaved population to rebel, was overridden by the unanimity of successive commanders-in-chief in the Caribbean and secretaries of state in Whitehall. The issue was never insufficient white troops, or the distance involved in transporting men from Britain to the West Indies. If those had been the most important factors then the case would surely have been made much earlier in the eighteenth century for the incorporation of slave men into the army. In fact, Britain recruited and shipped tens of thousands of soldiers to the West Indies in the 1790s, more than sufficient to achieve their military goals of conquering the French islands. The problem was that the army simply could not keep enough of them alive to do this. The new and virulent strain of yellow fever introduced in 1793 confirmed in military minds the need for a new approach. Amid much soul searching as to the best way to reduce mortality among white troops, including sending healthier men to begin with, improving diet and accommodation, while reducing rum intake, the solution that ultimately emerged was finding troops who simply did not die in such great numbers. Physicians and surgeons serving in the Caribbean were unanimous that the only men who could do this were Africans.

Notes

1 Dundas to Vaughan, 17 April 1795, WO1/83, The National Archives, London. [All subsequent references to WO materials are in The National Archives.]
2 Roger Buckley, *Slaves in Redcoats: The British West India Regiments, 1795–1815* (New Haven, CT: Yale University Press, 1979), 2–6.
3 John Bell, *An inquiry into the causes which produce and the means of preventing diseases among British officers, soldiers and others in the West Indies* (London: J. Murray, 1791), 1.
4 John Hunter, *Observations on the diseases of the army in Jamaica* (London: G. Nicol, 1788), 70–1.
5 Bell, *An inquiry into the causes*, 8.
6 Hunter, *Observations on the diseases*, 24, 192.
7 Maria Alessandra Bollettino '"Of equal or of more service": Black Soldiers and the British Empire in the mid-Eighteenth-Century Caribbean', *Slavery & Abolition* 38, no. 3 (2017): 521; Benjamin Moseley, *A Treatise on Tropical diseases on military operations*, 2nd edn (London: T. Cadell, 1789), 184; Patrick Mackellar, *A correct journal of the landing His Majesty's forces on the island of Cuba* (London: Green & Russell, 1762), 6.
8 Moseley, *A Treatise on Tropical diseases*, 181.
9 Hunter, *Observations on the diseases*, 36.
10 Alex Dirom, *Thoughts on the state of the militia of Jamaica Nov 1783* (Jamaica: Douglass & Aikman, 1783), 14.
11 John Gosling to The Marquis of Carmarthen, *c.* October 1787, British Library Add MS 28062 (f.378) in the correspondence of the 5th Duke of Leeds v.3, 1787.
12 'Of the Carolina, or Black Corps, serving in the Leeward Islands', CO101/31.
13 For a thorough account of the *Hankey*'s voyage, see Billy G. Smith, *Ship of Death: A Voyage that Changed the Atlantic World* (New Haven, CT: Yale University Press 2013).
14 Philip Beaver, *African Memoranda relative to an attempt to establish a British settlement on the island of Bulama* (London: C & R Baldwin, 1805), 104, 130, 159, 181, 190.
15 Beaver, *African Memoranda*, 471.

16 Colin Chisholm, *An essay on the malignant pestilential fever introduced into the West Indian Islands from Boullam, on the coast of Guinea, as it appeared in 1793 and 1794* (London: C. Dilly, 1795), 82–95.
17 Chisholm, *An essay on the malignant pestilential fever*, 95–6, 98.
18 James Clark, *A treatise on the yellow fever as it appeared in the island of Dominica in the years 1793-4-5-6* (London: J. Murray, 1797), 2; Chisholm, *An essay on the malignant pestilential fever*, 102; William Wright, *Memoir of the late William Wright* (Edinburgh: William Blackwood, 1828), 372.
19 *The Times*, 13 August 1793, The Times online database.
20 *Bury and Norwich Post*, 1 January 1794, British Newspaper Archive.
21 Chisholm, *An essay on the malignant pestilential fever*, 99.
22 Kenneth F. Kiple and Virginia H. Kiple, 'Black Yellow Fever Immunities, Innate and Acquired, as Revealed in the American South', *Social Science History* 1 (1977): 419–36.
23 Rana A. Hogarth, *Medicalizing Blackness: Making Racial Difference in the Atlantic World, 1780-1840* (Chapel Hill: University of North Carolina Press, 2017), 41–3.
24 Chisholm, *An essay on the malignant pestilential fever*, 97.
25 Chisholm, *An essay on the malignant pestilential fever*, 102.
26 Thomas Dickson Reide, *A view of the diseases of the army in Great Britain, America, the West Indies* (London: J. Johnson, 1793), 191.
27 William Pym, *Observations on Bulam Fever which has of late years prevailed in the West Indies, on the coast of America, At Gibraltar, Cadiz and other parts of Spain* (London: J. Callow, 1815), 128, 130–2.
28 Malouet to Duke of Portland, c. 20 September 1794, WO1/59.
29 Williamson to Dundas, 1 August 1794, WO1/60.
30 Bryan Edwards, *The History, Civil and commercial of the British Colonies in the West Indies* (London: John Stockdale, 1801), III, 174; Bryan Edwards, *An historical survey of the French colony in the island of St. Domingo* (London: John Stockdale, 1797), 164.
31 Hector M'Lean, *An enquiry into the nature, and causes of the great mortality among the troops at St. Domingo* (London: T. Cadell, 1797), 40.
32 Dundas to Williamson, 10 February 1795, Dundas to Williamson, 7 October 1794, both WO1/60.
33 Dundas to Williamson, 6 November 1794, WO1/60.
34 Williamson to Duke of Portland, 6 July 1795, WO1/61.
35 M'Lean, *An enquiry into the nature*, 2, 3, 5.
36 Robert Jackson, *An outline of the history and cure of fever, endemic and contagious* (Edinburgh, Mundell & Son, 1798), 249, 98–9.
37 Grey to Williamson, 10 May 1794; Henry Dundas, *Facts relative to the conduct of the war in the West Indies* (London: J. Owen, 1796), 132.
38 Grey to Duke of Portland, 5 November 1794, WO1/83; Vaughan to the Duke of Portland, 24 November 1794, WO1/31.
39 Vaughan to the Duke of Portland, 19 November 1794, WO1/83.
40 Vaughan to the Duke of Portland, 24 November 1794, WO1/31.
41 Vaughan to the Duke of Portland, 22 December 1794, WO1/31.
42 Robert Jackson, *A treatise on the fevers of Jamaica, with some observations on the intermitting fever of America* (London: J. Murray, 1791), 249–50.
43 Vaughan to the Duke of Portland, 22 December 1794, WO1/31; Vaughan to Dundas, 'Secret No 6', 25 December 1794, WO1/83.
44 Vaughan to the Duke of Portland, 24 November 1794, WO1/31; Vaughan to Dundas, 'Secret No 6', 25 December 1794, WO1/83.

45 Vaughan to the Duke of Portland, 26 January 1795, WO1/31; Vaughan to Dundas, 31 January 1795, WO1/83.
46 Vaughan to Dundas, 'Secret No 9', 11 January 1795, WO1/83.
47 Army surgeons to Vaughan, 23 March 1795, WO1/83.
48 Dundas to Vaughan, 17 April 1795, WO1/83.
49 See Vaughan to Dundas, 'Secret No 9', 11 January 1795, Vaughan to Dundas, 30 January 1795, Vaughan to Dundas, 31 January 1795, Vaughan to Dundas, 'Secret No 13', 25 February 1795, all WO1/83.
50 *The Times*, 27 February 1795.
51 Nicholls to Vaughan, 22 June 1795, WO1/83.
52 Irving to Dundas, August 1795, Leigh to Dundas, 2 October 1795, both WO1/84.
53 Leigh to Dundas, 8 October 1795, WO1/84.
54 Leigh to Dundas, 5 December 1795, WO1/85.
55 Dundas to Abercomby, 9 February 1796, WO1/85.
56 Return of a Brigade of Black Troops Barbadoes, 10 March 1796, WO1/85.
57 Abercromby to Dundas, 16 January 1797, WO1/86.
58 Abercromby to the Governors of Windward & Leeward Islands, 3 January 1797, Ricketts to Abercromby, 18 January 1797, both WO1/86; Abercromby to Dundas, 9 April 1796, WO1/85.
59 Abercromby to Dundas, 16 January 1797, WO1/86; Dundas to Abercromby, 28 October 1796, WO1/85.
60 Heads of Instructions to Major Genl Hunter, 26 January 1797, Instructions for the officers and medical staff, both WO1/86.
61 Cuyler to Dundas, 8 March 1798, WO1/86.
62 Cochrane to Dundas, 15 May 1798, Cochrane to Dundas, 7 June 1798, both WO1/88.
63 Buckley, *Slaves in Redcoats*, 55.
64 Abstract of British West Indian Trade and Navigation from 1773 to 1805, British Library, MSS Stowe 921, p32v.
65 Return of the West India Regiments, 6 September 1798, WO1/86; Dundas to Trigge, 17 May 1799, WO1/87.
66 Dundas to Trigge, 11 October 1800, WO1/89.
67 The earliest muster records of the West India Regiments are far from complete, but a few do survive; see, for example, WO25/653 for the 4th West India Regiment, 1796–1818, and WO25/657 for the 6th West India Regiment, 1797–1806.
68 John Poyer, *The History of Barbados from the first discovery of the Island* (London: J. Mawman, 1808), 624.

8

'A question between hiring and selling': Slave Leasing at Thomas Jefferson's Monticello, 1780–1830

Christa Dierksheide

In 1828, Thomas Jefferson's sister, Anne Scott Jefferson Marks, was on her deathbed, having lived in the North Octagonal Room at Monticello for seventeen years. By the summer, Jefferson's granddaughter, Cornelia Randolph, reported that 'her eyes were fixed, her features distorted, her breath came at long intervals her hands were cold & her pulse gone'. After battling a cancerous ulcer, 'Aunt Marks' looked 'so much like death that aunt Scilla sent for mama'. Indeed, it was Priscilla Hemings, an enslaved nursemaid and the sister-in-law of Sally Hemings, who 'has nursed her through the whole with a care & attention as unwearied as it is watchful, bearing patiently with the fretfulness & ill humour of disease & discomfort, sleeping in her room at night & watching by her during the greater part of the day'. Marks owned slaves at Monticello, but none of them had attended their mistress in the main house, or likely even crossed its threshold.[1]

While Marks resided on Jefferson's mountaintop among Hemings and Randolph family members, several of her own enslaved labourers lived at the bottom of the mountain, in close proximity to the overseer, Edmund Bacon, as well as Jefferson's own enslaved farm workers. From at least 1816 to 1824, Jefferson leased four different slaves from his sister: a man named Peter, and a woman, Sally, as well as her children, Fernil and Nancy. Sally bore a third child, Charlotte, at Monticello in 1816. Jefferson recorded that he paid a midwife for delivering the child for 'Mrs. Mark's Sally'. Jefferson hired Sally, who probably worked in the fields, for around $25 a year. She and her children were given clothing and food rations, and likely lived together in a single-family log dwelling located about a mile from the mountaintop. In the winter of 1817, Sally received a 'bed' – a burlap sack filled with straw – while her two daughters, one aged two and the other aged five, shared a new woollen blanket.[2]

The story of Marks and her human property sheds light on a relatively understudied aspect of slavery in the post-revolutionary era at Monticello and elsewhere in the Upper South: slave leasing. It also underscores another important point: Jefferson did not own all of the enslaved people who lived and worked at Monticello, and nor was he the only slaveholder. This runs counter to the image that Jefferson constructed of himself as the all-powerful master of Monticello, the 'most blessed of the patriarchs' who had 'my house to build, my fields to form, and to watch for the happiness of those who labour for mine'.³ On paper, Thomas Jefferson appeared to be the very autarkic slaveholder and elite planter that he imagined himself to be. When he was twenty-one, Jefferson inherited thirty enslaved people from the estate of his father, Peter Jefferson. And after his marriage to Martha Wayles in 1772, Jefferson acquired an additional 135 slaves and became the owner of over 14,000 acres of land that stretched across four plantations in the Virginia piedmont.⁴ By the time he drafted the iconic words of the Declaration of Independence in the summer of 1776, Jefferson, as the owner of several far-flung tobacco estates and 187 human beings, was one of the wealthiest men in the colony. A year before the truce with Britain was over, in 1782, Jefferson appeared to have maintained his privileged status – he was the second largest slaveholder in Albemarle County.⁵

But Jefferson's idealized image of himself as 'living like an Antideluvian patriarch among my children and grand children, and tilling my soil' was problematic.⁶ In reality, Jefferson embraced the market in rented slaves, hiring up to sixteen men a year, and leasing a total of approximately eighty-two slaves from thirty different owners between 1768 and 1824. He also hired out over 100 of his own slaves to local artisans and tenant farmers who leased portions of his 5,000-acre plantation, which was comprised of the Shadwell, Monticello, Lego and Tufton quarter farms. The complex hiring network at Monticello included Jefferson, his sons-in-law, his overseers, free white artisans, his own slaves, leased slaves and the owners of hired slaves. Over time, slaveholding at Monticello evolved to be far from the traditional and patriarchal one that Jefferson wanted outside observers to imagine. And the nature of slavery at Monticello, in Virginia and beyond, was changing and expanding in this period, often as a result of forces put into motion, knowingly or not, by planter-statesmen like Jefferson.⁷

Recent scholarship focusing on slave hiring has offered useful correctives to the more traditional, and certainly more static, view of a single planter lording over his extensive human property. One scholar contends that 'above 15 percent of enslaved people in the South as a whole could expect to be hired out at any one time';⁸ another historian estimates that slaves were three to five times more likely to be hired than sold.⁹ In the post-revolutionary era of declining tobacco profits in the Chesapeake, slave hiring allowed owners to generate a new form of income. Together with the abolition of entail and primogeniture, slave hiring further illustrated the democratization of slaveholding by giving more Whites the opportunity and shared interest in owning human property, whether temporarily or permanently. Still, scholars remain divided about whether slave hiring, which added a third party to the traditional master–slave relationship, weakened slavery by dividing 'mastery', or whether it strengthened and perpetuated the system.¹⁰

Recent literature on slave leasing in the Upper South has suggested that the growing hiring market underscored the increasingly commercial nature of enslavement.¹¹ But that slavery, and the markets that undergirded it, would expand in the post-revolutionary era was not a given. Many patriots, including Jefferson, assumed that slavery would end in America after it was divested of the transatlantic slave trade and the British tobacco market. As Walter Johnson has noted, 'slavery in the United States was a declining institution' at the end of the eighteenth century.¹² Soil exhaustion from tobacco monoculture, the switch to wheat production and the use of wage labour in the Upper South appeared to forecast slavery's demise. In 1785, Jefferson observed that in the North, 'emancipation is put into such a train that in a few years there will be no slaves Northward of Maryland'. He expected the ensuing diffusion of anti-slavery sentiment – what he called 'that interesting spectacle of justice' – to Virginia and Maryland, resulting in gradual emancipation laws.[13] Here Jefferson followed the predictions of Adam Smith, who had argued that only colonies cultivating tobacco or sugar could afford slavery, because of the 'exorbitancy of their profites'. By contrast, farmers growing 'chiefly wheat and Indian corn' who had no 'exorbitant returns' believed it 'not for their interest' to employ many slaves, if any at all. In these economies, Smith surmised, the switch to free labour was inevitable.[14]

But 'King Cotton' soon proved both Jefferson and Smith wrong. In the first decades of the nineteenth century, new 'free land' that became available in the south-west after US federal troops decimated or 'removed' the Creek, Chickasaw, Choctaw, Seminole and Cherokee tribes opened the door to cotton cultivation. Federal officials mapped and surveyed former tribal lands and then sold them to speculators or individuals through the General Land Office. This land was then cleared and drained in anticipation of what would later become the 'cotton belt', a vast swath of land that began in the upcountry of the Carolinas and extended westward through Georgia, Alabama, Tennessee, Mississippi, Arkansas, Louisiana and later Texas. The millions of 'hands' needed to build this cotton empire helped initiate a robust and tragic innovation of the antebellum era: the increased value and commoditization of slave bodies. As a result, the emergence of two new 'technologies' of the American slave empire – slave hiring and the domestic slave trade – indicated not simply the survival of slavery, but also the speed and scale of its expansion.[15] Indeed, as historian Calvin Schermerhorn has noted, 'rather than being domesticated, slavery was increasingly commercialized' and 'each new commercial technology presented new challenges and perils for the enslaved'.[16]

And Virginia lay at the heart of this transformation. With the self-reproduction of its slave population, which increased from 287,959 in 1790 to 453,698 in 1830, Virginia became, as the former slave Louis Hughes recalled, the 'mother of slavery'.[17] Not only did Virginia claim the largest slave population in the federal union, but it also served as the primary supplier of enslaved labourers to other states through the domestic slave trade, which transported nearly one million enslaved men, women and children to the Deep South between 1820 and 1860. Jefferson's neighbour, John Hartwell Cocke, also noted the insidious effects of a large 'surplus' slave population and the increased value of slave bodies in Virginia. Many plantations, Cocke suggested, were transformed into 'a sort of breeding Farm of human stock', with planters selling slaves to 'speculators for transportation to the South'. Increasingly, white Virginians, Cocke asserted, had come to believe that their 'profits consists in the increased number & value of their slaves', rather than in the crops they produced.[18]

But it was not just slavery that was changing in post-revolutionary Virginia; so too was slaveholding. In fact, by 1800, more than half of white households in the Piedmont and Tidewater regions of Virginia owned at least one slave, and the majority of slaveholding households looked nothing like Jefferson's. Indeed, of the 52,128 Virginians who held over 400,000 slaves in bondage by 1860, 11,085 of them possessed only one slave.[19] The diffusion of slaveholding across Virginia was a result of the post-revolutionary democratization of property laws. The abolition of entail in 1776 and primogeniture in 1785 meant that the ownership of both land and slaves became more feasible for non-elite whites in Virginia.[20] Jefferson, who drafted the statutes to abolish entail and primogeniture during and after the outbreak of the Revolution, wanted to break up the 'hereditary highhanded aristocracy'. He hoped that dividing the 'immense masses of property' would put an end to the division of 'citizens into two distinct orders of nobles and plebians'. But just as huge tracts of land had remained in the hands of the same dynastic families during the colonial era, so too had slaves. As real property, slaves had remained attached to estates as they passed from generation to generation of slaveholders within the same family. But after the Revolution, Virginia law redefined enslaved people as personal property, or 'distributable among the next of kin, as other moveables'.[21] The waning power of pre-revolutionary tobacco barons coupled with the liberalization of property laws gave rise to a new 'middle class' of slaveowners in Virginia. These 'successful overseers' and 'enterprising cultivators' were 'persons who own slaves without Land' or who 'hire their negroes out in the towns or elsewhere as they find employment, and live upon their wages'.[22] Jefferson had predicted that the democratization of property laws in Virginia would erode slavery – a system he believed to be perpetuated through 'aristocracy' – but this did not happen. Non-elite Whites, eager to use slave labour and slave bodies to accumulate capital and increase their social status, helped fuel the development of a burgeoning slave-hiring market in post-revolutionary Virginia.[23]

And yet, as this chapter will demonstrate, the practice of slave hiring at Jefferson's Monticello between the 1780s and 1826 did not indicate an inevitable expansion of the 'peculiar institution' in the eyes of all Virginians. Instead, a complex and nuanced portrait of slave leasing suggests just how contested, contingent and protean this new market really was. On the one hand, Jefferson viewed slave leasing as a mitigating force, a preferable alternative to the horrors of the slave trade: it prevented the separation of families and the certainty of hard labour or death in the Deep South while still allowing him to generate income. And crucially, while slave selling threatened Jefferson's image of himself as a benevolent patriarch, slave leasing only preserved and perpetuated him as a master who sought to 'ameliorate' not just his own slaves, but also those who belonged to others. Yet many of the white men and women who leased their human chattel to Jefferson did so for different reasons. Widows, overseers, and executors of indebted estates rented slaves to Jefferson rather than sell them through the domestic slave trade not because they harboured anti-slavery beliefs or sought to be more humane masters, but because they could make more money: the annual hire of slaves would likely net greater returns than the one-time sale of an enslaved person. But by engaging in the slave-hiring market and helping to democratize slaveholding in Virginia, Jefferson contributed to the evolution and entrenchment of the slave system in ways he had not anticipated.[24]

The problem of debt

Even with extensive holdings in land and slaves, the American Revolution had decimated Thomas Jefferson's wealth. After 1783, he and other debt-ridden American planters scrambled to satisfy their British creditors and rushed to develop new trade and credit networks in order to survive in the post-colonial world. Jefferson, responsible for ever-increasing debts incurred by himself, his parents and his father-in-law, the slave trader John Wayles, struggled to develop a plan to regain his solvency in the 1780s.[25] It was clear that Jefferson's Monticello plantation in particular was not generating enough income. The 'profits of the whole estate' were 'no more than' the profit generated by 'the few negroes hired out'.[26] The most plausible strategy, he wrote from his diplomatic post in France, was the 'idea of renting out my whole estate; not to any one person, but in different parts to different persons'.[27] Leasing out his 'plantations and all' seemed like the only viable option that would allow Jefferson to retain ownership of his lands and preserve them for future generations, particularly his two daughters. The realities of indebtedness forced Jefferson to endorse the 'idea of renting' out a portion of lands at his Albemarle, Goochland and Bedford plantations, a scheme that included the lease of his slaves. Indeed, between the 1790s and his death, much of the land and dozens of the slaves on the Monticello quarter farms were leased out to various tenant farmers.[28]

Jefferson argued that renting out his slaves with his land was preferable to selling them through the domestic slave trade. 'Hiring presents a hopeful prospect,' Jefferson declared in the wake of the Revolution, not because it represented a new way of expanding slavery in Virginia, but because it would allow him to retain ownership of his slaves and possibly free them at a future date.[29] Buckling under the weight of his crushing debts, Jefferson thought he had only two options. 'In a question between hiring and selling them [slaves] (one of which is necessary),' he wrote, the 'hiring will be temporary only, and will end in their happiness,' which Jefferson defined as improved material conditions and the ability to remain with their families. On the other hand, he wrote, 'if we sell them, they will be subject to ill usage without a prospect of change' and likely be sold south through the internal slave trade. Jefferson felt the 'weight of the objection' for either option, since 'we cannot guard the negroes perfectly against ill usage'. In the absence of any real solution, he believed that mitigation of the 'evil' was the only viable option.[30]

Despite Jefferson's knowledge of the domestic slave trade as a commerce that exacted terror on its victims and divided families, Jefferson did sell slaves in an effort to manage his debts. Between 1784 and 1794 he dispensed with eighty-four slaves. At his Elkhill plantation, in Goochland County, Jefferson directed that thirty-one slaves be sold in 1785. About seven years later, he sold three more groups of slaves from his Albemarle and Bedford estates. In December of 1791, twenty-nine enslaved people yielded over $4,000 on the auction block; another sale there a year later in Bedford brought nearly $2,000 for eleven people. And, in January of 1792, thirteen slaves were sold away from Monticello. Together, these sales netted Jefferson over $15,000. Still, to prevent further slave sales, Jefferson began to engage in slave hiring and also double 150 slaves to friendly creditors in 1796; this, he gambled, would shield his human property from being seized by men who were pursuing legal action against the estate of his father-in-law.[31]

But even if leasing his enslaved bondspeople was preferable to selling them, Jefferson worried that tenant farmers would mistreat them. Tenants, he knew, would have no motivation to 'watch for the happiness', as Jefferson put it, of the enslaved people that they hired from the patriarch of Monticello. These temporary slaveholders had an 'interest' in providing only minimal material comforts for slaves and in extracting as much labour from them as possible. In short, Jefferson recognized that hiring out his slaves was likely a recipe for death and cruelty. 'It would be their [tenants'] interest to kill all the old and infirm by hard usage,' Jefferson admitted. To counter this, he sought to mitigate the 'ill usage' of his slaves through a variety of means.[32]

Legal channels, Jefferson believed, would offer the best protection of human property. He hoped that leasing smaller parcels of his property, demanding rent payments in silver and limiting leases to five years would constitute a 'good rent' of his estate.[33] He inserted clauses in the lease agreement 'which had for their object the good treatment of my slaves', in particular 'that which denied a diminution of rent on the death of a slave' would help guard against ill-treatment of enslaved men, women and children. In his 1800 lease agreement with the tenant farmer John Craven, Jefferson stipulated that 'with respect to the negroes he will feed & clothe them well, take care of them in sickness, employing medical aid if necessary'.[34] In addition, 'should the negroes be treated with unreasonable severity, or not reasonably taken care of', then Jefferson would call in 'mutual arbiters' to annul the lease. Craven leased 500 acres of Tufton and Monticello and forty-five slaves from 1800 to 1809, paying an annual rent of $350. When Jefferson renewed his lease with Craven in 1803, he inserted clauses that he thought would guard against the overwork of young female slaves of reproductive age or older bondspeople.[35] And when Jefferson leased out the Tufton and Lego quarter farms in 1818 to his white grandson, Thomas Jefferson Randolph, he similarly stipulated that 'all the negroes', or sixty slaves, would be 'maintained, clothed and their taxes and levies paid', and that he would be prohibited from sub-leasing out any of the slaves.[36]

Additionally, renting land and slaves to tenants who were 'known to be kind and careful in their natures' would also help mitigate brutality and overwork, Jefferson thought. In the early 1790s, eager to embark upon a plan to ameliorate his farms and having immersed himself in the literature of agricultural improvement penned by the likes of Arthur Young, George Washington and George Logan, Jefferson sought to transition his lands from the 'slovenly business' of tobacco to wheat production. During his long journeys from Monticello to Philadelphia while serving as Secretary of State, Jefferson admired the diversified farming operations of eastern Maryland where the 'husbandry ... is in wheat and grazing: little corn, and less pork'.[37] On the flat land between the Susquehanna river and the Delaware border, he thought, the farmers understood the 'management of negroes on a rational and humane plan' since the 'labour there' was 'performed by slaves with some mixture of free labourers'.[38] Jefferson eventually hired Samuel Biddle and Eli Alexander from Maryland as overseers at Monticello, with Alexander later leasing Shadwell and Lego farms from 1806 to 1810. Jefferson explained to Biddle that he had 'come into another country' – eastern Maryland – to look for overseers and tenants for Monticello 'chiefly with a view to place them [his slaves] on the comfortable footing of the labourers of other countries'. In other words, he thought that 'over-lookers' from Maryland would treat slaves more like hired free workers than disposable chattel.[39]

Moreover, Jefferson sought to guard against the ill treatment of some of his more valuable domestic labourers, skilled artisans and older slaves by simply refusing to hire them out. In 1788, while Jefferson was in France, he specified to his steward that George Granger, Sr, Ursula Granger and Betty Hemings were 'not to be hired at all'. 'Great George', as Jefferson referred to him, was to remain at Monticello to 'take care of my orchards, grasses &c' while Ursula conducted domestic work in the main house and along Mulberry Row, the main plantation street at Monticello. Wanting to shield the 'negroes too old to be hired' from potential ill usage by temporary masters, Jefferson suggested that they remain at Monticello, where they might 'make a good profit by cultivating cotton' – a crop that either failed or was never planted.[40]

Slave leasing and patriarchy

In 1814, Jefferson outlined his plan to ameliorate his own slaves as a precursor to future emancipation. Until all slaveowners in Virginia consented to abolish slavery, planters 'should endeavor, with those whom fortune has thrown on our hands, to feed & clothe them well, protect them from ill usage, require such reasonable labour only as is performed voluntarily by freemen, and be led by no repugnancies to abdicate them, and our duties to them'.[41] Ironically, Jefferson's amelioration project at Monticello was facilitated by the hiring of outside slaves. While Jefferson worked to transform his own enslaved workers from unskilled field hands to artisans, managers and house servants on his mountaintop, he began hiring slaves to fill the labour vacuum created on his outlying farms. Most of the enslaved men hired at Monticello between the 1790s and Jefferson's retirement from the presidency in 1809 were 'employed in a little farming but mainly in other works about my mills, & grounds generally'.[42]

Jefferson's lease of four enslaved men, Essex, Isaac, Patrick and Peter, illustrates the unique roles that hired slaves played at Monticello. In 1794, Jefferson authorized the hire of 'four very able intelligent negro men'. At the end of January, '4 negro men arrive[d]' at Monticello, to comprise 'a good force for my works' at the canal for the toll mill on the Rivanna river.[43] Still, the blasting of rocks for the canal was not the only project that Essex, Isaac, Peter and Patrick worked on when they were hired at Monticello. In the summer of 1795, these men, all rented from the estate of Thomas Mann Randolph, Sr, were a major part of the 'force employed' during the wheat harvest.[44]

This workforce, which Jefferson imagined as a 'machine' moving in 'exact equilibrio', was comprised of fifty-eight men and women in July – eighteen cradlers, eighteen binders, six gatherers, three loaders, six stackers, two cooks and four carters. In addition, George Granger, Sr, outfitted with 'tools & a grindstone', drove a single mule cart 'from tree to tree as the work advanced' and was 'constantly employed in mending cradles & grinding scythes' as well as doling out liquor to the labourers. Patrick, Peter and Isaac worked as 'cradlers' during the hot July harvest; cradling wheat was the most onerous task, and consisted of men using a scythe attached to wooden 'fingers' to cut the wheat and lay it neatly in a row for collection by the 'gatherers' and 'stackers'. Essex, who was likely weaker than the other three hired men, was tasked with stacking the wheat cut by the cradlers. Jefferson noted that in three days in July, twelve cradlers harvested seventy-three acres of wheat at the Shadwell quarter farm; he calculated that each cradler could cut three acres of the crop, working sunup to sundown.[45] It seems clear that those slaves hired in the 1790s and 1810s often performed the most physically demanding work on the plantation, while many of Jefferson's own slaves became more skilled domestic labourers in the main house or along Mulberry Row, including blacksmiths, charcoal-burners, laundresses, parlourmaids, cooks, house joiners, carpenters and seamstresses.[46]

Jefferson believed that the amelioration of his own slaves reflected his conception of himself as an 'Antediluvian patriarch'. But this self was not just fashioned at home – it was also created, and endorsed by, outsiders. In this way, hired slaves and their masters played crucial roles in Jefferson's conception of patriarchy. Of hired slaves, Jefferson declared that he would treat them 'as my own, and better whenever any difference is made' when they took up residence at Monticello.[47] In 1810, Jefferson hired four slaves, Nancy, Tom Buck, Tom Lee and Frederick, all of whom had been previously leased by Thomas Mann Randolph, Sr. Although three arrived at Monticello in January per the lease agreement, Tom Buck 'contrary to orders went down the country'. When he finally appeared at Monticello about a month later, Jefferson 'found him neither in a condition to be received as a labourer, nor able to go away if rejected'. Both of the enslaved man's feet were 'frost-bitten and extremely bad'. Although Tom Buck was 'taken care of', and perhaps attended by a physician, after three weeks the feet 'had changed so as to threaten mortification and to require a more skillful treatment than we were competent to secure his life'. It is likely that the frostbite became gangrenous and that Tom Buck was threatened with sepsis. Jefferson eventually sent the hired slave to a boarding house in Charlottesville for three months, to be attended by a doctor there. Still, even when Tom Buck returned to Monticello, he required 'cloth shoes to protect his feet, which were entirely yet tender' and was unable to walk, 'except about the house'. The executor of the estate from which Tom Buck was leased, William Chamberlayne, initially balked at the high cost of the medical attention given to Tom Buck at Monticello and in Charlottesville. But he was also 'under an obligation' to Jefferson 'for the care & attention' given to a slave he did not even own. Despite Tom Buck being both a runaway and a leased slave who completed almost none of the work for which he was initially hired, Jefferson lavished expensive medical care and paternalistic oversight on him.[48]

Jefferson was anxious that hired slaves would not undermine or challenge the carefully cultivated 'self' that he fashioned in his private domain, that of humane and rational master. After two of Mary Daingerfield's hired slaves, Gabriel and another man, ran away from Monticello in the winter of 1807, Jefferson feared that 'they will make out a sad story' to their mistress. He urged his overseer, Edmund Bacon, that 'it would be well for you to set to rights by letting her know how little they have to complain of as to severity, food or clothing'. Bacon told her 'every Circumstance of the nigroes and their treatment. Also, she said she had heard from Good white Persons the treatment of your Nigroes which was as Good as she would wish.' Similarly, in the case of Tom Buck's frostbite, Jefferson was eager to prove his capacity for humanity, especially toward people he did not own. 'I acted for the owners of the negro,' he claimed, 'as I would have done for my own, as they were not here to take care of him. I could have no motive for recieving him, but that of humanity, and to save his life for his owners.' Jefferson not only wanted hired slaves to know his benevolent regime, but their owners as well.[49]

The hiring network

In central Virginia, most rented slaves were leased from the Richmond hiring grounds at the end of December; annual contracts, paid for with credit rather than cash, usually commenced on 1 January. Jefferson relied upon his overseers, directed by his sons-in-law, to secure contracts for hired slaves. In the winter of 1799, Jefferson entreated his overseer, Richard Richardson, to 'use every exertion to hire 6 men for me. On this everything depends.' The tasks for the 'Six men to be hired' would be to 'cut 200 cords of coal wood, dig out the canal, mend the fence at Shadwell' and 'quarry stone for the waggon'. And 'rather than let the plantation suffer greatly', the hired slaves 'must even interrupt their other work' to 'give all the assistance they can' to Richardson. Jefferson's overseers and relatives worked as intermediaries to secure lease agreements at Richmond or with local slaveowners eager to hire out their human property for income. In December, Jefferson told Thomas Mann Randolph, John Wayles Eppes or his overseers how many 'hands' he needed for the coming year and the rate that he would agree to pay. These men would then secure leases for hired slaves on Jefferson's behalf. Contracts usually stipulated that renters would be allowed twelve months' credit to pay the hiring fee. Jefferson 'gave his bond' for the hire of slaves in January, with payment expected one year later. To pay for these lease contracts, Jefferson drew on credit that he accrued from the sale of his crops in Bedford and Albemarle.[50]

During his lifetime, Jefferson hired slaves primarily from four types of owners: widows, minors, deceased and indebted planters, and overseers. In the summer of 1806, Monticello overseer John Holmes Freeman struck a deal with a widow who had lost her husband in the Revolutionary War. William Daingerfield, who served in the Continental Army, died in 1781, leaving his wife Mary and ten children at their Coventry plantation outside of Fredericksburg. Mary Daingerfield and her children inherited the land, livestock and slaves owned by her husband. But without remarrying, Daingerfield needed an income to retain the plantation and raise her children. This is likely why she consented to rent four of her own slaves, and five slaves belonging to her daughter Sarah, to Jefferson for the year. Leasing out these eight men and one woman for a full year at Monticello would generate $590. Jefferson even proposed to renew the contract and promised Daingerfield two things: timely payment for the hire and humane treatment of Tom, Edmund, Gabriel, Billy, Jack, George, Warner, Sampson and Polly. He assured Daingerfield that he would deposit payments in her Bank of Fredericksburg account and that her slaves 'shall be provided & treated with all the humanity which I can secure in my absence, and of which I am the more confident as the manager under whom they are is of a very mild & indulgent character'.[51]

But even with Jefferson's promise of 'all the humanity', one of Daingerfield's slaves died at Monticello. In October of 1810, Edmund had left his work at the Lego quarter farm where he, along with about a dozen other slaves, had been labouring in the fields, 'securing fodder & tops, and stacking them' for livestock feed. That day, he travelled a mile and a half to the Monticello home farm with a companion to fetch a repaired harrow. Although Edmund told no one, he likely suffered incredible pain as he crossed the Rivanna river and ascended the mountain. His fellow slaves at Lego farm had suspected that he was hiding an illness, though he 'always strenuously denied it'. But after returning home to his wife Sally that evening, he was 'taken very unwell with a pain in his breast and belly'. Still, he did not 'alarm his wife' or 'disturb the overseer'. When the overseer went to Edmund's 'house and found him abed', he saddled his horse and immediately rode to alert Jefferson. Only a few hours later, as Jefferson was preparing to visit the enslaved man himself, Edmund was seized by a fit of vomiting and died 'in a most sudden manner'. Jefferson, who commissioned an autopsy of Edmund's body by the physician who regularly treated his slaves, Dr Francis Carr, was unsettled by the slave's abrupt end. He was 'really much concerned at his [Edmund's] loss', since he was 'a most excellent fellow' and 'had taken a wife ... and had a child' at Lego farm. Indeed, Jefferson had intended to purchase Edmund from Daingerfield.[52]

Jefferson also hired slaves from widows in his neighbourhood. Lucy Wood, the sister of Jefferson's nemesis and the great orator, Patrick Henry, lived with her family at Buck Island, just seven miles from Monticello. Lucy Wood's husband, Valentine, had been a clerk in Goochland County, the colonel of the county militia and one of the first justices appointed in Albemarle County, before his death in 1781. From 1795 to 1797, Lucy Wood hired out her own slaves as well as those slaves inherited by her children in order to provide an annual income for the family. In 1795, Jefferson hired James from Lucy Wood, Dick from Jane Wood, and Reuben, Patrick and Bob from William Wood. Jefferson noted that he had 'been fortunate in getting 5. prime fellows', who worked on the initial construction of Monticello II, part of a gang of fifteen hired men in 1796.[53]

In 1797, the Wood family renewed their lease contract with Jefferson. James, Dick, Moses and Patrick were again hired out to Monticello. With each slave's annual hiring fee around $50, Lucy Wood was able to generate an income of about $200 for 1797 from the work of four men on Jefferson's mountaintop. In addition, the hiring agreement stipulated that Jefferson would feed, clothe and shelter the Wood slaves, thereby releasing Lucy Wood from the financial burden of providing for her human property. At Monticello, the Wood slaves were given wool and linen, shoes and stockings and from 1¼ and 1½ rations per week; a standard ration for an adult slave at Monticello was eight quarts of cornmeal and half a pound to a pound of pork. After 1797, the Wood slaves disappeared from Jefferson's records; presumably, they were hired out to other plantations or sold. Yet Lucy Wood's efforts to remain solvent through the hire of her slaves did not produce a high enough profit margin. In 1815, the Wood family was forced to sell their 1,500 acres in Albemarle County, relocating to Fluvanna, where Lucy died in 1826.[54]

Jefferson hired slaves from many other widows between 1790 and the 1810s. In 1795 and 1796, he hired two enslaved men, John Cain and Billy, from Sarah Champe Carter, the widow of Edward Carter and proprietress of Blenheim plantation.[55] In 1799, Jefferson leased an enslaved man named Jack, likely a brick mason, from the 'widow Mallory', or Lydia Mallory, in Richmond, paying $54.33 for his hire.[56] A year later,

Jefferson rented Mat from the 'widow Duke'; Mat served as a cradler during the summer wheat harvest.[57] In 1806, a hired man named Moses, owned by Mary Stevens of Caroline County, served as the miller for the Shadwell toll mill.[58]

Jefferson also frequently hired slaves from the executors of estates belonging to minor owners or deceased and indebted proprietors. After Thomas Mann Randolph, Sr, died in Richmond in 1793, many of his slaves were sold or hired out to pay his sizable debts. In 1794, Randolph's executors advertised for the sale of more than 100 of his slaves at Scottville in Powhatan County. Thomas Mann Randolph, Jr, as an executor of his father's estate, leased several slaves to his father-in-law, Thomas Jefferson, in order to help satisfy the debts. Between 1795 and 1798, Jefferson rented Patrick, Essex, Isaac and Peter Hawkins from Randolph. Jefferson also hired an additional three slaves from Randolph's estate, noting in the summer of 1797 that 'Wapping, Joe & Jame three negroe men from TMR begin to work.'[59]

Jefferson leased slaves from the estate of Lyne Shackelford, a Revolutionary War veteran and owner of Curls plantation in Henrico County. When Shackelford died in 1806, he named William Chamberlayne an executor of his will and a guardian of four of his five children. In 1810, Jefferson hired four of Shackelford's slaves. But he did not hire these enslaved individuals directly from Chamberlayne, a planter and Republican state senator from New Kent County. Instead, he subleased them from his son-in-law, Thomas Mann Randolph, Jr, who in 1809 'had in his possession, on hire, 4 negroes of the property' of the recently deceased Shackelford, but 'which he did not mean to keep another year'. Jefferson thus 'agreed to take them' at the same price paid by Randolph. Chamberlayne oversaw the collection of this hiring fee, which Jefferson adjusted to be a total of $127, rather than $166.67, since one of the slaves, Tom Buck, could only work for two months of his hire after contracting frostbite.[60]

Several Monticello overseers also hired their own slaves to Jefferson. From 1813 until at least 1817, Jefferson agreed to hire 'Bacon's man Lewis', a slave belonging to overseer Edmund Bacon, to work on the Monticello home farm for $80 per year. Bacon bought Lewis from his brother for $450 in 1814; he likely hired the slave out to Jefferson to recoup the expense. Lewis was given clothing and food rations by Jefferson and was also one of eleven enslaved workers to harvest the wheat at Monticello in the summer of 1815. It is likely that Bacon also leased out Lewis and his other slaves to neighbouring planters, including James Monroe and Arthur Brockenbrough. Hiring out slaves allowed overseers to supplement the annual income they earned from Jefferson. But Bacon was also a slave trader – between 1807 and 1818, he owned at least sixteen different enslaved men, women and children, buying and selling them at close intervals. Bacon may have used the savings he accrued through slave selling and slave leasing to buy land in Trigg County, Kentucky, where he moved in 1822.[61]

And it was Bacon who also secured the lease of the slaves owned by Anne Scott Jefferson Marks, Jefferson's impoverished sister who came to live at Monticello in 1811, dying there in 1828. From 1813 to 1816, Peter was leased out to Jefferson, perhaps to help offset the cost of supporting Jefferson's sister. He received a bed during the first year he was hired, in addition to his usual clothing allotment, as well as a hat during the second year of his lease. Peter worked as an agricultural labourer, rotating between the mountaintop and the plantation, although he harvested wheat at Lego farm in the summer of 1815. But in 1816, presumably acting on Marks's direction, Bacon sold Peter for $150.[62]

The more than eighty enslaved people that Jefferson hired from around thirty different widows, overseers, children and indebted estates demonstrates how multifaceted and deeply entrenched the market in slave hiring had become in post-revolutionary Virginia. Slave leasing provided previously marginalized members of Virginia society with the ability to 'improve' themselves or satisfy debts by garnering income from the bodies and labour of enslaved people. Widows like Mary Daingerfield leased out their slaves in the absence of a male head of household; slave leasing provided a larger, steadier income than cash crops or the sale of slaves. Executors like William Chamberlayne leased out enslaved people in order to support orphaned children until they came of age. And poor white artisans and overseers purchased and leased a small number of slaves to Jefferson to supplement their wages and generate money to purchase additional land and slaves. As historian Alan Taylor has noted, after 1776, 'common Virginians found it easier to buy or rent slaves' and to 'move west and south to make farms'. But it was the enslaved who 'suffered for the democratization and commercialization promoted by the revolution'.[63]

Conclusion

In the post-revolutionary period, leasing slaves, rather than selling them, allowed Jefferson to preserve the families of Herns, Hubbards, Gillettes, Grangers and Hemingses who lived and worked at Monticello. But avoiding the slave trade also served Jefferson's material interests. By renting out his human property, Jefferson could maintain his elite status and also preserve his sense of himself as the benevolent patriarch who watched 'for the happiness of those who labour for mine'.[64] Still, even if Jefferson embraced slave hiring as a 'hopeful prospect' that would allow him to retain his slaves with an eye toward liberating them at a future date, it was clear that Jefferson facilitated – and took part in – a system that was increasingly focused on the commodification of slaves. Seeing slaves as valuable collateral was key to understanding how the white men, women and children who leased their slaves to Jefferson viewed the practice of slave renting, as a means to accumulate capital, expand their access to credit networks and increase their independence and social status.[65]

Despite Jefferson's belief that slave leasing would keep his creditors at bay and preserve his slave property, the slave trade did come to Monticello. After Jefferson died in 1826, leaving $107,000 of debt to his white Randolph heirs, nearly everything from the house and plantation was sold, including '130 valuable negroes'.[66] Although Jefferson freed five slaves in his will, including his mixed-race sons Madison and Eston Hemings, 'all the rest of us were sold on the auction block' recalled Israel Jefferson Gillette. Wormley Hughes and Joseph Fossett, both granted freedom by the terms of Jefferson's will, watched as their wives and children were sold away to different bidders. David Hern, his children and grandchildren were auctioned off to at least eight different purchasers. In all, 126 slaves were sold in 1827, and a further thirty people were auctioned off in 1829. Although Jefferson's granddaughter Mary Jefferson Randolph maintained that most of the Monticello slaves were 'all sold to persons in the state', namely several faculty members at the University of Virginia, this was cold comfort to spouses, parents and siblings divided forever by the slave trade. As Peter Fossett, who was sold away from his family at the 1827 sale, later remembered, 'we were scattered all over the country, never to meet each other again until we meet in another world'.[67]

Notes

1 Anne Scott Jefferson Marks (1755–1828) was the twin of Jefferson's brother Randolph. 'Nancy' Jefferson married Hastings Marks in 1787. Following her husband's death in 1811, the childless and destitute Nancy Marks moved from Louisa County to Monticello where she lived until her death in 1828. Cornelia Randolph to Ellen Randolph, 6–8 July 1828, Ellen Wayles Randolph Coolidge Correspondence, Special Collections Library, University of Virginia.
2 James A. Bear, Jr, and Lucia C. Stanton (eds), *Thomas Jefferson's Memorandum Books: Accounts, with Legal Records and Miscellany, 1767–1826* (Princeton, NJ: Princeton University Press, 1997), II, 1325, 1318; Edwin M. Betts (ed.), *Thomas Jefferson's Farm Book: With Commentary and Relevant Extracts from Other Writings* (Princeton, NJ: Published for the American Philosophical Society by Princeton University Press, 1953; reprints, 1976, 1999), 156, 162, 164, 165, 169, 171, 172, 175, 176.
3 Annette Gordon-Reed and Peter S. Onuf, *'The Most Blessed of the Patriarchs': Thomas Jefferson and the Empire of the Imagination* (New York: Liveright, 2016); Thomas Jefferson to Angelica Schuyler Church, 27 November 1793, Founders Online, National Archives, http://founders.archives.gov/documents/Jefferson/01-27-02-0416.
4 Peter Jefferson will, 13 July 1757, Albemarle County Deed Book, No. 2, p. 33; Lucia Stanton, *'Those Who Labor for My Happiness': Slavery at Thomas Jefferson's Monticello* (Charlottesville: University of Virginia Press, 2012), 56.
5 Lester J. Cappon (ed.), 'Personal Property Tax List in Albemarle County, 1782', *Papers of the Albemarle County Historical Society* 5 (1944–5): 47–73.
6 Thomas Jefferson to Edward Rutledge, 30 November 1795, Founders Online, National Archives, http://founders.archives.gov/documents/Jefferson/01-28-02-0419.
7 Stanton, *'Those Who Labor for My Happiness'*, 7, 11, 43, 65–6, 85, 109, 120, 129, 135, 140, 153, 189, 248, 291.
8 Jonathan D. Martin, *Divided Mastery: Slave Hiring in the American South* (Cambridge, MA: Harvard University Press, 2004), 8.
9 John J. Zaborney, *Slaves for Hire: Renting Enslaved Laborers in Antebellum Virginia* (Baton Rouge: Louisiana State University Press, 2012).
10 For scholarship on slave hiring, see Frederic Bancroft, *Slave Trading in the Old South* (New York: Frederick Unger Publishing Co., 1959/1931), 147; Eugene D. Genovese, *Roll, Jordan, Roll: The World the Slaves Made* (New York: Vintage, 1974), 390; Robert W. Fogel and Stanley L. Engerman, *Time on the Cross: The Economics of American Negro Slavery* (New York: Norton, 1989/1974), 53, 56; Sarah S. Hughes, 'Slaves for Hire: The Allocation of Black Labor in Elizabeth County, Virginia, 1782 to 1810', *William and Mary Quarterly* 35 (April 1978); Randolph B. Campbell, 'Research Note: Slave Hiring in Texas', *American Historical Review* 92 (February 1988): 107–14; William A. Byrne, 'The Hiring of Woodson, Slave Carpenter of Savannah', *Georgia Historical Quarterly* 77 (Summer 1993): 245–63; Keith C. Barton, '"Good Cooks and Washers": Slave Hiring,

Domestic Labor, and the Market in Bourbon County, Kentucky', *Journal of American History* 84 (September 1997): 436–60.
11 Calvin Schermerhorn, *Money Over Mastery, Family Over Freedom: Slavery in the Antebellum Upper South* (Baltimore, MD: Johns Hopkins University Press, 2011), 16, 136.
12 Walter Johnson, 'King Cotton's Long Shadow', *New York Times*, 30 March 2013.
13 Thomas Jefferson to Richard Price, 7 August 1785, Founders Online, National Archives, http://founders.archives.gov/documents/Jefferson/01-08-02-0280.
14 Adam Smith, *An Inquiry into the Nature and Causes of the Wealth of Nations*, ed. R. H. Campbell and A. S. Skinner, 2 vols (Indianapolis: Liberty Fund Press, 1981/1776), 1:387, n. 27.
15 Peter S. Onuf, 'The Empire of Liberty: Land of the Free and Home of the Slave', in Andrew Shankman (ed.), *The World of the Revolutionary American Republic: Land, Labor and the Conflict for a Continent* (New York: Routledge, 2014), chap. 9; Sven Beckert, *Empire of Cotton: A Global History* (New York: Vintage, 2014); Joshua D. Rothman, *Flush Times and Fever Dreams: A Story of Capitalism and Slavery in the Age of Jackson* (Athens: University of Georgia Press, 2012); Walter Johnson, *River of Dark Dreams: Slavery, Capitalism, and Imperialism in the Mississippi Valley's Cotton Kingdom* (Cambridge, MA: Harvard University Press, 2013); Calvin Schermerhorn, *The Business of Slavery and the Rise of American Capitalism* (New Haven, CT: Yale University Press, 2015).
16 Schermerhorn, *Money Over Mastery*, 16.
17 US Census, 1790, 1830, *Historical Statistics of the United States: Colonial Times to 1970*, 2 vols (Washington, DC: US Dept. of Commerce, 1975); Louis Hughes, *Thirty Years a Slave: From Bondage to Freedom* (Milwaukee, WI: South Side, 1897), 31.
18 John Hartwell Cocke to unknown, 30 September 1831, Cocke Family Papers, Special Collections Library, University of Virginia.
19 Steven Deyle, *Carry Me Back: The Domestic Slave Trade in American Life* (New York: Oxford University Press, 2005), 31–3; Richard S. Dunn, 'After Tobacco: The Slave Labor Pattern on a Large Chesapeake Grain-and-Livestock Plantation in the Early Nineteenth Century', in John J. McCusker and Kenneth Morgan (eds), *The Early Modern Atlantic Economy* (New York: Cambridge University Press, 2000), 344–63; Lorena S. Walsh, 'Rural African Americans in the Constitutional Era in Maryland, 1776–1810', *Maryland Historical Magazine* 84, no. 4 (1989): 327–9; *Historical Statistics of the United States* (1970).
20 Alan Taylor, *The Internal Enemy: Slavery and War in Virginia, 1772–1832* (New York: W.W. Norton, 2014), 6, 43–6; Holly Brewer, 'Entailing Aristocracy in Colonial Virginia: "Ancient Feudal Restraints" and Revolutionary Reform', *William and Mary Quarterly*, 3rd Ser., 54, no. 2 (1997): 307–46; Richard S. Dunn, 'Black Society in the Chesapeake, 1760–1810', in Ira Berlin and Ronald Hoffman (eds), *Slavery and Freedom in the Age of the American Revolution* (Charlottesville: Published for the United States Capitol Historical Society by the University of Virginia Press, 1983), 67.
21 Thomas Jefferson's Thoughts on Lotteries, *c.* 20 January 1826, Founders Online, National Archives, http://founders.archives.gov/documents/Jefferson/98-01-02-5845; Samuel Shepherd (ed.), *The Statutes at Large of Virginia, from October Session 1792, to December Session 1806 . . .*, 3 vols (Richmond: n.p., 1835–6), I, 128–9; Thomas Jefferson, Query XIV, 'Notes on the State of Virginia', in Merrill D. Peterson (ed.), *Jefferson: Writings* (New York: Library of America, 1984), 263.
22 John Hartwell Cocke to unknown, 30 September 1831, Cocke Family Papers, Special Collections Library, University of Virginia.

23 David T. Konig, 'Thomas Jefferson, Slavery, and the Law', unpublished paper in the author's possession, 2015.
24 On Jefferson and amelioration, see Christa Dierksheide, *Amelioration and Empire: Progress and Slavery in the Plantation Americas* (Charlottesville: University of Virginia Press, 2014), 25–56.
25 On Jefferson and debt, see Herbert E. Sloan, *Principle and Interest: Thomas Jefferson and the Problem of Debt* (New York and Oxford: Oxford University Press, 1995).
26 Thomas Jefferson to Nicholas Lewis, 19 December 1786, Founders Online, National Archives, http://founders.archives.gov/documents/Jefferson/01-10-02-0466.
27 Thomas Jefferson to Nicholas Lewis, 29 July 1787, Founders Online, National Archives, http://founders.archives.gov/documents/Jefferson/01-11-02-0564.
28 Lucia C. Stanton, *Free Some Day: The African American Families of Monticello* (Chapel Hill: University of North Carolina Press, 2000).
29 Thomas Jefferson to Nicholas Lewis, 29 July 1787, Founders Online, National Archives, http://founders.archives.gov/documents/Jefferson/01-11-02-0564.
30 Thomas Jefferson to Nicholas Lewis, 29 July 1787, Founders Online, National Archives, http://founders.archives.gov/documents/Jefferson/01-11-02-0564.
31 Betts, *Jefferson's Farm Book*, 'Negroes Alienated from 1784 to 1794, inclusive', 25; Thomas Jefferson to James Lyle, 12 May 1796, Founders Online, National Archives, http://founders.archives.gov/documents/Jefferson/01-29-02-0063; Deed of Mortgage of Slaves to Van Staphorst & Hubbard, 12 May 1796, Founders Online, National Archives, http://founders.archives.gov/documents/Jefferson/01-29-02-0065; Shepherd, *The Statutes at Large of Virginia*, I, 128–9.
32 Thomas Jefferson to Angelica Schuyler Church, 27 November 1793, Founders Online, National Archives, http://founders.archives.gov/documents/Jefferson/01-27-02-0416; Thomas Jefferson to Francis Eppes, 30 July 1787, Founders Online, National Archives, http://founders.archives.gov/documents/Jefferson/01-11-02-0569.
33 Thomas Jefferson to Francis Eppes, 30 July 1787, Founders Online, National Archives, http://founders.archives.gov/documents/Jefferson/01-11-02-0569.
34 Agreement with John H. Craven, 22 August 1800, Founders Online, National Archives, http://founders.archives.gov/documents/Jefferson/01-32-02-0070.
35 Agreement with John H. Craven, 20 September 1803, Founders Online, National Archives, http://founders.archives.gov/documents/Jefferson/01-41-02-0298.
36 Thomas Jefferson to Thomas Jefferson Randolph, 15 September 1819, Founders Online, National Archives, http://founders.archives.gov/documents/Jefferson/98-01-02-0746.
37 Thomas Jefferson to Francis Eppes, 30 July 1787, Founders Online, National Archives, http://founders.archives.gov/documents/Jefferson/01-11-02-0569.
38 Thomas Jefferson to Nicholas Lewis, 11 July 1788, Founders Online, National Archives, http://founders.archives.gov/documents/Jefferson/01-13-02-0245.
39 Betts, *Jefferson's Farm Book*, 'Eli Alexander's Lease for Shadwell', 171–2; Thomas Jefferson to Samuel Biddle, 12 December 1792, Founders Online, National Archives, http://founders.archives.gov/documents/Jefferson/01-24-02-0710.
40 Thomas Jefferson to Nicholas Lewis, 11 July 1788, Founders Online, National Archives, http://founders.archives.gov/documents/Jefferson/01-13-02-0245.
41 Thomas Jefferson to Edward Coles, 25 August 1814, Founders Online, National Archives, http://founders.archives.gov/documents/Jefferson/03-07-02-0439.
42 Stanton, *'Those Who Labor for My Happiness'*, 71–89; Dierksheide, *Amelioration and Empire*, 25–56; Thomas Jefferson to John Strode, 5 June 1805, Founders

Online, National Archives, http://founders.archives.gov/documents/Jefferson/99-01-02-1851.
43 Authorization for J. P. P. Derieux, 26 December 1794, Founders Online, National Archives, http://founders.archives.gov/documents/Jefferson/01-28-02-0168; Thomas Jefferson to Thomas Mann Randolph, 26 December 1794, Founders Online, National Archives, http://founders.archives.gov/documents/Jefferson/01-28-02-0169; Bear and Stanton, *Jefferson's Memorandum Books*, II, 925.
44 Thomas Jefferson to Thomas Mann Randolph, 11 January 1796, Founders Online, National Archives, http://founders.archives.gov/documents/Jefferson/01-28-02-0450; Betts, *Jefferson's Farm Book*, 46.
45 Betts, *Jefferson's Farm Book*, 46.
46 Stanton, *'Those Who Labor for My Happiness'*, 71–89.
47 Thomas Jefferson to Edmund Bacon, 8 December 1807, Founders Online, National Archives, http://founders.archives.gov/documents/Jefferson/99-01-02-6934.
48 Thomas Jefferson to William Chamberlayne, 17 August 1810, Founders Online, National Archives, http://founders.archives.gov/documents/Jefferson/03-03-02-0009; William Chamberlayne to Thomas Jefferson, 6 February 1811, Founders Online, National Archives, http://founders.archives.gov/documents/Jefferson/03-03-02-0275; Bear and Stanton, *Jefferson's Memorandum Books*, II, 1251.
49 Thomas Jefferson to Edmund Bacon, 8 December 1807, Founders Online, National Archives, http://founders.archives.gov/documents/Jefferson/99-01-02-6934; to Thomas Jefferson from Edmund Bacon, 18 December 1807, Founders Online, National Archives, http://founders.archives.gov/documents/Jefferson/99-01-02-7017; Thomas Jefferson to William Chamberlayne, 6 January 1811, Founders Online, National Archives, http://founders.archives.gov/documents/Jefferson/03-03-02-0208.
50 Memorandum to Richard Richardson, [*c.* 21 December 1799], Founders Online, National Archives, http://founders.archives.gov/documents/Jefferson/01-31-02-0232.
51 Thomas Jefferson to John Minor, 10 August 1806, Founders Online, National Archives, http://founders.archives.gov/documents/Jefferson/99-01-02-4153; Lawrence MacRae, 'Descendants of John Daingerfield and his Wife, New Kent County, Virginia, 1640' [1928 typescript at VI]; [Fredericksburg] *Virginia Herald*, 25 August 1807, 25 February 1818; Thomas Jefferson to Mary Willis Daingerfield, 10 August 1806, Founders Online, National Archives, http://founders.archives.gov/documents/Jefferson/99-01-02-4150; Thomas Jefferson to Mary Willis Daingerfield, 7 November 1807, Founders Online, National Archives, http://founders.archives.gov/documents/Jefferson/99-01-02-6729. On widows and slave property in the post-revolutionary period, see St George Tucker, *Blackstone's Commentaries, with Notes of Reference to the Constitution and Laws of the Federal Government of the United States and the Commonwealth of Virginia*, 5 vols (Union, NJ: Lawbook Exchange, 1996 (1803)), vol. 3, note E.
52 Thomas Jefferson to Nathaniel H. Hooe, 20 October 1810, Founders Online, National Archives, http://founders.archives.gov/documents/Jefferson/03-03-02-0116.
53 Thomas Jefferson to Thomas Mann Randolph, 11 January 1796, Founders Online, National Archives, http://founders.archives.gov/documents/Jefferson/01-28-02-0450; Betts, *Jefferson's Farm Book*, 50–2; Enclosure: Memorandum for Samuel Arnold, 12 April 1798, Founders Online, National Archives, http://founders.archives.gov/documents/Jefferson/01-30-02-0183.
54 Thomas Jefferson to Thomas Mann Randolph, 11 January 1796, Founders Online, National Archives, http://founders.archives.gov/documents/Jefferson/01-28-02-0450; Betts, *Jefferson's Farm Book*, 50–2; Enclosure: Memorandum for Samuel Arnold, 12

April 1798, Founders Online, National Archives, http://founders.archives.gov/documents/Jefferson/01-30-02-0183; Edgar Woods, *History of Albemarle County In Virginia, giving some account of what it was by nature, of what it was made by man, and of some of the men who made it* (Heritage Books, 1989/1901), 347.
55 Bear and Stanton, *Jefferson's Memorandum Books*, II, 935.
56 Thomas Jefferson to George Jefferson, 18 May 1799, Founders Online, National Archives, http://founders.archives.gov/documents/Jefferson/01-31-02-0096; Bear and Stanton, *Jefferson's Memorandum Books*, II, 1013.
57 Thomas Jefferson to Richard Richardson, 8 January 1801, Founders Online, National Archives, http://founders.archives.gov/documents/Jefferson/01-32-02-0298; Betts, *Jefferson's Farm Book*, 58, 58a.
58 Bear and Stanton, *Jefferson's Memorandum Books*, II, 1186, 1207; Thomas Jefferson to Edmund Bacon, 13 May 1807, Founders Online, National Archives, http://founders.archives.gov/documents/Jefferson/99-01-02-5584.
59 *Virginia Gazette and Richmond and Manchester Advertiser*, 25 November 1793, 23 October 1794; *Virginia Gazette and Weekly Advertiser*, 29 November 1793; Betts, *Jefferson's Farm Book*, 43, 46, 49–53; Bear and Stanton, *Jefferson's Memorandum Books*, II, 943.
60 Henrico County Will Book, 5:260 [Vi microfilm]; Thomas Jefferson to William Chamberlayne, 17 August 1810, Founders Online, National Archives, http://founders.archives.gov/documents/Jefferson/03-03-02-0009; Thomas Jefferson to William Chamberlayne, 4 April 1811, Founders Online, National Archives, http://founders.archives.gov/documents/Jefferson/03-03-02-0404.
61 Between 1807 and 1818, Bacon owned at least sixteen different enslaved men, women and children. Only Lewis was listed as being hired out to Jefferson. Bear and Stanton, *Jefferson's Memorandum Books*, II, 1288; Betts, *Jefferson's Farm Book*, 144, 146, 148–9, 156; Edmund Bacon to Arthur Brockenbrough, 16 December 1821 and Bacon to Thomas Jefferson, 3 April 1822, *Memoranda Book of Edmund Bacon, 1802–22*, Special Collections Library, University of Virginia.
62 Betts, *Jefferson's Farm Book*, 144, 146, 148–9; Bear and Stanton, *Jefferson's Memorandum Books*, II, 1325, 1318; Betts, *Jefferson's Farm Book*, 156, 162, 164, 165, 169, 171–2, 175–6.
63 Taylor, *The Internal Enemy*, 52.
64 Thomas Jefferson to Angelica Schuyler Church, 27 November 1793, Founders Online, National Archives, http://founders.archives.gov/documents/Jefferson/01-27-02-0416.
65 Thomas Jefferson to Nicholas Lewis, 29 July 1787, Founders Online, National Archives, http://founders.archives.gov/documents/Jefferson/01-11-02-0564.
66 *Charlottesville Central Gazette*, 15 January 1827.
67 Israel Jefferson, *Pike County Republican*, 25 December 1873; Monticello dispersal sale receipts, Special Collections Library, University of Virginia; Mary Jefferson Randolph to Ellen Coolidge, 25 January 1827, Ellen Wayles Randolph Coolidge Correspondence, Special Collections, University of Virginia; 'ONCE THE SLAVE OF THOMAS JEFFERSON. // The Rev. Mr. Fossett, of Cincinnati, Recalls the Days When Men Came from the Ends of the Earth to Consult "the Sage of Monticello" – Reminiscences of Jefferson, Lafayette, Madison and Monroe' (Special to the *Sunday World*) Cincinnati, 29 January 1898.

9

Turmoil in the Cocoa Groves: Slave Revolts in Ocumare de la Costa, Venezuela, 1837 and 1845

Nikita Harwich

A slave revolt and its aftermath usually entail a logical process of disobedience, uprising and subsequent repression where, almost inevitably, the path that leads to a *status quo ante* is strewn with a display of violence, together with the predictable combination of blood, sweat and tears. It is not, however, always or necessarily the case. What happened in the region of Ocumare de la Costa in 1837 and 1845 shows that alternative solutions to violent conflict could be forthcoming, within a particular context. Slavery, though still a social reality in post-independence Venezuela, did not carry the same weight as in Brazil, Cuba or the United States' South. Even in areas where it maintained a relatively important economic significance, as was the case in Ocumare, slavery, as an institution of daily life, developed its own pattern of behaviour which affected masters and slaves alike in what could well be considered an atypical fashion.

The setting

The deep and narrow valleys, carved by the streams that surge from the heights of the *Cordillera* which runs through central Venezuela's entire coastline, that widen into small bays when entering into contact with the warm waters of the Caribbean, underline the particular features of the entire region of Ocumare de la Costa, located about 150 kilometres west of Caracas, as the crow flies.[1] An isolated region – navigation is often difficult since it is leeward and, by land, a two-day journey is usually necessary, either to cross the *Cordillera* or to reach the port town of Puerto Cabello[2] – Ocumare always fascinated its travellers whose eyewitness accounts insist on praising the luxuriant beauty of its landscapes:[3] a natural land for cocoa groves and, thus also, a land for slavery.

The *villa*[4] of San Sebastián de Ocumare – or Ocumare de la Costa as it is commonly known today – constituted, with 150 houses,[5] the most important population settlement area. With regard to the number of its inhabitants, Ocumare was followed, in decreasing order, by Cata, with twenty-six houses, Cuyagua and, finally, Turiamo, with only fifteen houses.⁶ This hierarchy, in terms of population, remained constant throughout the period. Another constant feature had to do with the population categories: the predominance of slavery and the fact that the near total of the micro-regional population settlement – more than 90 per cent in every one of the population centres throughout the period considered – was made up of black or mulatto inhabitants.⁷

By 1835, according to the available censuses, the population of the Ocumare *cantón* (district), with 3,363 inhabitants, had recovered its pre-independence level, while maintaining, from then on, a virtually non-existent population growth rate throughout the following decades. With a total of 1,432 people (including manumitted slaves subject to the 1821 law), according to the 1833 census, the Ocumare district slave population had more or less recovered its pre-war level.⁸ But the effects of the 1821 Manumission Law were soon felt, since the specific figure for slaves did diminish regularly until reaching in the end the level of the 460 individuals officially freed by the Abolition Decree of 1854.⁹ But even then, this figure represented only one-fourth of all registered slaves in the Carabobo Province – where Ocumare was located. If the number of standing manumitted slaves is added (some 540 persons), it could well be said that, on the scale of the district's total population, Ocumare still maintained one of the highest slave concentrations in all of Venezuela.¹⁰ This fact was linked to the traditionally inseparable relationship, established several centuries before, between slavery and work in the cocoa groves.

A cocoa *hacienda* is constituted by a given number of tree rows: various species of tall grown trees that provide the shade under which may, in turn, thrive the rows of fragile cocoa trees, each tree planted at a set distance from its neighbour. The size of the *hacienda* is thus always determined by the number of cocoa trees growing within its limits. Such size may vary: a 1,000 tree-grove may already be considered a *hacienda*, even though the average for the Ocumare region, at the turn of the nineteenth century, oscillated between 6,000 and 8,000 trees. The cocoa produced was of the pure *criollo* type, very similar to the one produced in the neighbouring Chuao valley, and therefore known in European markets under the brand name of *Grand Caraque*, synonymous with the highest quality.

At the end of the colonial period, the two most important cocoa *haciendas* in the Ocumare region belonged to the nuns of the Immaculate Conception Convent in Caracas, either through direct property – as in the case of the 25,000 tree 'Conception Nuns *Hacienda*', located in the Ocumare valley and parish proper – or through the form of an *obra pía*¹¹ donation, as in the case of the *hacienda* of that name, located in the Cata valley and parish, which totalled over 30,000 cocoa trees.¹² Another important group of properties belonged to the traditional patrician families of the Caracas province: the Tovars in Cuyagua and Turiamo; the Blancos, Osorios, de la Plazas or Cróquers in Ocumare. Concomitantly, from the last two decades of the eighteenth century onwards, the opportunities offered by cocoa cultivation had attracted new immigrants to the zone, seeking their fortunes in America, most – if not all – Canary islanders who soon became part of the local oligarchy.¹³

Contrary to other regions in Venezuela, the wars of independence in Ocumare did not witness any significant transfer of rural property into new hands. The one exception was the transfer, decreed in 1827 by Simón Bolívar himself, of the Cata *obra pía hacienda*, together with its benefits, as part of the endowment of the Caracas Central University. Thus, according to the slave census of 1833, which makes it possible to define with relative precision the major landowners within the area, the *Obra pía de Cata* and the Ocumare Conception nuns' *hacienda* remained the two most important individual properties in terms of the number of slaves and *manumisos* (manumitted slaves) labouring on their grounds (21 per cent of the total registered in the district).[14] With regard to a single family group, the Tovars – through their various family members – occupied the first place in terms of slave ownership. Then followed the combination of traditional patrician landowners from colonial times with the 'new' cocoa planters established just before independence – a situation that underlined the consolidation and permanence of local social structures. Most of the cocoa properties in the Ocumare region counted on the actual presence of their owners who formed the major nucleus of local notabilities, particularly those in charge of administrative or judiciary functions. There were, however, three major exceptions: the properties of the Tovar family, the Cata *Obra pía* and the Conception nuns' *hacienda*, which were run by appointed administrators and therefore lacked the 'personalized' master–slave relationship. This would indeed be one of the issues raised when turmoil hit the Ocumare cocoa groves.

The 1837 revolt

Slave 'insubordination' had always been a major worry for all Ocumare landowners. While individual escapes may have been fairly common, actual uprisings seem to have been relatively few – at least as far as the available documentation shows – which makes the two cases presented here stand out.

On 1 April 1837, Coronel Gualterio D. Chitty, administrator of the Cata *Obra pía hacienda*, addressed the following report to the local *Jefe Político*:[15]

> On the recently expired 30th, there has been an uprising of 15 slaves from this hacienda against the foreman's [*mayordomo*] authority; that they find themselves, since that date, in the hills near the Miranda hacienda; that through various trusted servants and with [the help of] the overseer José María Fragosa, I have sent them the order that they should return to their territory, which they paid no attention to and they continue in this state of insubordination, in such fashion that I consider this house and the lives of its inhabitants in danger, since the news I have obtained of their movements is that of a hostile attitude.[16]

Gualterio Chitty hoped that by informing the office in charge of public order in the district, the latter would 'take very effective measures to reduce these slaves to the sphere of their obligations, either calling upon the militia or through any other means deemed convenient'.[17] Attached to the report, Chitty listed the names of the fifteen 'runaway' slaves:

Francisco Plácido
Fermín
Silvestre
Lino
Juan Pío
José de la Concepción
José Gervasio
Francisco Antonio
Manuel Prudencio
Luis
José Hilario
Candelario
Juan Agustín
Juan Nepomuceno
Julián Antonio.[18]

Upon receiving Coronel Chitty's statement, which might be considered as an official complaint, the Cata *Jefe Político*, Manuel F. Delgado, immediately notified his Ocumare colleague, Luciano Benítez,[19] and forwarded, on 3 April, a copy of Chitty's initial document to the Governor of the Carabobo Province, accompanied by his own comments on the alleged uprising. Chitty had, indeed, on two occasions through one of his overseers tried to persuade the runaway slaves to return to their chores. Delgado further confirmed that, according to the information he had been given, 'The flight of these servants was executed without any motive, since while they were fulfilling their duties on March the 30th, during a short absence on the part of the foreman, they abandoned their work and fled.'[20]

Delgado then notified the provincial governor that orders had been issued to arm the local militia, 'in the numbers deemed necessary', so that it might proceed against the rebels, 'firing against them in case of resistance on their part'.[21] One of the local judges had even posted edicts inviting the runaways to surrender with a promise not to punish them for what they had done, but to no avail: 'on the contrary, they stroll in arms, openly and with insolence, up to the very outskirts of this town'.[22] Finally, Delgado indicated that the mayors of the Cuyagua and Ocumare parishes had been warned and that pickets had been placed on the road leading from Cata to both of the neighbouring valleys.

From a purely administrative point of view, all necessary steps had been taken. However, none of the measures considered seems to have borne any tangible result. On 6 April the Ocumare *Jefe Político*, Luciano Benitez, informed the Provincial Governor that the militia men who had been sent to help track down the runaways did not find them, which meant presumably that the latter had moved to another area.[23] The next documents in the archival file on the 1837 slave uprising are concerned with the arms, ammunition and field rations issued to the small militia force (two sergeants, two corporals and eight soldiers) involved in the chase.[24] Several months passed by without any additional news being reported.

But, by the end of the year 1837, a new dimension was added to what – so far – had mainly been a local incident. On 13 November, Gualterio Chitty decided to address directly a fully-fledged letter of complaint to General Carlos Soublette, the Vice-President of the Republic then in charge of the country's presidency. Chitty stated that within the entire Ocumare de la Costa district

> ...no protection whatsoever is provided as to the safety of property owners because there doesn't even exist the simulacrum of a police patrol that may guarantee in any way at all the population and the belongings of its inhabitants, consequently the slaves run away and may wander with total impunity throughout the entire district with no one to fear and no one to take care of their capture except only the owner to whom they belong to.[25]

At the same time, Chitty publicly levelled an accusation of potentially far reaching consequences: the runaway slaves were given 'indirect protection' by the employees and staff of the Aroa copper mines – then run by a British company – who

> ...either admitted them in their informal service for the type of work being carried out within such an establishment, with no regard for the requirements stipulated in the police regulation for the admittance of peon labourers, or finally even taking upon themselves to procure the freedom of some of these runaway slaves.[26]

To substantiate his charges, Chitty mentioned a letter he had received in August 1837 from Guillermo Irribarren, Office Manager of the Aroa mines, in which Irribarren mentioned having been given 300 pesos by a certain 'Juan Eugenio'. The latter had fled the Cata *Obra pía hacienda* some seven years earlier and believed that by offering this money, he was buying back his freedom from his former owner.[27] Chitty, of course, rejected the whole matter as a bad joke, while considering that, for a slave who had missed his duties for such a long time, a compensation of at least 700 pesos was due.[28]

Chitty continued: 'All of the coastal hacienda owners, and, better still, almost all those within the Republic have runaway slaves and the majority of these are to be found in the Aroa mines.' He then insisted that 'all the power and authority of the Nation' had to be exerted so that 'the Constitution and Laws be duly respected'.[29] While asking that a copy of his letter be forwarded to the Governor of the neighbouring province of Barquisimeto, where the Aroa mines were located, Chitty then added a printed list of all those slaves who had fled the Cata *Obra pía hacienda* between 1824 and 1836 (see Table 9.1), who numbered seventeen individuals, not including the fifteeen who had recently run away. All of them, according to Chitty, had now sought refuge and asylum in Aroa and needed to be tracked down, jailed, tried and brought back to their rightful owners.[30]

Chitty's letter was given due consideration and, within the next few weeks, instructions were personally issued by the Home Secretary, Diego Bautista Urbaneja, and the War Secretary, Rafael Urdaneta, to the effect that 'police dispositions' be fulfilled and the 'ills experienced by slave owners' be duly addressed.[31] The small Ocumare militia was again ordered to carefully patrol all neighbouring areas and Chitty's list of runaway slaves was circulated among the authorities of various neighbouring districts. But the available documents do not reveal what happened beyond the early months of

Table 9.1 List of the runaway slaves from the *Obra Pía de Cata Hacienda*

Date of flight	Names	Age	Status	Features
1824	José Simón	36	Married	Clear mulatto, regular height.
1824	Fulgencio	44	Single	Black, tall, thin, heated eyes, regular face.
1827	Jacobo Santana	44	Single	Little sambo, short body.
1828	José Narciso	23	Single	Clear little sambo, short and thin.
1830	Juan Eugenio	21	Single	Clear mulatto, regular height, thin, with a toupee.
1832	José de la Cruz	27	Single	Black, tall and thin.
1834	José Donato	27	Single	Sambo, with white spots on his face, regular height and thin.
1835	José María Evaristo	34	Married	Tall, thin, clear mulatto, with white spots on his face; very talkative.
1835	Pedro José Santos-pies	28	Single	Black, handsome features, regular body.
1836	José Felipe	29	Married	Clear mulatto, short and fat, frowning look.
1836	José de la Cruz Changala	41	Married	Sambo, regular height, with scars from sores on both legs.
1836	Cornelio el Viejo	53	Married	Light black, tall and thin, well-formed nose, scars from sores on his legs, and suffering from back rheumatism.
1836	Pablo	30	Married	Dark complexion, tall and thin, talkative, stutters slightly, a bruise on his left foot, a sign on his back like a mole.
1836	José Victorio	12	Single	Little sambo, short and thickset all around, flattened nose.
1836	José Félix	35	Single	Clear mulatto, curly hair, somewhat arrogant, usually complains about rheumatism in his back, tall and thin.
1836	José Gregorio	49	Married	Black, short body, round face.
1836	José Cecilio	36	Married	Clear mulatto, short, thickset and frowning look.

Coronel Gualterio D. Chitty, lessee of the aforesaid hacienda, offers a gratification of twenty pesos, and to pay the costs relating to the capture and conveyance to their hacienda, of each one of the slaves named in the list above, and fifty pesos for the arrest of José María Evaristo. The latter roams around the neighbourhood of Mariara or San Joaquín.
    Cata 3 April 1837
        Chitty
    Valencia, Valdes printing office.

Source: Carpeta, 'Fuga de esclavos', Expediente 'Alzamiento y fuga de los esclavos de la Hacienda *Obra Pía de Cata* en Ocumare', Archivo Histórico de Carabobo, 1837.

1838 and, at any rate, no news of any slave capture has remained on file. The case of the 1837 uprising seems to have simply died out and is mainly remembered because Chitty's detailed printed list has become a documentary landmark when dealing with the history and evolution of post-independence slavery in Venezuela.[32]

The 1845 uprising

On 12 February 1845, Santiago Almenar, the Justice of the Peace (*Juez de Paz*) of the Turiamo parish, notified his colleagues in the neighbouring parishes that a sizeable party of runaway slaves – around forty strong and partly equipped with firearms – were roaming across the hills into neighbouring jurisdictions.[33] Notification was immediately sent to the provincial governorship, in Valencia, which, in turn, issued orders for the local militia – originally based in Ocumare – to be armed and sent out. Accordingly, a police patrol (seven men strong) left Ocumare to patrol the mountains surrounding Turiamo.[34]

By 16 February, news arrived that three of the runaways who had been captured by a patrol of the National Guard near Guacara (on the other side of the mountain), and who were being brought back under a two men escort, were forcefully freed, almost upon their arrival in Turiamo, by an angry mob armed with machetes and stones. There were now over sixty slaves 'in hostile and threatening action'.[35] For Marcelino de la Plaza, the Ocumare *Jefe Político*, a major part of the problem was that the local militia did not have sufficient numbers to prevail in such cases. A force of at least 30 men would be required, not to mention the appropriate amount of arms and ammunition.[36]

It soon also became clear that the problem was not only one of lack of men and ammunition. The Carabobo governorship was soon informed by various sources that

> ... the event of the Turiamo slaves is to a great extent due to the bad behaviour on the part of the foreman who is the same person fulfilling there the office of Justice of [the] Peace and that the measures that should be taken pertain more to the hacienda owners than to the government.[37]

The accusations levelled against Justice Santiago Almenar were confirmed by several slaves captured a few days later in Guacara. His 'ill treatment' had indeed caused them to flee.[38]

Upon receiving the reports, particularly the one sent from Ocumare by Marcelino de la Plaza, the Carabobo governorship immediately dispatched a police force – ten men strong – under the leadership of National Guard Commander Simón García.[39] At the same time, instructions were also directed to the provincial Commander of Arms so that an additional contingent of twenty soldiers, led by Sub-lieutenant Antonio José Pérez, was immediately ordered to march to the Ocumare district.[40]

But from the start, the provincial authorities in Valencia suspected that the true causes of the uprising stemmed from the dual function assumed by Santiago Almenar: that of Justice of the Peace and *hacienda* foreman. The two functions were considered 'absolutely incompatible'.

> There was nothing improbable in that the Turiamo slave movement actually originated in complaints presented by the presently runaway slaves against Mr. Almenar, not because of his public authority functions but because of those as administrator of the haciendas to which they belong.[41]

While acknowledging the notifications made by Santiago Almenar regarding the flight of the runaway slaves and assuring him that all measures had been taken to ensure their capture and return to their rightful owners, Carlos Salom, acting on behalf of the Carabobo Governor, also officially instructed – on 26 February, two weeks after the uprising had actually started – the recently appointed Ocumare district *Jefe Político*, Ramón de la Plaza, to

> ...travel to the Turiamo parish so that, upon finding out the true nature of this business, he might take effective measures and put an end to such disorder, while duly and truthfully informing this Government as to what had actually happened so that, if need be, proceedings could be taken against those proven guilty.[42]

This latter task did not particularly appeal to de la Plaza, who complained that, due to the endemic fevers in the Turiamo area (because of the proximity to the Ocumare swamp), a trip there would be equivalent to a journey to his grave. Yet, if the Governor insisted, he had no choice but to sacrifice himself.[43]

For de la Plaza it was obvious that the situation in Turiamo was essentially due both to the population and production structure. The fact that '[t]he Turiamo parish has no free neighbourhood' was for de la Plaza the main reason that the *hacienda* foremen were, at the same time, Justices of the Peace. Furthermore, he observed, the *hacienda* owners were never there, which was

> ...the main cause, in my view, of the disorder noted in that valley. It truly appears, today... that if the owners do not cooperate in mending the evil, the consequences will be dismal, not only in the Ocumare district but in the entire Republic.[44]

By early March 1845, however, the situation in the Turiamo area seemed, slowly, to return to normal. On 8 March, the provincial authorities were notified that several runaway slaves from the Turiamo *haciendas* had already been returned to their masters' service. But the search was still going on, particularly for those who had been involved in the Guacara incident where three captured runaways had been forcibly freed by an angry mob.[45] At the same time, the issues raised concerning the implicit responsibility of the absentee owners in the whole matter now attracted official sanction. On 24 March, the Carabobo Governor officially asked his Caracas counterpart to arrange a meeting with the owners concerned, namely the heirs and/or representatives of Martín Tovar, Catalina Tovar, Concepción Tovar, Francisco Rivas and Juan Zérega.[46]

The ensuing meeting, held two weeks later in Governor Mariano Uztáriz's office, brought together Francisco Rivas; Ramón Monteverde, representing his wife, Concepción Tovar; Martín Tovar Galindo, representing the heirs of Martín Tovar and Juan Zérega; and Antonio Mijares, representing his mother, Catalina Tovar. The first three declared that, as far as they knew, their *haciendas* 'were in the best condition of order and peace, without having to take any particular disposition with regard to their slaves, since the latter were dedicated to their labours, with no runaway slave to single out'.[47] Only Mijares admitted that, in the *haciendas* belonging to his mother and under the management of Santiago Almenar

... about twenty or twenty-four slaves and manumitted workers had fled, in view of – from what he believes – were the painful tasks awaiting them, namely opening a drain and picking coffee.[48]

According to Mijares, eight of the runaways had so far been recaptured and an active search was presently underway to recapture those who were still missing.[49]

The meeting in Caracas with the Turiamo *hacienda* owners seems to have been a turning point in the 1845 slave uprising. The documentary evidence has a six-month gap, followed by an item in the file concerning the Primary Court of Claims of the Carabobo third judiciary circuit, based in Puerto Cabello, where Juan and Dionisio, two runaway slaves from the San Miguel and Santo Domingo *haciendas*, were being tried *in absentia* on the charges of having 'taken away under armed threat' the three slaves captured near Guacara on the previous 16 February.[50]

Based on information from various sources, it was clear to judge Rafael Martínez that the two defendants were not the only guilty parties involved in the matter. The Turiamo Justice of the Peace, Santiago Almenar, had also been guilty of negligence in his duties. He had sent the two defendants to the Puerto Cabello court without any kind of armed guard – so it was hardly a surprise that they didn't showed up for their trial – and he had not filled out the proper preliminary reports on the case.[51] These shortcomings were added to the various irregularities or suspicion of irregularities that had been mentioned since the beginning of the February slave uprising.

All was dutifully summarized in a report sent to the Valencia provincial government. It was Almenar's ambiguous attitude that was now under administrative scrutiny. He had obviously been the first to publicly denounce the uprising, but had delayed all judicial proceedings against the runaway slaves and had even officially shown favour towards them, on his own authority, by granting a seven-day amnesty – all in breach of established procedures and constituting 'an abuse of authority'.[52] At the same time, Almenar had refused to jail the runaways Juan and Dionisio, when captured, despite the latter having been publicly involved in an act of resistance against a constituted authority. Pondering over all these charges, the Carabobo governor Miguel Herrera decreed on 28 October that Almenar be immediately suspended from his office of Justice of the Peace, while administrative charges against him were drafted.[53] Paradoxically, the February 1845 slave uprising was now ending with the trial of the local representative of law and order.

Duly notified of his suspension and the charges he faced, Almenar was requested to present his case before the Primary Court of Claims of the Carabobo third judiciary circuit, based in Puerto Cabello.[54] His trial opened on 29 November 1845. Three charges were officially presented: first, that he had not immediately opened an official inquiry when the two slaves, Juan and Dionisio, had forcibly freed three of their companions, while in military custody; second, that he had granted a seven-day amnesty to all the runaways; and third, that he did not imprison Juan and Dionisio after they had been captured.[55]

In his defence, Almenar argued that he was unable to open an official enquiry because he had no clerks at hand to write out the necessary documents, but had immediately notified the Ocumare municipal authorities of the incident. As to the granting of an amnesty, Almenar explained that, as the foreman of the *haciendas* involved, he had chosen to offer the rebellious slaves a chance to return to their labours. In response to the third charge, the former Justice of the Peace declared that he did not jail the slaves Juan and Dionisio because he simply did not have the manpower to carry out the task.[56]

After hearing the defendant's defence, the court decided that only the third charge remained valid, but considered that a one-month suspension from his judicial duties and a fine equivalent to the cost of the trial was punishment enough.[57] Duly sent to the provincial authorities in Valencia, the sentence was confirmed by the Carabobo governor, Miguel Herrera, who, on 9 December, ordered that Santiago Almenar be reinstated as Turiamo Justice of the Peace.[58] Ironically, the final document on file relating to the 1845 slave uprising is a note from the third circuit court judge Rafael Martínez notifying the governor of Carabobo province that the slaves Juan and Dionisio were still on the run and that their physical description had been requested in order to continue their search.[59] It is not known whether they were ever recaptured.

Consequences

Even though these two slave uprisings appear to follow an overall and seemingly normal pattern of disobedience, revolt and repression, when viewed more closely, they do indeed shed new light on the type of peculiar master–slave relationship that prevailed within the context of a cocoa growing production unit in post-independence Venezuela.

The 1837 uprising took place in a *hacienda* that had been an *obra pía* for over a century and a half, before becoming part of the Caracas *Universidad Central* endowment. It can be assumed, therefore, that its management was traditionally less demanding on its slave workers than that of other *haciendas* directly supervised by their nominal owners and not considered as part of what was, after all, a charitable – or public service – institution. However, matters had changed since 1832, when the *hacienda* was given in concession to this 'Gualterio' Chitty, who merits further attention.

His real name was actually Walter Dawes Chitty, born in Deal (Kent) in 1794 and one of the many volunteers who had come to fight, in the so-called 'British Legion', for Venezuela's independence.[60] A sailor by profession, Chitty had arrived in 1818 to the island of Margarita and had distinguished himself in the July 1823 naval battle of Maracaibo, which ensured the surrender of one of the last royalist strongholds in the country.[61] During the *Gran Colombia* period (1821–30), he served as a captain in the young republic's navy, both in the Pacific and in the Caribbean.[62] A declared supporter of Simón Bolívar, Chitty, whose first name had now been Hispanicized to '*Gualterio*', was expelled from New Granada at the end of 1830, following the disintegration of the *Libertador*'s *Gran Colombia* scheme.[63] He then settled down in the port town of Puerto Cabello, in Venezuela, where he set up a coastal trading business and remarried.[64] It was probably though this line of business, as well as through his new wife's connections,[65] that he became involved with the Ocumare region cocoa *haciendas* and decided to place a bid for the administration of the Cata *Obra Pía*.[66] His reputation as a 'hero' of the Independence Wars certainly worked to his advantage and he was granted the concession on the *Obra Pía* for an 18-year period.[67] Chitty, who also owned a coffee *hacienda* in the valley of San Esteban, near Puerto Cabello, probably considered that the Cata *Obra Pía hacienda* would prove to be a most lucrative enterprise, once properly and 'efficiently' managed.

New instructions as to the duties to be performed in the *hacienda* as well as a new work timetable were probably introduced, which seemed to have been met with a certain degree of resistance. It is significant to note that twelve out of the seventeen runaway slaves reported by Chitty in his 1837 printed document had fled since 1832, that is to say from the date he had taken over as administrator.[68] If one were to add the fifteen runaways from 1837, this meant that over one-quarter of the *hacienda*'s entire slave workforce and over half of the male slave workforce (according to the figures of the 1833 slave census) had chosen to escape from their chores, thus probably leaving the *hacienda* critically short of workers.

As a former British subject, Chitty was aware of the involvement of fellow expatriates in the operation of the Aroa Copper Mines and was probably also aware that many of them, unlike himself, were active abolitionists who would readily lend a helping hand to runaway slaves. At the same time, by taking his claim to the country's President, who had been a former companion in arms, Chitty, while anticipating an immediate intervention, was also elevating the whole matter from a local issue to potentially a diplomatic incident.

The Aroa Copper Mines, once the personal property of Simón Bolívar, had been granted by his heirs to a British concern, representing the first direct foreign investment in Venezuela since independence.[69] Was it then possible to intervene to determine the fate of private property in which the territorial autonomy was not clearly defined? In other words, were a few runaway slaves and the complaints of a small group of cocoa growers justification for a potential conflict with one of Europe's great powers? Could strictly private interests, such as those governing the practice of slavery as an institution, justify intervention by the forces of the state? It seems that the answer was 'no' on both counts, particularly given the fact that Gualterio Chitty fell ill and died in November 1839.[70] His case was apparently buried with him and, presumably, a new bidder had to be sought for the administration of the Cata *Obra Pía hacienda*.

Similarly, in the 1845 Turiamo slave uprising, it was clear from the beginning that some form of administrative malpractice was at the core of the matter. The actual causes of the uprising seem to have been quite innocuous: 'opening a drain' or 'picking coffee' could hardly be considered particularly onerous tasks. Yet, they probably were at variance with long-established work routines. At the same time, the fact that Justice of the Peace Santiago Almenar, in other words, the local authority representative, would occupy the function of *hacienda* foreman caused jurisdictional problems. Once again, the conflict between public and private interests inevitably led to an imbroglio.

In his annual report presented to the Carabobo provincial legislature on 4 November 1845, Governor Miguel Herrera summarized the Turiamo events:

> Various slaves and manumitted workers escaped, being under the custody of the same person who exerted the function of Justice of the Peace ... [as a result of] what the owner declared to the Hon. Governor of the Caracas Province ... [to be] certain impending painful tasks; but the seemingly exaggerated warnings sent by this Justice to the neighbouring authorities and above all a dispatch sent by the Hon. *Jefe Político* from Ocumare informing that three of the runaways, captured and brought back to the haciendas to which they belonged, were forcefully taken away from the national guardsmen who were conducting them, by about sixty other slaves ... [who] remained ... in a hostile attitude, moved this Governorship to dispatch ten men of the same guard so that ... they might prevent that public order ... [from] being disrupted ... The Hon. *Jefe Político* from Ocumare returned the aforesaid force, while announcing a restored tranquillity in Turiamo ...[71]

Peace had been restored, which was the priority for the authorities, but the slave revolt had highlighted other problems, namely residual poverty and social inertia. According to Governor Herrera, these problems had a common cause:

> One may observe that the first necessity of this part of such a generally benign population is inaction; the summit of their pleasures is rest, and such ignorance which consists in not knowing about any other kind of life preferable to theirs, or in not appreciating the advantages of such better kind, or deeming it inaccessible, is what truly brands their character. These mixed causes and effects of the wretchedness in which they manage to satisfy all their needs, are, without any doubt, also the cause of the prodigality and improvidence with which they consume all the fruits of their limited work ... without thinking, usually ... [of] what tomorrow will bring ... Hence also, it seems to me, the reason for this constant clash between the entrepreneurs of large agricultural estates and the invincible apathy of those persons with whom they count as day labourers for the cultivation of their *haciendas*, and for their harvests.[72]

Even though the Carabobo governor's derogatory speech referred explicitly to free labourers, his words were equally applicable to slaves and manumitted workers.

The lessons to be drawn from the uprisings in Ocumare are that slavery, as an institution in post-independence Venezuela, while obviously a condition of personal servitude, could hardly be considered – at least in cocoa *haciendas* – as a particularly arduous condition in terms of the work that was required. This is in marked contrast to slavery in sugar plantations. In the cultivation of cocoa, the traditional master–slave relationship was mellowed by the type of labour involved, and remained temperate provided no unexpected modifications were made to the work regime. At the same time, while slavery was part of the public domain as a legal institution until 1854, its application – since slaves were 'legally' private property – remained confined to the private sector. Any involvement by the state, in the context of a liberalized economy, as was the case after independence, might be considered undue interference in private economic matters. It was not because they had fled their *haciendas* that slaves were pursued and prosecuted, but because they eventually represented a potential threat to public peace and contravened regulations geared to control public vagrancy and designed, in a situation of extreme labour shortage, to tie down – so far as possible – a labourer to his place of work. In this respect, the situation of a free labourer was not all that different from that of a slave. But the authorities *did* make the distinction and in the case of the Ocumare region, where slavery was an important part of the economy, measures were usually taken to try to resolve problems amicably before resorting to repression, which, apart from being costly, often failed to solve problems that arose between slaves and their masters or their master's representatives. Turmoil in the cocoa groves had to be subdued as peacefully as possible so that the social and economic system might be protected, a system rightly considered harmonious, precisely because it could – and would – remain unaltered.

Notes

1. Alejandro de Humboldt, *Viaje a las regiones equinocciales del Nuevo Continente* (Caracas: Ministerio de Educación, 1956), vol. 2, 233. From east to west, the Cuyagua and Cata coves, followed by the Ocumare and Turiamo bays, can thus be identified.
2. Francisco de Solano (ed.), *Relaciones topográficas de Venezuela 1815–1819* (Madrid: CSIC, 1991), 239–40.
3. Agustín Codazzi, *Resumen de la geografía de Venezuela* (Caracas: Ministerio de Educación, 1940), vol. 3, 65–6.
4. The Spanish word *villa* designated here an urban settlement that enjoyed a specific number of privileges: its inhabitants, at least initially, could only be of Spanish origin and benefited from certain rights, particularly fiscal exemptions.
5. de Solano, *Relaciones topográficas*, 240. This figure included the houses belonging to the neighbouring *haciendas*.
6. de Solano, *Relaciones topográficas*, 240.
7. Pedro Cunill Grau, *Geografía del poblamiento venezolano en el siglo XIX* (Caracas: Presidencia de la República, 1987), vol. 1, 357–9.
8. The Manumission Law, enacted in July 1821 and which aimed at the gradual extinction of slavery, stipulated that all future children of slaves would be considered free upon reaching the age of eighteen. By anticipating the gradual extinction of slavery as an institution, the Manumission Law also contributed – according to slaveowners – to increasing insubordination by those workers still bound to their slave status. See John V. Lombardi, *The Decline and Abolition of Negro Slavery in Venezuela 1820–1854* (Westport, CT: Greenwood Press, 1971), 41–2.
9. Nikita Harwich, 'Ocumare de la Costa, puerto de cacao venezolano : 1800–1870', in Michèle Guicharnaud-Tollis (ed.), *Caraïbes: Éléments pour une histoire des ports* (Paris: L'Harmattan, 2003), 70.
10. See Magnus Mörner, *Local Communities and Actors in Latin America's Past* (Stockholm: Institute of Latin American Studies, 1994), 94–7.
11. An *obra pía*, or 'pious work', was the donation of a given property, usually productive land, to a religious authority which would adminster the property and use its proceeds to fund a charitable institution, usually a hospital. Certain limitations were involved: in particular, an *obra pía* could neither be sold nor mortgaged.

12. Harwich, 'Ocumare de la Costa, puerto de cacao venezolano', 59–60.
13. Harwich, 'Ocumare de la Costa, puerto de cacao venezolano', 64–5.
14. 'Censos', Archivo Histórico de Carabobo (Valencia), hereafter referred to as AHC, May 1833.
15. The *Jefe Político* was the chief municipal officer within a given district.
16. Gualterio Chitty to Cata District *Jefe Político* as copied in dispatch sent by Manuel F. Delgado to Ocumare District *Jefe Político*, Cata, 1 April 1837, Gobierno de Carabobo, Carpeta 'Fuga de esclavos', Expediente 'Alzamiento y fuga de los esclavos de la Hacienda *Obra Pía de Cata* en Ocumare', AHC, 1837.
17. Gualterio Chitty to Cata District *Jefe Político*, 1 April 1837.
18. Gualterio Chitty to Cata District *Jefe Político*, 1 April 1837.
19. Manuel F. Delgado to Ocumare District *Jefe Político*, 3 April 1837.
20. Manuel F. Delgado to Ocumare District *Jefe Político*, 3 April 1837.
21. Manuel F. Delgado to Ocumare District *Jefe Político*, 3 April 1837.
22. Manuel F. Delgado to Ocumare District *Jefe Político*, 3 April 1837.
23. Luciano Benítez to Governor of the Carabobo Province, Ocumare, 6 April 1837, 'Fuga de esclavos'.
24. Antonio Osorio to Governor of the Carabobo Province, Puerto Cabello, 18 October 1837, 'Fuga de esclavos', AHC.
25. Gualterio D. Chitty to HE the Vice-President In Charge of Executive Office, Caracas, 13 November 1837, 'Fuga de esclavos', AHC.
26. Gualterio D. Chitty to HE the Vice-President In Charge of Executive Office, Caracas, 13 November 1837, 'Fuga de esclavos', AHC.
27. Gualterio D. Chitty to HE the Vice-President In Charge of Executive Office, Caracas, 13 November 1837, 'Fuga de esclavos'.
28. Gualterio D. Chitty to HE the Vice-President In Charge of Executive Office, Caracas, 13 November 1837, 'Fuga de esclavos'.
29. Gualterio D. Chitty to HE the Vice-President In Charge of Executive Office, Caracas, 13 November 1837, 'Fuga de esclavos'.
30. Gualterio D. Chitty to HE the Vice-President In Charge of Executive Office, Caracas, 13 November 1837, 'Fuga de esclavos'.
31. Diego Bautista Urbaneja to Governor of the Carabobo Province, Caracas, 13 December 1837, 'Fuga de esclavos', AHC.
32. See, for instance, Lombardi, *The Decline and Abolition*, 92, n. 38, and Mörner, *Local Communities and Actors*, 98.
33. Santiago Almenar to Second District Court of Justice of the Peace, Turiamo, 12 February 1845, as copied in Manuel Lovera to Governor of the Carabobo Province, Guacara, 14 February 1845, Caja 'Todos los Meses', Carpeta 'Orden Público', Expediente 'Sobre la fuga de una partida de esclavos de la Parroquia de Turiamo, amenazando la tranquilidad pública', AHC, 1845.
34. Marcelino de la Plaza to Governor of the Carabobo Province, Ocumare, 16 February 1845, Expediente 'Sobre la fuga de una partida de esclavos', AHC.
35. Marcelino de la Plaza to Governor of the Carabobo Province, Ocumare, 16 February 1845, Expediente 'Sobre la fuga de una partida de esclavos', AHC.
36. Marcelino de la Plaza to Governor of the Carabobo Province, Ocumare, 16 February 1845, Expediente 'Sobre la fuga de una partida de esclavos', AHC.
37. Luis Silva to Governor of the Carabobo Province, Patanemo, 17 February 1845, Expediente 'Sobre la fuga de una partida de esclavos', AHC.

38 Manuel Lovera to Governor of the Carabobo Province, Guacara, 17 February 1845, Expediente 'Sobre la fuga de una partida de esclavos', AHC.
39 C. Salom to *Jefe Político* of the Ocumare District, Valencia, 19 February 1845, no. 289, Expediente 'Sobre la fuga de una partida de esclavos', AHC.
40 C. Salom to Provincial Commander of Arms, Valencia, 19 February 1845, Expediente 'Sobre la fuga de una partida de esclavos', AHC.
41 C. Salom to *Jefe Político* of the Ocumare District, Valencia, 19 February 1845, no. 290, Expediente 'Sobre la fuga de una partida de esclavos', AHC.
42 C. Salom to *Jefe Político* of the Ocumare District, Valencia, 26 February 1845, no. 348, Expediente 'Sobre la fuga de una partida de esclavos'. Ramón de la Plaza was obviously related to Marcelino, presumably an older brother.
43 Ramón de la Plaza to Governor of the Carabobo Province, Ocumare, 1 March 1845, no. 52, Expediente 'Sobre la fuga de una partida de esclavos'.
44 Ramón de la Plaza to Governor of the Carabobo Province, Ocumare, 1 March 1845, no. 52, Expediente 'Sobre la fuga de una partida de esclavos'.
45 Governorship of the Carabobo Province Primary Court of Claims of the Carabobo 3rd judiciary circuit, Valencia, 8 March 1845, Expediente 'Sobre la fuga de una partida de esclavos', AHC.
46 Governor of the Carabobo Province to Governor of the Caracas Province, Valencia, 24 March 1845, Expediente 'Sobre la fuga de una partida de esclavos', AHC.
47 Mariano Ustáriz to Governor of the Carabobo Province, Caracas, 7 April 1845, Expediente 'Sobre la fuga de una partida de esclavos', AHC.
48 Mariano Ustáriz to Governor of the Carabobo Province, Caracas, 7 April 1845, Expediente 'Sobre la fuga de una partida de esclavos', AHC.
49 Mariano Ustáriz to Governor of the Carabobo Province, Caracas, 7 April 1845, Expediente 'Sobre la fuga de una partida de esclavos', AHC.
50 Rafael Martínez to Governor of the Carabobo Province, Puerto Cabello, 25 October 1845, no. 470, Expediente 'Sobre la fuga de una partida de esclavos', AHC. In his dispatch, Martínez included copies of all previous correspondence pertaining to the case.
51 Rafael Martínez to Governor of the Carabobo Province, Puerto Cabello, 25 October 1845, no. 470, Expediente 'Sobre la fuga de una partida de esclavos'.
52 Rafael Martínez to Governor of the Carabobo Province, Puerto Cabello, 25 October 1845, no. 470, Expediente 'Sobre la fuga de una partida de esclavos'.
53 Decree signed by Miguel Herrera, Governor of the Carabobo Province, Valencia, 28 October 1845, Expediente 'Sobre la fuga de una partida de esclavos', AHC.
54 José Medina to Governor of the Carabobo Province, Ocumare de la Costa, 3 November 1845, Expediente 'Sobre la fuga de una partida de esclavos', AHC.
55 Rafael Martínez to Governor of the Carabobo Province, Puerto Cabello, 29 November 1845, no. 566, Expediente 'Sobre la fuga de una partida de esclavos', AHC.
56 Rafael Martínez to Governor of the Carabobo Province, Puerto Cabello, 29 November 1845, no. 566, Expediente 'Sobre la fuga de una partida de esclavos'.
57 Rafael Martínez to Governor of the Carabobo Province, Puerto Cabello, 29 November 1845, no. 566, Expediente 'Sobre la fuga de una partida de esclavos'.
58 Miguel Herrera to *Jefe Político* of the Ocumare District, Valencia, 9 December 1845, no. 1798, Expediente 'Sobre la fuga de una partida de esclavos', AHC.
59 Rafael Martínez to Governor of the Carabobo Province, Puerto Cabello, 5 January 1846, no. 18, Expediente 'Sobre la fuga de una partida de esclavos', AHC.

60 The biographical information on Walter Chitty has been gathered primarily from an Argentina-based website, www.irishgenealogy.com.ar/genealogia/c/chitty/george.php.
61 www.irishgenealogy.com.ar/genealogia/c/chitty/george.php.
62 www.irishgenealogy.com.ar/genealogia/c/chitty/george.php.
63 www.irishgenealogy.com.ar/genealogia/c/chitty/george.php.
64 His first English wife, named Emily, had died some time before. His second wife, Ursula Matilde Liendo y Ascanio, daughter of Coronel Juan José Liendo y Larrea and María Mercedes Ascanio de Rada y Ponte, a distant cousin of Simón Bolívar, was – in turn – the widow of another foreign volunteer of the Bolivarian cause, the Prussian captain Ludwig Flegel von Sitzemburg, who had died of diphtheria in 1831 at age thirty-five.
65 It was her first husband, the Prussian captain, who had actually purchased a cocoa *hacienda* in Cata, registered in his Hispanicized first name, 'Luis' Flegel.
66 See *Actas del Claustro Pleno (1831–1833)*, *Boletín del Archivo Histórico* 4, Ildefonso Leal (ed.) (Caracas: Ediciones de la Secretaría de la U.C.V., 1985), 259–371.
67 *Actas del Claustro Pleno*.
68 See Table 9.1.
69 See José María Surga R., 'Las minas de Aroa', in Nikita Harwich Vallenilla (ed.), *Inversiones extranjeras en Venezuela. Siglo XIX* (Caracas: Academia Nacional de Ciencias Económicas, 1994), vol. 2, 8–64, and Paul Verna, *La minas del Libertador* (Caracas: Presidencia de la República, 1975), 187–247.
70 Information provided by www.irishgenealogy.com.ar/genealogia/c/chitty/george.php.
71 Miguel Herrera, 'Exposición que dirige a la honorable diputación de la Provincia de Carabobo sobre varios ramos de la administración municipal el Gobernador', in Antonio Arellano Moreno (ed.), *Memorias provinciales 1845* (Caracas: Ediciones del Congreso de la República, 1973), 74.
72 Herrera, 'Exposición que dirige', 80.

Part Three

Social Mobility on the Margins of Slavery, Freedom and Slave Ownership

10

Keeper of the Keys: Creole Management of a Nineteenth-Century French Plantation in New Orleans

Nathalie Dessens

In 1818, Henri de Ste-Gême left Louisiana forever and returned to his native castle of Bagen in south-western France, about sixty miles west of Toulouse. He left behind several pieces of urban property (land and houses) in New Orleans, as well as a plantation in Gentilly, on the outskirts of New Orleans, on which a handful of slaves remained in the care of Auvignac Dorville, a twenty-five-year-old Louisiana Creole. Over a period of fifty-five years, from 14 March 1818 to 12 September 1873, Dorville wrote 209 letters and a total of 399 pages, first to Ste-Gême and, after the latter's death in 1845, to his nephew Anatole de Ste-Gême, keeping them updated on the property Ste-Gême owned in New Orleans through regular (although sometimes infrequent) communication.[1] Dorville performed many tasks for Ste-Gême. He ran errands to obtain official documents and have them certified by the French Consul, for Ste-Gême himself but also, sometimes, for Ste-Gême's acquaintances who had family or business interests in Louisiana. He managed Ste-Gême's urban properties in New Orleans, keeping the houses in good repair, finding tenants, collecting rent, paying taxes, paving *banquettes* and making all the infrastructural improvements required by law; in short, running Ste-Gême's property in his stead.[2] He also collected debts for him, and even probably lent some of Ste-Gême's money, compiling interest for even greater gain. More importantly, he managed the Ste-Gêmes' Gentilly plantation and oversaw the life and work of the slaves, starting from Ste-Gême's departure, in 1818, until the sale of the plantation to John McDonogh, shortly before the latter's death, in 1850.[3] Despite the sale, Dorville remained on the plantation for five more years. Although he continued to manage the rest of the Ste-Gême family's assets until 1873, he left the plantation in October 1855 and settled in New Orleans for a few years, before retiring to St Bernard Parish at the end of the Civil War.[4]

The long history of this plantation, from its concession, in the early eighteenth century, to its sale, 125 years later, could be considered as 'traditional'. However, there are several unusual characteristics that make it depart from the norm or, at least, from what is considered as the norm in the Lower Mississippi Valley. First, the plantation by no means resembles the Louisiana plantation usually considered by historians. Most of the historiography on the Louisiana plantation economy focuses on the large cotton and sugar plantations of the Mississippi Valley which, if they did employ the largest populations of slaves and generate the largest economic exchanges, in particular compared to the rest of the United States, were, by no means the only model of plantation in Louisiana.[5] The Gentilly plantation corresponds to the model that prevailed in the peri-urban areas and has been largely neglected by the historiography.[6] Second, Ste-Gême was an accidental slaveholder, having acquired the plantation and its contents by marrying the widow of Louis Leufroy Dreux, the Louisiana Creole who had previously owned it. Moreover, if Ste-Gême could, at first sight, qualify as what has been the representation of a typical slaveholder (he was White, wealthy, educated and politically active), he gained no direct status and even no real revenue from his slaveholding and was an absentee planter. Yet, he never considered selling the plantation, although neither he nor his family ever returned to Louisiana. Finally, for a half-century, if the Ste-Gêmes remained the nominal owners of Gentilly, Auvignac Dorville, from a more modest Louisiana background, kept the keys to the Big House, having been given carte blanche by Ste-Gême. This constitutes the main anomaly in the ownership of the plantation and of its labour force. The 1818–73 correspondence from Dorville to the Sainte-Gêmes, archived at the Historic New Orleans Collection, reveals the strange (although not unique) position of Ste-Gême as a slaveholder. It also details the unconventional slave management Dorville exerted and the relationship he instituted with the slaves whose care he had been entrusted with.

After giving some contextual elements about the plantation itself, showing how it differed from the common depiction of a Southern Louisiana plantation, this chapter examines both the relationship of Ste-Gême to slaveholding and the actual slaveholding, in fact although not in name, of Auvignac Dorville, showing one of the many different ways in which atypical forms of slaveholding manifested themselves in the Atlantic world.

The Gentilly plantation

The history of the Dreux plantation is that of many plantations of the peri-urban New Orleans space. It was one of the earliest concessions, ceded by Jean Baptiste Le Moyne de Bienville, to Mathurin and Pierre Dreux, on 28 March 1725, a mere seven years after the foundation of New Orleans. It remained in constant use by the Dreux family throughout the eighteenth century. When Louis Leufroy Dreux died, in 1814, it became the property of his twenty-seven-year-old wife, Marguerite Delmas Dreux. When she married Henri de Ste-Gême, in 1816, the latter took charge of the plantation management, although he exerted it directly only for a short period of time.

The Gentilly plantation was located four and a half miles from the French Quarter, in what is today known as the East Orleans neighbourhood of Gentilly.[7] In the inventory established for the Dreux succession, in 1814, it is described as agricultural property belonging to the Dreux Braizé family, by Charter of Louis XVI, King of France. It was composed of two pieces of property that both spanned Bayou Sauvage.[8] The main property, where the plantation house was located, was a little over one mile in length, spread on both sides of the Bayou.[9] It was bounded 'on the northern side by the cypress groves of Lake Ponchartrain', and 'on the southern one, by those of the Mississippi River'. If the long history and size of the plantation might suggest one of the large plantations of the Lower Mississippi Valley, its detailed description does not correspond to what is typically expected of a plantation. Instead of a mansion similar to those that could be most frequently seen along the Mississippi river,[10] it contained 'an old half-timbered master house in bad condition, raised seven feet above the ground', one kitchen, a few outbuildings (one cowshed, one stable, one building for carts) and eleven slave cabins. The description of the master house reveals a relatively rudimentary lodging including only two rooms and a pantry. In 1814, the whole property was valued at 10,000 piastres.[11] There was a second piece of property, located one league (about three miles) from the other, also in Gentilly, on both sides of the Bayou as well, of which about fifty acres had been cleared.[12]

The workforce was composed of about twenty slaves, as indicated in the inventory of 1814. Dorville's letters mention a few purchases and a few deaths in the almost four decades of his management of the plantation, which suggests that the workforce remained relatively stable throughout the period, with very infrequent variations of one or two slaves. In 1814, there were nine male slaves, aged from twenty-four to sixty, six female slaves, aged fourteen to forty-five, two ten-year-old boys and four children under four. In 1829, Dorville speaks of his eleven male slaves and four female slaves working in the sugar cane fields, which suggests that there had been little evolution in fifteen years.[13] Many of the slaves' names inscribed in the 1814 inventory recur in Dorville's letters, which suggests that, beyond the numerical stability of the slave population, many of the original slaves remained on the plantation, at least until it was sold.[14]

The plantation was not one of those large sugar or cotton plantations of the Lower Mississippi Valley usually described in literature.[15] Although Dorville tried to turn it into a sugar plantation in the late 1820s, the climate was too uncertain for a sugar plantation with such a limited number of slaves to prosper. Dorville noted that they would have needed to at least double the number of slaves to guarantee a potential profit in sugar cane production. In 1828, when he decided to turn Gentilly into a sugar plantation, he mentioned the capital Ste-Gême had left in his hands 'with insufficient force to exploit it'.[16] Even with a larger workforce, profitability would not have been insured, since, for the next ten years, Dorville only mentioned the constant climatic catastrophes which destroyed his sugar cane crops, the cost of turning Gentilly into a sugar plantation, and the low prices and lack of demand for the sugar produced. The result is that, for most of its nineteenth-century existence, the plantation produced mainly cypress wood, firewood, hay and food products that the slaves sold on the New Orleans markets. Cattle and other livestock were essential in the enterprise. The 1814 inventory enumerates cows, oxen, calves, horses, mules and sheep. The livestock seems to have increased during the period of Dorville's management and he mentions several times the profits yielded by the sale of milk by the slaves at the market.

We are far from the image of the vast sugar or cotton plantations generally studied in Louisiana historiography.[17] The twenty slaves do not correspond to the representation generally conveyed of slaveholding in the Lower Mississippi Valley. Yet, when looking at the 1834 *Topographical Map of New Orleans and its Vicinity* by Charles F. Zimpel, it

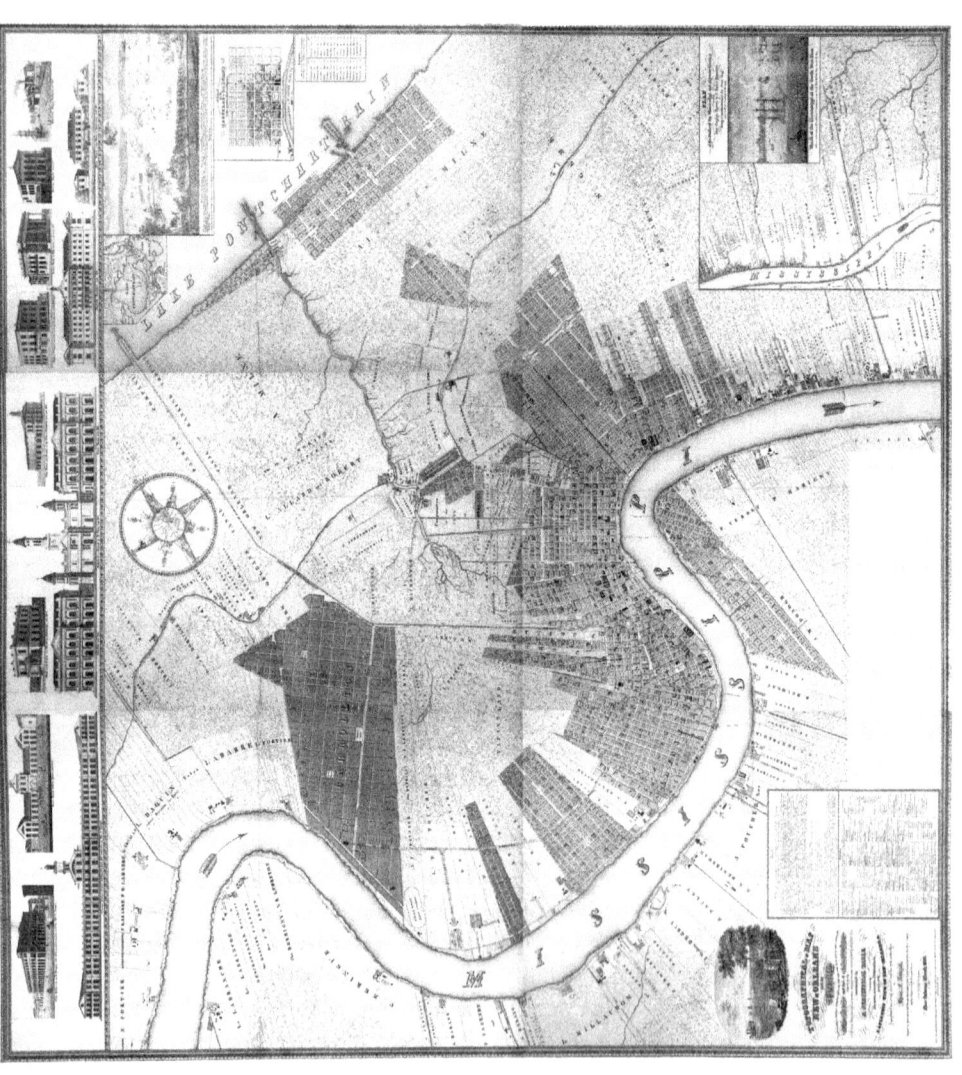

Figure 10.1 *Topographical Map of New Orleans and its Vicinity*, 1834. By Charles F. Zimpel.

is obvious that many plantations in the New Orleans peri-urban space in the early nineteenth century resembled the Ste-Gême one and that a number were even smaller, although others had more slaves than Ste-Gême's, Dorville evoking the fifty slaves of his neighbour, for instance.[18]

Although many of these small plantations attempted a conversion to sugar growing in the 1820s, most of them produced agricultural goods similar to Ste-Gême's. If we except the mention of sugar in the twenty years when Dorville was trying to produce cane (starting in 1828 but increasingly reducing the acreage of this commodity to less than three acres in 1846), most of the plantation products supplied the local markets.[19] Because it spread over the swampy area between Bayou Sauvage and Lake Pontchartrain, a large part of the land was hardly productive, save for the commercialization of wood (cypress wood and firewood) often mentioned by Dorville in his accounts. Some revenue also came from the renting out of slaves. In 1821, for instance, he mentions that Clarisse was rented out for $12 a month[20] and, several times over the years, he informs Ste-Gême that such and such slave was rented out, mostly women. Hay, cattle, sheep, poultry and dog breeding were other income sources on many of these plantations. In 1822, Dorville wrote, 'My fowl are superb, with many ducks, a few turkeys, about fifty geese, and more than two hundred hens, two-thirds of which are white.'[21] He often mentioned the sale of poultry and eggs, which is sufficiently important for some of the slaves to be devoted to this task. In a letter dated 28 May 1820, Dorville mentioned two slaves, Augustin and Honoré, designated as part-time *coquassiers*, which means, in French, persons selling poultry and eggs.[22] He also mentioned, in another letter, dated 5 February 1821, the necessity for him to replace Amazilie, whose task was to sell milk, with Zaïre, because the former had just given birth, explaining to Ste-Gême that this product was so profitable that he could not imagine losing its share of the plantation revenue.[23] Finally, as indicated in most of the letters and accounts, a large part of the benefits came from agricultural produce sold at the New Orleans markets. The production he enumerated in his letters and yearly accounts included corn, rice, oranges, plums and other kinds of fruit, milk, butter, cantaloupes, sweet potatoes, potatoes, beans, fava beans, all kinds of melons and gourds, cabbages, lettuce, pecans and other such goods. In 1822, for instance, he mentioned nineteen acres of corn.[24] In 1821, he informed Ste-Gême that he had a crop of 38,000 to 40,000 oranges.[25]

Some of Dorville's letters give a good measure of what was most profitable on the plantation. In 1820, for instance, he obtained more than $1,000 for milk, $996 for hay, $898 for wood, $700 for oranges, and $45 for corn, to which he added rice and sheep without more detail concerning the gains.[26] After over ten years of attempts at producing sugar, he reported that the profits in sugar for the years 1839 and 1840 were $1,028 and $841 respectively. In the same years, he earned $732 and $559 by selling melons.[27] In 1849, he added that his melons were 'one of the main sources of revenue'.[28]

The world of Lower Louisiana plantations was not exactly what is usually expected, and, in the peri-urban space, food production was an essential part of the plantation economy. This was the first peculiar or very specific character of some of the slave work in Lower Louisiana. The other myth the Gentilly plantation debunks is that all Louisiana planters were rich whites who dominated local economic, cultural and political life.

Ste-Gême, absentee slaveholder

Ste-Gême became the owner of the plantation when he married Marguerite Dreux, the young widow of the previous owner, in 1816. After barely two years, however, he returned to his home town in south-western France, Sauveterre-de-Comminges, where he settled in the family Chateau de Bagen, with his wife and her two teenage children, managing the family property for his aging parents. He kept ownership of the plantation until his death, in the mid-1840s, after which the property remained in the family, and his nephew, Anatole de Ste-Gême, who had never lived in Louisiana, became Dorville's correspondent, probably because Ste Gême's sons, born after their return to France, in the 1820s and 1830s, were too young for property management. If absentee planters were common in the Caribbean, especially the British Caribbean, there is little mention of them in the American South. And if absentee planters had plantations in the tropics, it was to reap the benefits of this lucrative ownership. Not so with Ste-Gême. Indeed, all of Dorville's accounts show that the benefits derived from the whole property, that is the plantation and the houses in town, were minimal if there were any at all. Most of the time, the plantation was barely self-sustaining, which means that Ste-Gême did not have to cover any cost on his Louisiana property but did not make any profit either. Several letters mention that the revenues were so low that Dorville could not clear enough money to pay his own salary. In July 1825, for instance, he wrote:

> I have been promising you for a long time a statement of your revenues and expenses. According to what I sent you last year, which concerned the year before, you could judge of the lowness of the gains. Those for last year, and until the present, have again been very little, as most of my slaves' time was spent building the house. These gains have nevertheless amounted to 2,000 and a few piastres that served to pay for the usual expenses, as well as those for the material for the house and the workers. I have not yet finished paying the whole. I owe $197.50. I have some money left but the taxes will take part of it. Despite all, I see with satisfaction the term approach when I entirely liquidate my debts. Then I will think of myself. My salary for last year is still unpaid. I am now painting the house, with the help of Laurent and once everything is finished, it will have cost me more or less $2,000. In a few days, I will know exactly how much to the last cent.[29]

Most yearly accounts confirm the meagre financial returns on Ste-Gême's Louisiana property. In 1832, for instance, Dorville informed Ste-Gême that 'The year that is ending will be the third in a row in which I have not received my salary.'[30]

Despite this absence of profit, Ste-Gême apparently never considered selling the plantation during his lifetime. The reasons why Ste-Gême kept his New Orleans property are unknown, although it is possible to speculate. The plantation had come from his wife's family-in-law and his wife might have been unwilling to sell it. Although her youngest Dreux child, her son Edgar (baptized Henry), died in 1823, her daughter Hermina (Marie Hermina) was still alive when Ste-Gême died.[31] She might have wished to keep it for herself and as a tribute to the Dreux family members who remained in Louisiana. Ste-Gême may also not have wanted to sever the links that still tied him to the New World, since he also retained the urban property he had himself acquired when he was in Louisiana. Finally, being a property and slaveowner in America may have added to his prestige in France. Some of Dorville's letters are addressed to 'Henry de Ste-Gême, the American', indicating that it might have been for Ste-Gême a means to increase his status and reputation. Importantly, he did not have to dispose of his Louisiana property since it was financially self-sustaining. He did not make money out of it, but did not lose money either.

The result is that the Ste-Gêmes were the owners of slaves they never saw again after their departure in 1818, and that they remained the owners of slaves after slavery was abolished in France in 1848. The correspondence shows that they were concerned about their slaves, apparently not only for financial reasons. Most letters include a paragraph about the slaves' health and occupations, very often in great detail. The reason for this inclusion might have been to keep Ste-Gême informed of the state of his property and financial interests, slaves included. It might also have been to account for the production of the plantation and thus the revenue it yielded. But there are, many times, clear indications that it was at the request of Ste-Gême's wife, and that she was concerned about slaves she had known and lived with for years before her departure for France. To cite only one of the many examples found in Dorville's correspondence, his letter of 28 May 1820 reads:

> Madame Ste-Gême is asking for detailed news of all the slaves. I will readily satisfy her request, starting with the oldest. Old Marie-Louise is peacefully living with César who rejuvenates at her cooking. Big and little Josephs, the two Basiles, Hector, Bacchus, and Charles are all good as far as health is concerned and relatively good as far as work is concerned. I am still satisfied with Laurent. I would not like to see him leave the plantation. I made a carter and a ploughman of him. He digs, shovels, and pickaxes well. Catherine is still a little crazy. Nérisse is not doing much. She is sometimes good[,] sometimes bad and, to be frank, she is a mean creature. Amazilie keeps getting pregnant. My doubts about Zaïre's pregnancy were confirmed. She is rented out in town for fifteen piastres a month. Clarisse is also rented out for twelve piastres a month. Her child is with her and he is in good health. Augustin and Honoré are the two greatest rascals I know. They are cowherds part of the day and domestics, gardeners, and egg and poultry sellers the rest of the day. With all that, they often give me the devil. Irma is still in perfect health. Victore, who is now only known under the name of Spanish gentleman, is also doing well. I take good care to instruct and nourish these two children.[32]

The familiarity with which he speaks of the slaves individually suggests that Mme de Ste-Gême knew them all or, at least for those born after her departure, knew of them.

Interestingly, the actual owners of the Ste-Gême Gentilly slaves seemed to correspond to a very typical representation of the slaveowning planters of nineteenth-century Louisiana. Ste-Gême was a wealthy white man, belonging to the French aristocracy. He had been a high-ranking officer in the French Royal Army, then served in the British Hussars in Saint-Domingue and, after the 1798 British evacuation from the former French colony, he became a captain in the 1st Regiment of the Colonial

Dragoons under Toussaint Louverture's rule. When Napoleon sent an expeditionary corps to try to regain control of the lost colony, Ste-Gême joined it and became squadron leader of the Gendarmerie of Saint-Domingue, in command of General Rochambeau's personal horse guard.[33] He retreated from Saint-Domingue and was discharged from the army. Among the flux of Saint-Domingue exiles, he started his second career as a privateer, first in Cuba, then, after 1809, in New Orleans. In the Louisiana capital, he was clearly among the renowned figures of the high society. Upon arrival in New Orleans, he became a high-ranking officer in the militia, commanding the *Dragons à Pied*. As major, he was second in command of the militia and distinguished himself during the Battle of New Orleans, for which he was officially acknowledged by General Andrew Jackson.[34] Ste-Gême was always part of high society, be it in Cuba, New Orleans or later in France, when he returned to his castle in the south-west. There, he held political power, becoming mayor of his home town, Sauveterre-de-Comminges, and a member of the General Council of Haute-Garonne. As a wealthy white slaveowning aristocrat, economically, socially and politically influential, Ste-Gême seems to fit perfectly the representation commonly held of a slaveowner. Except that he was an absentee slaveowner, a relatively unusual, although not exceptional, situation in nineteenth-century Louisiana; and except that, after his death, his French heirs still owned slaves although France had abolished slavery in 1848. Like his heirs after him, he was thus only the virtual owner of the Gentilly slaves. The one really managing them, acting and writing as if he was the real owner, was Auvignac Dorville, a Louisiana Creole, a member of the more modest white population of Louisiana.

Slaveholder by proxy

Auvignac Dorville, originally named Jean-Baptiste LaMolère Dorville, was born in 1793 in New Orleans, of parents both native to the parish; although Dorville's paternal grandfather was a native of Bordeaux, his maternal grandmother was also born in New Orleans. He himself did not own property when he accepted the keys to Ste-Gême's Gentilly plantation, but his family did. He was thus part of white Creole New Orleans society, although, in contrast to Ste-Gême, he was never part of high society.[35]

White people belonging to the non-propertied classes managing the plantations and overseeing the slave population of absentee masters were not uncommon in the Atlantic world. The phenomenon was even relatively widespread in the West Indian colonies of Britain and, to a lesser degree, France and Spain. It was not usual in the Anglo-American South, even if some extremely wealthy planters who owned several properties or spent the stifling Southern summers outside their plantations could, at least part of the time, leave their plantation management to others, especially on the large plantations of South Carolina. It was not even unheard of in Louisiana, although it was quite rare. The present case, however, is relatively out of the ordinary because both official documents and Dorville's letters to Ste-Gême often give the feeling that Gentilly and its slaves belonged to Dorville. The latter indicated many times in his letters that Ste-Gême had given him total control over the plantation, its crops and slave labourers. *Carte blanche* are the words he used to describe his status. In a long paragraph in which he apologized for not being more effective in his management, he referred to 'the time when [Ste-Gême] left [him] entirely in charge and with *carte blanche*'.[36] As long as he did not need any financial complement to run the plantation and as long as he was self-sufficient, he could make any decision he wanted concerning the management of the estate. He turned it into a sugar plantation without asking Ste-Gême, in 1828.[37] He turned it back to food crops a few years later, again without asking permission, progressively reducing the acreage of sugar from around forty in the early 1830s to less than four in 1846.[38] Many letters prove that he could invest in repairs, embellishments and slaves without seeking Ste-Gême's sanction. In a letter dated 25 September 1823, he gave an account statement, announcing a revenue of $980.25, and added, 'Which I keep and wish to use, without having asked your consent, to acquire two slaves. There is going to be an auction of seized Creole slaves next month who will sell on long term credit, and, with the cash, I could perhaps have three and the rest will reproduce little by little.'[39]

The result was that his management of the slaves resembled more closely what was practised in the small plantations of the Virginia backcountry than what was usual in the Lower Mississippi Valley. He lived in extremely close proximity to his slaves, one of whom, Irma, regularly mentioned in his correspondence, was his daughter. Listing the slaves in his 31 August 1819 letter, he noted that 'Irma whom I do not put in their number, because she calls me papa, also enjoys good health' (Folder 40). Another slave who clearly enjoyed a special status, Victor, was often mentioned, although no detail was given about his parentage.[40] He was apparently of mixed ancestry (hence nickname, 'Spanish gentleman'), and his task on the plantation was to serve Dorville's meals. Dorville emphasized that he took good care of Victor's instruction and food, and there can be little doubt that he took good care of all the slaves, if only because they were indispensable to the survival of the plantation. To give just one example, in a letter penned on 5 February 1821, he wrote:

> Last year, I repaired the main road of the plantation. The front of the slave cabins has been carefully elevated and drained, which has contributed to the good health that they have enjoyed this past summer, and even until the present. Amazilie is finally the mother of a pretty little girl who was born on the 22nd of September last at eleven o'clock at night. As she was sick for a long time before delivering and because this is her first baby, I will spare her until the weather is nice. Then I will rent her out. Instead of Amazilie, Zaire is now selling the milk because this activity is too profitable to be neglected. I was deceived twice about Zaire's pregnancy. I thought she was pregnant, but she was only late. Clarisse is still rented out at $12.00 a month on condition that the person who rents her maintains her child. In two or three months she will enrich you with another little slave, which means that she will not bring in any rent for some time. Nérisse is well at present. I hope that will continue. Victor is beginning to serve me at table. He already knows a lot. As for my daughter Irma, she is with Madame Dabévil who is showing her how to sew. She will remain apprenticed for two years and maybe more, unless, my dear monsieur Ste Gême, unforeseen circumstances bring you back to Louisiana with your family before that time.[41]

Dorville was informed of the smallest details concerning the slaves, including the most intimate ones of the enslaved women. In yet another letter, he detailed the gynecological problems of another enslaved woman in his care, Nérisse, asking Ste-Gême to try to get medical advice because the Louisiana doctors had been unable to cure her.[42]

This does not mean, of course, that the Gentilly slaves' status was more enviable than the rest of the Louisiana slave population. Indeed, Dorville several times mentioned punishments meted out to the slaves whose care he was entrusted with. But when examining the accounts of the plantation, it is apparent that the welfare of the slaves was an important part of Dorville's expenditures. Among the expenses listed in the accounts, a good share is devoted to the slaves. Dorville listed food, money spent to retrieve runaway slaves from jail, medical fees (for diseases, deliveries or dental care), New Year's gifts and clothes for slaves, and apprenticeships for some of them. Dorville's limited financial means may explain why he was so attentive to the health and reproduction of the slaves, the only way he had to maintain or even enlarge the workforce. But he also readily expressed feelings for all of the slaves he mentioned, varying according to the individual, showing that he did not consider them as mere chattels or as the equivalent of productive and reproductive cattle. For example, when announcing the illness of one of the older slaves, on 21 May 1822, he wrote, 'Your wife will learn with much distress that poor Basile has consumption.'[43] In October of the same year, he wrote, 'I am now awaiting with grief, at any moment, the hour when he passes away.'[44] A few months later, in a letter dated 16 January 1823, he shared the following:

> May God keep them and all the others in good health as long as possible, but especially till the moment when I must return them to you one day, so that I may not experience the sadness of having to write to you that this one is sick and that one is dead. I lost old César, on November 16th last of indigestion that complicated a diarrhea that nothing could stop. His old age and lack of strength did not make him very useful on the plantation, but he was an old servant and was always there. Poor Basile is still fighting his disease. I gave him a remedy from Dr Le Boy and it provoked a very advantageous change. I am short of this remedy but there is much in the river and as soon as possible I will continue this treatment, in the hope of announcing to you one day that I saved him.[45]

Dorville did not leave the plantation until 1855, not even when it was sold, in 1850, explaining to Ste-Gême that the new owner, John McDonogh, did not want him to leave. Although the specific arrangement he had made with the heirs of the latter is not known, he remained on the plantation for five years after McDonogh acquired it, until he left for New Orleans where he managed only the Ste-Gêmes' town property until the autumn of 1873.[46] For almost four decades, he was the de facto owner of the slaves of the Gentilly plantation, mostly using the first person possessive pronoun when he spoke of them, of the plantation or of anything pertaining to Ste-Gême's possessions. He called Hopkins 'my neighbour', spoke of 'my melons' when mentioning the plantation harvest and said 'my slaves' when discussing Ste-Gême's human property. This was clearly not a mistake, since sometimes he acknowledged the fact that some slaves were his own property. In a letter of 1846, for instance, he wrote, 'Your Caroline will before very long enrich you with another slave. I must warn you in advance that I claim half, because it is Charles, my servant, who did the work, and it would be unfair if you collected the whole.'[47] The constant use of the first-person possessive pronoun and the tone used to account for the management of the plantation leaves no doubt about Dorville's sense of autonomy and his power of decision.

Among the essays contained in the present collection, this one is slightly unconventional in that while it remains within the framework of white male slaveholding, the situation that pertained was much less conventional than may appear at first glance. Although Ste-Gême, an educated, politically involved white man belonging to the upper class, was the official slaveholder, his slaveholding was nominal, since the keys to the Big House were in the hands of a white Louisiana Creole who belonged to a less wealthy stratum of white Louisiana society. The total liberty and responsibility granted by Ste-Gême to Auvignac Dorville made him the actual slaveholder in Gentilly.

If absentee slaveholding was common in the West Indies, particularly in the British and, although to a lesser extent, French colonies, it was much less common in Louisiana. The Gentilly plantation knew the fate of many a plantation of the Atlantic world, and the division between ownership by a French aristocrat and totally autonomous management by a Louisiana Creole, with frequent exchanges of information and expertise from both sides of the ocean, gave it a definite Atlantic character.[48]

Although most of Ste-Gême's neighbours in Gentilly were not absentee planters, the types of plantation they owned were very similar to Ste-Gême's. They were all part of the small agro-urban world of New Orleans, comprising small plantations with limited slave workforces living in close proximity to the white person in charge, whether the actual owner or the *de facto* one, as in the case of Dorville. These were slaves who enjoyed considerable freedom of movement compared with the slaves of the larger plantations of the Mississippi Valley. If they did not represent the largest part of the Louisiana slave population in terms of numbers, they were not an insignificant presence either. Surely the time has come to add to the mainstream historiography on slaveholding in Louisiana, with its focus on the more traditional slave system, by dedicating research to the small plantations.

Notes

1 The letters are part of the Sainte-Gême Family Papers (MSS 100), hereafter SGFP, archived at the Williams Research Center of The Historic New Orleans Collection, in New Orleans (Louisiana). The present chapter is part of a larger research project conducted in collaboration with Louisiana historian Virginia Meacham Gould, which will produce a book tentatively entitled *The Keys to the Big House: A Creole Plantation in the Atlantic World*.

2 *Banquette* is the word from the French still used in New Orleans to refer to the sidewalk.

3 Dorville's letter, dated 2 August 1850, indicates the final settlement of the sale to McDonogh and the first payment of $13,250 (Folder 316).

4   Dorville's last letter from Gentilly is dated 18 September 1855 (Folder 351). He says he intends to leave Gentilly in October. His next letter, dated 20 November, was written from New Orleans (Folder 354). After 1865, all his letters were written from St Bernard.
5   The historiography of Louisiana plantations has essentially focused on the large plantations of the Mississippi Valley. See, for instance, Richard Follett, *The Sugar Masters: Planters and Slaves in Louisiana's Cane World, 1820–1860* (Baton Rouge: Louisiana State University Press, 2005), or Walter Johnson, *River of Dark Dreams: Slavery and Empire in the Cotton Kingdom* (Cambridge, MA: Belknap Press of Harvard University Press, 2013), which are probably the two recent works that most extensively cover plantation slavery in the Lower Mississippi Valley.
6   There are hints at the place of the slaves on the New Orleans markets (see, for instance, Rashauna Johnson, *Slavery's Metropolis: Unfree Labor in New Orleans during the Age of Revolutions* (New York: Cambridge University Press, 2016), 55–84), but in general the authors of these works focus on the slave economy rather than on food-producing plantations such as Ste-Gême's Gentilly one. See, for instance, Ira Berlin's *Many Thousands Gone: The First Two Centuries of Slavery in North America* (Cambridge, MA: Belknap Press of Harvard University Press, 1998), in particular the chapter entitled 'Slavery and Freedom in the Lower Mississippi Valley' (325–57). A few lines may be found in Thomas N. Ingersoll's *Mammon and Manon in Early New Orleans: The First Slave Society in the Deep South, 1718–1819* (Knoxville: University of Tennessee Press, 1999), when he mentions the fact that most of the Crescent City's slave population resided in the plantation neighbourhoods of the Orleans Parish (247), but there is no detailed treatment of what these plantations may have looked like in the early nineteenth century. The reason why no work has been dedicated to the peri-urban plantations, whose main revenue was produced by food crops grown for New Orleans's markets, can partly be explained by the fact that they were not included in the main capital-producing structures and that they did not produce much capital, but also that the slaves working on them did not constitute the majority of the Louisiana slave population.
7   All the descriptive elements are taken from the inventory of the plantation made on 24 May 1814, after Louis Leufroy Dreux's death. Inventory of the Estate of the Late Louis Leufroy Dreux, Register of Wills Office, Court of Probates, Parish of Orleans, State of Louisiana (a copy is available in MSS 100, Folder 626).
8   The plantation is clearly visible as 'St Gême' on Charles F. Zimpel's 1834 *Topographical Map of New Orleans and its Vicinity* (Historic New Orleans Collection, no. 1945.13), http://www.requestaprint.net/thnoc/gallery_hr/1955.19.a_f.jpg, and on the Maverick/Ogden 1829 *Map of the City of New Orleans* (Historic New Orleans Collection, no. 11921.21).
9   The inventory records '30 to 32 *arpents* facing both sides of Bayou Sauvage'. This indicates a width of one mile. The inventory does not give any measurement of width. All maps represent the property as more or less square, which would suggest that it was about one square mile, that is to say around 640 acres.
10 The description of the Ste-Gême plantation is very different from what can be found in most works related to Louisiana plantations, for instance the Laura plantation in Vacherie (Louisiana) in Laura Locoul Gore's *Memories of the Old Plantation Home and A Creole Family Album* (Vacherie, LA: Zoë Company, Inc., 2001). Following the same trend, see also S. Frederick Starr, *Une Belle Maison: The Lombard Plantation House in New Orleans's Bywater* (Jackson: University Press of Mississippi, 2013), or Craig A.

Bauer, *Creole Genesis: The Bringier Family and Antebellum Plantation Life in Louisiana* (Lafayette: University of Louisiana at Lafayette Press, 2011).
11 Throughout the correspondence, as was customary in Louisiana in the early American period, Dorville interchangeably uses dollars, gourdes and piastres.
12 The second piece of property was larger (about three miles in length and three-quarters of a mile wide on both sides of the Bayou), but only fifty acres had been cleared.
13 Sainte-Gême Family Papers (MSS 100), Folder 137. All further references to this correspondence will be abbreviated as SGFP. All quotations have been translated from the original French by the author of the present chapter.
14 There is nothing in Dorville's letters indicating what happened to the slaves when he left the plantation, a good five years before the beginning of the Civil War. They might have been freed or sent to Liberia with the rest of the McDonogh slaves. See G. Leighton Ciravolo, *The Legacy of John McDonogh* (Lafayette: Center for Louisiana Studies, University of Louisiana at Lafayette, 2002), 9.
15 See, for instance, David D. Plater, *The Butlers of Iberville Parish, Louisiana. Dunboyne Plantation in the 1800s* (Baton Rouge: Louisiana State University Press, 2015).
16 SGFP, Folder 118.
17 Because they were highly visible and because they influenced on a larger scale the economy of the American South (and even of the United States more generally), the plantations featured most often in historiography are the large cotton and sugar plantations. See, for instance, the works by Follett and Johnson referred to above. See also Edward E. Baptist, *The Half Has Never Been Told: Slavery and the Making of American Capitalism* (New York: Basic Books, 2014), or Scott P. Marler, *The Merchants' Capital: New Orleans and the Political Economy of the Nineteenth-Century South* (New York: Cambridge University Press, 2013).
18 See the map at http://www.requestaprint.net/thnoc/gallery_hr/1955.19.a_f.jpg.
19 In his letter of 16 February 1846, he wrote that he planted just four *arpents* of sugar cane (SGFP, Folder 296).
20 SGFP, Folder 48.
21 SGFP, Folder 59.
22 SGFP, Folder 42.
23 SGFP, Folder 48.
24 SGFP, Folder 61.
25 SGFP, Folder 48.
26 SGFP, Folder 41.
27 SGFP, Folder 288.
28 SGFP, Folder 299.
29 SGFP, Folder 99.
30 SGFP, Folder 210.
31 SGFP, Folder 77.
32 SGFP, Folder 42.
33 Nathalie Dessens, *Creole City: A Chronicle of Early-American New Orleans* (Gainesville: University Press of Florida, 2015), 12.
34 Dessens, *Creole City*, 14.
35 The Dorvilles would never have found space in Grace King's *Creole Families of New Orleans* (New York: MacMillan Company, 1921), while she dedicates a chapter to Ste-Gême (Chapter XXXVII, 443–5). From what we know of him, the Ste-Gême family could not be considered a Creole family and it is clearly his high status that made him acceptable in King's pantheon of New Orleans society.

36 SGFP, Folder 154.
37 SGFP, Folder 118.
38 SGFP, Folder 296.
39 SGFP, Folder 75.
40 He might have been a Dreux descendant. It is unlikely that he was fathered by Dorville, who would probably have said so, just as he did about Irma. And he cannot have been Ste-Gême's son, since the latter only arrived in Louisiana in 1809, where he fathered three free children of colour with his Saint-Domingue 'housekeeper'. Dessens, *Creole City*, 22–6.
41 SGFP, Folder 48.
42 SGFP, Folder 41.
43 SGFP, Folder 59.
44 SGFP, Folder 62.
45 SGFP, Folder 66. This is an exact translation of the sentence in French. The medicine he used might have been extracted from algae or fish, or any product found in the river.
46 His last letter is dated 12 September 1873, and was written from St Bernard, where he retired in 1865 at the end of the Civil War (SGFP, Folder 476).
47 SGFP, Folder 296.
48 Many of Dorville's letters mention his sending oranges, hot peppers, pecans and even ducks to the Ste-Gêmes. In exchange, he asked Ste-Gême to send him scythes and even hunting dogs.

11

João de Oliveira's Atlantic World: Mobility and Dislocation in Eighteenth-Century Brazil and the Bight of Benin

Mary E. Hicks

At nearly seventy years old, with a thick beard and white hair, richly dressed in a ruffled shirt, a waistcoat, pink pantaloons, a blue cloak, stockings and beaded Moroccan slippers, João de Oliveira returned to Salvador da Bahia after thirty-seven years on the west coast of Africa.[1] In 1770, when Oliveira made the maritime journey, it would have taken approximately forty-six days to traverse the South Atlantic waters between the ports of the Bight of Benin and colonial Brazil's most active slaving entrepôt – Salvador da Bahia.[2] Oliveira had been residing on the so-called Mina Coast – a region which stretched from Fort São Jorge da Mina in Elmina eastward to the western edges of the Niger delta – as a *cabeceira* or commercial agent of the African slave trade.[3] The wooden sailing ship also held seventy-nine enslaved men and forty-three enslaved women from the Bight of Benin, owned by Oliveira.[4] Also accompanying him were four West African *cabeceiras* sent by the 'King of Onim'.[5] They were identified as 'free men' acting as ambassadors to Portuguese commercial interests in the slaving ports of Recife and Salvador da Bahia in the north-eastern region of colonial Brazil.

Though Oliveira, in dress, connections and property, displayed all the trappings of an elite merchant, he was in fact not born in Europe or even Brazil. Far from an ordinary slave trader, Olivera's unlikely trajectory had begun in the same region of the West African coast where he resided as a *cabeceira*. Born in the Bight of Benin, more specifically on the Mina Coast, he was 'seized by countrymen younger' than himself as an adolescent, a traumatic memory that continued to linger into his old age.[6] On his face he bore the marks of his natal community: scarification in the form of three lines on each cheek.[7] Though Olivera never specified which community he had been born into, during the early eighteenth century most of the slaves trafficked from Bight of Benin originated in the Fon- and Yoruba-speaking communities living 100 miles from the coast.[8] Thereafter he was sold into bondage and transported to Brazil on a slaving ship destined for the north-eastern port of Pernambuco.[9] If Oliveira had been trafficked to Brazil in the 1710s, as his professed age and testimony of his abduction and enslavement would suggest, he arrived at the eve of one of the high points of Pernambuco's transatlantic slave trade. From the years 1701 to 1725, an estimated

121,301 men, women and children disembarked at the port, as slaving rapidly expanded in the 1720s.[10] An average of 5,054 enslaved Africans arrived annually in the early decades of the eighteenth century – the vast majority from the Mina Coast – making it the second most active period for the slave trade in the Captaincy of Brazil between 1560 and 1851, the date of the trade's cession.[11]

Most of the enslaved Africans who were disembarked in the Captaincy's capital, Recife, were destined for the sugar plantations and gold mines of the interior, where an insatiable demand for labour drove the transatlantic traffic in captives.[12] Oliveira, however, was fated for a different path. During his American enslavement he laboured in the 'resgate' or trade in slaves from West Africa.[13] His unlikely trajectory from enslaved African to freed *cabeceira* on the West African coast revealed that through his long life he had been enmeshed in the complex commercial currents and imperial politics that connected West Africa and Brazil during the mid- to late eighteenth century. Oliveira's remarkable geographic mobility illuminates the interconnectedness of the two regions, as well as the particularities of Brazilian slavery which allowed a small number of bondsmen and women the ability to travel and operate in contexts independent of their owners, even as far as the other side of the Atlantic Ocean. Within this context, Oliveira seized his remarkable geographic mobility, as he utilized imperial Portuguese institutions and customs in order to acquire superior legal statuses. During the course of his long lifetime, he evolved from free adolescent, to slave, to freedman to slave owner.

Though Oliveira's story could easily be construed as a linear unfolding of ever greater freedom and opportunity, it was the initial moment of his dramatic dislocation from his natal community – his enslavement and forcible removal from West Africa – that enabled such a trajectory in the first place. Ultimately it was his 'serial displacement', or multiple dislocations that began in Africa and continued to the Americas, which fostered his incredible geographic and social mobility.[14] Though his life was highly unusual, the intertwined nature of his displacement, disconnection, removal and mobility defined not only his experience of Atlantic slavery, but the experiences of many other enslaved Africans as well.[15] Oliveira's return to Bahia after his acquisition of freedom further illustrates this paradox; as he arrived in port, he was taken into custody, imprisoned, with his property confiscated, as he stood accused of participating in a smuggling operation on the West African coast. Once again, he was subject to captivity, perhaps in part because of his status. The targeting of Oliveira specifically may have been a result of prejudice against a formerly enslaved African-born man.

It was as a result of his detention in May of 1770 that Oliveira's voice enters the archive, as he authored a petition for clemency to the Portuguese Crown. The resulting legal protest is one of the few examples of a text created from the perspective of an African-born person in the Portuguese Empire in this era. It frames both his activities on the West African coast and his connections to a Brazilian slaving community, thus revealing his own understanding of the incentives of the colonial state and its commercial interests. He insisted that his 'unwavering contributions to Portuguese navigation' – in the form of his participation in the transatlantic slave trade – demonstrated his impeachable honesty and honour. His testimony illuminates the degree to which, even for people of African descent, slaveholding legitimated one's social status and sense of belonging within the empire. Crucially, Oliveira's freedom and mobility were also tied to the enslavement of others. Like many European slaveholders in the Atlantic world, his property holding and participation in the slave trade enabled his freedom and social ascendancy. Within the context of the early modern Atlantic, traffic in enslaved bodies acted as a form of social currency and power – especially for those born outside of traditional realms of status.[16] As a formerly enslaved slaveholder, however, Oliveira was unique. His ability to successfully operate within both African and Brazilian contexts made him a particularly effective trader. He boasted that he was able to 'open' the African ports of Porto Novo and Onim to Portuguese slaving interests, indicating his skill in cultivating commercial and political connections within the Bight of Benin. His multiple linguistic and cultural fluencies, like those of other Atlantic Creoles of the era, provided him with the means to escape slavery and social marginality, and eventually to make lasting ties with members of the white slave trading elite.[17] In the process he solidified the Brazilian commercial presence in port cities east of Ouidah, guaranteeing the perpetuation of the slave-based economy in Bahia and Pernambuco. Despite this, his African ancestry also made him particularly vulnerable to surveillance and imprisonment. He never truly became an equal to his white peers.

West African politics and a fractious trade

Long before João de Oliveira's arrival on the African coast, Bahian and Pernambucan slave traders had sought to re-establish themselves on the West African Mina Coast after their displacement by the militarily and financially powerful Dutch in 1637. Moving east from Elmina, the Portuguese constructed a trading fort in Ouidah in 1721, a port city which functioned as the 'the most important point of the embarkation for slaves' in the West African region, supplying an estimated one million enslaved men, women and children for transatlantic markets.[18] French, English, Danish and Portuguese slavers all competed for commercial advantage within the slaving port, and success often hinged on the ability to negotiate effectively with local African rulers and merchants. In contrast to other European empires, most slaving voyages arriving on the African coast originated in the colonies not the metropole, as Brazilian merchant ships from Bahia, Pernambuco and Rio de Janeiro spearheaded new transatlantic trading routes. This 'bilateral' rather than triangular trade provided Brazilian merchants greater control over slaving on the West African coast. It also meant that colonial settlements – not European cities – provided the critical personnel, trade commodities and infrastructure for slaving ventures in West Africa.[19] As Robin Law and Kristin Mann point out, the close connections between the Mina Coast and the north-east of Brazil fostered a continuous two-and-half-centuries-long cultural and commercial exchange that facilitated the slave trade.[20]

Brazilian merchants' effort to establish commercial relations in Ouidah coincided with a period of intense political volatility following the Dahomean King Agaja's conquest of Allada in 1724. This upheaval ushered in a period of increasing hostilities between that slave trading polity and surrounding ones, continually disrupting Atlantic commerce. The relative peace, efficiency and immense volume of the slave trade

Table 11.1 Slaves arriving in the north-eastern ports of Brazil

Time Period	Bahia	Pernambuco	Totals
1551–75	0	2,928	2,928
1576–1600	6,644	19,180	25,824
1601–25	54,449	90,694	145,143
1626–50	81,518	53,505	135,023
1651–75	111,633	45,776	157,409
1676–1700	117,932	92,326	210,258
1701–25	209,491	121,301	330,792
1726–50	264,094	80,993	345,087
1751–75	191,993	76,923	268,916
1776–1800	239,489	79,835	319,324
1801–25	282,043	191,529	473,572
1826–50	175,876	105,047	280,923
1851–75	1,146	438	1,584
Totals	1,736,308	960,475	2,696,783

Estimates courtesy of Stephen Behrendt, David Eltis, Manolo Florentino and David Richardson, *Voyages: The Trans-Atlantic Slave Trade Database*, www.slavevoyages.org.

controlled by Huedan middlemen based in Ouidah in the initial decades of the eighteenth century was instantly disrupted when Dahomey, based in Abomey, seventy miles from the coast, sacked and destroyed the city in 1727. Following the Dahomean military's successful drive to the coast – which included an attack on Savi months earlier during which thousands were killed and enslaved – Agaja and his army swiftly conquered Ouidah, driving out Huedan King Hufon and burning the Portuguese *feitoria* to the ground.[21] Agaja spared the remaining European trading forts, explaining to the resident personnel that the purpose of his military conquest was to gain access to the Atlantic trade. He claimed that the Hueden King had forbidden him to trade, and thereby precipitated Dahomey's hostilities.[22] This allegation was likely a reference both to Allada's control over the roads between Abomey and the Atlantic coast through which slave caravans travelled in the seventeenth century, as well as Hufon's continuing resistance to becoming a tributary of Dahomey.[23]

In the decades following the sack of Ouidah, Dahomey carried out its own blockades of these routes from the interior – where men, women and children were captured and enslaved – and the Atlantic seaports from which they were embarked by European ships. Though the war between Dahomey and Hueda ended in 1732, Bahian merchants continued to complain that the slave trade had slowed to a halt, with some ships returning to Brazil empty, and others whose voyages were delayed for over a year.[24] That same year, Dahomey attacked Jakin, levelling all the European trading forts there except for that of the Portuguese, and followed with a conquest of Badagry in 1737.[25] Each of these cities were rivals to Dahomey in the Atlantic trade, and they continued to be targets of the militarized kingdom's aggression along the coast along with the newly opened ports of Porto Novo and Ekpe until the end of the century.

The bellicose Agaja – who resided in the inland capital of Abomey – presented a particular challenge to slave traders stationed in Ouidah, at least according to Atlantic merchants and Portuguese administrators. Despite Agaja's overtures to the Portuguese, including an invitation to build trading forts on Dahomean controlled lands, royal administrators remained wary, opining that the African potentate 'destroys as many [African polities] as he conquers'.[26] Though this sentiment attempted to diminish the King of Dahomey's importance in the fortunes of European and American traders in the region, the military powerhouse wrought continuing commercial instability in the region.[27] Driven by Dahomey's persistent quest to control and monopolize the slave trade in the region, Bahian – and European – trading on the coast was periodically paralyzed. During this period Dahomey did not limit its aggression exclusively to other West African trading polities; slave traders, captains and their crews were regularly caught up in such violence, and sometimes imprisoned or killed. Mariners also faced dangers from pirates – both European and African – who plagued the coast.[28] In response to these dangers, Bahian traders moved eastward, to ports beyond the reach of Dahomey's army, especially those controlled by their powerful rival, the Oyo Empire.

This period of turmoil was a double-edged sword for the many Atlantic merchants who ventured to the coast to trade in slaves. The hostilities between displaced Huedans and the expanding slaving empire of Dahomey, which lasted until 1775, continued to produce war captives, some of whom were sold into the transatlantic slave trade. The ongoing instability, however, also endangered personnel stationed within the São José Baptista de Ajuda fort in Ouidah, the Portuguese Crown's only territorial foothold on the coast. The first attack on Ouidah saw the storekeeper of São José Baptista, Simão Cardoso, decapitated, with his head then reportedly delivered to Agaja.[29] In 1743, the director of the *feitoria*, João Basílio, was taken prisoner by Agaja's successor, Tegbessou, under suspicion of colluding with the exiled Huedan King by supplying him with weaponry to attack Dahomey. A Dahomean siege of the fort on the same day as Basílio's arrest led to its destruction, when the African 'head servant' tasked with running it in Basílio's absence set fire to the building with a keg of gunpowder after most of the Huedan refugees housed in the fort had been slaughtered.[30]

Though the fort was rebuilt in 1744, Tegbessou again riled Portuguese administrators by violating their claims to jurisdiction over management of the *feitoria* when he unilaterally appointed Francisco Nunes Pereira as director of São José Baptista. Pereira was a Portuguese trader who had likely orchestrated Basílio's arrest and expulsion from the Mina Coast, but he was able to ingratiate himself with the ruler, and bypass the approval of Portuguese authorities, in order to become the de facto lead trader. His tenure as director was short-lived, however.[31] Portuguese administrators found Tegbessou just as disagreeable as his father, going so far as to chastise the 'boldness and imprudence of the petty barbarian king'.[32] In these difficult decades, the *Conselho Ultramarino* – or Overseas Council – debated closing down the fort, reasoning that the value derived from the taxes paid by slave trading there were inadequate to reimburse the costs of maintaining the fort.[33] The second destruction of the São José Baptista fort prompted other European traders on the coast to assess their own vulnerability, with the director of the French fort in Ouidah exclaiming after the incident that 'if the Dahomeans (fierce people) once began to cut the throats of the whites, this country would become a slaughter house for us, and with the slightest discontent which these people might pretend to have, they would kill us like sheep'.[34] Brazil's viceroy intervened in 1751, appointing a new director for the rebuilt fort and reiterating the centrality of the Ouidian trade to Bahia's fortunes, arguing 'there should be no chance of suspending the trade which is so necessary for this State of Brazil'.[35]

Dahomey and its rivals' battles for regional supremacy periodically diminished trade on that portion of the Mina Coast, as did the increasing taxes levied by the King of Dahomey, requiring each ship captain to pay one slave to 'open the trade' as well as ten additional slaves upon the completion of a cargo. This was a much higher duty than the six slaves paid to the King, and two to his *caboceiras* that the Huedan ruler had mandated previous to his expulsion.[36] In the face of the declining favourability of trading terms, on 30 March 1756, the Portuguese Crown opened the Mina Coast to private traders allowing slavers to legally bypass the *feitoria* at Ouidah. Pierre Verger argues that this shift led to an overall decline of trade at Ouidah as well as an expansion of Bahian merchants slave trading activities eastward.[37] The ports of Badgary, Porto Novo and Onim already carried on a regional trade in slaves and other commodities with neighbouring communities on the lagoon, and each received slaves via caravans driven from the interior which were controlled by Oyo to whom these coastal African polities were tributaries.[38] As Brazilian slaving merchants scrambled to expand their commerce eastward, João de Oliveira's fluency in both Portuguese and West African languages and cultures became instrumental in establishing trade at Porto Novo in 1758.

João de Oliveira's West African diplomacy

As Oliveira would explain many years later, he first returned to the Mina Coast as an enslaved man, in 1733. Though Oliveira was vague about the labour he performed before arriving in Africa, his owner was likely involved in slaving as either a merchant or ship captain. Oliveira's entrance into the world of slave trading possibly occurred as he worked as a mariner or cabin boy on a vessel travelling to the African coast. By the slightly later date of 1775, royal administrators noted that Recife was home to 423 enslaved mariners – some of whom worked on the seven vessels that regularly travelled to the African coast.[39] In the nearby port of Bahia, as in Pernambuco, enslaved and freed African men made up 40.4 per cent of all registered sailors, while enslaved men comprised 35.8 per cent; of these 41.3 per cent of all African mariners laboured on vessels travelling to the West African coast.[40] In the port of Bahia, slaving ship owners and captains frequently employed their own bondsmen as seafarers.[41] Crucially, African mariners not only provided the skilled labour necessary to navigate sailing vessels to the West African coast, but also at times disembarked in African ports and engaged in small-scale trading of their own volition. Because of the long-standing privilege of allowing seamen a *caixa de liberdade* – an allotment of space within a ship's cargo hold to store personal trading goods – even enslaved mariners who laboured on routes to the African coast were able to accumulate money from both wages and transatlantic commerce.[42] In the initial years of his enslavement in Recife, Oliveira could have taken advantage of Portuguese legal custom which allowed enslaved people to hold property (*peculium*) as well as mariner trading privileges to begin to accumulate a modicum of personal wealth.[43]

Within a few years of arriving in Pernambuco, Oliveira's exceptional social ascent began as he utilized imperial Portuguese legal and cultural institutions to augment his status. He appears to have learned the Portuguese language, allowing him to receive the holy sacrament of baptism, and become 'unified with the people of the [Catholic] church'.[44] While Oliveira framed his conversion to Catholicism in terms of entering a community of fellow worshippers, his embrace of the religion indicated an attempt to recapture a sense of belonging through acculturation. In a petition to the Crown after his arrest, he argued that his entrance into the Catholic Church was one of the seminal moments of his life. He took pains to paint his exceptional devotion to Christianity as sincere and long-lasting – another sign of his fitness for the status of a vassal of the Portuguese Crown. His conversion thus entailed both performative and social dimensions.

His adoption of Christianity coincided with his eventual return to the Mina Coast on a slaving vessel where, under the auspices of his owner, Oliveira began work as a trader 'among his [former] countrymen'.[45] As a *cabeceira* and 'favourite' of African kings of diverse territories and ports where Portuguese merchants purchased slaves, he acted as an intermediary between slaving merchants and African potentates.[46] As a trader, Oliveira swiftly rose from an impoverished enslaved man to an influential middleman in the coastal slave trade in the Bight of Benin. His ascent began as he 'recuperated his primary and natal liberty' by purchasing his manumission from his owner – likely utilizing wealth he had accumulated from participating in slave trading while still enslaved. Like other urban and wage-earning slaves, Olivera's access to currency facilitated his manumission by self-purchase, which was the most common route to legal emancipation in colonial Brazil, and generally involved enslaved men and women paying their own market value to their owners periodically in small instalments.[47] As a freedman, Oliveira argued, he had led an exemplary life as a Portuguese subject, of which his enduring Catholic faith was a part. He recalled that he had 'always preserved the purity of his [C]atholic faith' through his many charitable acts, including donating money for the construction of the church *Nossa Senhora da Conceição dos Militares* and by gifting enslaved men and women as alms to various Catholic brotherhoods in the city of Recife. After he secured his manumission by paying for the 'value of his liberty' he '[in keeping with] Christian doctrine' provided financial support for the impoverished widow of his former owner.[48]

Following his manumission, Oliveira's intervention in the volatile imperial politics and commerce of the Mina Coast proved decisive for Portuguese commercial interests there. Oliveira argued that he had 'helped [Brazilian merchants] to affect their business with the most kindness'.[49] His activities included intervening in the 'assaults, and robberies' that African potentates had ordered their men to carry out against Brazilian traders.[50] Violence, a constant consideration within the slave trade, was particularly pointed during this period of Dahomey's and Oyo's expansion. Like its neighbour and tributary to the west, Dahomey, Oyo was an expansionist slaving empire which militarily subjugated other Yoruba-speaking city-states west of the Niger river, utilizing warfare to generate captives to sell to Atlantic merchants and making defeated polities into tributaries.[51] After Dahomey destroyed Oyo's principle Atlantic trading port, Jakin, in 1732, Oyo shifted its slaving routes to the coast eastward.

Olivera's return to West Africa coincided with Oyo's search for new oceanic outlets for its slaves and goods. By 1758 he had accumulated enough wealth to 'open' or establish commercial relations with the port of Porto Novo 'with his own labour and money'.[52] Inhabitants of the coastal city included Yoruba-speakers as well as refugees from Allada. Shortly thereafter he opened Onim, a port community 100 kilometres to the east, located on the Lagos river, which was conquered and governed by decedents of the royal dynasty of Benin.[53] Access to the trade in these two ports became especially vital in ensuring continuing profits for Brazilian slave traders. As the King of Dahomey periodically closed routes connecting slavers in the interior to Ouidah in 1758, the value of each slave sold rose from eight to twelve rolls of tobacco to thirteen to sixteen rolls.[54] In Porto Novo, meanwhile, one enslaved man cost eight to twelve rolls of tobacco.[55] Cargoes could also be completed 30 per cent faster at Porto Novo than at Ouidah, which prevented the spoilage of Brazilian tobacco before it could be sold for slaves.[56] Both of these ports, along with Badagry – which was opened by a Dutch trader in 1736 – became key outlets for Oyo commerce in the second half of the eighteenth century. Though Oliveira never detailed how he was able to secure trading rights to the two ports, he likely had some familiarity with Yoruba dialects from his youth. Also beneficial would have been his superior knowledge of culture on the eastern portion of the Mina Coast. Acculturated or *ladino* Africans like Oliveira, who had spent time in the Portuguese-speaking world, had long been central to the operation of Portuguese slaving in West Africa. In this regard, Oliveira was merely one in a long line of such Atlantic Creoles who were instrumental in transatlantic slaving.[57]

Oliveira, as an African man who circulated between Brazil and West Africa, built a series of relationships with African rulers and Brazilian merchants, and in the process provided crucial support in maintaining an active slave trade on a more hospitable portion of the coast. Unlike Ouidah, Porto Novo and Onim were not home to royally sponsored Portuguese *feitorias* or trading forts, so the necessary work of collecting slaves and goods for cargoes, as well as arranging provisioning and transportation for visiting slaving ships, had to be arranged by alternative means. The cultural and commercial expertise of intermediaries like Oliveira remained paramount in facilitating the day-to-day functioning of Brazilian commerce on the Mina Coast. As Robin Law and Kristin Mann argue, 'the need for efficient, reliable commercial networks' required 'business and social relationships that spanned the Atlantic world and linked political and commercial elites along the coast [of Africa]'.[58] Oliveira's actions in securing trade in Porto Novo and Onim allowed Bahian merchants to retain their advantage in the Mina trade, particularly his ability to secure lower costs and establish relationships with local African elites from whom to purchase slaves.[59]

During the 1760s, a transitional moment for the Brazilian slave trade on the West African coast, Oliveira was the most important Portuguese-speaking figure at either port. As a sign of his prominence, when he returned to Brazil in 1770 he was identified by the Governor-General of Bahia, Conde de Povolide, as an official *cabeceira* 'of letter' of the King of Portugal, a title which was 'one of the greatest favours of the Portuguese nation'.[60] The King of Onim also recognized Oliveira's official role, sending four ambassadors or *cabeceiras* with him to Bahia, presumably to solidify relations between the two Atlantic slaving ports. Pioneering trading relations in the eastern ports of Porto

Novo and Onim required significant diplomatic negotiation with West African potentates on behalf of the Portuguese Crown and Brazilian merchants.[61] Indeed, Oliveira's importance to the Bahian merchant community was further illustrated by the loyalty demonstrated by eighteen of its members who signed his petition for clemency in light of his 'unwavering contributions to Portuguese navigation'. The merchants noted that Oliveira had not only established commercial relations in two Yoruba ports, but had also safeguarded Brazilian slaving during several West African wars, prevented robberies of Brazilian trade goods, provided general aide and expedited embarkation through the collection of cargoes.[62] The merchants warned that Brazilian slaving would not have succeeded in the two ports if not for Oliveira, and that they, as the most prominent slavers of Bahia, had been very 'pleased with his residence' in West Africa.[63] During his time on the coast and in the following decade, trade at Porto Novo and Onim increased dramatically, and as a consequence traffic to Ouidah declined considerably.[64] In 1775, after Oliveira had returned to Brazil, Porto Novo's ruler attempted to further cement ties between his port and Brazilian merchants by requesting that the King of Portugal build a trading *feitoria* in his city. In his letter to the Crown, the King proclaimed, 'I am unable to personally look after everything that touches on the slave trade which is carried out by these ships from the absence of someone who takes care of all their needs'. His promise of tacit oversight was perhaps a veiled allusion to the domineering role that the King in Dahomey had played in an effort to extract greater profit from the Atlantic trade, and his intention of not doing so.[65] Portuguese administrators never responded however, and private traders like Oliveira continued to be solely responsible for managing trade in Porto Novo and Onim.

Oliveira's return to Bahia and incarceration

Despite Oliveira's prominence among the Pernambucan and Bahian slaving community in Onim, he was clear about the reasons for his return. The West African man, or as he was labelled in the legal records surrounding his petition, '*o preto*' or 'the black', had secured a new home in front of the Igreja (Church) do Pilar near Salvador's waterfront.[66] He was permanently returning to the city, in order to, in his words 'live among Catholics and receive the Sacraments of the Church'.[67] On 11 May 1770, upon arrival in the city, he disembarked from the ship *Nossa Senhora da Conceição e Almas*, owned by Jacinto Joze Coelho and captained by Manoel de Souza, which had travelled from the Mina Coast after a layover in São Tomé to collect provisions. Arriving in Bahia, Oliveira expected to receive 'the prize for the good service that he had always rendered for the [Portuguese] nation and the Crown' as a loyal vassal. Instead of being met with favour, he was arrested by the *Provedor* of the Customshouse several days after he disembarked and placed in the public jail, charged with possession of contraband in the form of cotton and linen textiles.[68] All the goods he had brought with him from the Mina Coast, including his slaves, were sequestered by the royal authorities, causing 'irreparable loss and ruin'.[69]

The circumstances of Oliveira's entrance into the city and his subsequent arrest remained contested, even after Oliveira had spent over two months in Salvador's local prison. Royal officials claimed that after arriving in port at 11 at night, the *Nossa Senhora da Conceição e Almas* was quietly met by a local cooper in his lighter, the trade goods housed on the ship belonging to Oliveira – including 122 slaves and other West African goods – were disembarked in the small vessel and brought to shore before the ship visited Bahia's customshouse to pay royal taxes on the imports. Shortly after, an official guarding the local Sea Fort, Sergeant Jozeph dos Santos Brandão, along with two soldiers, boarded Oliveira's ship. Witnesses later declared that the African man paid three *doblas* of gold coins to the sergeant, presumably as a bribe. Oliveira meanwhile, contended that he had seen no lighter approach the ship and that he possessed no satins or other textiles that were supposed to have been unloaded surreptitiously. Furthermore, Oliveira stated that he had not paid Brandão, and had only brought from the coast two enslaved boys and twenty-three *panos da costa* (African cloth fabricated in Yoruba-speaking city-states), which he had declared at customs.[70]

Royal officials argued that Oliveira had shipped much more to Bahia during his 1770 voyage, some of which was contraband. Following a search of his home, customs officers listed his extensive property holdings, which illustrated Oliveira's personal wealth as well as the cosmopolitan *milieu* in which he existed in the slave trading ports of the Mina Coast. He carried with him household goods such as a dining set which seated six made of jacaranda wood (native to South America, and likely imported from Bahia), a wardrobe, elaborate painted storage trunks, a large copper basin and a sink, and a large mirror embellished with gold, indicating the domestic comfort in which he had lived in West Africa. He also had accumulated a trove of religious objects illustrating the depth of his Catholic piety; they included a knife with an ivory and silver handle, a large gilded cross, a gold-embellished silver plate of *Nossa Senhora de Conceição* (Our Lady of the Conception), a silver circle with eight suspended cherub figurines, a small silver crown featuring the image of *Nossa Senhora da Conceição*, rosary beads made of mother of pearl, and a gold ring studded with emeralds and white and purple stones in the shape of a cross. As a well-connected slave trader, Oliveira had also accumulated luxury goods from all over the world: some were European in origin, such as 'Geneva brandy', a set of French silver spoons, finely painted English porcelain, a serving plate decorated with red paint and gold gilding; others were from Asia, such as a set of fine china from India, and packets of fine teas. Most of his wealth was held in slaves which included seventy-nine enslaved males valued at fifty milréis each, and forty-three enslaved females valued at forty milréis each, for a total of 5,670 milréis.[71] He also carried with him currency accumulated from his trading including 821.025 milréis, 104.985 milréis in silver, and several bundles of gold coins.[72]

At the heart of the royal officials' charges against Oliveira was the accusation that he had illegally smuggled textiles into the colony. An inventory of his goods revealed that he was indeed the owner of a dizzying assortment of fine fabrics from all over the world. He carried embroidered silks, Damasks, a taffeta gown embroidered with gold, another of velvet, three British shirts, fine table linens, yellow satin pants, green and red striped satin pants, silk scarves and belts, blue striped woollen cloth, blue flannels, decorated hats of taffeta, and various chambrays.[73] Many of these items appear to have been for his own personal use, imported to West Africa from Europe and India, to be used to purchase slaves from African merchants. Much to the Portuguese Crown's displeasure, contraband – or inter-imperial trading – was common on the West African coast, despite the illegality of exchanging Brazilian goods like tobacco and gold for European textiles. As Carl A. Hanson has argued, such activity 'accounted for a significant share' of contraband goods entering the Brazilian colonies and diminished royal coffers by circumventing the royal tax on European and Asian goods sold to the colonies.[74] Slave traders, hoping to avoid the inflated price of goods re-exported from metropolitan Portugal, instead dealt directly with English, Dutch and French slavers on the West African coast to purchase an array of untaxed goods.[75] A decade after Oliveira's detention, the governor of Bahia lamented that Bahian traders frequently utilized the slave trade as a cover to conduct an illicit trade in European textiles, which they then sold in Salvador's urban markets.[76] Thus Oliveira was only one of many transatlantic traders engaged in the practice.

Oliveira's ownership of an array of European and Asian goods indicated that he also participated in such illegal trans-imperial trading networks while living on the Mina Coast. Evidence of his wide-ranging trading activities in Porto Novo and Onim could be found in the goods he carried with him to Bahia. He possessed a scale – presumably used to weigh specie – and four folders full of old papers consisting of receipts and letters – remnants of Oliveira's complex commercial transactions on the coast with other African and European merchants. His dealings on the coast presumably entailed not only procuring slaves for Brazilian merchants, but also procuring foreign goods for Bahian markets. In addition to the collection of European and Asian textiles, Oliveira had also, according to royal officials, acquired a 'large cloth of three lengths called Mandy' and four additional 'painted' cloths of the same kind. These textiles were of West African origin, likely produced in Oyo and its environs, like the *panos da costa* that he also carried.[77] Oliveira pioneered not only eastern trading routes on the Mina Coast, but was also the first recorded importer of the African cloths to Brazil – a commodity that would become prevalent in transatlantic voyages from Onim to Bahia in the nineteenth century.[78]

Two months after his arrest, Oliveira petitioned Salvador's local *desembargador* (appellate judge) and *ouvidor geral do crime* (general magistrate of crime) for his release and the restoration of his sequestered goods. Denying the charges against him, he drew on his biography and the endorsement of other prominent merchants in the city to justify his release. His petition illustrated not only the factual outlines of a transient life, but also the strategies he had undertaken to forestall his own continual dislocation. Though Oliveira began his life as the consummate displaced outsider, the rhetoric he employed in his petition against his detention highlighted his identity as an 'insider' or vassal in the Portuguese Atlantic world.[79] His defence highlighted his desire to leave pagan lands and live as a good Christian, but also the value of his service to the Portuguese Crown. He implicitly characterized slaving as central to the King's commercial and political interests in the South Atlantic, thus maintaining that no one had been of greater service to the Crown in West Africa than he. Furthermore, Oliveira simultaneously emphasized his commercial kinship with the Brazilian merchant community, as well as his spiritual kinship with other Catholic parishioners at the church *Nossa Senhora da Conceição dos Militares*. At times he feigned innocence of his predicament, and despite his acumen securing commercial contacts on the West

African coast, Oliveira described himself not only as a loyal vassal but also as an 'ignorant' and 'rustic' individual incapable of misleading royal officials.[80] His legal strategies ultimately proved insufficient, however, and he remained incarcerated along with the ship captain, Manoel de Souza, the helmsman of the lighter, Sergeant Jozeph dos Santos Brandão, and soldiers Pedro Jozeph and Jozeph Pereira da Silva.[81] Despite the backing of Salvador's slave merchant community, Oliveira's defence did little to sway royal officials or cause them to reconsider testimony implicating him. His imprisonment and confiscation of his goods cut short Oliveira's social ascendancy. The aftermath of his detention is not documented. How he spent his final days and whether he achieved freedom and returned to his home in Bahia remains unclear. Just as he had begun his life, as a young boy forced from his homelands, living at the whim of others, so did his life likely end.

João de Oliveira's remarkable journey from enslaved adolescent to slave merchant complicates simplistic divisions between master and slave, trader and chattel, African and Brazilian. He was able to successfully integrate himself into a merchant community which had made him a slave and displaced him from his homeland. Through his own actions and commercial expertise, he in turn transformed that same merchant community and its trade. He embraced Portuguese cultural norms such as Catholicism, property-holding in slaves and patronage. It was through these strategies that he was able to negotiate his own path to freedom. Such a life trajectory blurs the lines between actions coded as either resistance or accommodation; instead, Oliveira successfully negotiated day-to-day life by understanding the contours of Portuguese merchant capitalism and colonialism in order to improve his individual life chances. He took advantage of the diffuse and often contradictory nature of power relations and status in the Lusophone South Atlantic, where race, wealth and imperial vassalage intersected but remained fluid. As such, Oliveira's story mirrors the complicated life trajectories of a multitude of African and Afro-Brazilian sailors and trading auxiliaries whose lives and labours were spread across the vast expanse of the Atlantic Ocean. However, his ability to acculturate, move freely within the South Atlantic spaces and utilize Portuguese institutions to his own advantage was not infallible. The same commercial acumen which had made him successful in West Africa – the ability to trade across boundaries of territory, culture and language – made him vulnerable to prosecution by a mercantilist colonial state in Bahia interested in policing imperial boundaries. The very factors which enabled his upward mobility – particularly his multiple cultural fluencies – also made him vulnerable. His life ultimately illustrates the very paradoxes which suffused the South Atlantic trade during the mid-eighteenth century.

Notes

1   Arquivo Histórico Ultramarino (hereafter AHU), Conselho Ultramarino-Bahia, Eduardo de Castro e Almeida, Caixa 44, Documentos 8246.
2   Alexandre Vieira Ribeiro, 'The Transatlantic Slave Trade to Bahia', in David Eltis and David Richardson (eds), *Extending the Frontiers: Essays on the New Transatlantic Slave Trade Database* (New Haven, CT: Yale University Press, 2008), 149.

3   The geographic designation of the 'Mina Coast' evolved over time as Portuguese commercial activity expanded eastward, but included coastal territories of contemporary Ghana, Togo, Benin and part of Nigeria. See Robin Law, 'Trade and Politics behind the Slave Coast: The Lagoon Traffic and the Rise of Lagos', *Journal of African History* 24, no. 3 (1983): 321–48.
4   Pierre Verger, *Os Libertos: Sete Caminhos na Liberade de Escravos da Bahia no Século XIX* (São Paulo: Corrupio Edições e Promoções Culturais Ltda., 1992), 12.
5   Onim is modern day Lagos, Nigeria.
6   AHU, Conselho Ultramarino-Bahia Eduardo de Castro e Almeida, Caixa 44, Documento 8246.
7   AHU, Conselho Ultramarino-Bahia Eduardo de Castro e Almeida, Caixa 44, Documento 8249.
8   Robin Law, *The Oyo Empire, c. 1600–1836: A West African Imperialism in the Ear of the Atlantic Slave Trade* (Oxford: Oxford University Press, 1977), 219–23.
9   Law, *The Oyo Empire*.
10 Daniel Barros Domingues da Silva and David Eltis, 'The Slave Trade to Pernambuco, 1561–1851', in David Eltis and David Richardson (eds), *Extending the Frontiers: Essays on the New Transatlantic Slave Trade Database* (New Haven, CT: Yale University Press, 2008), 119, and Stephen Behrendt, David Eltis, Manolo Florentino and David Richardson, *Voyages: The Trans-Atlantic Slave Trade Database*, www.slavevoyages.org.
11 Domingues da Silva and Eltis, 'The Slave Trade to Pernambuco', 95, 102; Stephen Behrendt, David Eltis, Manolo Florentino and David Richardson, *Voyages: The Trans-Atlantic Slave Trade Database*, www.slavevoyages.org.
12 Pernambuco, like other Brazilian slave trading entrepôts at the time, also re-exported large numbers of slaves to the gold mines of interior Minas Gerais via the Rio São Francisco. Merchants in Recife also sold approximately one-quarter of slaves who arrived in the port to Rio de Janeiro and Bahia in the period between 1742 and 1777. Domingues da Silva and Eltis, 'The Slave Trade to Pernambuco', 95–6, 108–9.
13 AHU, Conselho Ultramarino-Bahia Eduardo de Castro e Almeida, Caixa 44, Documento 8246.
14 For more on the slave trade as a form of serial displacement, see Alexander X. Byrd, *Captives and Voyagers: Black Migrants across the Eighteenth Century British Atlantic World* (Baton Rouge: Louisiana State University Press, 2008), and Sharla M. Fett, 'Middle Passages and Forced Migrations: Liberated Africans in Nineteenth-Century US Camps and Ships', *Slavery & Abolition* 31, no. 1 (2010): 75–98.
15 For the trajectories of similarly mobile enslaved Africans in the Atlantic, see Olaudah Equiano, *The Interesting Narrative and Other Writings: Revised Edition* (New York: Penguin Classics, 2003); Randy J. Sparks, *The Two Princes of Calabar: An Eighteenth-Century Atlantic Odyssey* (Cambridge, MA: Harvard University Press, 2009); Robin Law and Paul E. Lovejoy, *The Biography of Mahommah Gardo Baquaqua: His Passage from Slavery to Freedom in Africa and America* (Princeton, NJ: Markus Wiener Publishers, 2006); Verger, *Os Libertos*.
16 See Edmund S. Morgan, *American Slavery, American Freedom: The Ordeal of Colonial Virginia* (New York: W.W. Norton & Company, 1975), 4–6; Trevor Burnard, *Mastery, Tyranny, and Desire: Thomas Thistlewood and His Slaves in the Anglo-Jamaican World* (Chapel Hill: University of North Carolina Press, 2004), 38–67.
17 For more on the idea of Atlantic Creoles, or a group of men and women who as cultural and linguistic chameleons facilitated the early modern transoceanic trade by 'employing their linguistic skills and their familiarity with the Atlantic's diverse

commercial practices, cultural conventions, and diplomatic etiquette to mediate between African merchants and European sea captains', see Ira Berlin, *Many Thousands Gone: The First Two Centuries of Slavery in North America* (Cambridge, MA: Belknap Press, 1998), 17–39; Ira Berlin, 'From Creole to African: Atlantic Creoles and the Origins of African-American Society in Mainland North America', *William and Mary Quarterly* 53, no. 2 (1996): 255; Jane G. Landers, *Atlantic Creoles in the Age of Revolutions* (Cambridge, MA: Harvard University Press, 2010), 4–14.

18 Robin Law, *Ouidah: The Social History of a West African Slaving 'Port' 1727–1892* (Athens: Ohio University Press, 2004), 1–2.
19 For more on the bilateral connections between Africa and Brazil, see Luiz Felipe Alencastro, *O Trato dos Viventes: Formação do Brasil no Atlântico Sul, Séculos XVI e XVII* (São Paulo: Editora Schwarcz Ltda., 2000); José Honório Rodrigues, *Brazil and Africa* (Berkeley: University of California Press, 1965); Pierre Verger, *Trade Relations Between the Bight of Benin and Bahia, 17th–19th Century* (Ibadan, Nigeria: Ibadan University Press, 1968).
20 Robin Law and Kristin Mann, 'West Africa in the Atlantic Community: The Case of the Slave Coast', *William and Mary Quarterly* 56, no. 2 (April 1999): 307–34.
21 Law, *Ouidah*, 50–3.
22 Verger, *Trade Relations*, 122.
23 Edna Bay, *Wives of the Leopard: Gender, Politics, and Culture in the Kingdom of Dahomey* (Charlottesville: University of Virginia Press, 1998), 43; Law, *Ouidah*, 54.
24 Verger, *Trade Relations*, 124–6.
25 Verger, *Trade Relations*, 131–3, 139–41.
26 Verger, *Trade Relations*, 140.
27 Though Europeans and Brazilians perceived all political power in Dahomey to be concentrated in the hands of the King, as Edna Bay argues, royal power was in fact corporate, as the King of Dahomey represented to outsiders the power of a coalition of individuals and lineages whose support was necessary to secure any Dahomean King's assent to the monarchy. Bay, *Wives of the Leopard*, 7.
28 Verger, *Trade Relations*, 129
29 Verger, *Trade Relations*, 125.
30 Verger, *Trade Relations*, 147; Robin Law, *Ouidah*, 60.
31 Verger, *Trade Relations*, 153–4.
32 Verger, *Trade Relations*, 164
33 Verger, *Trade Relations*, 130.
34 Verger, *Trade Relations*, 147.
35 Verger, *Trade Relations*, 162.
36 Law, *Ouidah*, 127.
37 Verger, *Trade Relations*, 179.
38 Robin Law, 'Trade and Politics behind the Slave Coast', 323; Law and Mann, 'West Africa in the Atlantic Community', 307–34, 307.
39 Enslaved mariners comprised 69.4 per cent of the deep-sea maritime labour force. AHU, Conselho Ultramarino, Brasil-Pernambuco, Caixa 120, Documento 9196, Ofício do José Cesar de Menses.
40 A total of 1,096 deep-sea sailors were registered in the port in 1775, 'Mapa geral de toda a qualidade de embarcações que ha na Capitania da Bahia e navegam para a Costa da Mina, Angola', AHU Conselho Ultramarino, Brasil-Baia, Caixa 47, Documento 8812.

41 Mary E. Hicks, 'The Sea and the Shackle: African and Creole Mariners and the Making of a Luso-African Atlantic Commercial Culture, 1721–1835', PhD diss., University of Virginia, 2015, 145.
42 Mary E. Hicks, 'Financing the Luso-Atlantic Slave Trade: From Portugal to Brazil, 1500–1840, *Journal of Global Slavery* 2 (2017): 273–309, 286–7.
43 *Peculium* required the consent of the enslaved person's owner. Stuart Schwartz, *Sugar Plantations in the Formation of Brazilian Society: Bahia, 1550–1835* (Cambridge: Cambridge University Press, 1985), 252.
44 AHU, Conselho Ultramarino-Bahia Eduardo de Castro e Almeida, Caixa 44, Documento 8246.
45 AHU, Conselho Ultramarino-Bahia Eduardo de Castro e Almeida, Caixa 44, Documento 8246.
46 AHU, Conselho Ultramarino-Bahia Eduardo de Castro e Almeida, Caixa 44, Documento 8246.
47 Such arrangements were frequently exploitative, however, with owners charging above market prices for their slaves' self-purchase. Stuart B. Schwartz, 'The Manumission of Slaves in Colonial Brazil: Bahia, 1684–1745', *Hispanic American Historical Review* 54, no. 4 (1974): 603–35; Katia M. de Queirós Mattoso, *To Be a Slave In Brazil: 1550–1888* (New Brunswick, NJ: Rutgers University Press, 1991), 155–76; James H. Sweet, *Domingos Álvares, African Healing, and the Intellectual History of the Atlantic World* (Chapel Hill: University of North Carolina Press, 2011), 91–3.
48 AHU, Conselho Ultramarino-Bahia Eduardo de Castro e Almeida, Caixa 44, Documento 8246.
49 AHU, Conselho Ultramarino-Bahia Eduardo de Castro e Almeida, Caixa 44, Documento 8246.
50 AHU, Conselho Ultramarino-Bahia Eduardo de Castro e Almeida, Caixa 44, Documento 8246.
51 Law, *The Oyo Empire*, 148–9.
52 AHU, Conselho Ultramarino-Bahia Eduardo de Castro e Almeida, Caixa 44, Documento 8246.
53 AHU, Conselho Ultramarino-Bahia Eduardo de Castro e Almeida, Caixa 44, Documento 8246; Verger, *Trade Relations*, 167; Kristin Mann, *Slavery and the Birth of an African City: Lagos, 1760–1900* (Bloomington: Indiana University Press, 2007), 36.
54 Inferior quality Bahian tobacco – called *soca* – was dried and soaked in molasses, then rolled into large units for sale on the African coast. Verger, *Trade Relations*, 4, 12–14.
55 AHU, Conselho Ultramarino-Bahia Eduardo de Castro e Almeida, Caixa 19, Documentos 3494 and 3495; Verger, *Trade Relations*, 167; Law, 'Trade and Politics behind the Slave Coast', 328.
56 AHU, Conselho Ultramarino-Bahia Eduardo de Castro e Almeida, Caixa 44, Documento 8246.
57 Law and Mann, 'West Africa in the Atlantic Community', 315–20.
58 Law and Mann, 'West Africa in the Atlantic Community', 313.
59 Verger, *Trade Relations*, 167–8.
60 AHU, Conselho Ultramarino-Bahia Eduardo de Castro e Almeida, Caixa 44, Documento 8244.
61 Verger, *Os Libertos*, 9–13.
62 The merchants who signed the letter of support for Oliveira included Antonio Cardozo dos Santos, Clemente Jozé da Costa, David de Oliveira Lopes, Francisco

Bages dos Santos, Luiz Coelho Ferreira, Antonio Jozeph Coelho, Manoel Teixeira Bastos, Jozé da Costa Ferreira, João Antunes Guimarens, Agostinho Gomes, João Antonio Moncao, Francisco Ferndandes Vieira Guimarens, Luiz Gonçalves Lima, Francico Gomes Sores, Joze de Abreu Lisboa, João Perreira Lima. AHU, Conselho Ultramarino-Bahia Eduardo de Castro e Almeida, Caixa 44, Documento 8245.

63 AHU, Conselho Ultramarino-Bahia Eduardo de Castro e Almeida, Caixa 44, Documento 8245.
64 As Kristin Mann points out, slave trading from Onim began slowly in the early 1760s, but by the second half of the decade, an average of 575 slaves per year left the port. They declined in the first half of the 1770s after Oliveira had left the coast, but grew exponentially after 1780, peaking at 7,543 a year in the five years following 1846. Mann, *Slavery and the Birth of an African City*, 38–9.
65 Verger, *Trade Relations*, 180.
66 AHU, Conselho Ultramarino-Bahia Eduardo de Castro e Almeida, Caixa 44, Documento 8251.
67 Ibid.
68 AHU, Conselho Ultramarino-Bahia Eduardo de Castro e Almeida, Caixa 44, Documento 8246; AHU, Conselho Ultramarino-Bahia Eduardo de Castro e Almeida, Caixa 44, Documento 8244.
69 AHU, Conselho Ultramarino-Bahia Eduardo de Castro e Almeida, Caixa 44, Documento 8246; AHU, Conselho Ultramarino-Bahia Eduardo de Castro e Almeida, Caixa 44, Documento 8244.
70 AHU, Conselho Ultramarino-Bahia Eduardo de Castro e Almeida, Caixa 44, Documento 8244.
71 Royal officials perhaps undervalued Oliveira's enslaved property considering he had sold an enslaved man for 80,000 reis when he reached port. AHU, Conselho Ultramarino-Bahia Eduardo de Castro e Almeida, Caixa 44, Documento 8251; AHU, Conselho Ultramarino-Bahia Eduardo de Castro e Almeida, Caixa 44, Documento 8250.
72 These bundles amounted to four milréis, 709.200 milréis and 7.640 milréis respectively; AHU, Conselho Ultramarino-Bahia Eduardo de Castro e Almeida, Caixa 44, Documento 8249.
73 AHU, Conselho Ultramarino-Bahia Eduardo de Castro e Almeida, Caixa 44, Documento 8249.
74 Carl A. Hanson, *Economy and Society in Baroque Portugal, 1668–1703* (Minneapolis: University of Minnesota Press, 1981), 259.
75 Valença argued that 'instead of trading only with the natives of the country to obtain Negroes, gold, ivory and wax, [merchants] began also to trade with the English, the French and the Dutch who came to that Coast, receiving from the said nations European cloth, in exchange for Brazilian tobacco which they carried clandestinely to the ports of Bahia and Pernambuco. Trade on the Mina Coast was carried on in two different branches, one licit, legal and useful which was the slave trade, the other illegal, pernicious and prohibited which was trading in all sorts of foreign cloth which they took to Bahia under cover of trading in Negroes.' Verger, *Trade Relations*, 102, n. 74.
76 Verger, *Trade Relations*, 102, n. 74.
77 Colleen E. Kriger, 'Mapping the History of Cotton Textile Production in Pre-Colonial West Africa', *African Economic History* 33 (2005): 87–116, 102–3.

78 Oliveira was not the only passenger on the ship to traffic such goods. Testimony by a sailor aboard the *Nossa Senhora da Conceição e Almas* also suggested that the captain of the vessel had loaded 'five or six bales' of *panos da costa* each with twenty-five or thirty pieces of cloth onto the ship during a layover on the island of Fernando de Noronha off the coast of Pernambuco. AHU, Conselho Ultramarino-Bahia Eduardo de Castro e Almeida, Caixa 44, Documento 8248. J. Lorand Matory, *Black Atlantic Religion: Tradition, Transnationalism and Matriarchy in the Afro-Brazilian Candomblé* (Princeton, NJ: Princeton University Press, 2005); Flávio Gonçalves dos Santos, *Economia e cultura do Candomblé na Bahia: o comércio de objectos litúrgicos afro-brasileiros, 1850–1937* (Ilhéus, BA: Editus–Editora de UESC, 2013); Manuela Carneiro da Cunha, *Negros, estrangeiros: Os Escravos Libertos e sua Volta à África 2a Edição* (São Paulo: Editora Schwarcz, 2012).
79 For more on enslaved people claiming the status of 'insiders' or vassals of the Portuguese empire, see Mariana Candido, 'African Freedom Suits and Portuguese Vassals Status: Legal Mechanisms for Fighting Enslavement in Benguela, Angola, 1800–1830', *Slavery & Abolition* 32, no. 3 (2011): 447–59.
80 AHU, Conselho Ultramarino-Bahia Eduardo de Castro e Almeida, Caixa 44, Documento 8247.
81 AHU, Conselho Ultramarino-Bahia Eduardo de Castro e Almeida, Caixa 44, Documento 8249.

12

Gilbert Hunt, the City Blacksmith: Slavery, Freedom and Fame in Antebellum Richmond, Virginia

Elizabeth Kuebler-Wolf

For the first three decades of his life, Gilbert Hunt (1780?–1863) was enslaved. He worked as a blacksmith in Richmond, Virginia. Because the life of city slaves offered fewer restrictions and more opportunities to earn money on the side, by 1829 Gilbert Hunt was free, having saved $800 to purchase himself from his owner. Such a method of self-emancipation was a rare opportunity not available to most enslaved people, but one which Hunt was able to seize.[1] Eventually Hunt was able to save enough money to purchase his wife and free her, as well as purchasing two other people, almost certainly family members, as they were purchased after an 1832 law prohibiting free blacks from owning slaves who were not relatives.[2] Additionally, he amassed a considerable sum of real property by the time of his death. In 1860, Hunt was listed in the federal census as owning $1,300 of real property.[3] When he died in 1863, Hunt was free through his own efforts, a successful property holder, a thriving businessman and a prominent figure in both the free black community and white slaveowning community of Richmond. In the late antebellum period, he became not just locally known, but locally famous through a pamphlet biography and a widely circulated photographic portrait. In this way, Hunt's biography became fodder for public discourse about the benefits of slavery.

Photography and pro-slavery rhetoric

Gilbert Hunt's photographic portrait was first produced in Richmond in 1859 to coincide with the printing of a biographical pamphlet, written by Philip Barrett, called *Gilbert Hunt: The City Blacksmith*.[4] The image of Hunt was probably taken by George Cook. The glass negative remains in the George Cook collection at the Valentine Museum in Richmond. Cook was a noted photographer of Richmond's African Americans both before and after the war.[5] Multiple copies of this image exist to this day. Some are in archives and libraries while others can be found for sale on auction websites. Various copies of Hunt's photograph show how images live over time, generate a variety of meanings and are modified by texts and contexts, popular memory and

Figure 12.1 Cook Studio, *Gilbert Hunt*. Glass-plate negative. The Valentine, Richmond, Virginia.

historical context. In the case of Hunt's portrait, we can tease out how antebellum Richmond could conceive of Gilbert Hunt as a person whose unusual life experience actually justified the existence of slavery. First, it is important to examine the photograph itself (see Figure 12.1). In this image, we see Gilbert Hunt, sitting, facing the camera directly, with a sober expression on his face. Compare this image, destined to be reproduced for a white public, with a singular daguerreotype of Isaac Jefferson (1775–c. 1850) from the 1840s (see Figure 12.2)

While Isaac Jefferson had been a slave to Thomas Jefferson and his family, he had managed to purchase his freedom, although how and when this happened is not entirely clear. By 1847 he was working as a free blacksmith in Petersburg, Virginia. In this image, Jefferson wears the leather apron of his craft, standing in a confident pose with his legs apart. He fully inhabits the space of his portrait. He stands with his right

Figure 12.2 *Isaac Granger Jefferson*, c. 1845. Tracy W. McGregor Library of American History, Special Collections, University of Virginia Library.

leg bent, his right arm jutting out at the elbow as he rests his hand on his thigh, while his left arm rests comfortably on a support.

In 1847 a Charles Campbell of Petersburg, Virginia, interviewed Jefferson extensively and kept notes of their conversations. Campbell noted Isaac's appearance:

> Isaac is rather tall of strong frame, stoops a little, in colour ebony: – sensible intelligent pleasant; wears large circular-bound spectacles & a leather apron. A capital daguerreotype of him was taken by a Mr. Shew. Isaac was so much pleased with it that he had one taken of his wife...[6]

Isaac Jefferson's image was a private commission, made for the subject of the photograph. He had the option to dress and pose how he pleased for his portrait. The purpose of the photograph was for Jefferson's (and presumably his family's) own enjoyment.

These photos create small narratives. Compare Jefferson's pose and clothing to Hunt's. While Jefferson is standing, wearing the working clothes and protective leather gear of his trade, Hunt is neatly attired in a threadbare waistcoat and topcoat, with patched pants. Jefferson's posture is active and vigorous; Hunt sits with his hands in his lap. Although Hunt holds a blacksmithing hammer, it is clear that he is not about to jump up and begin work. Showcasing Hunt in a worn suit of clothes helped to promulgate the image of him as a destitute and needy old man, an idea also promoted in the biographical pamphlet of that year. The image effectively strips away Hunt's ability to work by taking him out of his protective blacksmithing gear. Jefferson, by contrast, looks as though he may have just taken a casual break from the shop for a minute to rest for a portrait. In both cases, the photographer would have spent a good deal of time working out the posture, clothing, properties and setting for the image, in discussion with his client. In Jefferson's case, the client was himself.

Hunt's portrait, unlike Isaac Jefferson's private daguerreotype, is made from a negative and was reproduced multiple times for public consumption. The intended audience for this image was the same as the audience for *The City Blacksmith*: the white population of Richmond. As such, both the text and the copies of Hunt's portrait were adaptations of Hunt's life story for an audience in a city saturated with pro-slavery sentiment and increasingly defensive of the institution. By 1859, Richmond, like the rest of the slaveowning South, was thoroughly alarmed by increasing abolitionist sentiment. It is in Richmond that the most extreme of the late antebellum pro-slavery writers, George Fitzhugh, published his works *Sociology for the South* (1854) and *Cannibals All!* (1857). Fitzhugh's anti-capitalist theories in favour of slavery argued that slavery was a preferable system to capitalism, because Northern factory owners did not have any economic reason to care about their workers. In contrast, Fitzhugh argued, slaveowners had to care about their slaves.

> Slavery protects the infants, the aged and the sick; nay, takes far better care of them than of the healthy, the middle-aged and the strong. They are part of the family, and self-interest and domestic affection combine to shelter, shield and foster them. A man loves not only his horses and his cattle, which are useful to him, but he loves his dog, which is of no use. He loves them because they are his. What a wise and beneficent provision of Heaven, that makes the selfishness of man's nature a protecting aegis to shield and defend wife and children, slaves and even dumb animals.[7]

It is in this environment of public discourse about the benefits of slavery, and in the same city where Fitzhugh's writings were pushing pro-slavery defences to an extreme, that Gilbert Hunt's fame was invented and his life transformed into a pro-slavery fable. According to the *Richmond Daily Dispatch*, Gilbert Hunt, with the support of a ladies' benevolent society, had 'been kindly permitted by authorities at the Fair grounds to dispose of some photographs of himself ... and the proceeds of which will help the deserving old man at a time when the weight of years has left him but little power to help himself. We trust every one [sic] will embrace such an opportunity to mark the general sense of his brave and loyal services.'[8]

According to the inscription on one print of the portrait now in a private collection (see Figure 12.3), Hunt was '[m]ade free by the inhabitants of Richmond for services rendered at the burning of the Theatre in Richmond at which he saved by his untiring exertions 36 lives. The fire occurred the 26th of September 1836.'[9] Legal and historical

Figure 12.3 *Gilbert Hunt*. Salt print, taken by Julian Vannerson, 5.25 × 7.375 in., 77 Main St, Richmond, Virginia, c. 1859–60. Image courtesy of Cowan's Auctions, Cincinnati, Ohio.

records make it clear that these statements are not quite in line with the facts. Both the date of the fire and the date and manner of Hunt's emancipation are incorrect. Hunt purchased his own freedom. One Richmond memoirist's account of the fire noted wryly, 'Gilbert, then a slave, afterwards obtained his freedom – I wish I could add, at the hands of a grateful community; but it was by his own industry.'[10]

Hunt was a free man by 1829, thanks not to the gratitude of white Richmond but owing rather to his own hard work and persistence. Rather than receiving reciprocal white generosity, he was obliged to purchase his own freedom, and that of some family members as well.[11] The fire in question happened in 1811, some eighteen years prior to Hunt gaining his freedom, which would make the grateful citizens of Richmond rather slow in their expression of gratitude even if they had freed him in 1829, and tardy by a quarter century if it were indeed 1836 when he was freed. Despite the factual inaccuracies of this inscription, the image is intended, through the force of words and the force of the 'objective reality' of a photograph, to shore up slavery as a benevolent and just hierarchy. The idea that he was 'made free' particularly appealed to a white Richmond audience, who, as claimed in the preface, were 'a people "*who have never been backward in the appreciation of whatever is true, and noble, and generous*"'.[12]

Interestingly, although Hunt's heroics at the 1811 fire at the Richmond Theatre were frequently cited as part of the reason that he was a worthy and noble soul, 'better' than the average slave, the contemporaneous historical record shows no evidence that Hunt was there at the time. The fire was a notable tragedy, killing at least seventy people, including the Governor of Virginia, and completely destroying the town's main venue of entertainment. In the years immediately after the tragedy, many pamphlets, sermons, historical accounts and private letters were written to record the event. No source mentions any slaves or slave heroics. In fact, rather than serving as proof that slavery was a healthy way to structure society, the theatre fire was treated as an object lesson in the inherent evils of theatrical amusements.

For instance, a pamphlet published in Philadelphia in January 1812 described the 'calamity at Richmond' in great detail, including several letters from survivors describing heart-wrenching scenes of death and destruction. This pamphlet seems to have had two aims: first, to give the reader a thrilling description of one of the largest urban calamities in the Early Republic and second, to admonish its readers that theatre fires were not unusual and were, perhaps, an indication of the inherent immorality of the pastime.[13] An 1813 sermon, published in pamphlet form, admonished that the fire proved that theatre was not just a physically but also morally dangerous entertainment, and remonstrated with its audience that

> ...the burning of the theatre at Richmond should have much weight upon your minds. It should induce you to consider the great danger of countenancing vain and sinful amusements, to grieve the hearts of those citizens, who wish to see the United States of America, flourish in virtue and religion.[14]

Several other pamphlets followed, all taking the same dual approach of recounting the thrilling specifics of the deaths of unfortunate victims while also deploring the sinfulness of attending the theatre.[15]

Dr McCaw, the white doctor who is described in Barrettt's 1859 pamphlet as working with Hunt to save people from the burning building, is mentioned in the *Calamity at Richmond*; however, there is no mention of Hunt or any enslaved person present at the fire as a rescuer in any of the pamphlets about the fire published in the decade after the event.[16] Dr McCaw is also cited for his bravery in *Remarks on the Theatre, and on the late fire at Richmond Virginia*, a pamphlet published in England which suggested that the theatre fire was divine punishment for the sin of slaveholding.[17] Neither Gilbert Hunt or even an anonymous slave is ever mentioned, even in this anti-slavery sermon. Eyewitness accounts of the fire and rescue, published in the *Richmond Enquirer* on 2 January 1812, make no mention of Hunt.[18] In William Dunlap's comprehensive history of theatre in America, published in 1832, the Richmond Theatre fire merits several pages of discussion, but nothing remarkable in the way of slave interventions in saving white patrons is mentioned.[19] Even when Dr James McCaw passed away in 1846, his obituary credited one of his sons with being his primary assistant during the theatre fire.[20]

One popular print was made to commemorate the fire. Called *The Burning of the Theatre in Richmond, Virginia*, the print was made by Benjamin Tanner, a Philadelphia engraver, and was likely meant to circulate to a national audience.

The image is a striking depiction of this early national disaster. The theatre is shown at an angle so that we can see the front and one side of the building. The composition is dramatic and energetic, with a dynamic diagonal orientation echoed through the flames coming from the roof, the drifting smoke of the fire and the general lean of figures toward the right upper-corner of the image. People climb, drop or jump from windows, or cannot escape because of crowding. Below, we see figures in distress – lying on the ground reaching for help, being carried away from the scene, reaching out in anguish for a child, or showing general despair at the horror of the scene.

On the left, a prominent figure faces the building with his arms raised outward, while a child falls in front of him; however, it is difficult to tell if the man is actually catching the girl or has simply fallen out of the window backwards before her. There is no clear scene where anyone is going into the fire or towards the building. Those who are rescuing victims are taking them from the ground in front of the burning structure and moving them towards relative safety.

Figure 12.4 John Lossing Benson, *The Burning of the Theatre in Richmond, Virginia, on the Night of the 26th. December 1811*. Philadelphia: Benjamin Tanner, 25 February 1812. Courtesy of the Library of Congress Prints and Photographs Division, Washington, DC.

The fact that there is no contemporaneous historical mention of Gilbert Hunt does not mean he was not there or that he was not a hero of the fire. At best, the lack of any discussion of Hunt only demonstrates that, even if he were at the fire in 1811, his actions were not considered remarkable. The Richmonders of 1811 simply did not remark upon Hunt in particular, or any slave more generally, in the rescue effort. Significantly, though, slaves were allowed to attend the Richmond Theatre and many enslaved individuals were likely present on the evening of the tragedy. Richmond in 1811 did not need a Gilbert Hunt. Almost no one who wrote about the fire and its aftermath commented on slavery, with one English exception mentioned above. In 1811, the ethical question that was germane was that of the moral (and physical) danger of attending the theatre.

Gilbert Hunt is first mentioned in conjunction with heroics at the Richmond Theatre fire only many decades after the fact. The first instance found by this author appears in a memoir from 1856, in which the author claims to have personally seen Gilbert Hunt and Dr McCaw working in tandem at the fire.[21] Two years later, the *Richmond Daily Dispatch* described

> the noble part which he [Hunt] bore in the memorable burning of the Richmond Theatre, in 1811. His brawny arm was the means of rescuing many a soul from the jaws of the devouring element, and some of the first families of our city now point to Gilbert Hunt with mingled pride and gratitude for his self-sacrificing conduct on that awful night which shrouded so many happy hearts with gloom.[22]

In the 1850s, Gilbert Hunt's story became a pro-slavery parable for white slaveowners and justifiers of slavery. Hunt had saved white slaveowners from the Richmond Theatre fire because slavery fostered good relationships between the races. Barrett's pamphlet quotes Hunt explaining his motivation for running to the burning theatre:

> My wife's mistress called to me and begged me to hasten to the theatre and, if possible, save her only daughter – a young lady who had been teaching me my book every night, and one whom I loved very much.[23]

In the perspective offered in Barrett's pamphlet of 1859, slavery had fostered an exceptional bond between master and servant. So close and loving a relationship could only exist within the confines of slavery, according to many theorists by the 1850s. At the time of the Richmond fire in 1811, such rhetorical strategies justifying slavery were not particularly important. The nation was not yet heavily engaged in a political or rhetorical battle over slavery's morality. If Hunt were present at the 1811 fire, it only mattered in the post-1830s debate over slavery. Copies of the Hunt portrait bear varying printed and handwritten inscriptions that suggest the ways in which Hunt's image was put to use to shore up an interpretation of slavery that stressed human, reciprocal relationships of respect and affection.

The photographic portrait of Gilbert Hunt, like the pamphlet biography, portrays a rather different, more docile, less vigorous man than the one who emerges from the historical record. Although Hunt was a relatively prosperous businessman at the time this image was taken, his image suggests a penniless old man, unable to ply his trade, in need of support. The old man's dignity is made more affecting by his clothing's patchiness and obviously worn quality. By rendering him thus poignantly in need, Hunt's freedom is made less dangerous to the established social and racial order. Here is a slave who was deservingly freed, goes the rhetoric, but though freed, he still needs the help of his white friends. Wearing threadbare clothing that hints of white gentility, Hunt can also be construed as emulating, though never fully measuring up to, his much-loved master, positioning the ex-slave as still subordinate and dependent, socially as well as financially. The 1859 pamphlet of Hunt's extraordinary rise to freedom and fame was sold in part to raise money for Hunt's retirement years.[24]

For white Richmond residents in the 1850s, the most fascinating aspect of Hunt's life was the episode in 1811 in which he allegedly helped rescue several members of the slaveowning classes, including some of his owner's family, from the devastating fire in the Richmond Theatre. For that heroic act, as his 1859 biography explained, 'Some of the first families in our state and city now point to him with feelings of

Figure 12.5 Smith and Vannerson, *Portrait of Gilbert Hunt*. Smith & Vannerson, 77 Main St, Richmond, Virginia, *c.* 1859. Courtesy of the Virginia Museum of History and Culture. Gift of Mrs Boykin, Mrs Crouch and Miss Colquist.

mingled pride and gratitude for his self-sacrificing conduct on that awful night.'[25] This copy of the portrait is also inscribed, 'Gilbert Hunt to his young friend and master, Henry Orth,' reinforcing the idea that Gilbert Hunt himself endorsed a subordinate and gratitude-laden relationship with his white 'benefactors', even after thirty years as a free man.

Another copy of the Hunt portrait, now in the collection of the Virginia Historical Society, bears the handwritten pencil inscription, 'This is the portrait of Gilbert Hunt, a faithful colored man who saved many persons from the burning theatre in Richmond in the year 1811.' The date of the inscription is unknown; however, the text offers an implicitly pro-slavery interpretation of the significance of Hunt's life. Hunt's 'faithful' daring and willingness to sacrifice his personal safety to that of white Richmond is the single salient fact that is recorded upon the portrait, despite Hunt's rather rich and eventful life. A third copy of the portrait was deposited at the State Library of Virginia in the early 1870s. The Petersburg *Appeal* noted the event and that Hunt was 'the colored blacksmith by whose efforts many persons were rescued from the flames at the burning of the Richmond theatre on the 26th of December 1811'.[26]

Good masters and the deserving slave

By twisting and tweaking the details, white Richmonders could see themselves reflected in Gilbert Hunt's life and his portrait as caring, generous and noble caretakers of the African Americans among them, and slavery as an institution that benefited those among their slaves who were deserving. Barrett described the affection that the crème of white society held for the old slave, thanks to his conduct at the Richmond fire, as 'mingled pride and gratitude for his self-sacrificing conduct'.[27] They were proud because Hunt's heroic actions on that night, in their view, reflected well upon Hunt's owners, who begged for his help and for whom Hunt willingly risked his own life and limb. Ultimately, they were proud not of Hunt, but of themselves. As the *Richmond Whig* exclaimed in an exhortation to readers to buy the pamphlet whose sales went to support the aged blacksmith, 'our citizens ... have never been backward in the appreciation of whatever is true, and noble, and generous'.[28]

That Gilbert Hunt was willing to risk life and limb to help white Richmonders while yet enslaved is the fact upon which white viewers repeatedly seized. This act was continually given as the reason why white Richmond owed him a debt of gratitude, why in some versions of the story white Richmonders freed him, why he should be supported in his old age, why his portrait should hang in the State Library and why there should be a memorial plaque raised to him in downtown Richmond at the site of his heroic deed. The blacksmith's heroics certainly deserved remembrance on their own merit, but for pro-slavery audiences, his selflessness proved that paternalistic slavery really existed.

To see how important this aspect of Hunt's biography became to white audiences, consider Hunt's later, very similar heroics during a fire at the State Penitentiary. While his rescue of inmates was similarly self-sacrificing and brave, this event is not typically remembered in connection with his photograph or memorials. Hunt himself provided a clue as to why. Remembering the prison fire, he told Philip Barrett,

> Oh! if you could have seen the poor fellows countenances, lighted up by the red light of the flames, and heard their piercing cries, you couldn't have helped doing something to save them, even though they were cutthroats, and rogues.[29]

Hunt reveals that he saved prisoners not because he owed them a debt of gratitude for their kindliness toward him, and not even because they were good people (rather, they were 'cutthroats, and rogues'), but out of simple human compassion. Perhaps that was the reason he saved those imperiled by the Richmond Theatre fire as well. In a climate in which the rightness of slavery, its beneficial effect on social relations between the races, and the decency of slaveowners had to be constantly upheld – Hunt's simple human compassion at the penitentiary was not as compelling a reason to celebrate the old blacksmith as the Richmond fire, which as we have seen featured most prominently in images of the blacksmith.

In the preface to the pamphlet about Hunt, Barrett used lines from Longfellow's famous poem, *The Village Blacksmith* (1840):

> Toiling, – rejoicing, – sorrowing,
> Onward through life he goes;
> Each morning sees some task begin,
> Each evening sees it close
> Something attempted, something done,
> Has earned a night's repose.[30]

This poem had been a staple of American literature since its publication in 1840. Sentimental authors of the day embraced Longfellow's language, which, according to a Longfellow scholar, 'was, by prevailing norms, a more feminine mode of self-carriage: chaste, patient, endlessly laboring and waiting.'[31] Charles Dickens quoted from it repeatedly in his own work, emphasizing the dignity of and nostalgia for the working-class way of life that he thought was receding into the past because industrialization was mechanizing so many jobs. Longfellow's poem remained significant in American culture and was not only set to music for home performances, but also included in lesson plans for children's school recitations until the twentieth century.[32]

By including this epigram in Hunt's biography, Barrett attaches a particular, sentimental meaning to the unusual story of Richmond's city blacksmith. Working tirelessly, performing honest labour, working dawn to dusk, Gilbert Hunt has 'earned a night's repose' in a way that was exceptional among free or enslaved blacks in Richmond. Interestingly, Longfellow's poem was also quoted in the introduction to Frederick Douglass's *Life And Times Of Frederick Douglass Written By Himself* (1892). In the introduction, George Ruffin comments:

> What can we say? Can he claim the well done good and faithful? The record shows this, and we must state it, generally speaking, his life had been devoted to his race

and the cause of his race. The freedom and elevation of his people has been his life work, and it has been done well and faithfully. That is the record, and that is sufficient. No higher eulogium can be pronounced than that Long-fellow says of the Village Blacksmith: –

'Something attempted, something done,
Has earned a night's repose.'[33]

Both men are credited with hard work and deserving of a good retirement. In the case of Hunt, however, the Longfellow poem is used to argue for his retirement on the grounds of poverty and dependence on white generosity. In an abolitionist context, by contrast, it was appreciation and respect for the indefatigable Douglass which prompted the use of Longfellow's poem.

Reducing a complicated life

For the thirty-five years that Hunt lived as a free man in Richmond, he was a prominent fixture in the public life of the city. In 1829, after gaining his freedom, Hunt travelled under the sponsorship of the American Colonization Society to Liberia to investigate its potential; however, upon arriving, he claimed that the local boatmen who took him to shore stole his tobacco, and reported that Liberia was not worth the trip.[34] The Manchester–Richmond Auxiliary of the American Colonization Society found Hunt a troublesome fellow, calling him 'a complete croaker' and expressing frustration that his public declarations did not help further the cause of Liberian migration.[35] For pro-slavery advocates, Hunt's rejection of the chance to emigrate to Liberia offered living proof of the benefits of the system in that slaves and ex-slaves preferred life in America. Barrett even has Hunt crying 'Carry me back to old Virginia' when he is wronged by 'African Yankees' on his trip to Liberia.[36] Returning to Richmond, he continued his work as a blacksmith and advised other free black inhabitants of Richmond not to bother making the trip. Hunt's explicitly expressed desire to return to Richmond was a point not lost on pro-slavery thinkers. Barrett noted in the pamphlet that this experience may have been the reason for his desire to return to Virginia, because, as Hunt says,

> They [the Africans he met in Liberia] were...perfect barbarians. They were as wise as serpents, but not as harmless as doves. Our people told me later they were perfect African Yankees. After this trick I could not help sitting down, looking towards America, taking a good cry, and saying to myself 'Carry me back to old Virginia.'[37]

As Hunt exclaims in the pamphlet, 'I have *lived* in Richmond, I have *labored* in Richmond, I hope to *die* and be *buried* in Richmond.'[38] In Barrett's view, Hunt's rejection of Africa reinforced the idea that bringing Africans to America as slaves had civilized them.

Hunt was also an important figure in Richmond's black community, albeit not always a universally loved one among either black or white society. Barrett skips over information available from public records which offers a different view of the blacksmith's life. As a deacon of the African Baptist Church, Hunt had acrimonious relations with other church members. In the late 1840s, the blacksmith was arrested for selling liquor without a license, and although he was eventually found not guilty of the charges, he delayed the trial for two years by his refusal to show up in court.[39]

Rather than a contentious, skilled litigant who also tangled with his own church's leadership, Hunt was, according to Barrett, 'a consistent member of the Baptist church'. In 'fifty years' walk and conversation', Barrett contended, Hunt was 'without reproach, in the midst of any people'.[40] Hunt's rather more complicated life is reduced to embody all of the prominent themes in defence of slavery: that slavery was civilizing; that slaves appreciated it, loved their masters, considered them family, and benefited materially, emotionally and spiritually from enslavement. Under such conditions, pro-slavery arguments would have contended, grow men like Hunt, who become worthy of emancipation.

What Barrett's pamphlet presents is a modified version of Hunt's life story made not just palatable, but even reassuring, for white Richmond. Hunt is rendered a 'palsied', helpless old man who needs the help of his white benefactors, whom he loves, in order to survive in his freedom. Portrayed as a docile, dependent old man who 'always loved my master – I love him now', Hunt epitomized what white Richmond hoped all slaves and former slaves would be.[41]

Hunt published two other books, which were moral stories for children. In one volume, *The Deaf Shoemaker: To Which Are Added Other Stories for the Young*, a shortened and sweetened life of Hunt makes only a passing remark that Hunt that 'purchased his freedom from his master' and goes on to discuss Hunt as the hero of the Richmond Theatre fire, setting a good moral example for children.[42] His other publication, *Flowers by the Wayside*, is confined to moral stories for Sunday school.[43] By 1859 there was a tidal wave of abolitionist magazines for children, while in contrast, Barrett barely mentions slavery at all in his two books for children; it would seem to follow that his sentiments were not particularly anti-slavery.[44]

Gilbert Hunt's story lives on, as do some rather convoluted memories of his life. One of the Library of Virginia's 'Virginia Memories' lesson plans, GILBERT HUNT AND THE RICHMOND THEATER FIRE, focuses primarily on the 1811 theatre fire and Hunt's role in it.[45] Students are asked to consider the question, 'Was Gilbert Hunt treated like a hero?' Certainly this is a promising road to venture down, but later in the lesson plan students are asked to 'research and discuss . . . other slaves who fought in the Civil War'. It is not clear from the lesson plan if the assumption is that Hunt would have fought for the Union or the Confederacy if he had still been living at the time. Hunt was involved in the War of 1812, not the Civil War (he died, an old man, in 1863). In 1812 he contributed both ironwork needed by the United States Army as well as protecting his master's property. As Hunt exclaims in Barrett's pamphlet,

> During the absence of the family, my master's residence and all its contents were left entirely in my charge, and had the English come upon us, no American would

have fought more bravely for the defence of his own home and fireside than I would have for the defence of my master's property; for he never treated me like a servant, but rather like a member of his own household. He never spoke a cross word to, nor struck me a lick during his whole life.[46]

Certainly if the assumption is that Hunt would have fought for the Confederacy, this is yet another, much more recent, instance of his biography being tweaked to support the slave system in the South.[47]

Gilbert Hunt lived an extraordinary life, one that was quite different from the experience of the vast majority of enslaved people. His position as a blacksmith in the city not only required that he attain some literacy, but also granted him a certain amount of leeway to accumulate his own money on the side. Even if he had never become 'famous' in Richmond, he was a prominent citizen and important leader of the free black community. His status as an outlier among the masses of enslaved people in the South is a worthwhile story in its own right. Examining the ways in which his image and biography became part of a larger rhetoric of pro-slavery ideology demonstrates the malleability of what, on the face of it, might be taken as simple facts.

In effect, Hunt's portraits are less about the individual in question and more about defining the nature of slavery itself. Hunt's biography as told in photographs and stories during his lifetime do not challenge the assumptions and ideals of slaveholding society, but rather reinforce those assumptions. Gilbert Hunt is unusual, his portraits say, which is reason to record him for posterity. Gilbert Hunt is unusual, his portraits say, which is reason to keep the majority of black Americans enslaved. What remains constant in these pictures is the concern that white society had for seeing itself reflected as benevolent, kind and just in the images of their slaves.

Notes

1 Marie Tyler-McGraw and Gregg Kimball, *In Bondage and In Freedom: Antebellum Black Life in Richmond, Virginia* (Richmond, VA: Valentine Museum, 1998), 58.
2 Tyler-McGraw and Kimball, *In Bondage and In Freedom*, 57.
3 Tyler-McGraw and Kimball, *In Bondage and In Freedom*, 58.
4 Philip Barrett, *Gilbert Hunt: The City Blacksmith* (Richmond, VA: James Woodhouse & Co., 1859), http://docsouth.unc.edu/neh/Barrett/Barrett.html.
5 Laura Wexler, *Tender Violence: Domestic Visions in an Age of U.S. Imperialism* (Chapel Hill: University of North Carolina Press, 2012), chap. 2, 52–93.
6 Rayford W. Logan (ed.), *Memoirs of a Monticello Slave / as Dictated to Charles Campbell in the 1840's by Isaac, one of Thomas Jefferson's Slave*s (Charlottesville, VA: Published by the University of Virginia Press for the Tracy W. McGregor Library, 1951), 36, https://babel.hathitrust.org/cgi/pt?id=uc1.$b534612;view=1up;seq=11.
7 George Fitzhugh, *Sociology for the South or The Failure of Free Society* (Richmond, VA: A. Morris, 1854), 46, University of North Carolina's Documenting the American South project, http://docsouth.unc.edu/southlit/fitzhughsoc/fitzhugh.html.

8   'A Colored Hero', *Richmond Daily Dispatch*, 30 November 1858, 1, https://www.encyclopediavirginia.org/_A_Colored_Hero_Richmond_Daily_Dispatch_November_30_1858.
9   https://www.cowanauctions.com/lot/exceptional-gilbert-hunt-freed-richmond-slave-salt-print-by-vannerson-146642.
10 Samuel Mordecai, *Virginia, Especially Richmond, in by-gone Days: with a glance at the present: being reminiscences and last words of an old citizen* (n.p.p.: n.p., 1860), 213–17.
11 Tyler-McGraw and Kimball, *In Bondage and In Freedom*, 57. Hunt is still being used by pro-slavery advocates: some white supremacists have seized on Hunt's ownership of slaves as 'proof' that slavery was not 'only' perpetrated by Whites – entirely missing the historical context, of course, but still deploying Hunt to polish up a white image.
12 Barrett, *Gilbert Hunt*, 4. This claim is quoted from a story in the *Richmond Whig*, 13 May 1859.
13 G. B. Barber, *Calamity at Richmond, Being a Narrative of the Affecting Circumstances Attending the Awful Conflagration Of the Theatre, in the City Of Richmond, on the Night of Thursday, the 26th of December, 1811* (Philadelphia: John F. Watson, 1812), x, https://ia800207.us.archive.org/18/items/calamityatrichmo00phil/calamityatrichmo00phil.pdf.
14 Rees Lloyd, *The Richmond Alarm: a plain and familiar discourse in the form of a dialogue between a father and his son; in three parts* (Philadelphia: Printed for the Author, J. Bioren, Printer, 1814), 117, https://cdn.loc.gov/service/gdc/lhbcb/16684/16684.pdf.
15 See, for example, Archibald Alexander, *A Discourse Occasioned by the Burning of the Theatre in the City of Richmond, Virginia, on the Twenty-Sixth of December, 1811* (Philadelphia: Printed by John Weldwood Scott for Daniel Wilson, 8 January 1812), James Muir, *Repentance; or, Richmond in Tears* (Alexandria, VA: n.p., 1812), or William Hill, *A Sermon, Delivered in the Presbyterian Meeting-House in Winchester, on Thursday the 23d Jan. 1812; Being a Day of Fasting and Humiliation, Appointed by the Citizens of Winchester on Account of the Late Calamitous Fire at the Richmond Theatre, Winchester Gazette*, 23 January 1812.
16 Barber, *Calamity at Richmond*, 27.
17 Ann Alexander of York, *Remarks on the Theatre, and on the Late Fire at Richmond, in Virginia* (York, VA: Printed by T. Wilson and Son, for the Author, 1812), 14.
18 'Statements', *Richmond Enquirer*, 2 January 1812, 2, https://www.encyclopediavirginia.org/media_player?mets_filename=evr11635mets.xml.
19 William Dunlap, *A History of the American Theatre* (New York: J. Harper, 1832), 370–3, https://archive.org/details/historyofamerica00dunl.
20 Dionna Mann, 'Gilbert Hunt (ca. 1780–1863)', *Encyclopedia Virginia*, Virginia Foundation for the Humanities, 5 April 2017, https://www.encyclopediavirginia.org/Hunt_Gilbert_ca_1780-1863#art_entry.
21 Samuel Mordecai, *Richmond in By-Gone Days, Being Reminiscences of an old Citizen* (Richmond, VA: George M. West, 1856), 144–9, https://cdn.loc.gov/service/gdc/lhbcb/02923/02923.pdf.
22 'A Colored Hero'.
23 Barrett, *Gilbert Hunt*, 29.
24 Barrett, *Gilbert Hunt*, 4. Quoted from the *Richmond Whig*, 13 May 1859.
25 Barrett, *Gilbert Hunt*, 20.
26 'Contribution to the State Library', *Petersburg [Virginia] Index and Appeal*, 16 November 1875, page 3, column 4.
27 'Contribution to the State Library', 20.

28 *Richmond Whig*, 13 May 1859, quoted in Barrett, *Gilbert Hunt*, 4.
29 Barrett, *Gilbert Hunt*, 9–10.
30 Henry Wadsworth Longfellow, *The Children's Own Longfellow* (Boston: Houghton Mifflin, 1908).
31 Eric L. Haralson, 'Mars in Petticoats: Longfellow and Sentimental Masculinity', *Nineteenth-Century Literature* 51, no. 3 (1996): 327–55.
32 Alice Sumner Varney, 'Henry Wadsworth Longfellow', *Journal of Education* (1 January 1915): 73–6.
33 Frederick Douglass, *Life and Times of Frederick Douglass, Written by Himself* (Boston: De Wolfe & Fiske Co., 1892), 19, https://docsouth.unc.edu/neh/dougl92/dougl92.html.
34 Barrett, *Gilbert Hunt*, 16.
35 Marie Tyler-McGraw, *An African Republic: Black and White Virginians in the Making of Liberia*, 141, n. 5, Tyler-McGraw, Minutes of the Manchester Richmond Auxillary Society of the ACS [1823–8], Benjamin Brand Papers, Virginia Historical Society.
36 Tyler-McGraw, *An African Republic*, 16.
37 Barrett, *Gilbert Hunt*, 15–16.
38 Barrett, *Gilbert Hunt*, 14–15.
39 Barrett, *Gilbert Hunt*, 14–15.
40 Barrett, *Gilbert Hunt*, 19.
41 Barrett, *Gilbert Hunt*, 8.
42 Barrett, *Gilbert Hunt*, 8.
43 Philip Barrett, *Flowers by the Wayside, A Book for Children and Youth* (Richmond, VA: Price and Cardozo, 1856).
44 Philip Barrett, *The Deaf Shoemaker: To Which Are Added Other Stories for the Young* (New York: M. W. Dodd, 1859), 141–59.
45 Library of Virginia, 'Gilbert Hunt and the Richmond Theatre Fire', http://edu.lva.virginia.gov/online_classroom/lesson_plans/gilbert_hunt_and_the_richmond_theatre_fire.
46 Barrett, *Gilbert Hunt*, 7.
47 Barrett, *Gilbert Hunt*, 7.

13

Nominal Slavery, Free People of Colour and Enslavement Requests: Slavery and Freedom at the 'Edges' of the Regime in the Antebellum South

Emily West

In 1856, Virginia became the first Southern state to formalize legislation on so called 'voluntary slavery' (the term is contentious), in keeping with its reputation as a torchbearer for laws about enslavement. Before this time, free people of colour could only become enslaved through special legislative acts, but from 1856 onwards, the state proudly proclaimed that any free man of colour over the age of twenty-one and every free black woman over the age of eighteen could choose their master via legislative or court petition if they so desired. Courts would then ascertain the value of the petitioner, after which the 'chosen' slaveholder would pay the court half the individual's value, and enter bond for the rest. Thereafter 'the condition of the petitioner shall in all respects be the same as though the Negro has been born a slave'.[1]

After this ruling, Virginia saw a flurry of petitions from free people of colour seeking enslavement, the majority of whom appear to have lived among the enslaved and who were anxious about forcibly being separated from them, especially when they were bound to enslaved people through spousal or other familial ties of affection. And the state was not alone – other Southern legislatures also enacted or debated similar laws about the expulsion or enslavement of free people of colour. Between 1856 and the outbreak of the Civil War, seven states made legislative provisions for the 'voluntary' enslavement of free blacks. These were Alabama, Florida, Louisiana, Maryland, Tennessee, Texas and Virginia. South Carolina and Georgia approved of it by means of special acts of the legislature in individual cases, and the issue was also debated in the legislatures of Delaware, Kentucky, Mississippi, Missouri and North Carolina. Essentially, all Southern states were moving in the longer term towards the enslavement of their free people of colour, and some also considered the forced expulsion of free blacks, including Mississippi, Missouri, Florida and North Carolina.[2] Inevitably, the outbreak of war diverted attention to the more pressing concerns of conflict, but despite these upheavals the Confederacy continued to regard the enslavement of free people of colour as a means of strengthening its regime. By early 1863, just four days after Lincoln's Emancipation Proclamation, Jefferson Davis decreed all free blacks in the Confederacy should be considered enslaved, although, as David Williams has noted, this move proved impossible to enforce as Blacks headed to Union lines in their thousands.[3]

Arkansas went further than all other Southern states in its discriminatory treatment of free people of colour. In February 1859, the state outlawed all emancipations and also famously declared 'no free negro or mulatto to reside in the State after January 1st 1860'.[4] Convinced that 'removal' was in the best interests of all concerned, late antebellum policymakers in the state seem to have considered the enforced removal of free blacks to be the only viable option to ensure the regime's survival. In this sense their actions can be compared to those of the federal government during the Jacksonian era a generation earlier, when policymakers presented the 'removal' of Native American tribes west of the Mississippi as being in the 'best interests' of both the white *and* Native American people.[5] The Arkansas legislature did not pause to question where these expelled free people of colour might go. Instead it offered only one route by which they might 'choose' to stay: namely by 'selecting' a master or mistress and entering slavery. Moreover, a failure to 'select' such an owner put free blacks at risk of being arrested and imprisoned by county sheriffs, and then hired out to the highest bidder, essentially subjecting them to enslavement in a different form whereby the state assumed 'ownership' and 'bidders' gained the labour of the people they hired. Arkansas was hence increasing the flexibility and malleability of its slave regime as it attempted to bring free people of colour into this system.[6]

This chapter explores the lives of the enslaved and free people of colour who lived on the 'edges' of the slave regime, an all-encompassing and useful term coined by the late historian Peter Parish to refer to free people of colour living in the antebellum South, many of whom were the nominal slaves of white people, or 'slaves without masters' according to Ira Berlin's seminal 1974 conceptualization.[7] Parish also applied the term to urban slaves, those who were hired out and slaves who worked in more industrial contexts. Essentially, Parish encouraged historians to look beyond the plantation paradigm: to shed light on the 'edges' to illuminate the flexibility and malleability of slavery as a whole. Exploring people's lives at the margins of the regime therefore allows historians to reject oversimplistic dichotomies of 'freedom' and 'bondage', and see more of the everyday realities of life for people who lived between the two. Their experiences reveal another 'face' of people's lives under the regime as well as the motivations of slaveholders. The chapter hence traces laws about expulsion and enslavement before considering why free blacks who already lived among the enslaved considered 'voluntary' enslavement a viable option. It will then elaborate on some of these experiences through a case study of some free black families in Mississippi who lived 'in between' slavery and freedom in forms of quasi-slavery, and the impact of Arkansas's 1860 expulsion law upon free people of colour.

The US denied all black people, whether enslaved or free, formal legal citizenship until after the Civil War. Yet with some notable exceptions (mostly focused around more localized studies), most historians of the antebellum South have tended to consider free people of colour and the enslaved in relative isolation from each other. In contrast, this chapter considers the bonds and interactions between free people of colour and the enslaved. And whereas a growing number of historians are devoting attention to the lives of free blacks, especially women, who tried to move from bondage to freedom, this chapter instead explores moves from freedom to enslavement.[8] Significantly, free people of colour did not always live apart from the enslaved. Evidence from the US census, from legislative and county court petitions submitted by free people of colour and from Works Progress Administration (WPA) interviews collated in the 1930s instead suggests that many free black people worked and lived within the households, farms and plantations of white slaveholders under informal systems of bondage, in positions of nominal or quasi-slavery. These people often had affective ties to the enslaved, from whom they did not wish to be separated, especially when Southern states imposed ever-more restrictive laws in relation to free people of colour's mobility over the course of the antebellum era. Moreover, the very existence of free blacks irked pro-slavery advocates who wanted to present enslavement as the most 'appropriate' situation for people of African descent. Hence lawmakers sought to create a clear binary division between Black and White, enslaved and free.

Southern slaveholders, too, increasingly aired their concerns about the existence of free people of colour over the course of the antebellum era. Pro-slavery ideologue George Fitzhugh, for example, even described the very notion of 'a free negro' as an 'absurdity'.[9] Hence the laws passed by Southern states in their attempts to regulate free blacks is testament to how much white slaveholding lawmakers perceived free people of colour as problematic. As early as 1806 Virginia passed a law decreeing that all former slaves manumitted by their owners had to leave the state within one year or else relinquish their liberty, unless they had the permission of county officials to remain.[10] And, despite free people of colour's valuable economic input, Southern legislatures, via local laws, statutes and ordinances, attempted to prevent the migration of free blacks into states, restricted emancipations, set up complicated systems of registration, taxation and guardianship, and attempted to send some free blacks 'back' to Africa via various colonization initiatives.[11] While these laws and ordinances were not always easy to enforce, legislative action escalated over time as rising sectional tensions led Southern lawmakers to debate and/or enact ever more restrictive legislation governing the lives of free people of colour, especially in the second half of the 1850s.

Following these legal debates and rulings across the South as a whole, a minority of free people of colour sought recourse to the law in an attempt to move from freedom to bondage. Their often poignant petitions for alleged 'voluntary' enslavement illustrate the sheer desperation and poverty of antebellum free blacks who fought not to move, but to 'remain still' with their families, in their homes, enmeshed in broader communities; they prioritized their immediate affective ties over and above their legal status, and sometimes even their freedom. For these people, there was no clear divide between slavery and freedom, but rather a continuum of racial oppression that also, of course, continued through the Civil War and thereafter when the era of Jim Crow segregation saw ongoing coercion and racialized violence. However, those who sought recourse to the law in an attempt to enter bondage are numerically highly insignificant. The author found just 143 enslavement petitions across the Southern states, while Ted Maris-Wolf's more recent and more focused case study of self-enslavement using evidence from Virginia's county courts found 110 enslavement petitioners within that state alone.[12] Compared to the total quarter of a million free blacks in the South in 1860, these numbers are very small indeed.[13] But these often very desperate people reveal much about a different face of enslavement upon its margins, as well as the nature of surviving written sources about slavery which are so often biased towards large, efficiently run plantations. Moreover, despite some regional differences in enslavement and expulsion laws as outlined above, free people of colour lived within enslaved communities in forms of quasi-slavery across the whole South, and their submission of enslavement requests also occurred across the region as a whole.[14]

The 1861 petition of Walker Fitch of Augusta County, Virginia, twenty-one years old in the census of 1860, is highly typical of these enslavement requests. In his petition to the state legislature, Fitch claimed to be 'weary of freedom'. He argued he wanted to belong to Michael G. Harman, the owner of his wife and children, and the holder of twenty-four enslaved people in total.[15] According to the 1860 census, which included free people of colour, Fitch did not live in the same household as his enslaved wife and children, although in practice it is highly likely he visited them frequently, especially at weekends. The relationship of Fitch and his wife (who could not legally marry under US law) probably operated in a similar way to those of enslaved couples in 'cross-plantation' or 'abroad' marriages, where husbands tended to partake in weekend visits sanctioned by slaveholders, but might occasionally also undergo additional 'illicit' midweek visits.[16]

Indeed, the fact that Fitch was not enslaved probably made little difference to Michael Harman. Every child that Fitch's wife bore would belong to him, following the precedent set by an earlier Virginian ruling of 1662, when, in a practice that deviated from most colonial lawmaking (which tended to follow British precedents that favoured patrilineal lines), the rule of *partus sequitur ventrem* decreed that the offspring of enslaved mothers followed the status of their mothers, and not their fathers.[17] Historians can do no more than hypothesize about the spousal relationship of Fitch, his wife and their family, but further light can be shed on this couple and their relationship by using census evidence in conjunction with Fitch's enslavement petition to speculate about why he might have wanted to enter slavery 'voluntarily'.[18]

The 1860 census reveals that Fitch lived in a free black household along with his mother, Margaret, and his sister, Elvira, both of whom laboured as washerwomen. Like many other free people of colour in the antebellum South, it is likely the family were poor.[19] Fitch himself is listed as a 'labourer', and in his petition, Fitch's potential owner, Michael Harman, explained that he owned Fitch's wife and children before describing how Fitch had worked for him for 'several years'. Harman subsequently explained in typically benevolent rhetoric that he was 'willing' to accept Fitch as a slave 'upon equitable terms'. Indeed, the fact that the entire petition is written in Harman's hand arouses suspicion that Harman simply wanted to acquire Fitch, a man of prime labouring and childbearing age, for free.

But Walker Fitch may have had his own reasons for wanting to become enslaved to Michael Harman. As is frustratingly the case for many other enslavement petitions, there is no recorded result for Fitch's request. But he could well have been acting pragmatically. Although his views and opinions are absent from the historical record, Fitch seems to have rejected the dichotomy between slavery and freedom. He was prepared to lose his right to the legal freedom yearned for by so many enslaved people, and he was prepared to work for Harman as a slave rather than as a poorly paid labourer. Furthermore, in accepting enslavement, Fitch also had something very important to gain, namely the ability to spend every night in the same bed as his wife, and to enjoy spending time with his children at the end of the working day and at weekends. In short, Fitch could be more immediately involved in the day-to-day life of his beloved family while his everyday labour stayed much the same as it always had. Walker Fitch's everyday life as a potential slave, rather than a free man of colour, can hence be characterized in terms of continuities rather than changes. For Fitch, like many others, there was no sharp delineation between slavery and freedom, but rather a continuum of oppression characterized by degrees of persecution. Walker Fitch was already a slave in all but name, a nominal slave of Michael Harman even before the submission of his enslavement request.

Like Walker Fitch, most free people of colour who submitted enslavement requests wanted simply to stay with their families, in their homes. They therefore responded to the threat of expulsion and/or enslavement in pragmatic ways that prioritized their immediate affective ties over and above their legal status, and sometimes even their freedom. Individual experiences of belonging in a sense of place via emotional attachments to people and areas assumed priority here. Historians often regard people's geographical mobility through a paradigm of positivity, but this does not hold true across time and space, especially in places with oppressive regimes where so much movement has been enforced. As argued by Edlie Wong, the right to movement is essential to modern conceptualizations of freedom, and certainly the freedom to partake in geographical mobility has, and continues to be, important for people.[20] But while the enforced curtailing of movement obviously negates one's freedom, the opposite is also true. For example, for enslaved people forced westwards as a part of the internal domestic slave trade, and for free people of colour reacting pragmatically to expulsion and enslavement laws, geographical mobility was something enforced and undesirable. These people simply wanted to be still, to remain with the people they loved.

Enslaved people and poor free people of colour were early pioneers in marrying for reasons of romantic love. Devoid of wealth and property, arranged marriages (informal or otherwise) bore no relevance for antebellum black Southerners, in contrast to patterns of wedlock among elite white Southerners, for whom the preservation of familial money was important to the maintenance of power networks.[21] Instead, antebellum black Southerners married for love. An unnamed formerly enslaved man from Henry County, Tennessee, told his Fisk University interviewer in the late 1930s that:

> I knowed a man named Wyatt who was free and he wanted to marry a slave girl name Carrie, and he gave himself to Carrie's master to marry her. That love is an awful thing, I tell you. What I woulda done was to go off and send for her later on. He was crazy to do that.[22]

The interviewee wrote off Wyatt as 'crazy', sacrificing his very liberty for the love of the woman, Carrie, whom he wanted to marry. But of course Wyatt didn't know that slavery would be abolished in 1865, and he made a pragmatic decision, albeit one governed by his heart, to live with his sweetheart in wedlock, by 'gifting' himself, as a slave, to Carrie's owner. Poignantly, all he had to offer was his own potential value as a black man who could become chattel. It is unknown how this arrangement worked at a practical level. Did Carrie's master seek recourse to the law in an attempt to formalize his ownership of Wyatt or did the arrangement operate on a more informal, ad hoc basis? Did Carrie's master simply 'assume' ownership of Wyatt and provide him with a home, food, clothing and other necessary items in return for Wyatt's unpaid labour and the 'freedom' to live with his wife? At the margins – the edges – of the regime, slavery was complicated and often raises more questions than it answers.

There are numerous instances of wedlock between enslaved people and free blacks contained within the Works Progress Administration (WPA) interviews with formerly enslaved (and free black) people in the 1930s, of which the case of Wyatt, detailed above, provides just one example.[23] Take Emma Stone, who lived with her free black mother, her nine siblings and her enslaved father on the Bell family plantation in North Carolina. 'We wuz,' she said 'just lak de udder slaves.'[24] In Texas, Mary Reynolds' free black father attempted to negotiate with his wife's owner to buy her from him. But Dr Kilpatrick was well aware of this woman's value to him both as a worker and reproducer. 'Dr Kilpatrick was never one to sell any but the old niggers who was past workin' in the fields and past their breedin' times,' Mary recalled. So 'my paw married my maw and works in the field the same as any other nigger'. They had six daughters, including Mary, and her father appears to have lived in quasi-slavery.[25] Likewise, Laura Hart, enslaved in Arkansas, described how her father attempted to buy her mother from her master, Sam Carson, who refused to sell. Laura Hart then explained how her father 'stayed with old man Carson till they was all free'.[26] Samuel Small explained how his free black father spent seven years working on the Florida plantation of his mother's master, unpaid, because he would not leave her.[27] These scattered examples among many others reveal the real strength of romantic ties of affection, as well as significant interaction along the blurred line between slavery and freedom for black Southerners.

Other cases of quasi-slavery at the edges of the regime can be found through a careful combination of archival research, supplemented by probing the US census and sometimes adding in a jot of speculation as well. The situation of the Lundy family of Pike County, Mississippi, provides a good example of this. In 1854 the Pike County Board of Police authorized a public auction to hire out a number of free blacks in the county with the surname Lundy. The policy was designed to raise a fund of some $6,000 to ship the Lundys to Liberia and provide for them for one year thereafter – so removing the 'problem' of these free blacks in the state – but it is unknown whether the Lundys themselves were instrumental in initiating this colonization request.[28]

The 1850 census shows twenty-six black or 'mulatto' people with the surname Lundy living in Pike County, fifteen of whom lived in one large multigenerational farming household – a common family formation for people living in poverty across a variety of different times and spaces. Extended families provide additional labour for financial support and women can share childcare responsibilities. But, looking up the other Lundys in the census reveals something more unusual. Spread throughout eight white headed households in the county were a number of free black Lundy children, of whom the eldest, John, was fifteen while the youngest, Celia and Bob, were six. These Lundy children seem to have already been hired out to white families, either alone or in pairs, either to earn additional money or to spare the Lundy household from the financial burden of raising then. They probably performed small domestic chores and helped with children. In short, their labour was practically the same as that of enslaved children.[29] Moreover, the Lundys were probably unaware of any legal rights they possessed as free people of colour rather than slaves because they were children or adolescents.

So the notion that these Lundy children were 'free' people of colour is rendered rather hollow by the realities of their everyday existence in which they laboured under systems of servitude and dependency despite their legal status as free people of colour and the limited protections under the law that status brought. Racial slavery meant many manifestations of exploitation, and not just for those legally enslaved. Moreover, using census and slave schedule evidence to track the family formations of the white families with whom the Lundy children resided reveals that all eight households held a number of slaves in addition to the 'free' black Lundy children. For example, fifteen-year-old John Lundy lived with the Stallins who owned five enslaved people. Sarah Lundy resided in the home of the Lamkin family along with their forty-two slaves. No doubt the Stallin and Lamkin families treated John and Sarah Lundy in much the same way as their chattel – they were slaves in all but name and part of broader enslaved communities despite their free status.[30] In the longer term, attempts to raise enough money to ship the Lundys to Liberia appear to have failed. Twenty members of the family appear on the 1860 census for Pike County, many of whom lived within the same white households for whom they still laboured.[31] The Lundy family's experiences suggest forms of *de facto* slavery and informal systems of hiring out for free people of colour both before and during the Civil War.

Across the border in Arkansas, the state's harsh expulsion law of 1860 meant that free blacks were not permitted to live within the state after that date. Those who stayed had to 'choose' slavery instead. Historians have estimated there were only around 700 free people of colour in Arkansas at the time of this ruling, most of whom chose to flee.[32] For example, Billy Higgins has illustrated how one free black community in Marion County diminished by 120, leaving only eight individuals in the area. Oppressive laws therefore rendered the free black population of Arkansas virtually extinct, but because these people often left no written sources, historians can only hypothesize about their movements. Higgins wrote:

> ... their [free people of colour's] decision to go raises several questions. Was their departure forced by Marion County whites ...? Did the community travel to a common destination together, or did they leave individually, each seeking to find new beginnings in another place?[33]

At the dawn of a new decade, free people of colour in Arkansas found themselves in a truly desperate situation. Leaving the state collectively – in groups that included beloved family and community members – was certainly an option. But what about free blacks whose primary affective ties were to the enslaved? They faced heartbreaking dilemmas including whether simply to 'lie low', to 'be still' and hope for better times ahead, or to leave, sometimes without their loved ones.

Choosing the former could be a risky strategy, however. County sheriffs caught at least a handful of free black people living illegally in Arkansas, all of whom were forced into slavery. For example, the Pulaski County sheriff captured Robert Deam in 1860 for living in the state 'contrary to law'. He appeared in open court and then 'selected' Thomas Yell as his new master. The language used is chilling since Robert Deam had no real choice beyond enslavement or expulsion. Aged fifty-five and valued at just $250, Thomas Yell had to pay just half that amount to the County treasury. Moreover, the 1850 census shows Robert Deam already living with the Yell family, where he worked as a labourer. So he 'chose' to stay with his family in the place he called home. Deam then poignantly disappears from the 1860 census because he had entered slavery, but the associated slave schedules show Thomas Yell owning eleven slaves, one a fifty-five-year-old man, presumably Robert, another a woman of sixty who may have been Robert's spouse and a number of other slaves, some of whom may have been their children (the slave schedules only give lists of enslaved people).[34] Robert Deam's move into bondage, although against his will, can be characterized in terms of continuities rather than changes. Faced with the stark and bewildering 'choice' of expulsion or enslavement, he accepted the latter in order to remain at home with his beloved family.

Conclusion

Arkansas went further than other Southern states in its restrictive legislation directed against free people of colour because no other Southern legislature passed a law designed to expel all free blacks. However, the fact that other states debated and sometimes legislated on what they termed 'voluntary' slavery suggests the South as a whole was attempting to make free people of colour's lives less tolerable, and ultimately to separate free people of colour from the enslaved by creating a bi-racial system of free whites and enslaved blacks. But despite these moves by the white men of government, slaves and free people of colour formed families, homes and communities across this often arbitrary divide, which they fought to preserve in pragmatic ways. Many free people of colour were already de facto slaves in the households of white families, families to whom some later sought enslavement. Ira Berlin famously described free blacks as 'slaves without masters', but ironically, some antebellum free people of colour were already subject to a kind of quasi-slavery *with* masters.[35]

Relatively overlooked by historians, understanding the lives of free people of colour in the antebellum South is important. As Ira Berlin has noted, the origins of various post-emancipation racial institutions such as the black codes, sharecropping and segregation can be found specifically in antebellum legislation directed against free blacks.[36] But despite the strenuous efforts by white Southerners to create a bi-racial system of plantation-based slavery, there remained diverse and contested middle grounds in between slavery and freedom where the enslaved, free blacks and poorer whites interacted in a variety of ways. During a climate of changing, and ever-more hostile, laws, exploring the lives of free people of colour along the 'edges' of the regime provides a useful 'way in' for historians interested in exploring further ties between the enslaved and free people of colour, relationships between free blacks and whites, and what these social and economic relationships reveal more broadly about interactions along the all-too hazy boundary between slavery and freedom.

Notes

1 'An Act Providing for the Voluntary Enslavement of Free Negroes of the Commonwealth', passed on 18 February 1856, chapter 46, 37–8. *Acts of the General Assembly of Virginia, 1855–1856* (Richmond: John Worrock, printer to the Senate, 1856), Library of Virginia, Richmond (hereafter LVA). See also Ira Berlin, *Slaves Without Masters: The Free Negro in the Antebellum South* (New York: Pantheon, 1974), 260–4, 371; John H. Russell, *The Free Negro in Virginia, 1619–1865* (New York: Dover, 1969), 107–9; June Purcell Guild, *Black Laws of Virginia: A Summary of the Legislative Acts of Virginia Concerning Negroes from the Earliest Times to the Present* (Richmond: Whittet and Shepperson, 1936), 121. Some of the arguments presented in this chapter are explored in more detail in Emily West, *Family or Freedom: People of Color in the Antebellum South* (Lexington: University Press of Kentucky, 2012).
2 Of the five states that did not legislate on 'voluntary' slavery, four were in the Upper South. But only Delaware's free black population stood at over 10 per cent of the total number of free people of colour. There was no correlation between the relative size of the free black population and legislative action on enslavement, nor was there a link between the geographic location of states and the desire to legislate. For more on these legal moves, see Thomas D. Morris, *Southern Slavery and the Law, 1619–1860* (Chapel Hill and London: University of North Carolina Press, 1996); and West, *Family or Freedom*, chap. 1.
3 David Williams, *I Freed Myself: African American Self-Emancipation in the Civil War Era* (New York: Cambridge University Press, 2014), 128–9.
4 'An Act to Remove the Free Negroes and Mulattoes from this State' (number 151), approved 12 February 1859. Acts Passed at the Twelfth Session of the General Assembly of the State of Arkansas, 1858–9. *Acts of Arkansas*, 175–8, Arkansas History Commission and State Archives, Little Rock (hereafter AHCSA).
5 Theda Perdue argues that Native American Removal was a process of ethnic cleansing. See 'The Legacy of Indian Removal', *Journal of Southern History* 77, no. 1 (2012): 3–36, esp. 28.
6 'An Act to Remove the Free Negroes and Mulattoes from this State', 175–8, AHCSA.
7 See Peter Parish, 'The Edges of Slavery in the Old South: Or, do Exceptions Prove Rules?', *Slavery and Abolition* 4, no. 1 (1983): 106–25. See also his book, *Slavery: History and Historians* (New York: Harper and Row, 1989), chap. 6; Berlin, *Slaves Without Masters*.
8 In addition to Berlin's *Slaves Without Masters*, see also John Hope Franklin, *The Free Negro in North Carolina, 1790–1860*, 3rd edn (Chapel Hill: University of North Carolina Press, 1995); Michael P. Johnson and James L. Roark, *No Chariot Let Down: Charleston's Free People of Color on the Eve of the Civil War* (New York: Norton, 1984). Jane Landers considers free blacks across Atlantic slave societies in *Against the Odds: Free Blacks in the Slave Societies of the Americas* (London: Frank Cass, 1996), as do David Barry Gaspar and Darlene Clark Hine (eds), in *Beyond Bondage: Free Women of*

Color in the Americas (Urbana: University of Illinois Press, 2004). For more recent works on free people of colour (especially women) in the US, see Wilma King, *The Essence of Liberty: Free Black Women in the Slave Era* (Columbia: University of Missouri Press, 2006); Jessica Millward, *Finding Charity's Folk: Enslaved and Free Black Women in Maryland* (Athens: University of Georgia Press, 2015); Amrita Chakrabarti Myers, *Forging Freedom: Black Women and the Pursuit of Liberty in Antebellum Charleston* (Chapel Hill: University of North Carolina Press, 2011); and Judith Kelleher Schafer, *Becoming Free, Remaining Free: Manumission and Enslavement in New Orleans, 1846–1862* (Baton Rouge: Louisiana State University Press, 2003).

9   George Fitzhugh, *Sociology for the South; Or, the Failure of Free Society* (Richmond, VA: A. Morris, 1854), 264.
10 Quoted in Peter Wallenstein, *Tell the Court I Love My Wife: Race, Marriage, and Law – An American History* (London: Palgrave MacMillan, 2002), 21.
11 For an overview of these laws, statutes and ordinances across the South, see West, *Family or Freedom*, chap. 1.
12 Ted Maris-Wolf, *Family Bonds: Free Blacks and Re-enslavement Law in Antebellum Virginia* (Chapel Hill: University of North Carolina Press, 2015), 21.
13 John Boles, *Black Southerners, 1619–1869* (Lexington: University Press of Kentucky, 1983), 135.
14 For a more detailed analysis, see West, *Family or Freedom*, esp. chap. 1.
15 Petition of Walker Fitch, Race and Slavery Petitions Project, University of North Carolina at Greensboro. Each petition holds a unique Petition Analysis Record number, in this case PAR 11686102. See https://library.uncg.edu/slavery/petitions/. 'Slave Inhabitants in Staunton District Number 1, County of Augusta, State of Virginia, Enumerated on 20th June 1860', 11. All US census information (including that from the slave schedules) has been obtained via ancestry.com.
16 1860 Census for Staunton, Augusta, Virginia, roll M653 1333, 786, image 266. Family History Library Film 805333. For more on the cross-plantation marriages of enslaved people, see Emily West, *Chains of Love: Slave Couples in Antebellum South Carolina* (Urbana and Chicago: University of Illinois Press, 2004), chap. 2.
17 Jennifer Morgan, *Laboring Women: Reproduction and Gender in New World Slavery* (Philadelphia: University of Pennsylvania Press, 2004), 71–2.
18 Stephanie Camp argues persuasively that historians use their imagination in the absence of written testimony: Stephanie Camp, *Closer to Freedom: Enslaved Women and Everyday Resistance in the Plantation South* (Chapel Hill and London: University of North Carolina Press, 2004), 95.
19 Julie Winch, *Between Slavery and Freedom: Free People of Color in America from Settlement to the Civil War* (Lanham, MD: Rowman and Littlefield, 2014), 63–71.
20 Edlie L. Wong, *Neither Fugitive nor Free: Atlantic Slavery, Freedom Suits, and the Legal Culture of Travel* (New York and London: New York University Press, 2009), 242–3.
21 For more on romantic love among enslaved people in the antebellum South, see West, *Chains of Love*, chap. 1.
22 George P. Rawick, *The American Slave: A Composite Autobiography*, vol. 18: *The Unwritten History of Slavery* (Westport, CT: Greenwood Press, 1972), 284.
23 Of course enslaved people (and enslaved people and free people of colour) could not marry under US law as they were not citizens. But most entered wedlock after undergoing some sort of formal ceremony. For more on black marriage, See Tera W. Hunter, *Bound in Wedlock: Slave and Free Black Marriage in the Nineteenth Century* (Cambridge, MA, and London: Belknap Press, 2017), especially chaps 1 and 3.

24 Emma Stone, *Federal Writers' Project: Slave Narrative Project*, vol. 11: *North Carolina, Part 2, Jackson–Yellerday*, 329. Accessed via the Library of Congress website: https://www.loc.gov/collections/slave-narratives-from-the-federal-writers-project-1936-to-1938/about-this-collection/ (hereafter LoC).
25 Mary Reynolds in George P. Rawick, *The American Slave*, Supplement Series 2, vol. 8: *Texas Narratives Part 7* (Westport, CT: Greenwood Press, 1979), 3284. Larry Koger has referred to the practice of free blacks purchasing enslaved spouses as 'nominal slavery'. See Larry Koger, *Black Slaveowners: Free Black Slave Masters in South Carolina, 1790–1860* (London: McFarland, 1985), 69. See also Hunter, *Bound in Wedlock*, 93–5.
26 Laura Hart, *Federal Writers' Project: Slave Narrative Project*, vol. 2: *Arkansas, Part 3, Gadson–Isom*, 192, LoC.
27 Samuel Smalls, *Federal Writers' Project: Slave Narrative Project*, vol. 3: *Florida, Anderson–Wilson* (with combined interviews of others), 303–4, LoC. These experiences are being developed into a further article by the author, '"We chilluns, long wid her, wuz lak de udder slaves": Free black families and "quasi-slavery" in the pre-Civil War US South' (in progress).
28 'An Act to Empower the Board of Police of Pike County to Remove the Lundy Free Negroes Living in Said County to Liberia', approved 10 February 1854. *Laws of the State of Mississippi, Passed at a Regular Session of the Mississippi Legislature Held in the City of Jackson* (Jackson, MS: E. Barksdale, State Printer, 1854), 287–8. Mississippi Department of Archives and History (MDAH hereafter).
29 For a detailed summary of the Lundy family children, see West, *Family or Freedom*, 68–9.
30 1850 Census, Police District 1, Pike, Mississippi, roll M432 380, 19A, image 42, and 1B, image 7. 'Slave Inhabitants in the County of Pike, State of Mississippi, Enumerated on the 30th August 1850', 3.
31 See West, *Family or Freedom*, 69–70.
32 Margaret Ross, 'Mulattoes, Free Negroes Ordered to Leave Arkansas on Eve of War', *Arkansas Gazette*, 15 February 1959, 3E. She claims only 144 free blacks remained, all of whom were rather elderly, a number also cited by Ira Berlin. See Berlin, *Slaves Without Masters*, 373–4, and Morris, *Southern Slavery and the Law*, 30–1.
33 Billy D. Higgins, 'The Origins and Fate of the Marion County Free Black Community', *Arkansas Historical Quarterly* 54 (Winter 1995): 440.
34 Entry for 17 May 1860, microfilm roll misc.39, Circuit Court Record Book 'Z' (Civil), May 1859–July 1863, Pulaski County, Arkansas, 281. AHCSA; 1850 census for Vaugine, Jefferson, Arkansas, roll M432 27, 75A, image 154; 'Slave Inhabitants in Campbell Township in the County of Pulaski, State of Arkansas, Enumerated on the 27th July 1860, 7.
35 See Berlin, *Slaves Without Masters*.
36 Ira Berlin, 'Southern Free People of Color in the Age of William Johnson', *Southern Quarterly* 43, no. 2 (2006): 10–15.

14

The Transition from Plantation Slave Labour to Free Labour in the Americas

Herbert S. Klein*

One of the most fundamental changes in the world economy in the nineteenth century was the transition from slave to free labour in the Americas. It was a century-long process, beginning in the late eighteenth century and ending in 1888.[1] It was a process that reallocated and destroyed large amounts of capital, reduced or increased the costs of commercial exports from America to Europe, shifted the centres of plantation agriculture in America and transformed labour relations throughout the Western hemisphere. It also had an impact on governments, destroying several of them in rebellions and civil wars. Slave emancipation itself also became the major impulse for the migration of Asian labourers to the Americas, as well as one of the important factors promoting the transatlantic migration of southern Europeans. It also introduced wage labour in large parts of the Americas and changed the nature of plantation agricultural labour. It even affected the rhythm of agricultural production, as the marked seasonal occupation of labour during harvesting and planting became a more pronounced aspect of plantation agriculture in the Americas.

Yet despite its importance, the whole process of the transition from slave to free labour has been little studied from a comparative and international framework until quite recently. But most of these detailed histories are of individual processes of abolition, emancipation and its aftermath and most of the comparative analyses have been confined to the North Atlantic communities.[2] Given the multiple outcomes, few have attempted to present a comparative analysis or to propose an explanatory model by which to account for the numerous variables that influenced the different emancipation processes and results.[3] It is the aim of this chapter to provide such a model, which takes into consideration the differing historical experiences with slavery, manumission and emancipation; ecological, technological, demographic and economic constraints; political power and race relations; and the competition of alternative sources of labour.

The transition from slave labour in the areas dominated by large plantations presented a number of variations within the Western hemisphere. Yet despite this diversity of post-emancipation arrangements, there was a common set of demands and constraints that operated everywhere, with the differing outcomes being determined by a combination of variables from local circumstances to world market conditions. It appears that the black ex-slaves everywhere had similar interests when confronting the planter class. They wished to set up as independent producers and abandon forever plantation labour. From being a supervised labour force organized in groups and employing women in all aspects of basic agricultural production, ex-slaves wanted to work in family units of production in which control over actual working conditions shifted to the individual workers themselves. The transition also meant an increasing sexual division of labour, as women shifted out of field labour which they had dominated in most of the plantation regimes.[4] The planters also had clearly defined aims, which they hoped to achieve despite the change in the legal status of their labour force. They wanted compensation for their financial loss, and wanted to maintain their plantation economies with some type of control over their former slaves. They were willing to use all possible instruments to prevent their ex-slaves from leaving the plantations and if they could not prevent this, they demanded that the governments help pay for an alternative labour force.

There were also external factors which would influence this clash between planters and ex-slaves. International markets for the traditional crops at the time of emancipation was one such factor. The level of demand and the prices for American produced plantation crops influenced whether planters could survive their lost capital and the higher price of free labour.[5] Another factor was the quality of the land itself. Given the low level of technology in most plantation regions, soil quality determined productivity. Older regions with much used soils tended to be higher priced producers, while those on virgin soils were far more competitive. There were also the very mechanics of the production process. Could production be developed in smaller units, or was the nature of the planting and harvesting of the crop difficult to break down to this level? The land to labour ratio in the individual region was fundamental in determining if the ex-slaves could have access to farming land away from the plantation. Without access to land, ex-slaves were more constrained in their opportunities to escape the plantation system. The pre- and post-emancipation composition of the population was also a significant factor. The numbers of poor landless or small farm Whites available to compete with the ex-slaves for land was a significant theme. Also the role and significance of a free coloured class in the pre-emancipation period already could influence opportunities or lack thereof for the ex-slaves.

For the ex-slaves the basic demand was for control over their own labour and access to their own lands to use for the production of food and possibly even commercial crops. Given the opportunity, ex-slaves withdrew from the production of sugar, cotton, coffee and other commercial plantation crops on the lands of the planters, preferring self-employment and the production of crops on their own lands. Thus, where possible, the ex-slaves withdrew their families and themselves from plantation field labour, especially when it was organized in the gang labour system. They obviously did not withdraw from the labour force itself since they were forced to feed themselves and their families which they could do only if they produced their food or were able to pay for it through the sale of their labour to others. In the majority of cases, rural-based ex-slaves desired first to produce their own food for consumption and sale in the local market. Some freedmen even tried to control and profit from production for export markets of some of the very goods they produced as slaves. In both cases, however, their prime concern was to obtain access to land, legally or more often illegally as squatters.

The planters had an opposing set of interests to their ex-slaves and in most areas were primarily concerned with maintaining the plantation system. They, and their governmental representatives (often for different reasons), were intent on maintaining pre-emancipation levels of production and of preserving as much as possible of the plantation structure with its organization into gangs in which women fully participated and even with some coercive central supervision if possible. Although some abolitionists thought that the ex-slaves might effectively produce the traditional commercial crops on their own lands, most assumed that the emancipated slaves would remain as landless labourers on the estates of the Whites. The planters would remain as managers of these estates. Although many of the arguments by abolitionists before emancipation may have been intended merely to dampen pro-slavery protests, they often reflected the general belief that with the end of slavery the slaves would be left as an 'uncivilized' and uneducated group that still had a long way to go before being integrated into the body politic. Moreover, the immediate increase of leisure time which the ex-slaves established, in which the freedmen emulated all other free workers, reinforced the elite conception of the ex-slaves as essentially lazy. No major group of planters, and few government officials, in any of the ex-slave societies accepted as legitimate the ex-slave demands for land and the imposed end to the plantation regime.[6]

Given these conflicting views of what post-emancipation societies should look like, bitterly fought battles resulted. Depending on a host of different factors, neither planters nor ex-slaves would fully dominate the outcome in any particular region, though the differing contexts and markets would favour either the ex-planters or the ex-slaves. In the majority of cases the ex-slaves would not be able to satisfy all of their demands, nor would the planters totally achieve their objectives. Nevertheless the frequent maintenance of planter class political power and land ownership meant that there were limits on what was obtainable by the ex-slaves. While slaves had great difficulty acquiring lands in many cases, in almost all instances the labour organization of the pre-emancipation plantations was totally destroyed and replaced by some form of family-based farm tenancy or voluntary wage labour without coercion.

Examining these causal factors in more detail, we can see how world market demand for the plantation crops at the time of emancipation greatly influenced the conflict. If demand was strong enough, even low productivity plantations could still survive. But if not, then planters were forced to liquidate their holdings. The higher the demand for the crop and its price, the greater the tendency was for the plantation system to be maintained, or for the production of the export commodities to be continued with some modifications of the production arrangements. World market conditions would be influenced by the availability of alternative sources of supply or alternative crops. The different circumstances of cane sugar (where there was competition not only from East Indian sugar but also from the development of beet sugar in Europe), coffee and cotton left a significant impact on the differing economic circumstances of the US South and the Brazilian South-east, where economic recovery was more rapid than in many of the sugar producing Caribbean islands in the nineteenth century.

The profitability of the plantation regimes would also be influenced by the relative costs of the factors of production. The greater the efficient scale of production, the more necessary would be the maintenance of the plantation system. The possibilities of developing production in smaller units could, however, permit maintenance of the production of the export crop albeit at some reduced level of productive efficiency. Such adjustment was possible in the production of coffee, cotton and tobacco, among other crops, but in general was not possible for sugar.[7] But in at least two crops, planting and processing revolutions which occurred prior to emancipation also significantly aided the planters through the crisis of loss of their slave labour force. This can be seen in the Cuban sugar industry and in the cotton plantation system in the United States. The early introduction of steam milling and then the creation of the large *ingenios* all constantly reduced costs to planters and increased productivity throughout the nineteenth century.[8] The same occurred in cotton, first with the gin, which allowed short staple cotton to be efficiently produced, and then the systematic improvement of seeds and plants led to a productivity revolution.[9] But there were no such improvements in other crops, and therefore access to virgin lands remained a crucial variable since such lands were systematically more productive per hectare than the older regions.[10]

If most of the planters were to survive or the ex-slaves become farmers, the crucial question in each of these slave plantation regimes was the availability of land and natural resources. For the planters relying on traditional production and plants, the quality of the soil and its history of usage influenced the costs of production. Equally, the amount of virgin soils determined future potential for profit. For the ex-slaves the relative availability of unused lands, their quality and water requirements, their location to markets and their legal status all influenced the potential development of small-scale freehold agriculture by ex-slaves. Thus, in societies such as British Guiana and Trinidad, with large quantities of virgin land just entering into sugar production, strong pressure for the maintenance of plantation agriculture was generated, while in older areas, such as Jamaica, or the old coffee counties of the Paraiba Valley in Rio de Janeiro and São Paulo, such pressures were more limited. Here land no longer viable for plantation agriculture could still be used for subsistence farming because it was well located in terms of markets. Even when much virgin land was available with an open frontier, such as in the coffee plantation regions of the western zone of São Paulo, it was relatively easy for ex-slaves to obtain frontier land beyond the plantations as squatters in the early development of these regions – a process long anticipating emancipation itself – though they would eventually be forced off these lands as the frontiers moved onward.[11] But on islands such as Barbados, with little available non-plantation-owned land, and good quality soils with much potential, the plantation system was able to continue without serious interruption. Equally, little land and high population density influenced the wage rates and the costs of production for the planters. Thus, for example, the high population densities on the islands of Barbados and Antigua meant that labour costs were kept low and, given all other potential inputs being of reasonable quality, plantation sugar production could persist after emancipation, and the Antiguan planters were even willing to do without the period of enforced apprenticeship. These islands were frequently pointed to as the successful examples of what emancipation would accomplish by metropolitan authorities who had favoured abolition. Even when land was available, as in Jamaica, the local governments tried to tax, restrict market access, apply vagrancy laws and otherwise pressure the ex-slave farmers (of whom a third had obtained land by the 1840s) so that they would still be forced to work the plantations. This was not that dissimilar from what occurred in the Southern United States.[12]

The ratio of Whites to Blacks in the population influenced the relative occupational opportunities open to the ex-slaves and even to some extent race relations between Whites and Blacks. In those zones where poor whites competed with the ex-slaves for land and semi-skilled and skilled occupations, such as the United States, ex-slaves had a more difficult time competing for land and labour than in places like Jamaica, Brazil and Cuba, where such large numbers of white working-class persons did not exist. Thus many ex-slaves in these societies were able to carry their skills with them and compete in the free market. In the United States this proved extremely difficult given the competition of abundant supplies of working-class whites.

The existence of a large free coloured class well before the end of slavery also aided in opening up social and economic mobility for the ex-slaves. If a large number of free coloured already owned urban and rural property, obtained credit, made contracts and had viable occupations well before abolition, then it was much easier for the ex-slaves to integrate into the free labour market even if they entered with no capital themselves. In Brazil, for example, the first national census of 1872 – sixteen years before final emancipation – reported that the slave and free coloured made up 60 per cent of the population, with the 4.2 million free coloured being the largest single group, followed by the 3.8 million Whites and just 1.5 million slaves.[13] Though Whites represented over half the population in Cuba in 1862, the 211,000 free coloured made up almost 40 per cent of the total coloured population and were already firmly established in the cities and rural districts well before final emancipation.[14] In Puerto Rico and Cuba, on the eve of emancipation, there were 885,000 non-whites of which 53 per cent were free coloured. In the West Indies and in the United States in contrast, such free persons were fewer in number and were often quite restricted in their physical mobility and their freedom to compete in the free labour market. Thus on the eve of emancipation the free coloured of Barbados were only 7 per cent of the entire non-white population,[15] and just 11 per cent of that same population in Jamaica. In all the British Caribbean the free coloured made up only 16 per cent of the total coloured population before emancipation. In the Dutch islands the figure was just 6 per cent and in the Danish islands they were probably a quarter of the coloured population. In total, all the non-Spanish European Caribbean islands had 1.3 million persons of African descent in the 1830s, of which only 15 per cent were free persons of colour.[16] The United States was little better, with only 11 per cent of the 4.4 million total coloured being freedmen in 1860, and this counts free blacks and mulattoes in the Northern free states.[17]

In only three large plantation countries – Cuba, Brazil and to some extent in the United States – was urban slavery significant, though it was primary in almost all the mainland Latin American colonies and republics. In these countries the role of slave and free coloured skilled and unskilled labour was fundamental and they were often the base labour force well past emancipation. In Havana, for example, there were over 45,000 persons of colour in the city in 1817 and 63,000 in 1868. In the former year the free coloured accounted for 47 per cent of this group, but by 1868 the freedmen were 60 per cent of the non-white and non-Asian population.[18] In the island as a whole in 1862, some 76,000 slaves lived in towns or 21 per cent of the slave population.[19] In Rio de Janeiro, free coloured made up a quarter of the 43,000 non-whites in the city, but slaves made up a much more significant 47 per cent of the total urban population. In the case of Rio in this period, the free coloured could be found in all occupations, even though they represented just 16 per cent of the total urban population.[20] Even in the Caribbean islands with their small urban centres, urban slavery was important and existed alongside the free coloured population. In Martinique in 1832, some 16,000 out of the island's 83,000 slaves lived and worked in towns.[21] Although these urban slaves represented half that ratio in the British islands (or just 9 per cent of the slave population), they numbered an estimated 43,000 in British islands in 1832, two-thirds of whom lived in towns with 2,000 or more slaves. Here too they lived with a larger share of the free coloured population of whom there were some 103,000 by the 1830s (or 13 per cent of the total coloured population).[22] In Matanzas Province of Cuba in 1877, almost two-thirds of the 38,000 free coloured lived in towns along with 12 per cent of the province's 70,000 slaves.[23] Thus for the minority of slaves found in these urban centres, the role of the free coloured before emancipation was fundamental. In Cuba and even more in Brazil and the non-Hispanic West Indies, urban slaves were able to practise their pre-emancipation skills as free persons. Given the lack of both guilds and a significant number of competitive white artisans in the West Indies and Brazil, there was a heavy reliance on these coloured workers whatever their status. Moreover, the extensive system of renting slaves and permitting them to set up separate households, something vigorously opposed in most towns in the United States, also gave these ex-slaves independence and skills which permitted them to better integrate into free society.[24] Though the white master craftsmen fought to prevent these artisans from taking exams or competing, they mostly were able to carry their skills into freedom.[25]

But even in the rural areas, free persons of colour could be found working in the plantations. They were often skilled sugar masters or even semi-skilled rural workers and for various reasons remained on the farms. Even as late as 1905 in São Paulo, 35 per cent of the coffee labour force were native born Brazilians and worked alongside the European families who had replaced the slaves. It is unclear how many of these workers were free coloured or slaves before emancipation, but it is evident that even in coffee some ex-slaves, now almost all males, continued to work in plantation agriculture even when land was available.[26]

In those regions where too few ex-slaves could be induced to work in the fields because of available land and labour opportunities, these plantations could persist if they could get access to alternative forms of labour, especially foreign-born labourers. The availability of cheap foreign-born indentured labour provided a basis for the maintenance of the plantation system in those cases where ex-slave labour costs were high (because of competing wage employment in farms or cities) or their labour not readily available due to their total withdrawal to small farming.[27] The possibility of this in-migration depended on cheap and mobile sources of labour (from Europe, India or China), on reduced transportation costs (much helped by the revolution in steam shipping), government subsidies and governmental willingness to enforce indenture contracts in one form or another. With varying degrees of importance, this alternative labour would be used in the West Indies, the Guyanas, Brazil and Cuba to maintain plantation production. In some cases, such as Cuba and North-eastern Brazil, the older work arrangements could be maintained with both ex-slaves and new contract workers through the conversion of plantation labour into a seasonal labour force, which in turn allowed the workers to be part-time subsistence farmers. Cuba is the only case where such Chinese 'coolies' and other indentured contract labourers were integrated into the field workforce alongside the slaves before emancipation. In all other cases this occurred after emancipation, as in the case of the other sugar plantations of the Caribbean region and the coffee fields of São Paulo. In turn, São Paulo is the only area where free European immigrant labour replaced the slaves in the post-emancipation plantation regimes. In these coffee *fazendas*, production would be maintained through family farm unit tenancy arrangements similar in terms of working arrangements – if not in modes of payments – to the sharecropping tenancy organized in the cotton fields of the US South after 1860.[28] There even emerged in post-emancipation Cuba roaming *cuadrillas* or hired gangs of ex-slave workers who moved from plantation to plantation during planting and harvesting seasons.[29]

Without question the local, regional and metropolitan governments were fundamental in carrying out emancipation itself. Since chattel slavery depended on enforcement of property rights, the end of that enforcement led to the end of slavery. Most governments were also willing to compensate the owners for their slaves, either in cash payments or through unpaid multi-year apprenticeships and often was anticipated with free womb laws, meaning all children born to slave mothers were free. Among the major plantation areas, only in the United States was emancipation begun without any compensation to the resident planter class, except in Washington, DC, in 1862. Haiti was, of course, a case with no compensation paid to landowners, almost all of whom left or died with the revolution, although some indemnity was paid to France years later.[30]

After emancipation there seems little significant difference in the attitudes of either colonial or independent governments toward their coloured populations, with again the obvious exception of the Haitian case. Most governments tried, at least initially, to provide for the continuity of the plantation structure, and undertook policies that helped reduce wage costs for the planters, either by limiting the bargaining power of the ex-slaves or by subsidizing alternative sources of labour (such as indentured labour). Yet the British government soon ended the special protection of its West Indian sugar producers, and it is argued that the end of the discriminatory sugar duties, not emancipation, generated the large-scale exodus from the Jamaican plantations and limited the pace of recovery in the British West Indies.[31] In the Brazilian case, it took major government subsidies to pay for the migration of European families to work in the coffee fields to replace their fleeing black workers. Planter concerns about continued government subsidization proved to be a major political issue for both the state and federal governments for many years after emancipation. However, it was only through this subsidization that the Brazilian producers could compete with the United States and Argentina for European, and above all Italian, workers.[32]

In countries like Brazil, which had offered no compensation for owners who had not freed their slaves beforehand, the government's dependence on the local plantation economy meant that they were more than willing to aid the planter class in their desire to keep plantation production from collapsing. But how far local planters could influence their governments depended on the nature of these regimes. There are differences between independent nations (such as Imperial Brazil and the United States) and those subject to colonial rule. In the latter case it is necessary to allow for differences between the local governments in the colonies and the metropolitan power (and, in the case of the British West Indies, between colonies with local legislatures and Crown Colonies). While some governments wholeheartedly supported the planters, from the British interest in allowing for post-emancipation apprenticeships to the massive funding by the Brazilian government of subsidized *colonos*, few governments deliberately developed major policies to promote the interests of the ex-slaves at the expense of the planters. Nor did all governments fully grant ex-slaves the same rights as free persons. Even Brazil would differentiate the legal rights of free coloured people between those initially born as slaves and those who were born free.[33] Others, such as the United States, went out of their way to isolate and deny basic rights to their ex-slaves and former free coloured, giving them a second-class citizenship. Already by the eighteenth century, free coloured persons in the United States were severely restricted in their mobility. Almost from the beginning, free coloured were explicitly denied the right to vote in all the southern and several Northern states. Once emancipated they were often required to leave the state and almost all Southern and some Northern states prohibited any free coloured persons from entering their states. Also their marriage partners were restricted. From early in the eighteenth century, mulattoes and Blacks were prevented from marrying Whites, and all such marriages were dissolved. Moreover, all states defined mulattoes as persons who had one ancestor who was a Negro to the third or fourth generation, and then made mulattoes identical to Negros in all laws relating to free persons of colour. As early as the mid-eighteenth century came the first severe limitations on manumission, and even the first of many temporary but total prohibitions of manumission (North Carolina, 1777; Georgia, 1801; and Maryland, 1860), and all Southern states progressively made emancipation more difficult for the slaveowners by requiring costly state courts intervention while many prohibited any manumissions by owners post-mortem (e.g. Georgia, 1849). Some went so far as to require that only the state legislature could approve any act of emancipation, taking this out of the hands of the slaveowner entirely. Restrictions on the geographic and economic mobility of the ex-slaves were universal from the eighteenth century onward. Most Southern slave states and many Northern ones required formal registration of all freedmen (Virginia, 1800; Tennessee, 1806; Illinois, 1811; Mississippi, 1822; Georgia, 1826; Michigan, 1827). Throughout the nineteenth century, freedmen were increasingly limited in their occupational mobility, with restrictions on the economic activities they could perform.[34]

Even where ex-slaves gained most political rights, and where land was available, out-migration from the former plantation areas was relatively limited. Except in Southeastern Brazil and to a lesser extent in western Cuba, mass migration of ex-slaves away from the plantation regions was quite limited, which in turn limited ex-slave economic options and aided plantation owners in their desires to keep their plantations in production. Migration from the Southern states to the North in the United States, from the north-east to the south in Brazil, and from Barbados to elsewhere in the West Indies, would only occur long after emancipation. Thus, in the case of the largest single emancipation process, that of the United States, ex-slaves did not move from their traditional homes to new land areas or to urban centres. Whereas 93 per cent of African Americans resided in the Southern slave states in 1860, as late as 1900 some 91 per cent of them still lived in that region.[35] All this meant that even if no longer tied to the planter class by work arrangements, ex-slaves remained in regions where the planter class tended to dominate politically and in which they defined the social norms.

In looking at the transition to freedom experiences, it seems clear that the Haitian case is the one instance in which ex-slaves achieved success and satisfaction of their most basic demands. The internal divisions between radicals and moderates, and between Whites and free mulattoes, provided a setting in which conflict led to the eventual elevation of the ex-slaves to a dominant power position. Slaves thus not only achieved freedom, but they seized power and destroyed much of the capital invested in the plantation economy, as well as most of the planter class. Despite the initial attempts of the republican regimes to restore some aspects of the plantation economy, the land reforms of the 1810s and 1820s led to the establishment of small, peasant-owned farms. The general collapse of an effective export agriculture and the relatively limited nature of the national market meant that no major influences were pulling the ex-slaves into a wage-labour system. This does not mean that they were outside the market economy. The existence of thriving local markets for foodstuffs and other commodities attests to the freedmen's willingness to respond to market incentives. The ex-slaves can be seen to have reacted as typical peasants, who can be drawn from their lands only if wages are high enough to provide a substantial income above the 'subsistence' level that could be achieved by production on their own plots.[36]

Compared to the Haitian experience, the transition histories of the sugar islands of the British West Indies saw a greater maintenance of export production and the plantation system. In these British possessions three different patterns can be discerned, detailed in 1841 by the Oxford economist, Herman Merivale.[37] On islands such as Barbados and Antigua, a lack of opportunity for land ownership precluded the large-scale withdrawal of ex-slave labour from sugar production. In these islands, sugar output continued to expand after emancipation. These were the areas from which, when sugar demand slowed and population increased, there was outmigration of labour to the expanding parts of the West Indies.

A second pattern was found in those regions undergoing rapid economic expansion at the end of the slave era, Trinidad and British Guiana. These areas were relatively 'underpopulated' (with high slave prices in the 1820s and 1830s). With emancipation, the ex-slaves generally either moved to unsettled land or to abandoned plantations, or else increased their labour input on the 'provision grounds' from the period of slavery, and total sugar output declined. These declines were reversed within two decades in British Guiana, more rapidly within Trinidad, as an expanding plantation sector re-emerged, based on specialization in sugar production. The attempts to restrict the ownership of land by ex-slaves were, however, generally unsuccessful, and the new basis for estate labour was indentured labour, drawn mainly from India, under governmental subsidy and regulation.

The third pattern was typified by Jamaica. Sugar output fell dramatically, and this shortfall persisted for at least several decades – in Jamaica for about a century. Moreover, the availability of lands, either from the decline of estates or from available public lands, allowed the ex-slaves to rapidly develop a peasant-like economic base, free from plantation requirements. The increasing cost of production rendered the Jamaican estates less competitive than plantations in the new regions (British Guiana and Trinidad) or those that had better control over their labour force (Barbados, Antigua and St Kitts). Other islands in the British group such as St Vincent and Grenada had a pattern similar to that in Jamaica. In these islands, the declining relative productivity of the sugar economy meant that planters were unable to replace slaves with contract labourers from Asia, while, at the same time, the continued importance of plantations for sugar production meant that a viable system of sharecropping could not be developed. Some variants of sharecropping were attempted on St Lucia and Tobago, but they failed.

The pattern in the French West Indian colonies of Martinique and Guadeloupe combined aspects of several of the British islands. As in most other societies producing sugar, there was an immediate drop in production as the plantation system adjusted to the end of slave labour. Unlike the Jamaican experience, however, production returned to pre-abolition levels within approximately one to two decades. But while the planters were able to use various mechanisms to maintain production, including the importation of indentured labour mainly from Africa, the relatively lesser importance of indentured labour here – compared to the British islands – meant that the French planters had to work out alternative labour arrangements with their ex-slaves, many of whom were able to establish subsistence farms.

In the Dutch West Indies, above all in the plantation sugar society of Suriname, the Jamaican pattern dominated, with production taking over a half-century to recover its pre-emancipation levels. What was left of the sugar plantation regime was able to survive through the use of contract labour imported from Asia, but the ex-slaves were able to escape the plantations because of the availability of alternative lands.

The final abolition history among the smaller Caribbean producers worth noting is the case of Puerto Rico. Though the island's relatively small number of slaves were concentrated in the sugar industry and production was profitable to the end, the sugar industry was in decline from the middle of the nineteenth century. Thus the late nineteenth century saw a shift to coffee with a reorientation of Puerto Rico's international trade back to Spain. When abolition occurred, therefore, the economy was in a process of reorganization. The relatively low demand for labour and the availability of a large local free labour pool due to the extraordinary population growth in the nineteenth century meant that when the sugar industry revived in the post-abolition period, it could provide itself with abundant labour at low costs without the need to import workers or control its ex-slaves. The Crown was not reluctant to assist the planters with special vagrancy laws and other mechanisms that cut down on the mobility of the rural labourers and limited their ability to respond to alternative opportunities.

In the larger plantation slave economics of Brazil and Cuba, their post-emancipation experiences – at least in the earliest stages – seem to resemble the Trinidad–British Guiana pattern. In both cases, land availability made it difficult for the planters to force the ex-slaves into labouring on the old plantations. Ex-slaves initially moved off the plantations in large numbers and in the case of Brazil they were totally replaced by European workers. Although the coffee planters had tried various contract labour arrangements prior to the 1880s, these usually failed over the debts contracted by the workers for their transport and the limited wages which were granted the free workers.[38] In the 1880s, as abolition became a serious threat, a new systematic effort at government organization and financing of a contract labour system developed which was able to supply large quantities of workers at subsidized prices for the planters. Unlike the West Indies, which used African and Asian indentured workers, the Brazilians were able to exploit European immigrant labour through government subsidized contract arrangements. But the massive replacement of slaves by Italians in the coffee plantations led to a new labour arrangement which totally reorganized plantation labour, with work divided into family units of production and workers paid by piece work.[39] Able to find alternative employment in the cities or in other American nations, and with strong support from their government representatives, the Italians refused to accept indentured contracts, and the planters were forced to compromise. Moreover, the technical nature of coffee production was such that the shift from gang labour to more acceptable family production units and piece-wage arrangements could be made without loss of productivity or any serious change in total output. Having worried about allowing Italians into favourable contracts for fear of their becoming competitors, by the last decade of the nineteenth century Brazilian planters began to experience that competition, particularly as the coffee frontier continued to expand into the west *paulista* plains and slowly moved toward Paraná in the twentieth century.

In the Brazilian North-east, the history of emancipation fitted more closely to the Jamaican model. Here the process of emancipation occurred while the economy was experiencing relative stagnation, due both to increased competition in the sugar markets of Europe because of the expansion of beet sugar and increased competition for slave labour because of the expansion of coffee production in the south. Moreover, the availability of land allowed the ex-slaves to move off the plantations quickly into small-scale commercial, as well as subsistence, agriculture. While the plantation system in the Brazilian North-east remained intact, planters were forced to work out complex wage agreements with the ex-slaves to attract them into plantation labour, and in fact this was the only region in Brazil where mixed free and slave labour had worked together on plantations even before abolition had occurred. In some ways this was similar to what was occurring in some of the Cuban sugar plantations before abolition. This region was probably the last major sugar area in the Americas to introduce modern steam mills (*usinas*), this taking place only in the first decades of the twentieth century.[40]

The Cuban case is an even more complex variant, for it involves a reorganization of the means of production, an introduction of foreign workers and the successful incorporation of much of the ex-slave labour force into the sugar plantation industry on a part-time basis – all in the context of the ongoing growth and expansion of the sugar economy.[41] As early as the 1840s, when Trinidad and British Guiana were turning toward East Indian labourers, the Cuban planters were beginning to import Yucatan Indians, and by the middle decades of the century large-scale importation of Chinese contract labourers had begun. Here the introduction of non-slave labour preceded the demise of slavery, and the transition had begun even before the ultimate legal end of slavery.

At the same time, the costs of conversion of the mills into modern steam-driven *centrales* led many of the planters to abandon direct control over the land and production of the cane, in return for maintaining control of milling and processing of sugar. Thus to some extent the great estates had become amalgams of sub-estate producing units in which intermediate-size farmers (the *colonos*) brought in their own work groups to till the land, and in which the larger ex-planters controlled milling.[42] Even before the final legal abolition of slavery in the 1880s (and especially after the Ten Years' War), free landless blacks, Chinese contract labourers and slaves were working side by side on these complex units.[43] By the time of emancipation, slave labour, while still dominant, was no longer the only source of labour even on the most advanced estates in the western half of the island.

Given the extraordinary vitality of the Cuban sugar industry, which dominated world sugar production by this time and was constantly expanding into the virgin areas of the western half of the island, the landowners were able to offer wages attractive enough to draw workers into the labour force. Many of the ex-slaves found themselves working on the lands of their old plantations, and others worked on smaller farms providing cane for the *centrales* even though alternative land was available in the eastern part of the island for small-scale subsistence agriculture. Here many ex-slaves were able to obtain land, and by the twentieth century this region shared many features of peasant agriculture common to the other West Indian islands. But the dynamism of the sugar industry meant that in the western half, wages were sufficiently high to attract many of the ex-slaves on the old estates. Finally, the very organization of sugar production in the post-emancipation period changed dramatically. With no need to maintain labour over the entire year, and the voracious demands of the mills, the industry became far more seasonally based than previously. Now during the 'dead season' – when no workers were needed to either plant, cultivate or harvest sugar – many of the sugar workers either engaged in small scale agricultural activity on their own plots or entered the wage labour market for a large part of the year.[44]

The example of the United States shares several of the characteristics of other areas. A sharp decline in output and a withdrawal from the plantation labour force occurred, although unlike the outcome in most other areas, export production increased as a share of total Southern agricultural output. The continued vitality of the international cotton market after abolition guaranteed that some type of persistence of the plantation would be attempted. But since the cotton crop could be produced on smaller farms because of the low capital investments needed, eventually an alternative of small tenant farming organization replaced gang labour on the large plantations. The planters kept their lands but now divided them, like the Brazilian coffee planters, among family production units. But instead of adopting piece-work payments, they ended up working out sharecropping arrangements where the tenants were able to keep half of their output from the lands of the ex-planters.[45]

Although ex-slaves attempted to work their own farm plots as squatters or owners, the lack of capital or access to credit, the lack of transport for what lands were available for food exploitation, and white hostility toward land sales which created differential land markets by race all worked against land ownership by ex-slaves. Moreover, the continued high price being paid for cotton on the international market allowed the ex-planters to offer incentives high enough to attract black workers back to the old plantations, though in completely new working arrangements.[46] The result in the United States, particularly in the case of cotton, was a failure of the slaves to obtain land, but given both black and white worker hostility to gang labour, the planters were also forced to end the old slave-style labour arrangements and mostly rented their lands to ex-slave tenants and sharecroppers. Given the large number of poor whites in these old plantation regions, there was also a substantial increase in the amount of cotton production from the small white-owned and operated farms within the South, as well as some increase in the production of the other plantation crops by white labour in the late nineteenth century.

Thus the US Southern planters were able to maintain the old staple production with new labour organization, just as the planters in many of the Caribbean islands and Brazil were able to do so. But in the case of the United States the ex-slaves and Southern Whites were the major sources of agricultural labour rather than immigrants or contract workers, and long-term sharecropping arrangements were the norm rather than short-term piece-work contracts, which became the staple of Brazilian plantation agriculture, or money wages, which dominated in Cuba. The United States' planters initially could not pay the standard daily wages which became the means of attracting the ex-slaves into part-time sugar production in Cuba, nor could the US South compete with the North and the West for immigrant labour. The ex-planters did not have the political power to force the central government to subsidize a flow of directed immigration, as in Brazil and the various Caribbean areas, nor did the defeated planter class have the capital to enable it to purchase labour with high wages, as in the Cuban experience. At the same time, more limited land availability, the lack of credit, education and useful skills among the ex-plantation slaves and the more active competition from the majority poor white workers closed off many of the potential economic opportunities for the ex-slaves in terms of alternative labour activity.

There are a few issues worth stressing in this comparative analysis. It is doubtful that, in any major case, slave emancipation, however achieved, reflected a prior decrease in the profitability in the use of slave labour on the plantations. Even those producing on older lands could still achieve positive returns based on their slave labour force. Broadly considered, emancipation usually came at times of expanding production, not stagnation, and this influenced the planters' desires to maintain plantation production.[47] Apparently, as far as sugar production was concerned, in those areas without extremely high population densities, only the use of contract labour could maintain that pace of expansion of production. In a few cases, growth and expansion of production could be achieved even without the need to import contract labour from abroad. In the coffee and cotton fields, production could be maintained or even expanded after emancipation without the need to maintain the plantation form of organization. In the case of sugar, adjustment to a seasonal labour force and or new contract labourers was the answer, for even the *colono* farms in Cuba which had no mills were extensive plantations using a variant of the old gang-type labour.

Second, while the slaves in only a few cases succeeded in capturing the land that they had previously worked as slaves, emancipation – however uncompensated it was for the slaves – was unqualifiedly a highly desirable condition in itself. Though the ex-slaves remained poor and politically weak in the great majority of ex-slave societies, the ending of slavery made considerable difference in their ability to choose living and working conditions. In almost all cases, ex-slaves now determined the types of work arrangements they would accept. Gang labour and the unrestricted use of female labour in the fields were the first things to go, along with corporal punishment, even in situations where the ex-slaves had to return to their old plantations to work in groups. Moreover, the amount of free time that could be devoted to one's family or increasing income through alternative wage labour was considerably expanded. Although some post-abolition governments attempted to restrict mobility of the ex-slaves through vagrancy laws, at the time of emancipation or even much later as in the case of the United States, in the end freedmen would obtain significant economic, geographic and social mobility.[48]

Finally, ex-slaves were free to obtain education and organize their own family lives as they saw fit, without the oversight of the plantation owners. Thus, however limited the practices of emancipation were, with no state ever providing the slaves with compensation for their slavery or offering them land and credit, the process began a fundamental change in the lives of the ex-slaves which would eventually lead to their full integration as citizens and free persons in all the old slave societies.

Notes

* The author would like to thank Laird Bergad and Stanley Engerman for their helpful comments.

1 An earlier version of some of the ideas presented here appeared in Herbert S. Klein and Stanley Engerman, 'The Transition From Slave to Free Labour: Notes on a Comparative Economic Model', in M. Moreno Fraginals et al. (eds), *Between Slavery and Free Labour: The Spanish Speaking Caribbean in the Nineteenth Century* (Baltimore, MD: Johns Hopkins University Press, 1985), 255–69. This chapter also draws on arguments and detailed references to sources presented in Stanley L. Engerman, 'Economic Adjustments to Emancipation in the United States and British West Indies', *Journal of Interdisciplinary History* 12 (Autumn 1982), and Herbert S. Klein and Ben Vinson III, *African Slavery in Latin America and the Caribbean*, 2nd edn (New York: Oxford University Press, 2007).

2 For general reviews of these questions – mostly based on the experience of the British West Indies and the United States – see Eric Foner, *Nothing But Freedom: Emancipation and Its Legacy* (Baton Rouge: Louisiana State University Press, 1983); Frank McGlynn and Seymour Drescher (eds), *The Meaning of Freedom: Economics,*

Politics and Culture after Slavery (Pittsburgh: University of Pittsburgh Press, 1992); and Frederick Cooper, Thomas C. Holt and Rebecca J. Scott, *Beyond Slavery: Explorations of Race, Labour, and Citizenship in Postemancipation Societies* (Chapel Hill: University of North Carolina Press, 2000).

3   One of the few who have attempted this is Stanley L. Engerman, who has published several articles on this theme as well as a book, *Slavery, Emancipation, and Freedom: Comparative Perspectives* (Baton Rouge: Louisiana State University Press, 2007).

4   Slave women made up the majority of field hand gangs in almost all the plantation areas, as they were excluded from almost all semi-skilled and skilled non-field labour. See, for example, Lucille Mathurin Mair, 'Women Field Workers in Jamaica during Slavery', in Brian L. Moore, B. W. Higman, Carl Campbell and Patrick Bryan (eds), *The Dynamics of Caribbean Society: Slavery, Freedom and Gender* (Barbados: University of West Indies Press, 2003), 182–96; and B. W. Higman, *Slave Populations of the British Caribbean, 1807–1834* (Baltimore, MD: Johns Hopkins University Press, 1984), 189.

5   Price trends of the three major plantation crops differed. For coffee there was a long-term steady but modest rise of prices through emancipation to 1896; see Francisco Vidal Luna and Herbert S. Klein, *The Economic and Social History of Brazil since 1889* (New York: Cambridge University Press, 2014), 355–6, table A.1. For cotton, the high prices during the Civil War were followed by a long-term decline in world prices; see Gavin Wright, 'Cotton Competition and the Post-Bellum Recovery of the American South', *Journal of Economic History* 34, no. 3 (September 1974): 611, table 1. For sugar, the trend in production, if not in prices, was long-term growth after 1850; see Manuel Moreno Fraginals, *El ingenio*, 3 vols (Havana: Editorial de Ciencias Sociales, 1977), III, 35–8, table 1.

6   For a detailed analysis of pre-emancipation debates about expected outcomes, see Stanley L. Engerman, 'Comparative Approaches to the Ending of Slavery', *Slavery & Abolition* 21, no. 2 (August 2000): 281–300; and Seymour Drescher, *The Mighty Experiment: Free Labour versus Slavery in British Emancipation* (New York: Oxford University Press, 2002). These expected outcomes were also part of the economic arguments used by the abolitionists; see Howard Temperley, 'Capitalism, Slavery and Ideology', *Past and Present* 75 (May 1977): 109 ff.

7   For a discussion of British policy after emancipation, see William A. Green, *British Slave Emancipation* (Oxford: Clarendon Press, 1976), while for a discussion of Jamaica, see, in particular, Douglas Hall, *Free Jamaica, 1838–1865* (New Haven, CT: Yale University Press, 1965).

8   Fraginals, *El ingenio* I, chap. 5, on the impact of mechanization of the mills on productivity.

9   On the increase of productivity of US cotton output in the nineteenth century and its causes, see Alan L. Olmstead and W. Paul Rhode, *Creating Abundance: Biological Innovation and American Agricultural Development* (New York: Cambridge University Press, 2008).

10 See Herbert S. Klein and Francisco Vidal Luna, *The Economic and Demographic History of São Paulo, 1850–1950* (Stanford, CA: Stanford University Press, 2018), chap. 4.

11 For a detailed analysis of the process of frontier settlement in the West Paulista region, see Alida C. Metcalf, *Family and Frontier in Colonial Brazil, Santana de Parnaíba, 1580–1822* (Berkeley: University of California Press, 1992).

12 Swithin Wilmot, '"We not slave again": Enslaved Jamaicans in Early Freedom, 1838–1865', in Marc Kleijwegt (ed.), *The Faces Of Freedom: The Manumission and*

Emancipation of Slaves in Old World and New World Slavery (Leiden: Brill, 2006), 220–1. These actions sometimes led to major strikes of workers; see Drescher, *The Mighty Experiment*, 158–9.
13 Directoria Geral de Estatistica, *Recenseamento da população do Imperio do Brazil a que se procedeu no dia 1o. de agosto de 1872* (Rio de Janeiro, 1873–6). On the multiple roles of the free coloured in pre-emancipation Brazil, see Herbert S. Klein and Francisco Vidal Luna, 'Free Coloured in a Slave Economy: The Case of São Paulo and Minas Gerais, 1829–1830', *Hispanic American Historical Review* 80, no. 4 (November 2000): 913–41; and Herbert S. Klein and Clotilde Paiva, 'Freedmen in a Slave Economy: Minas Gerais in 1831', *Journal of Social History* 29, no. 4 (June 1996): 933–62.
14 *Noticias estadisticas de la isla de Cuba, en 1862* (Habana: Imprenta del gobierno, 1864).
15 Melanie J. Newton, *The Children of Africa in the Colonies: Free People of Colour in Barbados in the Age of Emancipation* (Baton Rouge: Louisiana State University Press, 2007), 40, table 1.
16 Alex Moreaux de Jonnès, *Recherches statistiques sur l'esclavage colonial et sur les moyens de le supprimer* (Paris: Bourgogne et Martinet, 1842), 43–4, 50–1. The Danish data is only available from 1815.
17 See Klein and Vinson, *African Slavery in Latin America and the Caribbean*, 274, table 3.
18 Ramon de la Sagra *Historia económico-política y estadística de la isla de Cuba o sea de sus: de sus progresos en la población la agricultura el comercio y las rentas* (Havana: Imprenta de las Viudas de Arazoza y Soler, 1831), 5; and Jacobo de la Pezuela, *Diccionario geográfico, estadístico, histórico de la Isla de Cuba*, 4 vols (Madrid: Imprenta Méllado, 1863–6), III, 372.
19 Rebecca J. Scott, *Slave Emancipation in Cuba: The Transition to Free Labour, 1860–1899* (Princeton, NJ: Princeton University Press, 1985), 12, table 1.
20 Mary Karasch, *Slave Life and Culture in Rio de Janeiro, 1808–1850* (Princeton, NJ: Princeton University Press, 1987), 65, 69. For an equally detailed study of slaves and free coloured in the city life, see Luiz Carlos Soares, *O' povo de cam' na capital do Brasil: a escravidão urbana no Rio de Janeiro do século XIX* (Rio de Janeiro: 7 Letras, 2007).
21 Dale W. Tomich, *Slavery in the Circuit of Sugar, Martinique and the World-Economy, 1830–1848*, 2nd edn (Albany, NY: SUNY Press, 2016), 145, table 3.4.
22 Higman, *Slave Populations of the British Caribbean*, 77, table 4.2; 94, table 4.4; and chap. 7.
23 Laird W. Bergad, *Cuban Rural Society in the Nineteenth Century: The Social and Economic History of Monoculture in Matanzas* (Princeton, NJ: Princeton University Press, 1990), 97, tables 5.1 and 5.2.
24 For the contrast, see Ynael Lopes dos Santos, 'Alem da Senzala: Arranjos escravos de moradia no Rio de Janeiro (1808–1850)', MA thesis, Universidade de São Paulo, 2007; and Richard C. Wade, *Slavery in the Cities: The South 1820–1860* (New York: Oxford University Press, 1967).
25 For a detailed discussion of the free coloured in Brazil, see Herbert S. Klein and Francisco Vidal Luna, *Slavery in Brazil* (New York: Cambridge University Press, 2009), chap. 9.
26 Francisco Vidal Luna, Herbert S. Klein and William Summerhill, 'The Characteristics of Coffee Production and Agriculture in the State of São Paulo in 1905', *Agricultural History* 90, no. 1 (Winter 2016): 30, table 3.
27 See K. O. Laurence, *Immigration into the West Indies in the Nineteenth Century* (St Lawrence, Barbados: Caribbean Universities Press, 1971). For a discussion of

indentured labour, and further references to sources, see Stanley L. Engerman, 'Contract Labour, Sugar and Technology in the Nineteenth Century', *Journal of Economic History* 43, no. 3 (September 1983): 635–59, and Stanley L. Engerman, 'Servants to Slaves to Servants: Contract Labour and European Expansion', in E. van den Boogart and P. C. Emmer (eds), *Colonialism and Migration: Indentured Labour Before and After Slavery* (Dordrecht: Martinus Nijhoff, 1986). For a general survey of this theme of Asian contract labourers in the Caribbean, see Walton Look Lai, 'Two Asian Diasporas and Tropical Migration in the Age of Empire: A Comparative Overview', in Walton Look Lai and Tan Chee-Beng (eds), *The Chinese in Latin America and the Caribbean* (Leiden: Brill, 2010), 35–63.

28 The standard explanation for the rise of sharecropping in the US post-emancipation South is found in Roger L. Ransom and Richard Sutch, *One Kind of Freedom: The Economic Consequences of Emancipation*, 2nd edn (Cambridge: Cambridge University Press, 2001). For a detailed analysis of the reorganization of labour in the post-emancipation Brazilian coffee fields, see Warren Dean, *Rio Claro: A Brazilian Plantation System, 1820–1920* (Stanford, CA: Stanford University Press, 1976); Thomas H. Holloway, *Immigrants on the Land* (Chapel Hill: University of North Carolina Press, 1980); Chiara Vangelista, *Le braccia per la fazenda: Imrnigranti e 'caipiras' nella formazione del mercato del lavoro paulista (1850–1930)* (Milan: Franco Angels, 1982); and Zuleika Alvim, *Brava gente! os italianos em São Paulo 1870–1920* (São Paulo: Brasiliense, 1986). For the Cuban experience, see Bergad, *Cuban Rural Society*, chap. 15; and on the pre-1860 use of non-slave immigrant workers, see Fraginals, *El ingenio*, I, chap. 6.

29 Scott, *Slave Emancipation in Cuba*, 229.

30 Engerman, *Slavery, Emancipation, and Freedom*, 37–8.

31 Although at times rice was grown on small farms, there was generally a need for heavy capital expenditures to control the water supply. For the development of the rice industry in British Guiana, after the arrival of indentured labour from India, see Jay R. Mandle, *The Plantation Economy* (Philadelphia: Temple University Press, 1973).

32 On the comparative American labour markets for Italian workers, see Herbert S. Klein, 'A integração dos imigrantes italianos no Brasil, na Argentina e nos Estados Unidos', *Novos Estudos CEBRAP* 25 (São Paulo: Outubro, 1989), 95–117.

33 Sidney Chalhoub, 'The Politics of Silence: Race and Citizenship in Nineteenth-Century Brazil', *Slavery and Abolition* 27, no. 1 (April 2006): 73–87.

34 All these references come from the standard summary of these laws in John Codman Hurd, *The Law Of Freedom and Bondage in The United States*, 2 vols (Boston: Little Brown & Co, 1858–62), II, 2–150. After examining these laws, which became more draconian after 1800, one scholar concluded that 'whites had pushed free Negros into a place of permanent legal inferiority. Like slaves, free Negros were generally without political rights, were unable to move freely, were prohibited from testifying against whites, and were often punished with the lash.' Ira Berlin, *Slaves without Masters: The Free Negro in the Antebellum South* (New York: W.W. Norton, 1874), 97. For the post-emancipation laws, see Franklin Johnson, *The Development of State Legislation Concerning the Free Negro* (New York: n.p., 1916).

35 Herbert S. Klein, *A Population History of the United States*, 2nd rev. edn (Cambridge: Cambridge University Press, 2004), 125.

36 On the Haitian experience, see most recently Laurent Dubois, *Avengers of the New World: The Story of the Haitian Revolution* (Cambridge, MA: Harvard University Press, 2004); and Laurent Dubois, *A Colony of Citizens: Revolution and Slave Emancipation*

in the French Caribbean, 1787–1804 (Chapel Hill: University of North Carolina Press, 2004). For discussions of the Haitian case, as well as of developments elsewhere in the Caribbean, see Sidney W. Mintz, *Caribbean Transformations* (Baltimore, MD: Johns Hopkins University Press, 1984).

37 Herman Merivale, *Lectures on Colonization and Colonies* (London: Longman, Green, Longman, & Roberts, 1841). Another useful contemporary source, making a similar distinction, is William G. Sewell, *The Ordeal of Free Labour in the British West Indies* (New York: Harper & Brothers, 1861).

38 For a detailed analysis of these first experiments, see Dean, *Rio Claro*.

39 For details of the piece-work payments system and the family work arrangements on the Brazilian coffee fields, see Holloway, *Immigrants on the Land*; Vangelista, *Le braccia per la fazenda*; and Alvim, *Brava gente! os italianos em São Paulo*. On the early evolution of the coffee slave economy, see Francisco Vidal Luna and Herbert S. Klein, *Slavery and the Economy of São Paulo, 1750–1850* (Stanford, CA: Stanford University Press, 2003).

40 See Peter L. Eisenberg, *The Sugar Industry in Pernambuco* (Berkeley: University of California Press, 1974).

41 Bergad, *Cuban Rural Society*, chap. 15; and Scott, *Slave Emancipation in Cuba*, chap. 10.

42 For an analysis of this new organization of the sugar industry, see Alan Dye, *Cuban Sugar in the Age of Mass Production: Technology and the Economics of the Sugar Central, 1899–1929* (Stanford, CA: Stanford University Press, 1998).

43 For an analysis of the Chinese experience in Cuba, see Juan Perez de la Riva, *Para la historia de las gentes sin historia* (Barcelona: Editorial Ariel, 1976).

44 Bergad, *Cuban Rural Society*, chap. 15.

45 Ransom and Sutch, *One Kind of Freedom*, chap. 4.

46 For a detailed discussion of why ex-slaves did not become freehold farmers on a large scale in the US South. see Gavin Wright, 'The Economic and Politics of Slavery and Freedom in the U.S. South', in Frank McGlynn and Seymour Drescher (eds), *The Meaning of Freedom: Economics, Politics, and Culture after Slavery* (Pittsburgh: University of Pittsburgh Press, 1992), 85–111; and Ransom and Sutch, *One Kind of Freedom*, chap. 5.

47 A useful discussion of the profitability question on the eve of emancipation in the three big plantation regions is found in Laird Bergad, *The Comparative Histories of Slavery in Brazil, Cuba, and the United States* (New York: Cambridge University Press, 2007), chap. 5.

48 On the difficulties the ex-slaves had to establish independence in various of the Southern states even in the 1860s, see Bruce E. Baker and Brian Kelly (eds), *After Slavery: Race, Labour, and Citizenship in the Reconstruction South* (Gainesville: University of Florida Press, 2013).

Index

Abercromby, Ralph 109
Abolition Decree (1854) 134
abolitionism (*see also* emancipation)
    abolition of slavery in Britain 6, 75, 76, 83n.3
    abolition of slavery in France 157
    emergence of 20
    Henry Bibb and 40
    transatlantic Jewish 20–2
absentee slaveholding 7, 71–82, 156–8
acculturation 171
activism, anti-slavery 40
African American people, notions of the inferiority of 50 (*see also* people of colour)
African Baptist Church 195
Afro-Europeans, Suriname 18–19
Afroiberians 15
Agaja, King of Dahomey 167–9
agency, of slaves 7–8, 16, 17, 41–6, 66
agriculture (*see also* plantation system; sugar production)
    Antigua 214
    Barbados 214
    Cherokee people and 42, 46
    cocoa cultivation 134, 144
    coffee production 217, 221, 223–4
    cotton cultivation 117, 214, 217, 222, 223, 224
    by ex-slaves 214
    Gentilly plantation 153, 155
    Jamaica 78–9, 214
    new technologies and 214
    sharecropping tenancies 217, 220, 222, 223
    South Carolina 57–8
    tobacco cultivation 116
    transition from slave to free labour and 212
Alexander, Eli 120
Allada 167, 171
Almenar, Santiago 138–9, 140, 141–2, 143
amelioration, of slaves 122
America. *See* United States
American Anti-Slavery Society 40
American churches, support of slaveholders 48
American Civil War 26, 31, 62, 201
American Colonization Society 194
American Revolution 62, 66, 118
American slavery, the rethinking of 26–8
Americas, transition from slave to free labour in 211, 222
amnesia, colonial trick of 42
Andrews, William L. 41
Anthony, Lysbet 95
anti-slavery activism 40
Anti-Slavery Society 40
Antigua 214, 219
Anzilotti, Cara 58
apprenticeships 75, 160, 217
Arkansas, free people of colour and 200, 205–6
Armitage, David 2
Aroa Copper Mines 137, 143
artisans, ex-slaves 216
asiento 90, 97n.12
Atlantic paradigm, slavery and 2
Atlantic slavery 13–17
authority
    challenges to by slaves 62–2
    maternalism and 61
    of slaves 44

Bacon, Edmund 115, 122, 125, 126
Badagry 168, 170, 171
Bahia 15, 16, 168, 170, 173
Barbados 214, 215, 219
Barbados Slave Code (1661) 98n.42
Barrett, Philip 183, 190, 192, 193, 194–5

Bartlett, Mary 58, 59
Basílio, João 169
Bayou Sauvage 152, 153, 155
Beckles, Hilary 77
Bell, John 102
Ben-Ur, Aviva 18
Benin, royal dynasty of 171
Benítez, Luciano 136
Benson, John Lossing 189
Berlin, Ira 2, 200, 206
Bibb, Henry Walton 5 (*see also* chapter 3)
Biddle, Samuel 120
Bienville, Jean Baptiste Le Moyne de 152
Bight of Benin 165, 167, 171
black militias 101–11
black people. *See* people of colour
Black Seminoles
    capitalism and 33–5
    defining/controlling their own labour 32–3
    in Florida 25–36
    Seminoles and 5
    specific context of 31–2
Boddicott, Mary 57
Bolama island 103
Bolívar, Simón 135, 142, 143
Bonaparte, Napoleon 158
Boot, Nicholaes 95
Brandão, Jozeph dos Santos 174, 176
Brazil
    Bahia 15, 16, 168, 170, 173
    coffee production 221
    Pernambuco 165–6, 167, 168, 170–1, 177n.12
    population of 215
    Recife 165, 166, 170, 171
    Salvador da Bahia 7, 165, 173
    slave trade and 167–8, 171–2
    transition from slave to free labour and 217–18, 221
    West Africa and 166
British Caribbean. *See* British West Indies
British Guiana 214, 219
British Legion, Venezuela 142
British West Indies (*see also* names of individual islands)
    population of 215
    sugar production in 74–5, 217, 219
    transition from slave to free labour and 219
    urban slavery 216
Buck, Tom 122, 125
Buckley, Roger 101, 110
Bucknor, Eliza Rose 76
Bullock, Elizabeth 63–4
Bullock, Hannah 63–4
Burnard, Trevor 72, 74–5
The burning of the theatre in Richmond, Virginia 189

cabeceiras 7–8, 165, 170, 171, 172
Calamity at Richmond 188
Campbell, Charles 185
Campo, Elvira del 14, 15
Canada West 40, 51n.7
Canary islanders 134
Cannibals All! 186
capitalism 33–5, 186
Caracas Central University 135
Cardoso, Simão 169
Caribbean islands (*see also* British West Indies; Dutch Caribbean; French West Indies; Leeward Islands; names of individual islands)
    population of 215
    under development in 78
    yellow fever in 104–6
Carolina Corps 103, 108
Carr, Francis 124
Carson, Sam 204
Cartagena expedition (1740) 102
Carter, Sarah Champe 124
Cata *Obra Pía hacienda* 135, 137–8, 143
Catholicism (*see also* Christianity; religion)
    João de Oliveira and 171, 173, 175
    slaves converting to 171
    Spanish and Portuguese Inquisitions 14–17, 19
Celes, Jan 92
Chamberlayne, William 122, 125, 126
Charlemount Pen, Jamaica 77
Charter of Liberties and Exemptions, Dutch West Indian Company 94
chattel system 26, 29, 59
Cherokee people
    agriculture and 42, 46

Cherokee Nation v. Georgia (1831) 42
   forced emigration of 42, 49
   slave codes adopted by 47
   slaveholding of 5, 29, 39–51
   sovereignty of 42, 49
Chisholm, Colin 104, 105
Chitty, Gualterio D. 135–7, 142–3
Christianity (*see also* Catholicism; religion)
   American churches support of slaveholders 48
   Conversos/New Christians 13–20
   converted Christians with impure blood 15
   female slave ownership and 60, 65
   forced conversion to 13–14
   religion and Christian slaveholders 48
   slaves and 171
citizenship, people of colour and 200, 208n.23
Clark, James 104
class
   classes of Indian negroes 30
   'middle class' slave owners in Virginia 118
   planter class 219
   ranking of social status 31
   white non-proprietied classes 158
   working-class Whites 215
Claypoole, Catherine 79
clothing, slaves and 47, 92
Cockburn, Charles Seymour 77
Cockburn, Isabella 76–7
Cocke, John Hartwell 117
cocoa cultivation 134, 144
Coelho, Jacinto Joze 173
coffee production 217, 221, 223–4
Colonial Office Slave Registration Office, London 76
colonization
   colonial trick of amnesia 42
   colonization initiatives 194, 201, 204
   legacies of 78
   slavery and 90
Colville, Andrew 80
commerce (*see also* trade)
   New Christians and 14
   sugar and 20
commercialization, of slavery 117

Commissioners of Arbitration, Britain 76
commodification, of human beings 15, 25, 126 (*see also* property)
compensation
   compensation claims, Jamaica 76–82
   paid by Great Britain 6, 76–82
   transition from slave to free labour and 212, 217
Conception Nuns Hacienda' 134, 135
consumer goods, of slaves and owners 34, 174
control
   maternalism and 61
   ownership and 28–9
   by slaves 44
conversions
   forced conversion to Christianity 13–14
   to Judaism 19
   slaves converting to Catholicism 171
Conversos/New Christians 13–20
Cook, George 183–4
corporate slavery, New Netherland/New York 6, 89–96
cotton cultivation 117, 214, 217, 222, 223, 224
Craven, John 120
Creoles
   Creole management of a French plantation in New Orleans 151–61
   transatlantic slaving and 172
Crow, Jim 201
Crowley, John 56, 57
cruelty, towards slaves 41, 47 (*see also* violence)
crypto-Jews 14
Cuba 102, 215, 216, 217, 221–2
culture(s)
   acculturation 171
   cultural construction of ownership 28–31
   cultural fluency 167
   of Native people 49–50
   religious-cultural identity 15
   trade and 172
Cuyler, Gereral 109

Dahomey 167, 168–70, 171, 173, 178n.27
Daingerfield, Mary 122, 123, 126

Daingerfield, William 123
Davis, Jefferson 199
De jure belli ac pacis ('On the Law on War and Peace') 91
The Deaf Shoemaker: To Which Are Added Other Stories for the Young 195
Deam, Robert 206
debt, of Thomas Jefferson 118–21
Declaration of Independence 116
Delgado, Manuel F. 136
democratization
    of property laws 118
    of slaveholding 116
denunciations, by slaves 16–17
Detroit 40
diasporas, Sephardic 13–14, 17
Dickens, Charles 193
Dijck, Hendrick van 95
diplomacy, of João de Oliveira 170–3
Dirom, Alex 103
discourse, pro-slavery 183–92
discrimination
    Arkansas 200
    against black people in New Netherland 94
diseases effecting white people 102, 103–7, 110, 111
dislocations 166, 175
domestic slaves, vulnerability of 17
Dorville, Auvignac 7, 151, 152, 153, 155, 156–7, 158–61
Douglass, Frederick 40, 193, 194
Dragons à Pied 158
Draper, Nicholas 71
Drescher, Seymour x, 4 (*see also* chapter 1)
Dreux, Louis Leufroy 152
Dreux, Marguerite Delmas 152, 156, 157
Dreux, Mathurin and Pierre 152
Dundas, Henry 101, 108, 109, 110
Dunlap, William 188
Dutch West Indian Company. *See* Netherlands

economic agency, of slaves 7–8
economic mobility of ex-slaves 215, 218
economic wellbeing, of Indian slaveholders 47

economy(ies)
    Jamaica 74–5, 78–9
    post-slave societies 8, 211–12
Ekpe 168
elites
    African 172
    Cherokee society 42
    marriage and white elites 203
    slave traders 174
    women 58–60, 65, 66
Ellis, Mary 65
emancipation (*see also* abolitionism; manumission)
    American Civil War and 26, 31
    Britain and 75
    Dutch West Indian Company and 93, 96n.3
    families and 224
    gradualist movements 21
    self-emancipation 183
emigration, forced 42, 49
empowerment
    of slaves through 'trickster tactics' 41–6
    of widows 57
England. *See* Great Britain
entail, abolition of 118
entrepreneurs, female 79–81
Eppes, John Wayles 123
equality, racial 49
equity, rule of 56
Eurafricans, Suriname 18–19
Evance, Rebecca 62
exploitation, sugar plantations and 75
expulsion, of free people of colour 199–200, 201

families
    Dutch West Indian Company and 92
    emancipation and 224
    Indian slaveholders and 48
    voluntary slavery and 201, 202–4, 206
    widowarchy 56–7
Fitch, Walker 202–3
Fitzhugh, George 186, 201
Florida
    attempt to make a a free labour plantation 20–1
    Black Seminoles in 25–36

free people of colour 30–1
   slavery in 27–8
Flowers by the Wayside 195
food, slaves and 47
Forbes, John 65
Fort Mose 31
Fossett, Joseph 126
Fossett, Peter 127
Fragosa, José María 135
France
   abolition of slavery (1848) 157
   indemnity paid to 217
   sugar production in the French West Indies 220
free people of colour
   Arkansas and 200, 205–6
   citizenship and 200, 208n.23
   concept of freedom and 2
   Dutch West Indian Company and 93, 96n.3
   employing white servants 93
   expulsion of 199–200, 201
   Florida 30–1
   freedman status 31
   labour and 94
   land ownership of 93
   marriage and 208n.23
   restrictive legislation against 8
   rights of 218
   seeking enslavement 199, 201
   social conditions of 98n.41
freedom, concept of 2
Freeman, John Holmes 123
French West Indies, sugar production in 220

Gaines, General 33
García, Simón 139
Garrison, William Lloyd 39, 40
Gatewood, William 44
Geggus, David 106
gender, labour and 32–3
General Land Office 117
gentility, Lowcountry female 59, 65, 66
Gentilly plantation 151, 152–5
geographical mobility of slaves 166, 202, 215
Georgia 42
Germany, Jewish problem 20

Gerrit, Manuel de 93
Gibraltar 20
Gilbert Hunt: The City Blacksmith 183, 186, 190
Gillette, Israel Jefferson 126
The Good Lord Bird 31
Gosling, John 103
government subsidization, transition from slave to free labour and 217
gradualist movements 21
Granger, George Sr. 121
Great Britain (*see also* British West Indies)
   abolitionism 6, 75, 76, 83n.3
   British Guiana 214, 219
   compensation claims 6, 76–82
   English common law 56
   Industrial Revolution 75
   invasion of Saint Dominique 105–6
   Jamaica and 71–82
   militarized slavery 6, 101–11
   slaveholders living in Britain 71–82
   slavery and 26–7
Green, Keith Michael 40, 48, 50
Grenada 104–5, 220
Grey, Charles 107
Grotius, Hugo 91
Guadeloupe 107, 220

Haiti 217, 219
Halachic principle 13
Hall, Douglas 71–2
Handlin, Oscar and Mary 93–4
Hankey 103–4
Hanson, Carl A. 175
Harman, Michael G. 202–3
Hart, Laura 204
Harvey, Elizabeth 64
Havana 102, 216
health and wellbeing
   disease effecting the military 102, 103, 104, 105–7, 110, 111
   diseases effecting white people 102, 103–6, 111
   of slaves 60–1, 64, 92, 159–60
Hemings, Madison and Eston 126
Hemings, Priscilla 115
Hemings, Sally 115
Henry, Patrick 124

heresy 16
Hern, David 126
Herrera, Miguel 141, 142, 143–4
Hewson, Barbara 81
Higgins, Billy 205
Higman, Barry 74
hiring out slaves 64, 155, 205 (*see also* leasing, of slaves)
Historia dei riti Ebraice 13
A Historical Study of Women in Jamaica 77
History of Barbados 110
History of Jamaica 77
Horry, Daniel 61
Hueda 168, 169
Hufon, King of Hueda 168
Hughes, Louis 117
Hughes, Wormley 126
Hunt, Gilbert 8 (*see also* chapter 12)
Hunter, John 102

identity(ies)
    Jewish 19
    of Native people 42
    religious-cultural 15
Immaculate Conception Convent, Caracas 134
indentured labour 216–17, 218, 220, 221
Indian peoples. *See* Native Americans
Industrial Revolution, Great Britain 75
inequality, social 28
inheritance, of widows 57
Inoyoseph, Alexander d' 95
Inquisitions, Spanish and Portuguese 14–17, 19
Irribarren, Guillermo 137
Irving, Major-General 108
Italian labourers 221

Jackson, Andrew 42, 49, 158
Jackson, Robert 106, 107
Jakin 168, 171
Jamaica
    agriculture in 78–9, 214
    Britain and 71–82
    compensation claims 76–82
    diseases effecting white people 102
    economy of 74–5, 78–9
    Jamaican female slaveholders 6, 77–82

    Kingston 79, 82
    livestock farming 78–9, 80–1
    population of 215
    sugar production in 220
Jansen de Salee, Anthony 92
Jansz Ringo, Philip 95
Jefferson, Isaac Granger 184–6
Jefferson, Peter 116
Jefferson, Thomas 6 (*see also* chapter 8)
Jesup, Thomas 30
Jewish peoples (*see also* Judaism)
    black slaves in Jewish homes 13
    crypto-Jews/secret Jews 14–15
    Jewish identity 19
    Jewish oppression in Russia 20, 21
    'Jewish problem' in Germany 20
    Jewish slaveholders 4–5, 13–22
    Judaizing 16, 17
Jodensavanne 18
Johnson, Eliza 64
Jozeph, Pedro 176
Judaism
    Book of Esther/Purim holiday 19–20
    jehidim and *congregantes* 19
    rabbinical law 18, 19

Kentucky 40
Kilpatrick, Dr. 204
Kingsley, Zephaniah 27–8, 30
Kingston, Jamaica 79, 82
kinship ties, Indian slaveholders and 48 (*see also* families)
knowledge work 32

labour
    apprenticeships 75, 160, 217
    city slaves 183, 200, 215–16
    contract labour system 221, 222
    female labour on plantations 225n.4
    free labour plantations 21
    free people of colour and 94
    gender and 32–3
    indentured labour 216–17, 218, 220, 221
    knowledge work 32
    piece work 221
    sexual division of 212
    slavery as 1

transition from slave to free labour
  in plantations 211–12, 213,
    214–15, 222
  white labour in the plantation
    system 223
land ownership
  Cherokee people and 42
  ex-slaves and 212–13, 220, 221,
    222, 223
  of free people of colour 93
  of women 80–1
language skills. *See* linguistic skills
Law, Robin 167, 172
Lawes, Nicholas 77
law(s)
  Abolition Decree (1854) 134
  Barbados Slave Code (1661) 98n.42
  Cherokee Nation v. Georgia (1831) 42
  English common law 56
  the expulsion or enslavement of free
    people of colour 199, 200, 201, 205
  female slave ownership and 56
  free womb laws 217
  Indian Removal Act (1830) 41–2
  legal rights of company slaves 92
  legal status of slaves 6
  Manumission Law (1821) 7, 134,
    145n.8
  property laws 7, 118
  rabbinical law 18, 19
  restrictive legislation against free
    people of colour 8
  rule of equity 56
  rule of *partus sequitur ventrem* 202
  Slavery Abolition Act (1833), Britain
    75, 76, 83n.3
  slaves/servants and 93–4
  vagrancy laws 224
  Worcester v. Georgia (1832) 42
leasing, of slaves 6–7 (*see also* chapter 8;
    hiring out slaves)
Lebsock, Suzanne 60
Leeward Islands 101
Legacies of British Slave-Ownership
    Project (LBS) 71, 72–4, 81
Leigh, Major-General 108–9
Levine, Lawrence 44–5
Levy, David (Yulee) 21–2, 24n.33
Levy, Moses Elias 4, 20–1, 24n.33

The Liberator 39, 40
Liberia 194, 204
Liberty Party 40
*Life And Times Of Frederick Douglass
    Written By Himself* 193–4
linguistic skills, social mobility and 33,
    167, 171, 172
literacy, of slaves 58–9
livestock farming, Jamaica 78–9, 80–1
Long, Edward 77
Longfellow, Henry Wadsworth 193–4
Louis XVI of France 152
Louisiana, absentee slaveholding 7, 156–8
Lower Mississippi Valley 153
Lundy family 204–5
luxury goods 174

MacManus, Edgar 89
Mahamad 19
Mair, Lucille 77
Malcolm, Robert 108
Mallory, Lydia 124
Mann, Kristin 167, 172
Manual I of Portugal 15
Manuel, Cleijn 92
manumission (*see also* emancipation)
  in exchange for silence 17
  by female slaveholders 69n.60
  Florida 27
  limitations on 218
  Manumission Law (1821) 7, 134,
    145n.8
  mixed race relationships and 18–19
  by self-purchase 171, 183
mariners, enslaved 7–8, 170, 171, 176
Maris-Wolf, Ted 201
market conditions, the plantation system
    and 213–14
Marks, Anne Scott Jefferson 115, 125,
    127n.1
maroon or maroonage communities 31
marriage
  black Southerners/white elites 203–4
  Dutch West Indian Company and 92
  extramarital relations 19
  mixed race 18–19, 21, 218
  people of colour and 208n.23
  Seminole/Black Seminole 35
  wealth accumulation by women and 77

Marshall, John 42
Martínez, Rafael 141
Martinique 109, 216, 220
Maryland 120
masculinity, black 40
Massey, Rebecca 65
maternalism 6, 55–66
Matlack, Lucius 48
Matthewes, Anne 64
McCaw, James 188–90
McDonogh, John 151, 160
McLoughlin, William G. 46–7, 48, 50
Merivale, Herman 219
Methodism 40
Micanopy 33
Michaelis, Johann David 20
Michaelius, Johannes 94
Michigan State Anti-Slavery Society 40
migration
    of ex-slaves 219
    forced emigration 42, 49
    out-migration from the plantation system 218–19
    transition from slave to free labour and 211
Mijares, Antonio 140–1
militarized slavery, Britain 6, 101–11
military, diseases effecting the 102, 103, 104, 105–7, 110, 111
Mina Coast 165, 167, 170, 172, 177n.3
Mississippi Valley 152, 153
M'Lean, Hector 106
mobility
    economic mobility of ex-slaves 215, 218
    of ex-slaves 224
    free people of colour and 201
    geographical mobility of slaves 166, 202, 218
    of slaves 7–8
    social mobility of ex-slaves 215
    social mobility of slaves 8, 18–19, 33, 166, 170–1, 172, 174, 176
    status mobility 18
Modena, Leone da 13, 22
Monteverde, Ramón 140
Monticello 6 (*see also* chapter 8)
morality, of Native people 50, 51
Morgan, Edmund 56

Morgan, Philip 65–6
mortality rates
    among the military due to disease 102, 105–7, 110, 111
    in the southern colonies 56
Moxham, Ann 79
mulattos, *congregantes* 19
mutualism 31

Narrative of the Life and Adventures of Henry Bibb, An American Slave 5, 39, 40
Native Americans
    Cherokee people. *See* Cherokee people
    culture of 49–50
    disposssession of 42, 117
    'Five Civilized Tribes' 41–2
    identity of 42
    Indian Removal Act (1830) 41–2
    Indian Territory 41, 43, 46, 50
    misconceptions surrounding 50, 51
    New Netherland and 94
    oppression of and by 42–3
    Seminoles in Florida 5, 25–36
    slaveholding of 5, 25, 29–30, 39, 46–9
    social hierarchy in Indian societies 29
Negretto, Pedro 92
Netherlands
    Dutch Caribbean, Sephardim slaveholders and 17–20
    Dutch Reformed Church 92
    Dutch War of Independence 90
    Dutch West Indian Company 89, 90–2, 93, 94, 96n.3
    Dutch West Indies, sugar production 220
    slavery and 89–90, 95
New Amsterdam 89, 92
New Christians/Conversos
    Atlantic slavery and 4, 13–17, 19
    the Dutch Caribbean and 17–20
New Echota, Treaty of (1835) 42
New Granada 142
New Netherland
    corporate slave ownership 6, 90, 91
    'half-freedom' status of slaves 94
    service slaves 92
New Orleans 43, 151–61

new technologies
  agriculture and 214
  late introduction of 71, 221
  steam shipping 217
New York, corporate slavery in seventeenth-century 89–96
New York Historical Society 89–90
Nicholas I of Russia 20, 21
Nichols, Charles H. 44
Nossa Senhora da Conceição e Almas 173, 174, 181n.78

Ocumare de la Costa
  geography and population of 133–5
  slave revolts 7, 135–44
Oklahoma 26
Oliveira, João de 7–8 (*see also* chapter 11)
Onim 167, 170, 171, 172–3, 175, 180n.64
Opauney 33
oppression
  Jewish in Russia 20, 21
  of and by Native Americans 42–3
  racial 201
  by slaveholders 40
Oswan, Mrs 81–2
Ouidah 167–70, 171, 173
overseers 48, 57–8, 123, 125
owner-in-fees 76–7
ownership, cultural construction of 28–31
Oyo Empire 169, 171–2

Paramaribo 19
Parish, Peter 200
paternalism
  Lowcountry male 65–6
  slavery and 48, 192–4
patriarchy
  of husbands 57
  slave leasing and 121–3
  of Thomas Jefferson 116, 118, 119–20, 122, 126
Paynes Landing, Treaty of (1832) 30
people of colour (*see also* Black Seminoles; free people of colour)
  Afro-Europeans, Suriname 18–19
  Afroiberians 15
  citizenship and 200, 208n.23
  marriage and 208n.23

Perdue, Theda 46, 47
Pereira, Francisco Nunes 169
Pérez, Antonio José 139
Perez, Manuel Bautista 16
Pernambuco 165–6, 167, 168, 170–1, 177n.12
Petley, Christer 74
Philadelphia 104
piece work 221
Pike County, Mississippi 204
Pilaklikaha 32, 34
Pinckney, Charles 57
Pinckney, Eliza Lucas 55–66
Pinckney, Thomas 62
piracy 91, 169
Plan for the Abolition of Slavery, Consistently with the Interests of all Parties Concerned 21
'plantation economy' school 78
plantation system
  absentee owners 71–82
  denunciations by slaves 16
  the development of 1
  factors of production and 214
  female labour 225n.4
  Florida 27
  free labour plantations 21
  indentured labour and 217, 218
  Jewish slaveholders 19
  maintenance of 8
  management by women 57–8
  out-migration from 218–19
  the Seminoles and 33
  transition from slave to free labour and 211–12, 213, 214–15, 222
  white labour 223
  world market conditions and 213–14
Plaza, Marcelino de la 139
Plaza, Ramón de la 140
political power, of the planter class 213
politics, West Africa 167–70, 171–2
Porto Novo 167, 168, 170, 171, 172–3, 175
Portrait of Gilbert Hunt 191
Portugal 15, 90, 165–6
Portuguese, Anthony 92
post-slave societies 8
pottery, Seminole 34–5

power
  political of the planter class 213
  socio-economic of southern colonial widows 56–7
Poyer, John 110
The Price of Emancipation 71, 74
Price, Richard 19
Primero, Jan 93
primogeniture, abolition of 118
privateers 91–2 (*see also* piracy)
pro-slavery rhetoric 183–92
property
  enslaved people and 170, 183
  people as 28, 29–30, 31, 118 (*see also* commodification of human beings)
  property laws 7, 118
  transition from slave to free labour and 217–18
  women and 56
Protestant Reformation 90
Protestants, the Sephardic diaspora and 17
public sphere, women and 58
Puerto Rico 215, 220
Purim 19–20
Pym, William 105

Quakers 27
quasi-slavery 200, 201, 202, 204, 206

race
  mixed-race marriage 18–19, 21, 218
  racial hierarchy of the South 49–51
  racial oppression 201
  slavery and 28
Ragatz, Lowell 71
Randolph, Cornelia 115
Randolph, Mary Jefferson 126–7
Randolph, Thomas Jefferson 120
Randolph, Thomas Mann Jr. 123, 125
Randolph, Thomas Mann Sr. 121, 122, 125
rebellions, of slaves in Indian Territory 47 (*see also* slave revolts)
Recife 165, 166, 170, 171
Refugee Home Society 40
Reide, Thomas 105
relationships (*see also* marriage)
  between Africans and Indians 25
  extramarital relations 19

mixed race 18–19
slave–master 16, 47–8, 142, 144
slave–mistress 58–60
religion (*see also* Catholicism; Christianity)
  African Baptist Church 195
  and Christian slaveholders 48
  Dutch Reformed Church 92
  Judaism 19–20
  Protestants, the Sephardic diaspora and 17
  Quakers 27
  religious-cultural identity 15
  slaves and 48, 90, 92
Remarks on the Theatre, and on the late fire at Richmond Virginia 188
Rensselaer, Jeremias Van 95
resistance
  of slaves 44
  to tropical diseases 102
revolts by slaves. *See* slave revolts
Reynolds, Mary 204
rhetoric, pro-slavery 183–92
Richardson, Richard 123
Richmond Daily Dispatch 186, 190
Richmond Enquirer 188
Richmond theatre fire 186–90, 191–3
Richmond, Virginia 123, 183–4, 186–8, 192–5
Richmond Whig 192
rights
  of ex-slaves 218
  legal rights of company slaves 92
Rio de Janeiro 214, 216
Rivas, Francisco 140
Ross, William Potter 49
runaway slaves 63–5, 135–40, 143
Russia, Jewish oppression in 20, 21
Ryden, David 80

Saint Augustine 34
Saint Domingue 6, 104, 105–6, 158
Saint George 104, 108
Saint Lucia 105, 108, 220
Saint Vincent 220
Salom, Carlos 140
Salvador da Bahia 7, 165, 173
São José Baptista 169
São Paulo 214, 217

São Tomé 15
Savi 168
Schermerhorn, Calvin 117
Schorsch, Jonathan 13, 17, 19
Scott, James 2
seamen of African descent 7–8 (*see also* mariners)
segregation 201
self-emancipation 183
self-enslavement. *See* voluntary slavery
self-purchase, manumission by 171, 183
Seminole Indians 5, 25–36
Sephardim slaveholding 4–5, 13–22 (*see also* Jewish peoples)
sexual violence 64
Shackelford, Lyne 125
sharecropping tenancies 217, 220, 222, 223
Shepherd, Verene 74, 78
Sheridan, Richard 74
Sibley, Albert G. 44, 52n.36
Silva, Jozeph Pereira da 176
Simmons, Mary 65
slave codes, adopted by the Cherokee Nation 47
slave revolts (*see also* rebellions)
  Ocumare de la Costa 7, 135–45
  St Domingue 104
  St Lucia 108
slaveholding
  atypical forms of 1–2, 4–5
  good masters and deserving slaves 192–4
  by non-white peoples 28
Slavery Abolition Act (1833), Britain 75, 76, 83n.3
Slaves in Redcoats 101
Small, Samuel 204
Smith, Adam 117
Smith, Elizabeth 63
smuggling 174–5, 180n.75, 181n.78
social conditions, of free people of colour 98n.41
social distance 18
social hierarchy, in Indian societies 29
social inequality 28
social mobility, of slaves 8, 18–19, 33, 166–7, 170–1, 172, 174, 176, 215
social status 18, 31

socio-economic power, of southern colonial widows 56–7
Sociology for the South 186
Song of the Shank 31
Soublette, Carlos 137
South Carolina 5–6, 55–66
South Carolina Gazette 63, 64, 65
Souza, Manoel de 173, 176
sovereignty, of the Cherokee people 42, 49
Spain
  the Netherlands and 90
  purge of Portuguese peoples 16
  slavery and 26–7
  Spanish Inquisition 14–15
status mobility 18 (*see also* social mobility)
Ste-Gême, Anatole de 151, 156
Ste-Gême, Henri de 7, 151, 152, 155, 156–7, 161
stereotypes, of the drunken Indian 50
Stevens, Mary 125
Stone, Emma 204
sugar production
  commerce and 20
  difficulties of cultivation in New Orleans 153, 155
  monoculture 78
  sugar plantation system 71
  transition from slave to free labour and 214–15, 223
  in the West Indies 74–5, 79, 217, 219, 220
  women and 80
Suriname 4–5, 18–19, 220

Tanner, Benjamin 189
Taylor, Alan 126
technology
  absentee owners and 71
  agriculture and 214
  late introduction of 221
  steam shipping 217
  technological knowledge 32
Tegbessou, King of Dahomey 169–70
Thirty Years' War (1618–48) 90, 91
threat, felt by New Christians/Conversos 14
Times 104
To Tell a Free Story 41
tobacco cultivation 116

Tobago 220
Topographical Map of New Orleans and its Vicinity 153–4
torture, the Spanish and Portuguese inquisitions 14–17, 19
Tovar family 135, 140
trade (*see also* commerce)
    cultures and 172
    by enslaved mariners 170, 171
    inter-imperial 174–5, 180n.75
    Jamaica and 79
    in sugar 74–5, 79
    transatlantic 7–8
The Trade, The Owner, The Slave 78
Trail of Tears 42
transatlantic slave traders (*cabeceiras*) 7–8, 165, 170, 171, 172
transnational histories 2
'trickster tactics', empowerment of slaves through 41–6
Trinidad 214, 219–20
Twiller, Wouter van 92
Tyler, John 30

United Provinces 91, 92, 95
United States
    American Anti-Slavery Society 40
    American churches' support of slaveholders 48
    American Civil War 26, 31, 62, 201
    American Colonization Society 194
    American Revolution 62, 66, 118
    Declaration of Independence 116
    poor Whites competing with ex-slaves 215
    population of 215
    the rethinking of American slavery 26–8
    rights of ex-slaves and 218
    transition from slave to free labour and 211, 222
urban slavery 183, 200, 215–16
Urbaneja, Diego Bautista 137
Urdaneta, Rafael 137
Uztáriz, Mariano 140

vagrancy laws 224
value, of slaves 43
Vannerson, Julian 187

Vaughan, John 101, 107–8
Veen, Pieter Cornelis Van der 95
Venezuela
    Aroa Copper Mines 137, 143
    British Legion 142
    Ocumare de la Costa slave revolts 7, 135–45
    slavery in 133–4
Verger, Pierre 170
The Village Blacksmith 193
violence
    Indian slaveholders and 47
    racialized 201
    to runaway slaves 64–5
    sexual violence towards slaves 64
    the slave trade and 171
    towards slaves 41, 47, 64–5, 66, 95
Virginia (*see also* Monticello)
    atypical forms of slavery 7
    the expulsion of free people of colour 201
    the hiring network 123
    'middle class' slave owners in 118
    slavery and 91, 116
    Thomas Jefferson and 117
    voluntary slavery 199
Voice of the Fugitive 40, 44
voluntary slavery 199, 200, 201–4, 206, 207n.2
vulnerability 14, 16, 17

Walvin, James 78
war(s)
    American Civil War 26, 31, 62, 201
    between Dahomey and Hueda 168, 169
    Dutch War of Independence 90
    first Anglo-Dutch war 93
    Second Seminole War (1835–1842) 21, 29–30, 33
    slavery and 91
    Thirty Years' War (1618–48) 90, 91
Wayles, John 119
Wayles, Martha 116
wealth
    accumulation of by women 77
    British West Indies and 74–5
welfare, of slaves 60–1 (*see also* health and wellbeing)

wellbeing, economic of Indian
    slaveholders 47 (*see also* health and
    wellbeing)
Wesleyan Connection 40
West Africa
    Brazil and 166
    Mina Coast 165, 167, 170, 172, 177n.3
    politics 167–70, 171–2
    service slaves/coast slaves/castle
        slaves 92
    slave trade 167
West India Regiments 6, 101–11
West Indies (*see also* names of individual
        islands)
    sugar production in 74–5, 79, 217,
        219, 220
    trade with Gibraltar 20
Western Citizen 44
white people
    diseases effecting 102, 103–7, 110, 111
    poor Whites competing with
        ex-slaves 215
    white female slaveholding 5–6
    white labour in the plantation
        system 223
    white non-propertied classes 158
    white servants employed by free people
        of colour 93
Whitfield, Francis 41, 43, 44
Wilberforce, William 108
Williams, David 199–200
women
    elites 58–9, 65, 66
    entrepreneurs 79–81
    female labour on plantations 225n.4

Jamaican female slaveholders 6, 77–82
    labour of 32
    land ownership by 80–1
    management of plantations by 57–8
    manumission by female slaveholders
        69n.60
    maternalism of female slaveholders
        55–66
    property and 56
    public sphere and 58
    sexual violence and 64
    slaveholders 5–6, 27, 55–6, 69n.60,
        77–82
    socio-economic power of southern
        colonial widows 56–7
    sugar production and 80
    wealth accumulation by 77
    widowarchy 56–7
    women's history 78
Wong, Edlie 203
Wood, Jane 124
Wood, Kirsten 58
Wood, Lucy 124
Wood, William 124
Worcester v. Georgia (1832) 42
Works Progress Administration (WPA)
    201, 204
Wynter, Charlotte Phillips 79

Yell, Thomas 206
yellow fever 103–4, 111
Yulee, David 21–2, 24n.33

Zérega, Juan 140
Zimpel, Charles F. 153–4